Commodification of Global Agrifood Systems and Agro-Ecology

This book explores the shifting relations of food provisioning in Turkey from a comparative global political economy perspective. It offers in-depth ethnographic analysis, interviews and historical insights into the ambiguities and diversities that simultaneously affect the changing conditions of food and agriculture in Turkey. Specific issues examined include the commodification of land, food and labour; the expansion and deepening of industrial standardization; the expansion of a supermarket model; and concomitant changes in, as well as the simultaneous co-existence of, traditional methods of production and marketing. Contrasting observations are drawn from diverse locales to provide examples of convergence, divergence and cohabitation in relation to transnationally advocated industrial models.

Commodification of Global Agrifood Systems and Agro-Ecology employs a form of comparative perspective that allows the particular processes of restructuring of agrifood relations in Turkey to be simultaneously distinguished from, yet related to, changes taking place in global power dynamics. Yıldız Atasoy explores agrifood transformation in Turkey with a unique approach that considers a plurality of intertwined normative influences, ontological beliefs, cultural–religious narratives, political struggles and critical–interpretive positions. Based on original research, the book treats changes in food provisioning as an analytical thread capable of uncovering how the normative acceptability of capitalized agriculture and techno-scientific innovation is entangled with processes of class formation, growing inter-capitalist competition and Islamic politics. Such processes, in turn, frame income/wealth generation, landscape management, agro-ecological dynamics and labour practices, as well as the taste and smell of place.

Yıldız Atasoy is professor of Sociology, Associate Member of the School for International Studies and Associate Member of the Department of Geography, Simon Fraser University, Canada. Her books include: *Global Economic Crisis and the Politics of Diversity* (edited); *Islam's Marriage with Neoliberalism: State Transformation in Turkey*; *Hegemonic Transitions, the State and Crisis in Neoliberal Capitalism* (edited); *Turkey, Islamists and Democracy: Transition and Globalization in a Muslim State*; and *Global Shaping and Its Alternatives* (edited).

Routledge Studies in Governance and Change in the Global Era
Edited by Daniel Drache, York University, Canada

Harold Innis, one of Canada's most distinguished economists, described the Canadian experience as no one else ever has. His visionary works in economic geography, political economy, and communications theory have endured for over 50 years and have had tremendous influence on scholarship, the media and the business community.

The volumes in the Innis Centenary Series illustrate and expand Innis's legacy. Each volume is written and edited by distinguished members of the fields Innis touched. Each addresses provocative and challenging issues that have profound implications not only for Canada but also for the new world order, including the impact of globalization on governance, international developments, and the environment; the nature of the market of the future; the effect of new communications technology on economic restructuring; and the role of the individual in effecting positive social change.

The complete series will provide a unique guide to many of the major challenges we face at the beginning of the twenty-first century.

Proposals for future volumes in the series are actively encouraged and most welcome. Please address all enquiries to the editor, by email drache@yorku.ca or by fax 1.416.736.5739.

8. Europe, Canada and the Comprehensive Economic Partnership Agreement
Taming globalization?
Edited by Kurt Hübner

9. The Governance Gap
Extractive industries, human rights, and the home state advantage
Penelope Simons and Audrey Macklin

10. Commodification of Global Agrifood Systems and Agro-Ecology
Convergence, Divergence and Beyond in Turkey
Yıldız Atasoy

Other titles in this series include:

Health Reform
Edited by Daniel Drache and Terry Sullivan

Democracy, Citizenship and the Global City
Edited by Engin F. Isin

The Market or the Public Domain
Global governance and the asymmetry of power
Edited by Daniel Drache

Commodification of Global Agrifood Systems and Agro-Ecology

Convergence, Divergence and Beyond in Turkey

Yıldız Atasoy

LONDON AND NEW YORK

First published 2017
by Routledge

2 Park Square, Milton Park, Abingdon, Oxfordshire OX14 4RN
52 Vanderbilt Avenue, New York, NY 10017

Routledge is an imprint of the Taylor & Francis Group, an informa business

First issued in paperback 2020

British Library Cataloguing in Publication Data
A catalogue record for this book is available from the British Library

Library of Congress Cataloging in Publication Data
A catalog record for this book has been requested

ISBN: 978-0-415-82050-9 (hbk)
ISBN: 978-0-367-59516-6 (pbk)

Typeset in Bembo
by Deanta Global Publishing Services, Chennai, India

For my father,
Mehmet Nedim Atasoy (1934–2015)

Contents

List of Figures   viii
List of Tables   x
Acknowledgements   xi

1   Agrifood Systems and Supermarketization   1

2   Breaking from the Past: Changes in Agricultural Land Use   36

3   GLOBALGAP and Agro-Biotechnology: Syngenta and
    Rijk Zwaan in Turkish Villages   61

4   Farming Imaginaries: Convergence, Divergence and Beyond   93

5   The Taste and Smell of Place   131

6   Trust and Trustworthiness: Paternalist Labour Relations
    in Agriculture   169

7   Supermarkets and *Pazars*: Divergent Paths   211

8   A Discussion on Diversity   246

References   261
Index   283

Figures

2.1 Wheat Production in Turkey (1940–2013)   45
2.2 Regional Wheat Production (1995–2012)   46
2.3 Amount of Registered Immovables of the Treasury   51
3.1 Tolga Tabur, Syngenta Vegetable Portfolio Manager for
Southeast Europe (Kayabükü, Beypazarı, 28 May 2014)   74
3.2 Protected Plant Varieties (2014)   88
3.3 Protected Plant Varieties (2014)   88
3.4 Protected Vegetable Varieties (2014)   89
4.1 Diverse Knowledge Bases and Emerging Ambivalences   98
4.2 Mesut (Kayabükü, Beypazarı, 28 May 2014)   103
4.3 Hidayet Taş (Karacaören, Güdül, 10 May 2014)   107
4.4 Hidayet and His Wife, İlknur Taş (Karacaören, Güdül,
9 July 2016)   107
4.5 Carrot Sorting, Grading and Packaging at Hidayet's Cold
Storage Facility (Harmancık, Beypazarı, 17 June 2015)   113
4.6 Sadettin Ayık (Beypazarı, 19 May 2014)   116
5.1 Nuri (Fasıl, Beypazarı, 20 May 2014)   134
5.2 Halit (Karacaören, Güdül, 17 June 2015)   142
5.3 Musa (Kamanlar, Güdül, 21 May 2014)   148
6.1 Agricultural Labour in Turkey   170
6.2 Horizontally Established Ties of Trust and Paternalist
Labour Regimes   173
6.3 A Kurdish Migrant Worker at Syngenta's Open-field Day
(Kayabükü, Beypazarı, 28 May 2014)   179
6.4 Tents of Kurdish Migrant Workers (Beypazarı, 20 May 2014)   184
6.5 Ömer, a Farmer and a Kurdish Migrant Family
(Fasıl, Beypazarı, 20 May 2014)   184
6.6 Male Members of the Kurdish Migrant Family Working for
Ömer (Fasıl, Beypazarı, 20 May 2014)   185

6.7   Female Members of the Kurdish Migrant Family Working
      for Ömer (Fasıl, Beypazarı, 20 May 2014)   185
6.8   Children of the Kurdish Migrant Family Working for Ömer
      (Fasıl, Beypazarı, 20 May 2014)   186
6.9   Members of a Labouring Kurdish Migrant Family
      (Güdül, 13 June 2015)   189
6.10 A Group of Female Greenhouse Workers at Bey Fide
      (Fasıl, Beypazarı, 20 May 2014)   201
6.11 Saniye (Fasıl, Beypazarı, 20 May 2014)   202
6.12 Women's *Kaşıklama* (Spooning) Work (Fasıl, Beypazarı,
      20 May 2014)   202

Tables

1.1   Summary Information of Interviewed Individuals   27
1.2   GAP Practices in Large Agricultural Towns in Ankara (2014)   28
1.3   Some Important Crops Grown in Ankara and Their Share of the Overall Production in Turkey (2013)   29
1.4   Registered Farmers in Ankara (Number of Applications, 2013)   30
2.1   National Registry of Farmers   44
2.2   Land Consolidation by Year(s)   57
3.1   GAP Project Implementation in Turkey (2012)   65
3.2   Contract Farming in Plant Production   67
3.3   Plant-Production Areas Under Contract Farming (2011)   67
6.1   Average Daily and Monthly Wages of Workers in Agriculture (2013–2014)   175
7.1   Weekly *Pazars* in the Province of Ankara (2013–2015)   221
7.2   National Supermarkets, Turkey (2015)   232
7.3   Fastest Growing PERDER-Member Local Supermarkets, Turkey (2015)   238
7.4   Local Supermarkets, Ankara (2015)   240

Acknowledgements

My deepest thanks to all of the individuals who made this book possible through their generosity and support. I am particularly grateful to the many farmers who shared their rich experience and profound knowledge with me. Hidayet Taş, a farmer from the village of Karacaören in Güdül, deserves a special thank you. Our conversations, which often took place over delicious meals served on his farm, were both personally and professionally rewarding. Hidayet introduced me to many other farmers in Beypazarı and Güdül with an immense caring and commitment. I am proud to call Hidayet my friend, along with his wonderful wife İlknur, daughter Elif and extended family. Thanks also to Halit, who warmed our stomachs and our souls with his *tarhana çorbası* (peasant soup), cooked over an open fire and shared around a common farm table with his elderly father, young son and other local farmers who 'dropped by'. It was a delight to meet them all. I only hope I was able to convey something of their wisdom and their aspirations in this book.

Kurdish migrant and local workers all generously shared their ideas and time. Their experiences are often not included in discussions on what constitutes good food, and I am indebted to these workers for their important contribution.

My thanks go to the mayor of Güdül, Hava Yıldırım, whom I have known for many years. She made many of my meetings with farmers and officials possible. I am grateful to the mayor of the village of Çağa, Muzaffer Yalçın, who assisted me in exploring the geographical indication patenting of local heirloom tomatoes. My access to official government reports and documents was facilitated by Muhsin Temel, director of Ankara Agriculture in the Ministry of Food, Agriculture and Livestock. I am grateful for his insights and guidance. In Kırşehir, I would like to thank Banu and Onur, who provided me with the opportunity to meet farmers and agricultural workers in the village of Savcılı Büyükoba in Kaman, where farmers kindly shared their unique experiences of seed saving and heirloom production of local crop varieties.

I would like to thank Ataman Avdan and Esin Gözükara, my PhD students in Sociology at Simon Fraser University (SFU). This book benefitted from their proficiency in providing research assistance locating official documents and literature resources and preparing tables and figures. I also would like to acknowledge SFU's SSHRC-GRF grant, which provided me with financial support to carry out my research trips to Turkey.

At Routledge, I am indebted to Andy Humphries and Emily Kindleysides, commissioning editors; Daniel Drache, editor of the *Governance and Change in the Global Era* series; and Elanor Best, Natalie Tomlinson and Lisa Thomson, editorial assistants, for their support and excellent work on this project. I also thank the anonymous reviewers who offered their thoughtful suggestions.

At home, I am inspired by and grateful to Ken Jalowica, my husband, who is also a sociologist. He always found the time to read various drafts of the manuscript and to provide numerous insightful comments, even when busy teaching at Kwantlen Polytechnic University. As usual, Ken shared his critical observations with generosity of spirit and love. He remains my greatest critic. Of course, the shortcomings in this volume remain mine alone.

1 Agrifood Systems and Supermarketization

This book examines the structural transformation in Turkey's food-provisioning system, including producer–distributor–retailer relationships, from a comparative global political economy perspective. The remaking of agriculture and food in Turkey is taking place through intensified commodification of land, food and labour; the expansion of a supermarket model; and concomitant changes in, as well as the simultaneous co-existence of, traditional methods of production and marketing. This remaking is consistent with what the World Bank (WB), in its *2008 World Development Report*, calls a 'new agriculture for development' – a policy that advocates the ascendancy of large-scale commercial farmers and a profit-driven orientation in global agriculture (World Bank 2007) tied to national economic growth (Li 2009; McMichael 2009). While the report anticipates a gradual disappearance of small-scale farming, it also encourages the integration of small producers into out-grower schemes as suppliers for large commercial farms through contract farming (White et al. 2012, 625–6). The WB presents a largely linear perspective on the remaking of food and agriculture that posits an inexorable tendency toward commodification. Alternatively, this book offers a systematic presentation of the tensions, ambiguities and diversities that simultaneously affect the changing conditions of food and agriculture in Turkey.

Overall, the WB sees large-scale commercial farming as essential for economic growth in the global South. Support for the dominance of large-scale commercialized farmers in the 'new agriculture' is typically justified by the assertion that small-scale farming is inherently unproductive and that small producers are incapable of acting as economic agents for sufficiently increased yields (the 'yield gap') (de Ponti et al. 2012; FAO 2015; *Field Crops Research* 2013). It is assumed that the crop 'yield gap' between large-scale and small-scale farmers is already large and increasing. This assumption reflects a belief in farmers' differentiated ability to integrate into more input-intensive production systems, to adopt gap-reducing and productivity-enhancing technologies (i.e. input of soil nutrients, plant genetics and improved crop varieties) and to be responsive to various risk-management issues and environmental constraints. The fundamental criticism levelled at small-scale farmers in relation to the crop yield gap is their general *lack* of efficiency in achieving higher returns on labour, land and water, according to the rules of economic competitiveness. The yield gap is seen to constitute a general poverty trap for many smallholder farmers. In fact, it is believed that those who cannot increase yields and generate income from agriculture should abandon agriculture altogether.

The structural transformation in food and agriculture does not necessarily mean that governments design rules and policy mechanisms that involve an endless profit-driven pursuit of wealth generation and accumulation through market exchange – a process elaborated by Adam Smith (1991 [1776]) more than 200 years ago. The remaking of food and agriculture not only represents *all* of these market-oriented changes but *also* a new value orientation to *economization* (Brown 2015; Dardot and Laval 2013). This process hinges on the normative activation of economization as a mode of thinking and acting. Economization 'injects' food and agriculture with a new 'value system' that applies market metrics to the conception/regulation/management of everything in terms of its contribution to economic growth. Such a value system conceives of humans (i.e. farmers) as 'enterprising subjects', mobilized to improve their performance values in competition. It also perceives agriculture (and land) as an 'enterprise entity' – an instrument and space of competition, the use of which is subject to the systematic pursuit of efficiency. Thus, this book draws in particular from scholarship that focuses on a specific understanding and reasoning of economization in its analysis of the neoliberal nature of agrifood transformation in Turkey.[1] Such reasoning connects individuals, material and normative/discursive resources and relationships, and institutions, into the dominant 'knowledge structure of political economy' (Gill 2000), which, in its totality, is conceived as economization. Thus, economization is *the* knowledge structure of the neoliberal capitalist economy.

A neoliberal remaking of agriculture is expected to reach deep into its political, ethical and moral dimensions in ways that are more significant than the mere institutionalization of market-economic principles in food relationships based on cost–benefit calculations. This remaking requires a normative logic that is capable of integrating economic policy and individual behaviour. Economization signifies that individual activity is entrepreneurial in its very essence. Its value is appreciated and enhanced in the market, *as if* individuals have always been calculatively engaged in market-based economic relations of competition that filter out winners and losers (Dardot and Laval 2009, 148–91, 264–8). This meaning of neoliberal reasoning and its remaking of subjects, relations and worldviews goes well beyond the expansion of market relations into agriculture. Rather, it encompasses an enduring process of remaking agrifood relationships and a political, normative redeployment through the logic of economization *as if* the self was a business and individuals were a coherent entrepreneurial unit (Gershon 2011).

The normative account of neoliberalism conceives of economization as a *global norm* affecting global agriculture by altering the rules of economic behaviour around the competitive principles of a market economy. It anticipates the gradual disappearance of small-scale farming and traditional, customary methods of food provisioning. This account remains an empirical question, given the globally valid conditions of geo-historical diversity and context specificity. It is important to ask if economization is a useful concept for an analysis of the structural transformation that is underway in Turkey's food-provisioning system. Further, it remains an empirical question, because the normative power of economization does not pre-exist the place-specific and historically bound power dynamics, political struggles and conflicts that reshape the political and cultural conditions of accumulation (Atasoy 2009; 2016). Questions must be asked concerning the shared and divergent perceptions that frame the existing tensions and ambiguities in agrifood relationships in Turkey and may complicate economization as the dominant mode of neoliberal reasoning. As a neoliberal value system, economization is sometimes embraced and sometimes pushed aside, leading to possibilities for commodification in land and food *without certainties*. Within these possibilities, both old and new ways of thinking co-exist in framing the transition.

The WB's 2008 report (World Bank 2007, 2) acknowledges that development trajectories vary in different parts of the world and that there are multiple pathways in the pursuit of a market-oriented agriculture for development. Despite its acknowledgement of global diversity, the report continues to identify 'development' in terms of a *generalized path* for the production of high-value agricultural commodities directed toward global demand. It would seem that the mere existence of diversity in the global economy would be expected to generate more subtle and complicated outcomes than that of a generalized, market-based pathway based solely on efficiency and entrepreneurial fitness in the 'competitive business' of farming.

The neoliberal remaking of agriculture and food in Turkey is the central empirical question of this book. It requires us to rethink how normative conformity to a market-oriented model and economization logic is established *through* geo-historically differentiated considerations of time and place. This in turn allows us to critically examine how agriculture is being reorganized in a way that generates a space within which individual farmers are regarded as neoliberal units of competitive, 'entrepreneurialized subjects'. Space-making for these neoliberal subjects involves a process that melds a multitude of culturally specific and politically charged issues into a logic of economization (Atasoy forthcoming). Hence, we observe emerging possibilities for uncertain neoliberal complexities. This book shows that the remaking of agrifood relations lies *within* the process of making a neoliberal history in Turkey and in confrontation with the state-centric developmentalist past, thereby enabling people to 'sense-make' within a specific ontological orientation of economization.

We can advance our understanding of the interplay between deepening economization in agriculture and divergent positions, perceptions and practices by being more attentive to the socio-spatial differences in multifaceted relationships, broader histories and discourses. Through my example of Turkey, these relationships are connected to European Union (EU) accession, Ottoman history, the republican state-led developmentalist project, Islamic politics and the recent policies of the ruling Justice and Development Party (AKP). I detail several ways in which the neoliberal remaking of agriculture and food through a competitive economic logic is *not* exterior, in the Turkish context, to long-held views, religious orientations, policies and struggles that have arisen in the course of cultural, economic confrontations with the developmentalist state. This remaking under the AKP government is attached to the deep structure of the neoliberal global economy and the dominant knowledge mode of economization. Within this attachment, a plurality of normative influences, cultural–religious narratives, political struggles and critical–interpretive positions are simultaneously intertwined to form the substance of a neoliberal condition against the cultural, economic and social fundamentals of statist developmentalism.

The present work endeavours to uncover the uneven processes of connectivity that situate locally and regionally scaled variegations *within* the broader relations of agrifood transformation in Turkey. An analysis of this complexity, with contrasting and complementary examples drawn from various regions of the world, also offers insight into how we might make sense of farmers' integration into this transformation beyond the currently dominant dualistic perspectives based on market-confirming behaviour. I will show that small-scale producers are neither marginalized relics of the past (cf. Lerner 1958; Rostow 1960) – which constitute shadow markets for subsistence food outside the commercialized relations of capitalist agriculture (cf. Bernstein 1996, 2010) – nor subjects mobilized to form a political force for creating an alternative ontology that challenges the market episteme in agriculture (cf. McMichael 2008). My analysis depicts small producers as a dynamic element in the deepening commodification of agriculture. They partially adopt agro-industrial production methods, gradually embody a normative logic of economization, and act as 'personal enterprises' who create alternative 'niches' in marketing their food with a taste and place-based claim to its locality. Small producers are players in a particular structural context of neoliberal history-making. A neoliberal condition in agriculture, then, does *not* generate a pathway that resembles what Paul Collier (2008) calls the 'Brazilian model', with its associated changes in the livelihood conditions of smallholders toward large-scale dispossession and displacement from agriculture. A different complexity emerges, one that reflects the twists and turns of both convergence and divergence in regard to neoliberal ways.

Multiple pathways of commercialization exist in Turkish agriculture. What we observe is a diversification in food provisioning whereby smallholders and large-scale producers operate through their own differentiated, but also frequently converging, entrepreneurial practices of land and labour management and integration into globally advocated agro-industrial methods of production. These pathways simultaneously and unevenly converge into the process of commercialization in agriculture. Based on original research (with methodological details to follow later in this chapter), the book uncovers how commercialization is entangled with a diverse set of orientations, standards and practices.

Further, the book provides a nuanced examination of agrifood restructuring by revealing the significance of particular local/regional/national/global dynamics of power.

The structural transformation and neoliberal remaking of Turkey's agriculture and food relationships intersect with broader histories, deeply rooted normative inclinations and long-held ideas about national development and modernization. This does not imply that individuals act as 'neoliberal subjects' by acquiring the necessary set of productivity-enhancing skills through training, nor does it suggest that they subscribe to an interest-bound, old liberal-style utilitarian ideational system of cost–benefit calculation to bring about such a change. Rather, this book explores how the interpretative processes of developmentalism enable people to cognitively 'sense-make' according to a specific ontological orientation that frames their conformity within the logic of economization and deepening commercialization in food provisioning. It expresses an entirely historical and deeply 'messy' phenomenon of turning away from the path of statist-developmentalism that has shaped the particular content of political struggles over inclusion, exclusion, domination and subordination. The main problem in making sense of this messiness lies in the interconnectivity between individual farmers (expressed in their desire to take part in commercialization) and neoliberal restructuring. While neoliberal reasoning allows various farming groups to articulate their position in the social hierarchy of developmentalism as unequally endowed groups, neoliberalization of the economy also enables them to work their way into a more favourable position in the middle class.

The approach presented here brings forth the dynamic interplay between neoliberal subjects/agents and the process of neoliberalization by reference to the economic, political and cultural–religious dimensions [sites] of power. As this power is reconfigured at a historical conjuncture that permits the social hierarchy of developmentalism to be reorganized, the relations and mechanisms of accessing resources are also restructured to allow various groups to reposition themselves in the economy (Atasoy 2009). Thus, the book situates the neoliberal remaking of Turkish food and agriculture within the contingent conjunction of power reconfigurations in a developmentalist social hierarchy. This is important for understanding what a neoliberal conception of change entails in relation to the cultural, normative reconfiguring of social and ecological relationships.

A comprehensive review of the literature on regional diversities and country-specific variations in the remaking of global agriculture is beyond the scope of this book. Nonetheless, I have referred to numerous examples from global political economy throughout the book. These examples further highlight the significance of a spatially and historically multilayered analysis of agrifood restructuring in Turkey. The present book does not offer a conventional, formal comparative approach between Turkey and any other country (or countries). Conventional comparisons typically select a case (or a group of cases) to draw parallels and establish cause-and-effect relationships. They do so through an examination of convergent and divergent outcomes in relation to institutions and forms of change, or in terms of the experiences of producers with capitalized agriculture. This book, alternatively, provides a meso-level *multilayered analysis* of the current conjuncture of neoliberalization in global agrifood relations through context-specific historical variegation *within* Turkey and *across* time (cf. McMichael 1990). Different patterns of variegation involve alterations in land use and cropping practices, land access and common property resources, changing livelihoods and agro-ecological dynamics, as well as emerging values, perspectives and ideas. Agrifood transformation, including supermarket expansion and the persistence of traditional methods, is analyzed as expressing an unevenly combined process in the interconnectivity between a generalized path and the context specificity of place. It is out of this uneven process that the changing conditions of capital generation and accumulation in agriculture are forged.

A Generalized Path

A generalized neoliberal path in agrifood transformation involves the restructuring of land and food for large-scale commercial production in order to fuel economic development. A market-oriented agriculture is often promoted in non-traditional, high-input production of animal feedstuffs and biofuel energy crops, off-season fresh fruits and vegetables, and livestock and aquaculture products. It primarily serves high-value markets in urban areas and in the global North rather than the subsistence needs of producers (Borras Jr. 2009). Those who are unable to re-organize their production under the general transformative processes of commercialization are encouraged to leave agriculture. They are believed to underutilize land for food production and as pasture. Therefore, their lands can, and should, be reconfigured and transferred for commercial use in agriculture and as real estate (Atasoy 2016).

Significantly, the WB's 2008 report does not diminish the role of the state in agriculture. In fact, a strong state capacity is preferred in the formulation, implementation and institutionalization of the 'new agriculture' under a market-driven model of development. This preference is clearly specified in the WB's *World Development Report 1997: The State in a Changing World*, which promotes an efficient and strong public administration to oversee commercialization in agriculture (Gill 1998). The report further advocates the dissolution of small-scale subsistence-based food production and reconfiguring of land and resource access and use.

Although the WB expects the state to play an active role in the re-organization and management of the new agriculture, this is not an easy task. It requires many things to be devalued and revalued in *contracting* small-scale production and *expanding* commercial agriculture. A change in state-policy intervention affects much that people 'value' in their lives and livelihoods and is therefore a politically, socially, culturally and emotionally sensitive issue. Land use, land access, common property resources, housing, biodiversity, agro-ecological integrity, water management and livelihood practices, among other things, become subject to revaluation by the state. This generates a multiplicity of outcomes, including large-scale dispossession, (partial) repossession, displacement, informalization, marginalization, exclusion and diminished rights, along with actual or potential resistance (Atasoy 2016). As a result, the reorganization of agriculture and associated changes in land and resource access and use are closely connected to 'accountability politics', citizenship dynamics and social–redistributive justice (Fox 2007). As governments attend to redistributive challenges, the power dynamics in society are also reconfigured, with significant implications for the re-organization/re-categorization of property as well as the accessing and gaining of benefits from resources and livelihood practices (Lund 2009; Ribot and Peluso 2003; Scoones 2015).

The WB's 2008 report closely ties alterations in land/resource use and access patterns to the question of small-scale producers' efficiency in achieving competitiveness in agriculture (World Bank 2007, 138–9, 143–5). The transfer of lands to large-scale commercial producers is encouraged out of a conviction that they are better positioned to reflexively enhance their fit with the market rationality of neoliberalism and adapt to the cost-efficiency creating methods of competition. Large-scale farmers are viewed as 'neoliberal agents' who can conceive of themselves as 'self-investing entrepreneurial businesses' (Gershon 2011), in contrast to the cultural unfitness of small producers.

This conception of farmers is central to economization as a normative orientation and ethic of neoliberalism. It identifies 'neoliberal selves' both *within* and *without* the European liberal discursive view of *human nature* that has been exemplified since the seventeenth century by Thomas Hobbes, John Locke, Jeremy Bentham and Adam Smith, among others. John Locke developed an understanding of society as an aggregate of rational market actors. Thomas Hobbes believed that these actors are motivated by calculations of competitive positioning and survival, and Jeremy Bentham viewed them as calculating utilitarian subjects in pursuit of self-interest. The dominant classical liberal view is that the market rationality of self-interested subjects instigates the creation and accumulation of wealth. Neoliberal economization does not reject these liberal assumptions nor does it conceive of humans merely as an elaboration of 'old-style' liberal subjects involved in wealth generation (Brown 2015, 79–111). Rather, such subjects are also regarded as 'entrepreneurial', as 'investment capital'. Neoliberal selves are thus considered 'personal enterprises', capable of enhancing their investment-capital value and taking responsibility for contributing to economic growth (Dardot and Laval 2013, 264–8). The question remains as to how the normative deepening of formal rationality and market metrics intersects with the remaking of the social to establish new political conditions and a reorganization of past and present in the neoliberalization of agriculture.

It is noteworthy that the WB pays little attention to state responsibility in furthering redistributive social justice. The *2008 World Development Report* is clear in its expectation that states expand their market-oriented policy intervention into a broad range of economic activities across sectors. However, it seems that the long-held belief that the state also has a meaningful role to play in realizing the 'common good' is now diminished (cf. Abrams 1988). The WB appears far more interested in encouraging states to have 'greater coordination across international agencies ... [and] with ... new actors in the global arena' (World Bank 2007, 24). These international agencies include international governmental and multilateral institutions such as the International Monetary Fund (IMF) and the WB itself, which require that governments open up to global trade, investment and capital movement. The new actors include private organizations and networks, including international non-governmental organizations (NGOs), philanthropic foundations and financing agencies, research and development (R&D) institutions, business networks, biotechnology companies, consultative groups, agribusiness enterprises and supermarket chains (World Bank 2007, 261–5). The expectation that national states will coordinate policy more effectively with international governmental agencies, multilateral institutions and private players is intended to ensure that commercialization becomes deeply rooted within a general global governance structure.

Despite the fact that the WB's 2008 report identified market-oriented commercial agriculture as 'new agriculture', the WB actually laid out this policy preference more than 25 years earlier in its *1982 World Development Report*. The 1982 report connected the economic development of countries in the global South to a shift away from state-led developmentalism toward a market-led model of change. The 2008 report aims to 'rectify' the implementation failures of the 1982 report.

The 2008 report attributed the 'failure' in the global implementation of the 1982 recommendations to the inadequacy of post-war global governance institutions in framing and enforcing a comprehensive market-oriented agricultural policy. The 2008 report views the post-war Bretton-Woods regime as offering a 'shallow' form of multilateralism (Rodrik 2011), permitting individual governments to respond in their own ways to the needs and demands of citizens as producers and consumers. Post-war institutions embodied a national conception of economic regulation that allowed the public authority of the state to control and channel the processes of economic liberalization (Gill 1998, 29–30). The 2008 report advocates more effective policy coordination at the global level through the deployment of a stronger state capacity to restructure and insert agriculture into a globalized system of governance.

The General Agreement on Trade and Tariffs (GATT) established in 1947 was one of the key Bretton-Woods institutions, although it had minimal relevance for the global governance of agriculture (Pritchard 2009, 298). Due to the fact that GATT's priorities were entangled in the domestic policy agendas of individual states, what emerged, according to the WB, was a lack of global agreement on the rules pertaining to international trade, product standards, intellectual property rights, new technologies and environmental and ecological concerns (World Bank 2007, 22–4). Consequently, the WB's 2008 report advocates the introduction of effective mechanisms for global rule making and policy coordination that will facilitate the expansion of commercialization and profit-driven thinking in agriculture.

Global policy coordination requires 'bargained compromises' among governments to ensure policy harmonization and create complementary expectations among a variety of actors through multilateral agreements. It was hoped that the creation of the World Trade Organization (WTO) and its Agreement on Agriculture (AOA) protocol in 1995 would change the least institutionalized dimension of the post-war international economic order – global agriculture. However, the collapse of the Doha Round of trade negotiations (which began in 2001 and is still ongoing) has cast doubt on the ability of WTO-led policy coordination of agriculture to realize a greater market orientation (Pritchard 2009, 304), largely because of disagreements over agricultural subsidies, sustainable economic growth and access to global markets for exports by countries from the global South (European Commission nd.). In addition to the rise of agricultural protectionist policies and the emergence of regional alternatives to a multilateral deal (*The Economist* 2012), the global economic crisis that began in 2008 has further complicated the ability of WTO-led multilateralism to act as a 'supra-national entity'. Nonetheless, the WB's policy framework remains anchored by the WTO's leadership in standardizing regulatory rules and tackling challenges in the global governance of agriculture. As new private actors demonstrate their power more forcefully in the present neoliberal conjuncture of global agriculture (McMichael 2009), another mechanism may be utilized for more effective institutionalization of 'corporate self-governance' and compliance with private industry standards (Brown and Woods 2007; Busch 2011). As will be examined in greater detail in Chapter 3, the GLOBALGAP – a consortium of transnational supermarket chains – provides such a mechanism for reorganizing agriculture.

Tensions within the Model

There are two aspects to the neoliberal restructuring of agriculture and food under the deepening logic of economization: one concerns the historical centrality of small-scale production for meeting local–regional subsistence needs; the other relates to the increasingly dominant role played by supermarkets and agribusiness firms in expanding commodity relations in society, where 'needs' are increasingly defined and met in terms of mass-produced packaged goods and services.

Smallholders, Subsistence Production and Dispossession

The concept of subsistence encompasses 'self-sufficiency' and 'self-reliance' as key attributes of an 'autonomous' existence at the local level, where agricultural production is often small-scale (Bennholdt-Thomsen and Mies 1999, 21, 65–108). It is well known that small-scale production can rarely sustain the self-sufficiency of rural households and therefore, according to *The Rural Poverty*

Report of 2011, published in 2010 by the International Fund for Agricultural Development, the majority of rural populations live in poverty (van der Ploeg 2012). The world's rural populations live in vastly different agro-ecological regions characterized by uncertain rainfall, different conditions of soil fertility and varied infrastructural resources and levels of risk. This agro-ecological diversity necessitates vastly different livelihood strategies, which may include the use of a rural commons, seasonal out-migration, off-farm employment and many other strategies (Bernstein et al. 1992; Harriss-White and Garikipati 2008). Rural people creatively combine different activities, use a variety of resources, follow different survival strategies and actively engage in negotiating the terms of living, 'vertically and horizontally', with or without state involvement, at the household, village and regional levels (Eriksen and Silva 2009; Hutchinson 2012; Scoones 2015).

Small-scale production remains the dominant form for acquiring locally based subsistence food in many regions across the global South. *The Rural Poverty Report* of 2011 advocates a market-oriented transformation of agriculture to systematically reduce rural poverty. This is consistent with the 2008 WB report on global agriculture. According to the rural poverty report, smallholder agriculture must become more commercial, and small-scale farms should operate as businesses, increase their productivity and adopt more sustainable land and water-usage practices. In addition to these measures, the report suggests that rural people should increasingly seek non-farm employment in micro enterprises and large agribusinesses (van der Ploeg 2012, 441). The strategic assumption of the report is that small-scale agriculture may co-exist alongside large-scale agro-enterprises (van der Ploeg 2012, 442), as long as it can be integrated into market-oriented non-traditional commodity production of cotton, coffee or fresh fruits and vegetables through contract-farming arrangements, with more limited involvement in on-farm subsistence food production.

This assumption draws on the 'agrarian question', which constitutes a core issue for scholarship on the neoliberal restructuring of agriculture. 'Classic' literature on the 'agrarian question' regards small-scale agricultural producers as 'peasants' (Shanin 1971). In contrast to farmers who fully enter the market, peasants most often keep the market at 'arm's length' in order to ensure continuity upon the land and household sustenance (Wolf 1969, xiv–xv). Peasants primarily have access to land that is either owned or rented. Thus, according to Eric Wolf, the category of peasants also covers tenants and sharecroppers as well as owner–operators. They generally control their means of production, make autonomous decisions regarding the process of cultivation and, with the help of simple equipment and family labour, aim for subsistence before producing for sale on the market (Wolf 1969).

According to Wolf (1969, xiv), social, cultural and political arrangements rooted in agrarian life that support access to land and the labour of immediate family, kin and neighbours are essential to sustaining subsistence-oriented production in agriculture as a source of livelihood. This is an important reminder of how, historically, under the greater intensification of economization and deepening commercialization in agriculture, subsistence-oriented cultivators of food became severed from their ties to one another and disembedded from the land, thereby losing a direct connection to their means of sustenance. The disintegration of the subsistence-based social realm and the inability to live from the earth is traceable to the historically bound, linear pattern of capitalist development in Europe, which completely reorganized all aspects of social life in industries and cities. Increasingly, people became tied to one another and to the land only indirectly through the market and the bonds of money (Marx 1954 [1887]; Polanyi 1944). Karl Marx (1954 [1887], 667–712) aptly described this process in European history as 'primitive accumulation', the forcible dispossession of the peasantry from the land, a process facilitated by state legislation.

Studies in agrarian political economy explore contemporary processes of corporate-led restructuring of food relationships in terms of an accelerated commodification of agricultural lands, contraction of its usage in subsistence agriculture and a generalized dispossession of smallholders from their land and resources, along with the dissolution of subsistence-based food production (Bernstein 1996, 2010; Byres 2009; Li 2009). This generates large surplus rural populations that are often expelled from agriculture – a process the significance of which has been described as 'the great enclosure of our times' (Araghi 2000). Pushed into a marginalized existence within the current crisis economy, these surplus rural populations are forced to negotiate a generalized condition of ontological precarity as they become wageless and dis-employed (Atasoy 2014, 293–4; Ferguson 2006). The separation of farmers from their means of production and reproduction represents an instance of what David Harvey (2003, 144–5) has called 'accumulation by dispossession' – a term that essentially delineates the contemporary processes of Marx's primitive-accumulation concept. Accumulation by dispossession entails an upward redistribution that restores the class dominance of an economic elite while threatening the material, social and cultural well-being of the subordinate masses, including their attachment to the land, 'habits of the heart' and ways of living.

Literature on the 'agrarian question' considers the continuing usefulness of the concept of peasantry *today* in relation to the dispossession and differentiation of agricultural producers under the general class-transformation processes of capitalist accumulation (Bernstein 1996; 2010). Philip McMichael (2009; 2012a) redefines these processes in the current context as being governed by supermarket-driven corporate agriculture and in relation to the dominant development narrative of neoliberal capitalism. For Jack Kloppenburg (2010), the erosion of seed self-provisioning, together with the knowledge of seed saving, constitutes an important aspect of the current process of agrarian dispossession. Commodified, patented/protected, high-priced, privately owned corporate seed production separates farmers of all types in the world from their most fundamental means of production, the seed, and their ability to propagate and disseminate the seed for future use in planting.

Recent scholarship has also highlighted *land grabbing* as an aspect of agrarian dispossession by reference to agro-industrial restructuring (Borras Jr. et al. 2010;

White et al. 2012). This concept explores contexts, causes and mechanisms of the contemporary refiguring of access to, exclusion from, and claim over common resources, as well as the role of the state in the reorganization of property relations (Wolford et al. 2013). The literature on land grabbing often focuses on large-scale domestic and transnational interests acquiring land and resource access rights to be used for various purposes, ranging from commercial food, bio-fuel and biomass production to protection of global biodiversity and greenspace (Holmes 2014). Land grabbing sustains the deepening of commodification in agriculture, with implications for land-property and access dynamics, labour regimes and the re-organization of production and markets. It extends to farmers' increasing dependency on external, agrochemical and industrial providers of inputs and instruments, as well as to the epistemic dispossession of genetic and agro-ecological knowledge (i.e. knowledge separated from experience in relation to cropping the land for subsistence).

With a clear change in livelihood from one relying on an immediate, deeply sense-based connection to the earth to another based on a techno-scientifically driven separation from that connection, the stage has been set for small producers' increasing inability to maintain their autonomy from the forces of the market economy, to control their means of production, access resources (including land and water) and achieve self-sufficiency in agriculture. With the loss of access to their resource base, coupled with a complex set of interactions with 'the metabolic rift in soil nutrients' (Foster et al. 2010, 76), many small producers must 'combine commodity and subsistence production to varying degrees' in order to survive (Bryceson 2000, 299). According to Deborah F. Bryceson (2000), the effects of the contemporary processes of 'primitive accumulation' in the current neoliberal conjuncture have been nothing short of de-agrarianization and de-peasantization.

Bryceson (2002, 726–7) defines *de-agrarianization* as a long-term occupational adjustment. It involves an income-earning reorientation and the social identification and relocation of rural dwellers away from an agriculture-based mode of livelihood. *De-peasantization* is a specific form of de-agrarianization in which peasantries lose their economic capacity and social coherence and shrink in demographic size. The re-organization of farming thus involves a shift from a 'socially driven' (also referred to in the literature as 'peasant-driven') mechanism of increasing yields for local/regional consumption to a 'technologically driven' intensification of productivity, fuelled by corporate agribusiness practices (van der Ploeg 2012, 444–5). This process often expels people from rural areas into a 'planet of slums' (Davis 2006) and a life on the margins of cities as informal, precarious labour (Ferguson 2006).

'Capitalism's Modernity' and Neoliberal Economization: The Inefficiency of Smallholder Agriculture

For the purpose of clarifying neoliberal accumulation and agrifood regime restructuring, it is important to recall a pro-market critique of smallholder agriculture found in post-Second World War development discourse. At the heart of this critique is the ontology of a capitalist modernity, as described by Barrington Moore, Jr. (1966) in his classic work on the fate of the peasantry in England.

Barrington Moore's description of the 'English road' to modernity is the description of capitalist development in agriculture. The English road was dependent on the forceful clearing of the land of its original owners and users by robber barons – the process of land privatization via enclosures, which was ultimately controlled and sanctioned by parliament, as elucidated in Marx's primitive-accumulation concept. '[T]he intrusion of commerce into a peasant community' (Moore 1966, 26), stimulated by the urban growth of manufacturing industry, finally destroyed the medieval peasant society – a process that ultimately forced the English peasantry into a change of livelihood as they began to work as wage-dependent labourers in urban industrial and rural agricultural capitalist enterprises.

The English road represents a spatial, sectoral reorganization of the rural–urban divide in the development of capitalism as well as the incorporation of newly privatized village lands into the profit-driven processes of agricultural production (Brenner 1982). This pushed more and more peasants into wage labour in industrial cities where they became dwellers of 'jerry-built houses' or 'slums' constructed around industrial work sites (Engels 1872). The process was significantly aided by the Poor Law Reform Act of 1834. By abolishing the 'right to live' policy of the Speenhamland, the law contributed to the creation of a free, competitive labour market (Polanyi 1944, 81–9). For Marx, the notion of the 'free' labourer is inseparable from capitalism, and the 'freedom' of that labourer amounts to dispossession.

The elevation of the 'English road' to the zenith of twentieth-century development thinking via post-Second World War theories of modernization instituted a mono perspective of development based on a sectoral rural–urban divide. This perspective saw peasant production in agriculture in relation to the question of productivity by reference to scale economies of cost-efficiency in a manner virtually identical to that described by Walt W. Rostow (1960) as 'catch-up developmentalism'. Rostow's notion of 'catch-up developmentalism' is characterized by the unleashing of an entrepreneurial spirit and mass commercialization, aided by the state, with an emphasis on a rising efficiency that increases productivity and creates new wealth. Similarly, Daniel Bell (1979, 10), in *The Cultural Contradictions of Capitalism*, has identified 'rationality' as governing the growth-oriented economic life. 'Rationality' consistently functions to minimize cost and optimize output through efficiency for the purpose of increasing productivity and productiveness. This type of growth regime requires 'competition which commands a decisive cost advantage … [with] its usual disciplining influence' (Schumpeter 2008 [1942], 84–5), thereby weeding out presumably low-performing small-scale producers and inefficient economic activity in a process of 'creative destruction' that creates the optimal conditions for economic growth (Schumpeter 2008 [1942], 81–6). The *modernist* imagery of economic development exemplified in the works of Rostow (1960) and Bell (1979) considers the dispossession of small-scale subsistence-oriented agricultural producers from the land a necessary condition for successful capitalist development. It persists and prevails today in the early twenty-first century as an essential narrative in the global governance of corporate agriculture.

A modernist imaginary of social change assigns two meanings to capitalist development. The first is cultural and the second is economic. Cultural modernization is thought necessary to increase 'rationality' in the organization of economic and social activity by reference to market-economy principles of competition. Market competition is assumed to mobilize resources and stimulate the impetus required for economic change and growth, in contrast to the immobility and conservatism ascribed to 'traditional' peasant culture, which 'blocks' development. Early examples of this perspective can be seen in Daniel Lerner's *The Passing of Traditional Society* (1958).

Lerner further points out that a change from the subsistence-based social arrangements of the village to the emergence of a market society requires a shift in the social–psychological orientation of the members of society. He identifies three stages (1958, 45) in the reordering of this orientation for the modernization process to occur: tradition, transition and modernity. For Lerner, transition implies that the *psyche* in members of a traditional, rural society is turned away from an attachment to the land and its subsistence-based cultivation toward modernity as shaped by physical, social and psychic mobility. A mobile personality is characterized by rationality and empathy. The latter is defined as the capacity to reflexively see oneself in the other's situation, which enables newly mobile persons to operate efficiently in a changing world by being more responsive to market economic conditions and the pressures of commercialization (Lerner 1958, 49–50). For Lerner, as with Rostow, the unleashing of an *entrepreneurial spirit* via the state's cultivation of mobility in personhood is the cultural backbone of a market society. This mobility is achieved through *human capital* creation by individuals who succeed in gaining productivity-enhancing skills. Such skills are necessary for active engagement in wealth generation and accumulation and, if necessary, in order to reflexively manage one's departure from agriculture (Becker 1962; Coleman 1988). This meaning of modernity is virtually identical with the neoliberal logic of economization in regard to reorienting human behaviour in accordance with the competitive, cost-efficient and formal logic of rationality required for 'being a success' in the market.

There is a widespread use of the concept of *human capital* in elaborations on the meaning of cultural modernization. It is viewed as essential for the remaking of individual identity as a self-governing and self-investing unit within the market. This fits well into neoliberal economization logic, which conceives selves as 'personal enterprises' within the market economy, not merely as subjects acting within the calculative, utilitarian liberal logic of self-interest but also as 'self-investing entrepreneurial human capital' motivated to increase performative values within a process of self-valorization (Brown 2015; Dardot and Laval 2013). The notion of human capital entails a shift of the self away from being solely concerned with earning a wage and maximizing returns in the economy (cf. Marx 1954 [1887]; Weber 1984 [1930]) toward becoming a value-enhancing personal enterprise that desires to increase self-worth and appreciation and prevent its depreciation within the market.

This view of the neoliberal self contrasts with Max Weber's conception of capitalists as expressing a calculative, instrumental rationality – not as an end for self-realization through work – but as a means of assurance for otherworldly salvation through ascetic abnegation and self-renunciation (Weber 1984 [1930]; 1946 [1915]). If we extend Daniel Bell's (1979) understanding of the cultural tensions of capitalism to neoliberal economization, one might argue that a neoliberal deviation from the Puritan roots of capitalism described by Weber would constitute a contradiction within the culture of capitalism. This is because Bell would argue that an emergent neoliberal culture of self-enhancement, promoted by the principles of market economics and economization (i.e. efficiency, productivity, optimization, rationality), would be dominated by a *hedonism* that undercuts the relationship between the ascetic values of work and a Weberian-style break with the self (i.e. through disdain for consumption and this-worldly pleasures). However, I contend that it is the normative expansion and deepening of market metrics and rationality in all spheres of existence that elevates the 'ethics' of competition and the 'spirit' of enterprise to the status of epistemic privilege as a critical condition in the neoliberal remaking of the social, hence resolving the cultural contradiction anticipated by Bell. As a form of rationality, economization allows the social to be re-made and operated like a 'business', with the self as a 'personal enterprise'. This reconstitution amounts to what is described in the title of a book published by Colin Leys in 2007 – *Total Capitalism*.

Economic modernization refers to the issue of production and productivity. It focuses attention on the most efficient ways of determining and organizing surplus product so that profits can be re-invested for expansion and improved production. The goal is to achieve the lowest production cost and greatest comparative advantage in world markets. This perspective on modernization entails a process of increasing 'rationality' through the development of large-scale firms in all sectors of the economy. According to Daniel Bell (1979, 12–3), 'the nature of change in techno-economic order is linear in that the principles of utility and efficiency provide clear rules for innovation, displacement, and substitution. A machine or a process that is more efficient or more productive replaces one that is less efficient.' The meaning of *modernization* here is similar to the concept of capitalist industrialization modelled on the nineteenth-century transformation in England from agrarian to industrial economic structures, as described by Barrington Moore.

In weaving together the cultural and economic meanings of modernization, Walt W. Rostow (1960) argues that once an *entrepreneurial spirit* is unleashed by the cultivation of a culture of rationality, there is ample opportunity for economic development to begin. International institutions of the post-Second World War development regime, including the WB, the IMF and the

United Nations (UN), have already acted to support the process. However, it requires turning some of the peasantry into capitalist farmers through techno-scientifically driven modifications in their farming practices. It also necessitates the destruction of low-yielding peasant farming on the grounds that peasant production cannot sustain significant productivity increases in agriculture (Terres et al. 2015).

There is a convergence of Marxist theoretical approaches to capitalism with non-Marxist interpretations of capitalism's modernity, as demonstrated by their shared assumption that the emergence of more efficient productive forces has gone hand in hand with the institution of large-scale private property and the production of commodities. This is exemplified in the work of Robert Brenner (1982) and Henry Bernstein (2010). From a Marxist perspective, Brenner (1982, 17) argues that the pre-industrial property system of Europe was incompatible with the requirements of economic growth, and that subsistence-based production by peasants, rooted in an attachment to the land, generated a widespread trend toward declining productivity of labour. Henry Bernstein (2010) suggests that the logic of peasant 'elimination', viewed as an aspect of rural class differentiation, lies in the historically bound, path-dependent processes of capitalist accumulation, which reduce all social forms into capital–labour relations, initially in sixteenth-century England and then more dramatically with the emergence of industrial capitalism in eighteenth-century Europe. Subsequently, if unevenly, this logic spread across the world economy via development projects, particularly after the end of the Second World War. According to Bernstein, rather than conceptualize peasants as being in possession of an enduring and distinctive internal logic of subsistence-based production expressed through 'core elements' of peasant society – household, kin, community or locale – it is better to consider their transformation within capitalism through an underlying process of proletarianization or semi-proletarianization. Since peasants cannot reproduce their means of production in the face of multiple pressures – including competition with other peasants over land, labour or access to inputs, to credit or to markets – they are ultimately marginalized, dispossessed and proletarianized.

The assumed modernity of capitalism commonly shared in social theory, establishes a link between private-property rights, land consolidation and economic growth, which includes processes directed toward the gradual dismantlement of peasant possession of land, including the commons, and subsistence-oriented production systems. It ultimately naturalizes the logic of economization for assessing productivity through a market calculus. While cumulative environmental impacts and ecological costs have been assessed as externalities, occurring outside of markets and outside of cost-pricing (Hawken 2010), the efficiency of small-scale agricultural production is placed well within the market calculus (Borras Jr. 2003). Therefore, the elimination of inefficient, 'low-performing' small-scale producers is justified for agro-industrial purposes in favour of large-scale land ownership and farmers conceived as private businesses. Research has shown that in Brazil, for example, market-led reforms and specialized large-scale production of agro-exports and biofuels have been driving peasant elimination and dispossession through land privatization and high concentration of landownership, both of which threaten agrarian liveli-hoods (Fernandes et al. 2012; Mueller and Mueller 2010). Similar interpreta-tions can be found in studies on the Movement of Landless Rural Workers (MST) in Brazil, the Zapatista Army of National Liberation movement in Mexico and the transnational peasant movement *Vía Campasina,* all of which represent a grassroots agrarian response to dispossession (Altieri and Toledo 2011; McMichael 2008; Wolford 2005).

In short, the persistent narrative of capitalist modernity is that the peas-antry is an economically static and inefficient group that embodies a position of cultural immobility and marginality, barely surviving poverty and failure. Viewed as economically inefficient and culturally unsuitable for the modern market-economic requirement of calculative rationality, peasants must be released from the land and turned into wage-earning labourers. Those who do not embody the norms of efficiency and productivity necessary for economic competitiveness in the market will be assigned to a realm of the *anti-economy* (Cameron 2004, 130–51). The anti-economy refers to a form of social spatial-ity, of social exclusion and marginalization created in the countryside and inner cities, beyond the norms of the competitive society. It is inhabited by those who cannot be accommodated within the enterprise culture of neoliberalism. Thus, these people may find themselves in the precarious category of wageless and dis-employed members of the informal economy, reclassified not in terms of their poverty as the poor but as the *shadows* of neoliberal capitalism socially excluded from the norms of neoliberal economization (Ferguson 2006). This process also results in the growth of megacities with large urban slums (Davis 2006), the expansion of legal and illegal international labour migration (Phillips 2009) and pervasive unemployment, poverty and marginalization in rural areas (Araghi 2000).

My research leads me to believe that it is a mistake to represent the neolib-eral remaking of agriculture as a homogeneous and monolithic phenomenon marked singularly by its dispossessing effects on the livelihood of small produc-ers. To do so fails to account for the situated variations and differentiated, une-venly experienced consequences of 'actually existing projects of neoliberalism' (cf. Brenner et al. 2010). Neoliberalism reflects a multiplicity of pathways and a great deal of variegation. Its policy recommendations and technical mecha-nisms are deployed in diverse political contexts that often exhibit historical continuity with the past, with varied political projects, social–cultural norms, inherited institutional frameworks, regulatory practices and political struggles (Atasoy 2009; 2016; Collier 2005).

Historically, the defining feature of agriculture in Turkey has been the consolidation of small-scale land ownership and a decline in the propor-tion of village families who do not own their land (Keyder 1993; Pamuk 1988). Notably, the Ottoman lineage has produced a counter-trend against the large-scale displacement and dissolution of smallholders in republican

Turkey (Atasoy 2016). While capitalist relations have gradually penetrated into agriculture and while the 'core of the *differentia specifica* of peasanthood' has been undermined since the beginning of state-led developmentalism in the 1930s (Keyder and Yenal 2011, 83), Turkey's re-organization of agriculture has not translated into a more permanent, large-scale *de-agrarianization* in terms of differentiation (i.e. increasing land concentration) and displacement (i.e. smallholders turning to wage work). Restructuring was only gradually undertaken in the 1980s under the Motherland Party (ANAP) government (1983–9), and successive governments have not completely retracted the earlier agricultural support policies of the national developmentalist era (Güven 2009). Although the most dramatic changes began to take place after the AKP came to power in 2002, small-scale agricultural producers continue to prevail in the more commercialized regions of Turkey, and a 'traditional' peasantry persists in the subsistence-oriented Eastern and Southeastern regions (Keyder and Yenal 2011). The present book examines the complicated relations of a *gradual shift* that has been occurring in Turkey since the 1980s, particularly since 2002, toward the intensified commodification of agricultural lands and commercialization in agriculture. The outcomes are differentiated between varied categories of farmers and uneven for the expansion of supermarkets in Turkey's food-provisioning system.

Expansion of Supermarkets into Agriculture

With its emphasis on performance values such as efficiency and high productivity, capitalist modernity embraces the growing power and influence of large corporations in food processing, agrochemicals, seeds and retailing. Indeed, the dominant trend in the current global agrifood economy is unquestionably marked by the exceptional concentration, growing influence and market power of transnational supermarket chains. Supermarkets constitute a unified presence in the commercialization of production, distribution and consumption of food and are now increasingly dominant in food processing and agrifood supply chains (Burch and Lawrence 2007). Accompanying this trend is the proliferation of private standards designed by supermarkets to regulate the behaviour and market access of farmers and processors. These developments signify the intensification and deepening of market rule and commodification, which, according to Harriet Friedmann (1992, 379), points to the 'suppression of particularities of time and place in both agriculture and diets'.

> (M)ore rapidly and deeply than before, transnational agrifood capitals disconnect production from consumption and relink them through buying and selling ... Farms would adapt production to demand for raw materials by a small set of transnational corporations ..., and in order to meet quality standards would buy inputs and services from (often the same) transnational corporations.
>
> (Friedmann 1992, 379)

Rural producers, it is argued, experience the commodification process as newly created producers of raw commodities, 'upstream' in the supply chain. They are increasingly subject to governance through private, non-elected market operatives of transnational supermarkets and agrifood corporations (Busch 2010; 2011).

Following their inception in the United States (US) in the early 1900s, supermarkets have seen relatively rapid growth in countries of the global North. Supermarkets have also proliferated in the global South since the 1990s, yet their growth rates and influence on the restructuring of agrifood chains have varied across regions and countries (Berdegue and Reardon 2008). Wal-Mart from the US, Carrefour from France, Ahold from the Netherlands, Tesco from the United Kingdom and Metro Group from Germany are among the largest international supermarkets. In Turkey, supermarkets have been expanding significantly since the late 1980s. Initially, supermarkets' entry into food retailing occurred through the market consolidation of joint ventures with transnational food retailers by Turkish holding conglomerates. Since the 1990s, the growth in the number of supermarkets has been due to the rising number of Turkish-owned domestic supermarkets. Supermarket expansion in Turkey occurred during the same time period as in Latin America, which Reardon, Timmer and Berdegue (2004, 17–9) define as the 'first wave'. The 'second wave', affecting East and Southeast Asia and Central Europe, occurred 5–7 years later. The 'third wave' of expansion occurred in smaller countries in Latin America, Central America, Asia, and especially South and East Africa, while the 'fourth wave' is now occurring in South Asia and West Africa. These waves correspond in large measure to changes in income distribution, rate of urbanization, women's entry into paid work, the popularization of credit-card use and policy changes favouring supermarkets over traditional food-provisioning systems.

Recent scholarship explores various aspects of this general trend. The areas examined include the extensive agrifood value/commodity chains that globally link producers and consumers in a new international division of labour (Bair 2009; Goodman and Watts 1997); genetic modification, agricultural biotechnology and intellectual property rights protocols (Deibel 2013; Kloppenburg 2010; Pechlaner and Otero 2008); the environmental consequences of new technologies and regional ecological sensibilities (Campbell 2009); food safety, nutritional problems and health concerns including obesity (Dixon 2009; Otero et al. 2015); the increasing influence of finance capital on the agrifood system (Burch and Lawrence 2009; 2013); supermarkets' role in rural community well-being (Dixon and Isaacs 2013); and private standards and the transformation of the agrifood supply chain (Atasoy 2013; Burch and Lawrence 2007; Davey and Richards 2013; Friedmann and McNair 2008; Reardon et al. 2009; Richards et al. 2013).

Research reveals that supermarkets play a major role in the production, distribution and consumption of food throughout the world. This research shows that there is a shift from traditional subsistence-based food production to luxury, supermarket-owned private label products and new types of manufactured 'ready meals' – a trend that tends to undercut small-scale farmers and wholesalers from local and regional markets (Burch et al. 2013). These changes undermine local farming systems and food sourcing in diets while paving the way for corporate-controlled homogenization and standardization of food tastes and diets. By shifting from food retailing to food production, supermarkets increase their power over a highly controlled and monitored industrialization of agriculture that includes food quality and ecological sustainability standards (Burch and Lawrence 2007; Jansen and Vellema 2004; Winson 2013). Supermarkets' growing involvement in the production of 'own brand' and rationalized meals represents increased inter-firm integration in food provisioning among retailers, biotechnology companies, food-brand manufacturers, suppliers and farmers (M. Harvey 2007). Such developments change food-provisioning systems and associated processes of capital accumulation throughout the world by incorporating some large farmers while marginalizing and dispossessing many small producers (Magdoff et al. 2000).

In reorganizing 'local production for distant consumers' (Fonte 2006), supermarkets are establishing linkages with farmers in most areas of the world through formally established 'contract farming' (Watts 1990), and informally applied 'implicit contracts' and 'preferred supplier lists' (Reardon and Timmer 2007). However, their impact on small producing communities and traditional production methods is open to debate (Reardon et al. 2009). Some scholars argue that small and medium-sized farms producing for domestic and export markets are not disappearing (Berdegue and Ravnborg 2007, 2). Small producers in Mexico, for example, prefer contract farming in non-traditional export avocado production, which they view as a viable survival mechanism to gain market access for their produce (Echanove-Huacuja 2006). In Turkey, due to the gradual dismantling of state support for small-scale agriculture, smallholders producing tomatoes for the processing industry have begun to participate in contract farming as an alternative source for credits, inputs and other forms of technical assistance (Ulukan 2009). However, my research shows that the likelihood of contract farming expanding in Turkey's agriculture is uncertain. For example, fresh fruits and vegetables continue to be supplied to supermarkets *mainly* through wholesale markets without the use of contracts (Atasoy 2013).

Challies and Murray (2011) point out that in Chile, small-scale raspberry producers' integration into supply chains increasingly depends on their capacity to comply with retailers' quality standards. Small-scale producers often lack reliable information on a diversity of quality standards, means of grading and certification, and types of inputs to be used. They also lack the infrastructure, technology and capital necessary for cooling, storage, sorting, packaging and transport requirements. Consequently, they cannot readily meet the quality, consistency and volume requirements of supermarkets. Supermarkets also have difficulty cultivating direct ties with a large number of small producers. Research confirms that similar patterns are observed in many other countries in the global South, including historically significant agro export–producing countries such as Brazil (Mainville and Peterson 2005). However, recent research on Australian citrus-fruit growers indicates that these often mandatory standards have not resulted in uniform impacts or responses across agrifood systems (Tennent and Lockie 2011). Different types of supply chains also co-exist (Atasoy 2013; Hueth et al. 1999; Pritchard et al. 2010). In light of these competing interpretations, it is important to be context-specific about the 'power' of supermarkets in reorganizing and controlling supply chains, from seeds and seedlings to retailing and consumption (Morgan et al. 2006). Even if supermarkets are becoming globally dominant, as this book shows, their influence across the agrifood sector may take a variety of forms. An emphasis on context-specific diversity establishes the futility of positing a linear, singular and homogeneous transformation in agrifood systems across distant and diverse areas.

Turkey shares the general historical pattern of global agrifood restructuring, which began in the early 1980s in many places in the global South, when market-oriented economic restructuring measures were introduced in response to the global economic crisis. Many countries adopted the common structural adjustment policy criteria, which profoundly altered the state-led developmentalism implemented between the 1930s and the 1970s (McMichael 2012b). However, there is great variation among these countries in terms of the national/local trajectories of agrarian change experienced during both the state-led developmentalist era and the current, ongoing period of market-oriented economic restructuring. Such shifts in policy orientation have affected agriculture and food-provisioning systems in all countries of the world, though in different, socio-spatially variegated ways.

In Turkey, the traditional food provisioning system consists of small-scale producers, small independent family-run retailers, wholesalers, traders and neighbourhood-based street markets (known as *pazars*). However, shifting relations of food provisioning under the influence of global biotechnology companies and the recent expansion of a supermarket model remain largely neglected in social science research in Turkey. To the best of my knowledge, no books or journal articles on the subject of supermarket proliferation have been published in Turkey, with the exception of my own article, 'Supermarket Expansion in Turkey: Shifting Relations of Food Provisioning', published in the *Journal of Agrarian Change* (2013). Given the paucity of such research, it is difficult to assess the impact of these changes on production and consumption, land use and class relations, which have historically been tied to traditional ways of organizing food-provisioning activities.

Existing research on food relationships largely focuses on trade liberalization and transformation in foodstuff retailing as associated with marketing structure and market capitalization (Özcan 2008). Recent research on Turkey also examines the market access of growers and the business dynamics of supermarket supply (Codron et al. 2004; Lemeilleur and Tozanlı 2007; Lemeilleur and Codron 2011). It identifies the current links between supermarkets and small producers as weak and suggests the need for improvement in marketing structures. My work offers a more comprehensive and critical re-thinking of the neoliberal remaking of agriculture and the shifting relations and practices of food provisioning in Turkey, with comparative and complementary observations drawn from various regions of the world.

A Brief Overview of Recent Developments in Turkish Agriculture

It is worth noting a few key areas of importance for agricultural production in Turkey. A particularly significant case in point is fresh fruits and vegetables (hereafter FFV). According to the Ministry of Food, Agriculture, and Livestock, agriculture's GVA (gross valued added) contribution to Turkey's overall economy is 9 per cent. This also represents 25 per cent of employment. The 9 per cent GVA contribution is high compared to the 6 per cent figure in Brazil, 3 per cent for Spain and 1 per cent for Germany and the US (Republic of Turkey Ministry of Investment Support and Promotion Agency [RTMISPA] 2014, 4). Turkey has become a major global producer and exporter of FFVs since the 1980s. It remains among the top ten producers globally in almost all types of fruits and vegetables. FFV production constitutes 40 per cent of the value of total agricultural production in Turkey (Bignebat et al. 2009, 807). According to the Ministry of Food, Agriculture, and Livestock, the gross value of Turkey's agricultural production rose from US$ 27 billion in 2000 to US$ 63 billion in 2012, with export contributions increasing from US$ 4 billion to US$ 15 during the same 12-year period. The Turkish agrifood industry recorded a US$ 5.6 billion trade surplus in 2014. As part of its target for the agricultural sector for 2023 (the centennial of the founding of the Republic), Turkey aims to be among the top five global producers with a gross production value of US$ 150 billion (RTMISPA 2014, 6). In addition to effectively feeding a population of 78 million people, Turkey has become an important FFV exporter (and leader in the case of tomatoes) in some regional markets, including the Russian Federation and the EU (RTMISPA 2014, 19).

More specifically, with a total production of 29.5 million tons (TÜİK May 2015), Turkey is the fourth largest vegetable producer in the world, after China, India and the US (Abak et al. 2010). With a total production of nearly 10 million tons per year since 2005, Turkey is the third largest tomato producer in the world after China and the US (Bignebat et al. 2009, 809). Tomato production increased by 26 per cent between 2000 and 2010. Turkey has also become a major exporter of processed fruits and vegetables. It is fifth in canned FFVs, first in jams and fourth in dried fruits and vegetables (RTMISPA 2014: 41). Turkey is also the world's leading producer of cherries, hazelnuts, sultanas/raisins, dried apricots and figs.

Overall, domestic food demand grew 14 per cent between 2007 and 2012. It is forecast to grow 6 per cent between 2012 and 2017, due mostly to urbanization and the growing population (RTMISPA 2014, 8-9). Although no single food group dominates, FFV is the basis of the Turkish diet, followed by cereals (mostly wheat). As compared to 40 kilograms of FFV consumed per person in Brazil (Mainville and Peterson 2005, 131) and 180 kilograms in

France and the US (Codron et al. 2004, 594), FFV consumption in Turkey is 338.1 kilograms per person, with 107.6 kilograms of fruits and 230.5 kilograms of vegetables consumed per person in 2003. This constitutes a 43.6 per cent increase from 1960 levels of consumption in Turkey (Akbay et al. 2007, 210). As compared to approximately 2.5 per cent of income spent on FFVs in Brazil and 4 per cent in the US (Mainville and Peterson 2005, 131), FFV accounts for 26 per cent of the total food budget of Turkish consumers. In 2003, the average consumption of cereals in Turkey was 217.5 kilograms per person, a 4.1 per cent increase from the 1960 level, representing 9.1 per cent of total food expenditures. Cereals (mostly wheat) are the basis of several staple foods in Turkey, including bread, macaroni and bulgur. Pulses, including lentils, chickpeas and dried beans, are also widely consumed, with a 2003 consumption rate of 10.9 kilograms per person (a 17.2 per cent increase from the 1960 level of consumption) (Akbay et al. 2007, 210, 217). The share of processed food is estimated to be 10–20 per cent of food consumed in Turkey (Rehber 2000, 27), although this may have changed since the early 2000s. Still, Turkey appears to have the lowest per capita consumption of packaged food in Europe (Berk 2013, 2).

The case of Turkish agriculture, supplying both domestic and export markets, demonstrates the continuing importance of small-scale producers in commercial agriculture – producers who have a relatively low level of vertical integration with supermarkets and agribusiness firms (Atasoy 2013). Although contract farming for international and domestic processing companies and domestic exporting firms has recently begun in tomato, tobacco, sunflower, and corn seed production (Ulukan 2009), FFV production is still dominated by small producers, and the FFV supply chain is organized mainly through specialized traders, wholesale markets and *pazars*, often without the use of written contracts. Informal networks of street vending also continue to be a significant aspect of commercialization in food provisioning.

The expansion of 'modern, organized trade' in food retailing is taking place within this system of food provisioning dominated by small-scale producers and retailers. 'Modern, organized' trade is comprised of corporate chain entities.[2] The share of 'modern trade' in food retailing, including supermarkets and discount stores, increased from 33 per cent in 2007 to 47 per cent in 2012, with corresponding declines in 'traditional, unorganized trade' from 67 per cent in 2007 to 53 per cent in 2012. Traditional trade includes *pazars* as well as stand-alone 'mom and pop' shops. Informal marketing of food by farmers themselves through street vending is excluded from these definitions. A 6.8 per cent increase in the share of modern trade and a 5.5 per cent decrease in traditional trade is forecast by 2016 (RTMISPA 2014, 16), with supermarkets and discount stores being the main drivers in the growth of modern trade in food retailing (RTMISPA 2014, 17). The continuing significance of traditional food provisioning and informal retailing and the growing importance of supermarket and discount chains in food retailing, together with concomitant changes in agricultural production, constitute areas that have not been systematically studied in Turkey. This book represents an effort to fill that important gap in the literature.

Turkey's path to a market-oriented agriculture differs sharply from the 'Brazilian model' of global agriculture (Collier 2008). Brazil has become a global powerhouse of agro-industry and agro-exports in biofuel and biodiesel crops, including soybeans, sugarcane and palm oil, as well as high-value animal protein products and fresh fruits and vegetables, in addition to its more traditional exports crops of coffee and sugar (Wilkinson and Herrera 2010). Many of the agro-export projects of Brazil are vertically integrated with large agribusiness firms and supermarkets (Selwyn 2010). Brazil has one of the world's most concentrated land-holding structures, with large national and transnational corporations increasingly concentrating market power while extending into new 'frontier' lands in the Amazon rain forest, displacing many smallholder farmers in the process (Wilkinson and Herrera 2010). Such differences in global agriculture, as highlighted here through the example of Brazil, illustrate the co-existence of heterogeneous commodity networks in global agrifood systems. In the case of Turkey, each path in the neoliberal making of agriculture expresses a different type of food production and supply chain, which creates different localized challenges and opportunities for producers and consumers. Moreover, each path has been differentially consolidated into the long-term and unevenly combined processes of global agrifood restructuring.

Methodology

How do we explain why a country follows both similar and divergent policies over time within the commonly encountered restructuring of global agriculture and food? How does a general trend become a practice in a specific location? What are the locally/regionally particular, distinct rationales in producing certain outcomes? In searching for answers to these questions, this book employs a form of comparative perspective that allows the spatially and temporally particular processes of neoliberal restructuring of agriculture and food in Turkey to be simultaneously distinguished from, yet related to, changes taking place in global agrifood dynamics.

Henisz et al. (2005), among others, argue that international pressures of coercion, normative emulation and competitive mimicry constitute key aspects of the international diffusion of policy and the domestication of ideas, principles and norms. However, a market-economy model has not taken hold to the same degree nor have its effects been uniform across all countries (Brady et al. 2005). Its broader trends and general processes often unfold differently across contexts. This is important if we are to critically reflect on continuities as well as divergences across cases within the general world historical context of market intensification in agriculture. Indeed, recent scholarship has brought forth the broader historical contexts of interrelationships between global agrifood systems and the place-specific relationships of rural food producers and networks (Morgan et al. 2006).

Even our understanding of the words 'global' and 'local' has become increasingly nuanced and complex, arising from the question of location in relation to a range of food-related activities as well as the production of value and meaning that accompany these activities (Eriksen and Sundbo 2015; Feagan 2007; Mandelblatt 2012). Rather than a general policy convergence on the practices of the market economy, which transfers 'the model' from one jurisdiction to the other in a 'one size fits all' manner of standardization, there are great space-specific variations, divergent patterns and context-bound particularities among villages, town and regions *within* and *among* countries in regard to its deepening. This book contributes to critical political economy by shedding new light on the continuing importance of diversity across and *within* a geo-historical context, as well as the uneven nature of systemic change in global agriculture.

Attention to 'diversity' is a key concept in this book's approach to agrifood restructuring. However, it should not be conflated with the institutional orientation of the 'varieties of capitalism' approach developed by Peter A. Hall and David Soskice (2001). The 'varieties of capitalism' perspective is primarily concerned with the contrasting features and logics of 'diversity' expressed by national manifestations of capitalism that are seen as more or less institutionally coherent (Lane and Wood 2009). It tends to cluster country-specific institutional similarities and differences comparatively to show that the national institutions that support their markets differ substantially, thus generating different regulatory outcomes between 'liberal market economies' and 'the coordinated market economies' of the global North. The countries examined include Britain, France, Germany, Japan and the US. Diversity itself may provide clues that are useful for exploring the workings of an unevenly combined variegation within global capitalism. However, a formal comparative study of unitarily conceptualized, bounded cases (nation or firm-based cases), as Hall and Soskice have conducted, cannot prepare us for such an exploration.

In addressing the question of diversity, and thus problematizing the notion of a globally valid market-centred view, this book exposes the political content of the model as a time-specific and locally instituted project. There are always discrepancies and disjunctures between a general, externally designed, diffused and/or imposed set of policy recommendations, rules and normative standards and their domestic interpretation, internal mediation and implementation at the national and local levels. The global process of policy convergence is therefore frequently imperfect, contested and discontinuous and the forms of complementarity often varied. The uneven processes observed across geographically and historically diverse contextual conditions indicate that a complicated political process is currently underway within the general conjuncture of the global economy (Atasoy 2014). The present book attributes the *variegated* nature of global agriculture to the diverse forms of interaction with, and relational interpretation of, policy-making and policy-implementation sites and activities, which have their own histories and geographies. The combination of policies, redesign of local/national trajectories of development and re-alignment of the relations of capital and culture all further attest to this variegation. These complexities involve not only an economic policy-regime change across a socio-institutional landscape but also ontological changes in the *thinking* of social, cultural and ecological relationships.

The primary evidence for this book is drawn from Turkey. It examines diversity through locally, regionally differentiated processes and practices of agrifood restructuring across cases in Central Anatolia. My contextual analysis of official documents and histories is complemented by information gathered from fieldwork in several commercial FFV-producing villages and agricultural towns in the provinces of Ankara and Kırşehir in Central Anatolia. I conducted my fieldwork during the summer between 2011 and 2015. The fieldwork provided me with the essential qualitative data needed to examine people's own experience and understanding of the ongoing agrifood restructuring process. The book also draws from interviews that I conducted with 122 individuals in the provinces of Ankara and Kırşehir. Table 1.1 provides information on the individuals interviewed. Details regarding my meetings with respondents and specific interviews will be provided in each of the relevant chapters. A majority of my respondents are small-scale producers; only five describe themselves as large-scale. All are commercial farmers. The agricultural workers I interviewed include both local men and women and seasonal migrant workers of Kurdish origin from villages in Eastern Turkey. Producers in my sample are in their thirties and forties, with the exception of three who are in their fifties and late sixties. Participants were recruited through personal contacts in the community and snowball sampling. This was due to the challenges of finding different categories of farmers who implement different production methods and follow different commercialization strategies. In regard to workers, snowball sampling was required due to linguistic difficulties. Many of the agricultural workers I interviewed are Kurdish migrants with limited ability to speak Turkish. I conducted face-to-face, open-ended interviews with each of my informants. Interviews were approximately 2–3 hours long and digitally recorded. They have been subsequently transcribed and analyzed. All respondents consented to be interviewed and photographed. The Turkish farmers wished to have their names used in the book. Agribusiness managers and owners also gave consent to have their names used, as did the elected officials. Other respondents have been given pseudonyms.

Ankara is the third largest agricultural region in Turkey, after the Harran region in Southeast Anatolia and Konya in central Turkey. It contains 1,221,408 hectares[3] of arable land and land under cultivation with permanent crops,[4] of which 43,529 hectares are used for vegetable production.[5] The case locations (towns and villages) in Ankara and Kırşehir were selected to provide ethnographic detail and illustrative examples of the complexities and difficulties of agrifood restructuring in Turkey, where small-scale production remains dominant.

Both Beypazarı and Güdül are territorially adjacent towns within the province of Ankara, located in the north-west Central Anatolian basin. They are both connected to the Kirmir River, a branch of the Sakarya River. The Sakarya

Table 1.1 Summary Information of Interviewed Individuals

Province	ANKARA								KIRŞEHİR	Total
Town	City Centre	Güdül Centre	Güdül			Beypazarı Centre	Beypazarı		Kaman	
Village			Çağa	Karacaören	Kamanlar		Kayabükü Köyü	Fasıl Köyü	Savcılı Büyükoba	
Respondents:										
State Officials and Mayors	1	3	1							5
Turkish farmers		30	8	7	2		1		3	51
Syngenta officials							6			6
Rijk Zwaan officials							1			1
Foreign farmers (from Romania, Greece, Italy and Spain)							10			10
Agricultural workers		4					8	10	10	32
Greenhouse owners/ managers								3		3
Seed distributors						3				3
Agro-traders	1	1					3			5
President of Wholesale Markets of Turkey	1									1
Homemade food producers	2	3								5
Total	5	41	9	7	2	3	29	13	13	122

River is the second longest river within Turkey, after the Kızılırmak. The towns share commonalities in natural resource and watershed management issues. As shown in Table 1.2, Beypazarı has the largest number of farmers with Good Agricultural Practices (GAP) certification in Ankara, specializing in the commercial production of carrots and salad varieties for consumption in various regions of Turkey. There are five GAP-certified farmers in Beypazarı, one of whom I interviewed. Rather than enter into contracts with supermarkets, producers in Beypazarı prefer to market their crops themselves and through regionally recognized and trusted agro-traders and wholesale commissioners. Beypazarı also attracts large global biotechnology companies, such as Syngenta and Rijk Zwaan, which are engaged in the experimental cultivation of newly developed biotech seeds for vegetables and salad varieties (see Chapter 3). I have interviewed company managers and representatives of Syngenta and Rijk Zwaan in the village of Kayabükü in Beypazarı during an experimental farming day organized by Syngenta, as well as a number of foreign guest farmers invited by Syngenta to introduce their newly developed seeds and crops.

Table 1.3 shows the share of important food-crop varieties produced in Ankara in relation to overall production in Turkey. While I do not have official data on Beypazarı's contribution to overall production in Ankara, I assume it to be significant because Beypazarı has the largest concentration of farmers in the commercial production of salad, spinach and carrot varieties in Ankara. Güdül, on the other hand, has no farmers with GAP certification. Nonetheless, it produces a sizeable amount of commercially oriented hybrid and traditional heirloom varieties of FFV, often locally marketed by producers themselves.

As shown in Table 1.4, 45,717 farmers applied for registration with the National Registry of Farmers in the province of Ankara in 2013. Ankara contains 25 towns, seven of these within city boundaries (Altındağ, Çankaya, Etimesgut, Keçiören, Mamak, Pursaklar and Yenimahalle). Beypazarı has the sixth-largest concentration of farmers registered with the national registry in Ankara (2,160), while Güdül has the ninth lowest (615). Considering that seven of the towns with the lowest concentration of registered farmers are located within city boundaries, Güdül actually has the third lowest concentration of registered farmers in the province. Thus, the comparison between Beypazarı

Table 1.2 GAP Practices in Large Agricultural Towns in Ankara (2014)

Town	Number of Farms	Crop	Farm Size/da	Production/Ton
Gölbaşı	3	Mixed Fruits	4,380	1,500
Nallıhan	1	Lettuce, Carrots	1,330	5,394
Beypazarı	5	Lettuce, Spinach, Carrots, Onion	293	2,030
Polatlı	4	Onion	306	2,240
Çubuk	1	Mixed Vegetable and Fruit	25	30

Source: Umut Karakuay, Ankara Agriculture (official correspondence, 2014).

Table 1.3 Some Important Crops Grown in Ankara and Their Share of the Overall Production in Turkey (2013)

Crop	Amount of Production in Turkey (ton)	Amount of Production in Ankara (ton)	Share (%)	Ranking in Turkey
Safflower	45,000	24,876	55	1
Pumpkin	95,076	11,498	12	1
Lettuce (iceberg)	64,625	35,721	55	1
Melon	1,699,550	196,295	12	1
Green onion	153,478	18,454	12	1
Cooking onion	1,904,846	427,971	22	1
Cumin	17,050	10,239	60	1
Sunflower seeds (appetizer)	143,000	22,200	16	2
Spinach	220,274	26,268	12	2
Carrot	569,855	131,800	23	2
Green lentils	22,000	2,789	13	2
Sour cherry	179,752	28,183	16	2
Barley	7,871,618	683,764	9	2
Vetchling (fiğ)	114,218	17,333	15	3
Lettuce (with hub)	212,189	23,133	11	3
Marrow squash	293,709	26,312	9	3
Oat	235,000	20,447	9	3
Pear	461,826	17,749	4	3

Source: Umut Karakuay, Ankara Agriculture (official correspondence, 2014).

and Güdül provides important qualitative detail for a better understanding of agricultural variegation under neoliberal restructuring. A contrasting example is drawn from the village of Savcılı Büyükoba in Kaman, in Kırşehir province, which is also a significant FFV producer for local consumption.

In Beypazarı, I conducted my interviews in the villages of Fasıl and Kayabükü, and Beypazarı Centre. Beypazarı is both a town and a district. The district includes three other smaller towns and 64 villages. It has a population of approximately 47,000 people, 67 per cent of whom are engaged in agriculture. The Office of the Beypazarı District Governor (Beypazarı Kaymakamlığı in Turkish) lists information on its webpage pertaining to land use and areas of production for the year 2009.[6] According to the data, Beypazarı covers a total of 1,868,000 dekars of land (or approximately 186,800 hectares)[7], 35 per cent of which are agricultural lands equalling approximately 653,800 dekars (65,380 hectares). Approximately 15 per cent of these lands are irrigated. While 85 per cent of agricultural lands are used for grain production (nearly 55,573 hectares), 13 per cent are used for vegetable production (nearly 8,499 hectares) and 2 per cent for fruit and vineyards. Carrots and salad varieties are produced on nearly 4,000 hectares of lands, or half of the total land used for all vegetable production. In 2009, Beypazarı produced 110,000 tons of carrots and 44,000 tons of salad varieties. The district produces 60 per cent of Turkey's carrots. There is also significant spinach, radish and green onion production in Beypazarı.

Table 1.4 Registered Farmers in Ankara (Number of Applications, 2013)

Towns	Number of applications
Akyurt	939
Altındağ	123
Ayaş	2,080
Bala	4,823
Beypazarı	2,160
Çamlıdere	42
Çankaya	317
Çubuk	1,491
Elmadağ	1,091
Etimesgut	35
Evren	520
Gölbaşı	3,522
Güdül	615
Haymana	6,985
Kalecik	2,138
Kazan	1,114
Keçiören	84
Kızılcahamam	186
Mamak	148
Nallıhan	1,568
Polatlı	8,626
Pursaklar	176
Sincan	2,307
Şereflikoçhisar	4,283
Yenimahalle	344
Total	45,717

Source: Umut Karakuay, Ankara Agriculture (official correspondence, 2014).

In Güdül, I conducted my interviews in the villages of Kamanlar, Karacaören and Çağa, in addition to Güdül Centre. Güdül consists of 23 villages and three *belde*,[8] and it has a population of approximately 8,500 people. Kamanlar, Karacaören and Çağa have the largest concentration of agricultural land allocated for commercial vegetable production in Güdül. Çağa has the largest amount of land allocated for vegetable production, followed by Karacaören and Kamanlar. Çağa also produces geographical indication (GI)-certified local heirloom tomato varieties for commercial sale. According to official data, which I obtained from Agriculture Güdül,[9] there are 790 hectares under commercial vegetable production in Güdül out of a total of 23,800 hectares of agricultural land. Çağa has 600 hectares out of a total of 790 hectares of land under vegetable production, while Karacaören has 150 and Kamanlar 20. Güdül Centre has 10 hectares of land allocated for vegetable production. Regardless of the scale of production, farmers in Beypazarı and Güdül are heavily reliant on store-purchased inputs for their production.

The village of Savcılı Büyükoba in Kaman, Kırşehir, is in the Kızılırmak river basin. It shows much similarity with the farming practices of Güdül producers from the villages of Çağa and Karacaören. Producers in Savcılı Büyükoba also use self-saved seeds for the commercial production of local varieties. The population of Savcılı Büyükoba is approximately 2,500. Over 20 per cent of residents are vegetable and livestock farmers, while 50 per cent are involved in grain production.[10] It is common practice for producers in both Güdül and Savcılı Büyükoba to market their produce in local *pazars* through both formal and informal channels and via street vending. Producers in Beypazarı rely largely on the formal channels of agro-traders and wholesale commissioners. Kurdish migrants are informally employed by all the farmers in my case locations as a cheap source of labour. Situated along fertile river basins, none of the towns and villages noted has problems with accessing water for agricultural use – hence the commonly experienced indifference to water conservation.

This book provides a meso-level analysis. The goal here is not primarily to show locally/nationally scaled distinctions and institutional coherence. Rather, it is to reveal the contradictions, divergences and disjunctures, as well as complementarities and convergences, that emerge in conversation with the general processes and governance framings of global neoliberalism as it affects agriculture and food provisioning.

Organization of the Book

This introductory chapter addresses broad theoretical and methodological issues in relation to the neoliberal restructuring of agrifood systems. It also identifies the significance of the book.

Chapter 2, 'Breaking from the Past: Changes in Agricultural Land Use', explores the profoundly transnational dimension of agrifood industry transformation in Turkey. It does so in relation to the WB's articulation of 'new agriculture' through a 'direct payment aid' (DPA) policy and the unfolding history of the Customs Union (CU) in the larger context of the General Agreement on Tariffs and Trade (GATT, 1947–94), the Uruguay Round of GATT (1986 to 1994), the subsequent Doha Round of trade talks within the WTO, and the WTO's 1995 AOA. The various institutional and technical innovations adopted by the AKP government (since 2002) represent, for the first time in Turkish history, a *gradual* break from the (semi)subsistence-oriented small-scale grain production established during the previous developmentalist era, with its roots in the old Muslim–Ottoman traditions. The break from the past through the reorganization of landscapes, although gradual, encompasses the commodification of small-scale agricultural lands and contraction of rain-fed grain producing areas, with associated changes in land use, land access and reconfiguration of common-property resources, including public lands, water and bio-information. The emerging picture reflects a gradual disentanglement of land and natural resources from the long-established pathways of self-provisioning. The normative activation of *economization* as, increasingly, the dominant ethos and valuation of conduct can be best described by means of

Marx's concept of alienation and Polanyi's notion of 'fictitious commodities', supported by Weber's instrumental rationality thesis.

Chapter 3, 'GLOBALGAP and Agro-Biotechnology: Syngenta and Rijk Zwaan in Turkish Villages', provides data on the significance of efficiency and rationality values within the market economy model for the *optimization of performance* in agriculture. In combination with data analyzed in Chapter 2, Chapter 3 illustrates the practice of *techno-scientific economic management* of land, plants and bio-information as tradable commodities. It provides a detailed account of the growing expectation of farmers' conformity with biotechnology innovation in seeds and high-technology input-intensive agricultural production methods. Specific issues covered include government encouragement of GLOBALGAP standards and contract farming through the enforcement of privately established industrial food-quality standards and product innovation, as tied to the entrepreneurial rules of a competitive market economy model. The chapter elaborates on global homogenization of crop production by examining developments in global agricultural biotechnology and patents and trade in biotech seeds, including the expansion of an intellectual property rights regime. In addition to data drawn from official government documents, the chapter provides an in-depth analysis of interviews conducted with representatives of global biotechnology seed-industry companies such as Syngenta and Rijk Zwaan. It examines how corporate-driven pressure for standardized differentiation in food varieties and profit-oriented reorganization of farming practices is *brokered* in the remaking of agrifood systems. Interviews are conducted with company managers and officials from Syngenta and Rijk Zwaan at open-field trial demonstration days organized by Syngenta for its newly innovated seed varieties and breeds grown in Beypazarı. Additional interviews are conducted with farmers (both Turkish and foreign) invited to the demonstration days to examine the experimental growing of these varieties.

Chapter 4 and Chapter 5 demonstrate the co-existence of multiple pathways of commercialization in Turkish agriculture and food provisioning. Chapter 4, 'Farming Imaginaries: Convergence, Divergence and Beyond', draws information from interviews conducted with large-scale farmers in Beypazarı and Güdül in Ankara, as well as the owners of seedling greenhouses and seed distribution companies in Beypazarı. It reflects on the ways in which input-intensive capitalized farming practices are becoming a dominant productivist form. The chapter introduces the concept of *farming imaginaries*. It refers to the perceptions, aspirations and evaluations of farmers in relation to the normative acceptability of the techno-scientific ways which frame income/wealth generation and landscape management, including the use of soil/plants/water resources. The path followed by large-scale producers and seedling growers typically reflects a growth-oriented commitment to capitalized agriculture and techno-scientific innovation. It is based on a formal *institutionalized* commercial trust in the production of food by reference to GAP food-quality standards, even if farmers are not GAP-certified producers. The farming imaginaries of my respondents reinforce a transnationally advocated industrial agriculture, often implemented without vertical contract-based ties with supermarkets and agro-traders. However, the picture that emerges from my interviews is more complex. Even when farmers demonstrate significant conformity to the industrial model, they reveal divergent narratives rooted in the *duality of assessments* arising from their farming imaginaries, particularly in regard to sensitivities concerning agro-ecological landscape-management issues and conservation of natural resources.

Chapter 5, 'The Taste and Smell of Place', draws from interviews that I conducted with mayors and producers in the villages of Beypazarı and Güdül in Ankara, and Kaman in Kırşehir. It shows that although 'organic' and small-scale producers (both heirloom and conventional growers) share the farming imaginaries and ambiguities associated with industrial farming, they also 'distrust' agro-industrial methods of production. This distrust signals a more pronounced cultural dissonance in farming, which articulates a history of the senses, local food culture and heritage and the place of food. Although smaller-scale farmers do not entirely diverge from the scientifically driven, global agro-industrial system, they rely mainly on *personalized* relations of trust established informally with consumers and wholesale market commissioners. I call this form of trust *participatory certification by consumers*. It is through personalized trust networks that small producers secure their market viability as informal street vendors, *pazar* merchants and alternative producers of village products. Taken together, Chapters 4 and 5 reveal that the simultaneous co-existence of two modes of trust engenders different types of supply chains co-mingled within a market-oriented, profit-driven reshaping of food provisioning in Turkey, into which supermarkets are melded. The existence of different types of supply chains reflects variegation in farming imaginaries through which producers normatively frame their ambivalent attitudes over agricultural biotechnology and input-intensive agriculture, on the one hand, and interpretative assessments of modernity for national development and income generation, on the other.

Chapter 6, 'Trust and Trustworthiness: Paternalist Labour Relations in Agriculture', examines the labour practices employed by large-scale, organic and small-scale producers. Only a small number of farmers use unwaged family members. While the majority of open field work is done by Kurdish migrants, locals are often employed in enclosed areas. The chapter demonstrates that Kurdish migrants from Eastern and Southeastern Turkey constitute a highly exploited, informally employed reserve-labour pool in Turkish agriculture, largely due to their internal displacement. They are typically considered undifferentiated, bounded members of entire households. This chapter further shows that agro-labour contractors are the key institutional mechanism involved in the informal organization of a particular labour regime for Kurdish migrants, mediating the expansion of a capitalized agriculture equipped with the delegated power of labour control and management. The labour regime for Kurdish migrants connects horizontally established social relations of kin networks, geographic–regional connections and migration and household livelihood strategies into labour loyalty and management. I conceptualize the informal labour of migrant workers in terms of the *entire household as a labouring unit* with little or no gender or generational effect on wage determination and labour management. It is this block of labour that constitutes the site of exploitation. I compare the 'entire household as a labouring unit' concept with the employment of local workers who are viewed independently of household bounds and are differentiated along gender lines with corresponding wage inequalities. The gender effect on wages is based on the position of local workers in vertically established relations of production. To illustrate my argument, I draw from the in-depth interviews that I conducted with local and Kurdish-migrant agricultural workers, as well as agro-labour traders, in the towns and villages of Ankara and Kırşehir provinces in Turkey. In addition to my interviews with independently operating commercialized small and large-scale producers and a greenhouse grower, I offer data from interviews with workers employed on a farm subcontracted by the biotechnology firm Syngenta for the experimental growing of its newly innovated seeds.

Chapter 7, 'Supermarkets and *Pazars*: Divergent Paths', shows how different types of production methods and supply chains that co-exist simultaneously qualify supermarkets' ability to take hold in Turkey's food relationships, where small-scale production and neighbourhood *pazars* dominate and written contracts with supermarkets and agro-traders are of limited use. The chapter argues that supermarket expansion in Turkey involves both convergence with and divergence from the transnationally advocated model of new agriculture – as varying perceptions, ambivalences and power configurations interact. This is illustrated through an analysis of the domestic appeal of a supermarket model to various groups in Turkey, including Islamic capitalists. Supermarket expansion reflects the competitive growth of Islamically oriented capital groups in giving voice to the specific ways in which non-market value-based politics are also crafted in processes of capital accumulation and the political reconfiguring of class relations in Turkey today. The links between a market-economy model and moral–symbolic attachments are contingently centred on refiguring class relations in the context of a change from state-led national developmentalism (which historically marginalized Anatolian, small-scale Muslim capitalists) to a market-oriented model of development. While this change is in keeping with what the WB calls the 'new agriculture', it also represents the repositioning of Islamic capitalists in the economy in competition with large joint ventures owned by transnational corporations and Turkish holding companies. Thus, supermarket expansion in Turkey expresses *commonality* in the transnationally advocated development model and *difference* in terms of the culturally varied conditions of development.

Chapter 8, 'A Discussion on Diversity', weaves the foregoing strands of analysis into a general account of the commodification process in agrifood systems, in all its complicated multidimensionality and diversity. The cohabitation of these complexities contains an immense background context of knowledge systems and cognitive orientations with their roots in late Ottoman and early republican lineages. This context presents historical continuity with, and commitment to, a science and technology–intensive modernity *and* spiritual–emotive referents to Islamic principles that foster a holistic worldview. Both influences play a key part in shaping consciousness and agencies in terms of ambivalences, accommodations and mixed associations, interpenetrating with the deepening of an agro-industrial model that fragments and decontextualizes life.

Notes

1 I use the term *agrifood* to refer to both agriculture and food.
2 For the definitional distinctions between 'organized' and 'unorganized' retailing, see Chapter 7.
3 One hectare is equal to 2.47 acres.
4 https://biruni.tuik.gov.tr/bolgeselistatistik/tabloOlustur.do (accessed 19 January 2017).
5 https://biruni.tuik.gov.tr/bolgeselistatistik/tabloOlustur.do11 (accessed 19 January 2017).
6 http://www.beypazari.gov.tr/default_b0.aspx?content=1004. (accessed 4 March 2012).
7 One *dekar* is approximately one quarter of an acre.
8 *Belde* in Turkish refers to a large village with its own municipal status, typically having a population exceeding 2,000.
9 I obtained the data in an excel file via an e-mail communication in 2013.
10 http://ysf40.tr.gg/SAVCILI-B-Ue-Y-Ue-KOBA.htm (accessed 3 March 2014).

2 Breaking from the Past

Changes in Agricultural Land Use

This chapter places the expansion of a market-oriented agro-industrial model in Turkey in the context of land configuration by the state. It elaborates on the increasing commercialization in land use and land access and the concentration of landholdings through the various institutional and technical innovations adopted by governments. In Turkey, the state does not typically demand the expropriation of lands from small-scale agricultural producers. Rather, it uses land surveys, land registration, and cadastral techniques in the reclamation of public lands to be brokered for private commercial use. The state reclamation of public lands, land-titling and land-consolidation schemes – as a reworking of land commodification for private use – represents a *historical break* from the long-held practices of the old Muslim–Ottoman and early republican traditions on agricultural production and small producers' access to lands for subsistence needs. In drawing a general picture of this historical break, the chapter addresses the issue of state reclamation of public lands and their redirection toward private-investment projects in agriculture. Land-consolidation schemes that re-group privately owned, small-scale agricultural lands into larger parcels are also discussed in relation to the nature of the transfer of ownership and use rights. Future implications are considered as well. Finally, the chapter explores the promotion of a neoliberal development project by successive governments since the 1980s, setting in motion, for the first time in Turkish history, the state-led commodification of land for the expansion of large-scale capitalized commercial agriculture.

The long genealogy of Ottoman-republican continuity in regard to producers' land access and use for subsistence represents a departure from the patterns more commonly experienced in the global South. The problem of lack of access to land by the rural poor has been a prevalent historical trajectory inherited from the colonial past in much of the global South. There is a rich literature debating land use and access issues in postcolonial contexts. Characteristically noted is the variation in the trajectories and historical processes of reconfiguring land access and use patterns, as demonstrated by work on Africa, Australia, Brazil, China, Colombia, India, Mexico and Vietnam (Bair and Hough 2012; Dasgupta 2008; Godden 1999; Hall et al. 2011; Nuijten 2003; Sikor 2012; Sugden and Punch 2014; Vergara-Camus 2012). A range of contributions to the literature points to the importance of examining the spatially specific processes through which accumulation interacts with the historical characteristics of local, national and regional economic formations, resulting in outcomes that are varied and not easily generalizable. This insight strongly suggests that we should focus research on the actually existing relations of neoliberalism to reveal its continuities as well as ruptures with geo-historically existing practices and rationalities.

The historically specific trajectory of state exercise of power and authority over land use, access and common property resources in Turkey has discouraged the private concentration of wealth and power. Small-scale (semi)subsistence-oriented agriculture has been the dominant trajectory, although there have been many different practices and strategies within that type of farming. It is through these varied practices and in light of the historical dominance of small-scale farming that the very conditions of neoliberal capital restructuring in Turkey are embraced. The processes of neoliberalization do not redirect or turn capital restructuring against small-scale agriculture in the transformation of farmers as subjects of neoliberal agriculture. Small and large-scale producers *cohabitate* the same neoliberal condition, acting as agricultural businesses in their own differentiated ways.

In short, this chapter analyzes the complexities of a contextual shift carried out through the neoliberal policies of successive governments as they reconstitute commercial agriculture in Turkey. This shift should be understood as historically grounded and ideationally mediated. It cannot be reduced to the mere calculus of a market-based, performance-oriented valuation of neoliberal agriculture. The world-historical context that has influenced the twists and turns of Turkey's agrarian transformation, the adoption of associated institutional innovations and the importance of domestically rooted discourses, cultural practices and implementation challenges are the subject of this chapter. I also consider whether we might advance our understanding of deepening commercialization under the general processes of neoliberalism by examining the state's reconfiguring of land use and access in the geo-historical context of Turkey's agricultural practices. The implication here is that neoliberalism does not necessarily engender uniform impacts or responses in regard to property-ownership dynamics and distributive effects; it must be continuously supported by the state's active involvement in reconfiguring and deepening commodification.

In general, however, neoliberal global agriculture achieves broad distinguishing effects, mutating from within and 'nesting', perhaps uneasily, with other historical practices. As a performance-oriented model, neoliberal agriculture is *specialized* in the large-scale agricultural cultivation of selected plants and animal species and in terms of using relatively fewer ingredients for food processing by virtue of their relative cost. It is *intensive*, with a heavy focus on increasing capitalized, technical output per hectare in agriculture; per square meter in supermarkets and food-processing factories; and per worker. It is also *concentrated* in the hands of only a few corporations for production, distribution and retailing; and *financialized* through stock-exchange and shareholding arrangements with links to banking systems (Rastoin 2009, 15–16). These are generally agreed-upon characteristic features of capitalized agriculture and commercial agro-industrial food systems. Governments in Turkey have implemented a number of policies to reconfigure land use, land access and common property resources for the expansion of large-scale specialized and capitalized input-intensive commercial agricultural production by professional farmers. Nevertheless, small-scale production continues to be the dominant form, marked by genealogical roots in the modalities of the past while having strong aspirations for competitive growth in the future. Turkish agriculture, with its continuing reliance on small-scale production, is less dependent on private finance-capital markets and more dependent on non-commercial, non-profit-oriented public banks (Marois and Güngen 2016, 9). An increasingly generalized industrial method of agricultural production is taking hold and is being directed toward the commodity-intensive expansion of food provisioning aimed at 'distant consumers' (Fonte 2006, 215). This also has significant consequences for a geo-historically differentiated account of neoliberalized agriculture and food.

An analysis of the implementation of institutional and technical innovation in Turkey's agriculture requires a rethinking of the variegated farming practices within a state-led structuring of the neoliberal condition. This variegation is due to the already existing multitude of 'farming scripts' and 'styles' of farming (Vanclay and Silvasti 2009). Vanclay and Silvasti use the term *farming scripts* to explain the persistence of small-scale, family-based farming and its common features of production, along with the cultural character of a 'traditional peasant way of life' consisting of various habits, values, ethics and emotive aspects of living, working and gardening. Vanclay and Silvasti refer to *style of farming* to reflect the social differences between farmers in relation to differing bodies of knowledge, ideas and worldviews, as well as varying strategies and rationales – the physical expression of which is differentiation in farming practices. Different styles of farming are created through sociocultural processes as well as government policies and market relations. This suggests that farmers do not necessarily conform to a singular productivist agro-industrial notion of agriculture but rather manoeuvre themselves into various positions (van der Ploeg 2013). Both 'farming scripts' and the 'style/practice of farming' represent useful heuristic devices for examining the *cohabitation* of small-scale farming with a deepening agro-industrial model in the neoliberal transformation of agriculture.

In advancing this argument, I diverge both from Bernstein's (2010) argument that capital subordinates agriculture, which implies the end of a classical 'agrarian question'; and from McMichael's (2008) position, which assumes a farmer-led opposition against agrifood capital. My emphasis on cohabitation remains useful for interpreting variegation in the neoliberal practices of farming across and within regions and in relation to specific crops, types of farmers and landscape conditions. This suggests that relations are more complicated than a binary split between agrifood businesses, corporate bodies and large-scale farmers, on the one hand, and 'peasants', on the other, would suggest.

Turkish agriculture has experienced several periods of restructuring in its history (Aydın 2010), but one of the most significant occurred when Turkey entered into a customs union (CU) with the European Union (EU) in 1995 and subsequently signed a bilateral trade agreement in 1998. With capital accumulation through commercialization of agriculture as the objective, a number of significant changes have been advocated since the Justice and Development Party (AKP) government came to power in 2002 and as Turkey has proceeded on its long, tangled path to full EU membership. Among a myriad of policy initiatives, three are especially noteworthy in their capacity to initiate a break from the past and create a decidedly neoliberal trajectory. These include the commodification of agricultural lands, the introduction of a good agricultural practices (GAP) project, and the penetration and proliferation of agricultural biotechnology. They express differentiated instances of a combined process of instituting a 'new way of agriculture' through the neoliberal agenda to deepen capital accumulation in agriculture. The GAP project of 2004, the Agriculture Law (No. 5488) of 2006 and the Seeds Law (No. 5553), also of 2006, are instrumental in fostering deeper integration into global agro-industrial processes, including agricultural biotechnology (Atasoy 2013). I will examine the specific policy tools developed for this integration in Chapter 3.

The policy tools created to reconfigure land include the Land Conservation and Usage Law (No. 5403) of 2005, the 'Documentation and the Betterment of Problematic Agricultural Land' (STATİP) project of 2006, and the 'Prediction of Harvest and Drought Tracing in Agriculture' (TARİT) program of 2008. Taken together, these tools contribute to the simultaneous *expansion* of lands for large-scale commercial agriculture and the *contraction* of small-scale (semi) subsistence-oriented agriculture – developments that are critical for an inquiry into the overall transformation and commodification of land (Atasoy 2016; McMichael 2012a). Before analyzing land-use reconfiguration by the state, I describe the world-historical context of agricultural change in Turkey, which consists of the policy-implementation requirements that emerge from Turkey's EU membership bid, the World Trade Organization (WTO) enforcement of market rules and relevant World Bank (WB) loan agreements.

The Reorganization of Agriculture: World-Historical Context

The Helsinki Summit of 1999 officially positioned Turkey within the EU enlargement process. After the Copenhagen Summit of 2002, which accelerated the process, and with the beginning of accession talks in 2005, Turkey undertook a number of policies to implement EU-membership criteria. These criteria, established by the Copenhagen European Council of 1993, are commonly known as the Copenhagen criteria. A market-oriented neoliberal development model has been the dominant economic policy perspective framing the EU's Copenhagen enlargement criteria. Member-candidate states are required to institutionalize a neoliberal market economy model and enhance their capacity to compete with the EU (Eder 2003), including full participation in the customs union. The customs union (CU), which consists of all EU member states and a number of surrounding non-member states, entails free movement of goods between countries within the CU without customs duties and tariffs; the application of a 'Common External Tariff' (CET) on imports entering the union from third countries; and the application of a 'Common Agricultural Policy' (CAP) (Atasoy 2013, 551). Together, they establish the basis of EU economic conditionality for membership, which is moored in the market-oriented dynamics of EU policymaking for a single market (Pinder 1989). Given that Turkey aspires to full EU membership, CU requirements significantly affect Turkey's policy options in favour of a particular development model that leads to intensive agro-industrial agriculture.

Turkey's implementation of CU requirements for manufactured goods began at the end of 1995 and was extended to agricultural products with the signing of a bilateral trade agreement on 25 February 1998 (*Official Journal of the European Communities* 1998). With the start of EU-Turkey membership negotiations in 2005, the CU objective has been included in the negotiating guidelines as part of EU membership conditionality. From this perspective, the EU acts as an agent of external coercion for the enlargement and deepening of neoliberal economic policies in member-candidate states.

The Treaty of Rome (signed in 1957) had envisaged the institution of a single market as a phased programme to be completed by 1992 (Pinder 1989). Because the Treaty of Rome was neither approved nor disapproved by the General Agreement on Tariffs and Trade (GATT) (1947–94), both the CET and CAP policies were formulated through agricultural support policies outside GATT jurisdiction (Raghavan 1990, 160). Given that the United States (US) was also unwilling to keep agricultural products within the GATT system of tariff reduction, agriculture was excluded from trade negotiations, enabling both the US and the then European Economic Community (EEC) (1957–93) to pursue a protectionist policy in agriculture (Rosset 2006, 20) until the Uruguay Round of GATT (1986–94). Consequently, the post-Second World War figuring of the international agrifood system generated chronic surplus commodities, particularly in cereals, meat and dairy, both in the US and the EEC. This underlined a key historical contradiction in the system, which is rooted in strong state protectionism and the US-led restructuring of a global market economy (Friedmann and McMichael 1989).

The EU (established in 1993) and the US formulated different responses to this overproduction problem, which tends to lower prices. There was no common ground for policy compromise at the Uruguay Round of negotiations. The EU pursued a commodity-by-commodity 'exchange of concessions' strategy for products in oversupply. In contrast, the US pursued a market-oriented approach, asking all agricultural products to be included in negotiations for the complete removal of all agricultural subsidies by 2000. Direct payment aid

(DPA) to farmers was the only exception to the removal of subsidies, replacing support policies (Raghavan 1990, 171–4). Although a commitment to rolling back protection was the basis for the establishment of the WTO in 1995, which replaced the GATT (1947–94), the EU and the US have not committed themselves to subsidy removals. Consequently, old trade issues have continued to persist, bringing the subsequent Doha Round of trade talks within the WTO to a standstill.

The EU implements its trade-liberalization policy by obtaining commodity-based trade concessions on its surplus products through negotiating regional and bilateral free-trade agreements. Turkey's entry into the CU in agriculture occurred in this context of a standstill within the WTO. The signing of the bilateral trade agreement in 1998 enabled the EU and Turkey to exchange trade concessions in agricultural products: the EU obtained concessions from Turkey on its oversupply products, which include live bovine animals, meat, dairy and cereal; and Turkey received concessions for some of its products of export interest, including fruits and vegetables (fresh, chilled, dried and prepared) and olive oil (*Official Journal of the European Communities* 1998, L-86/4 and L-86/10). These reciprocal concessions have effectively framed the conditions for Turkey to shift its agriculture from one based on production of staple crops for subsistence to commercial production of FFVs (fresh fruits and vegetables) for consumption by distant consumers. Turkey's implementation of a WB- and WTO-induced DPA policy was also an integral part of that restructuring, which began in 2001 and lasted until 2009.

The DPA policy initiated by the WTO's 1995 Agreement on Agriculture (AOA) signalled a new period, invoking a market-oriented policy that commenced a reduction in surpluses in agricultural products through removals in trade protection, farm subsidies and government intervention. The AOA advocated that the DPA and its associated trade reforms be phased in over 6 years for countries from the global North and over 10 years for countries from the global South (WTO 1995). The reframing of the international agrifood system through the DPA policy has involved 'breaking the link between support payments and actual production (so-called "decoupling")' (Thomas 2008, 43). Decoupling was dependent on government guaranteed stable-income provisioning to producers. The decoupling of price support mechanisms, along with DPA, is envisaged, particularly within the EU, under the assumption that farmers adjust production in accordance with fluctuations in market demand, such that the removal of obstacles to trade liberalization is assured. Decoupling was expected to produce a better alignment for domestic agriculture of CU member states with world prices (Lee 2014, 67). Although DPA policy implementation was supposed to mitigate the adverse impacts of trade liberalization and price alignment on small-scale producers, AOA trade liberalization generated a context for competition among producers everywhere to produce and sell cheaply (McMichael 2012b, 138–40). In the process, those who could not enhance their competitive capacity were driven out of farming, especially in subsistence-oriented cereal production in market-adjusted agricultures.

Under the changed conditions of world cereal markets after the 2008 food crisis, when surplus crops were no longer a function of market prices, the CAP shifted its policy orientation from direct agricultural payments to rural development projects (Vaz et al. 2009). These projects are evaluated by policy makers in relation to their 'income-generation capacity' – a capacity now adapted to the efficiency, rationality and technological innovation requirements of a competitive market economy. Such requirements are teased out over the farming styles/practices, associated knowledge base and cultural perspectives of intensive and specialized agricultural production.

Market 'efficiency' and economic 'rationality' have been recurring themes that permeate discussions on institutional innovation for market-oriented agricultural restructuring. These themes have become the leitmotif used to justify policies that support large-scale capitalized farming reliant on input-intensive techniques and marginalize small-scale producers utilizing extensive farming practices. However, a policy position for or against large and small-scale farming reveals little on *how* a market model has been implemented and *what the effects are* in facilitating economic competition and growth. In Turkey, the government's preference for a certain development model is entangled with *both* styles of farming. In advancing this argument, I provide a brief illustration of the land-reconfiguration reform policy that has been implemented to contract small-scale agricultural lands and open a space for commercial activity.

Agricultural Reform and Contraction of Small-Scale Agricultural Lands in Rain-Fed Dry Farming

Turkey's integration into European food governance within the CU after 1998, and its adoption of the DPA policy in 2001 after signing the 'agricultural reform implementation project' (ARIP) aid agreement with the WB (World Bank 2001), paved the way for the removal of agricultural subsidies formerly paid to farmers in the form of price, input, credit and import–export supports (Özkaya et al. 2010, 10–1). ARIP, also designed to promote the harmonization of Turkey's agricultural policies under the CAP regime (ARIP Project Brief 2007, 1), was a means of decoupling subsidies from production in order to eliminate inefficiencies in farming practices. Thus, ARIP became the backbone of Turkey's structural-adjustment and stabilization program adopted during the 2000–01 economic crisis. The agreement identified agriculture as the driver of economic growth, which heralded a re-intensification of governmental mobilization for a market-economy model. Agricultural restructuring was perhaps not solely undertaken because of Turkey's commitment to the WTO's AOA and the EU's CAP but was largely driven by the need to increase productivity in agriculture to fuel economic growth – a response to the 2000–01 economic crisis, which triggered a 9.4 per cent fall in Turkey's GDP (Atasoy 2009, 109).

Tied to a WB structural-adjustment loan of US$ 600 million, the Turkish government committed itself to the abandonment of subsidies to stimulate surplus production for exports. ARIP, which was to be implemented over a 7-year period between 2001 and 2008, represented a government-led productivist attempt to liberalize agriculture. This policy shift reduced agricultural subsidies by approximately US $5.5 billion by the end of 2002 to only US $0.6 billion. Approximately 70 per cent of subsidy cuts were intended to remove government support guarantees for agricultural commodity prices, and the remaining 30 per cent for reducing agricultural-input support for credit and fertilizer (World Bank 2004, viii). In addition to a total elimination of the US $956 million in agricultural credits provided in 1999, government subsidies for fertilizer also came to an end, dropping from US $183 million in 1999 to zero by 2002 (TMMOB 2004). In 2001, the government also stopped its policy of purchasing cereals (TZOB 2005, 14).

These reductions in government support for agriculture were intended to be offset by the maintenance of direct payments, which, since 2001, had constituted 75 per cent of government support for agriculture in Turkey (OECD 2010, 18, 25). However, in reality, the implementation of the ARIP policy of restructuring agricultural subsidies resulted in decreased incomes for farmers, which fell by 16 per cent (US $2.7 billion) between 1999 and 2002 – and were disproportionate to agricultural outputs, which declined only 4 per cent (World Bank 2004, viii–xii). An estimated 80 per cent of the 16 percent decline in agricultural income is explained by this realignment of agricultural production without government support guarantees. The remaining 20 per cent decline derives from lower agricultural output as farmers reacted to lower profitability, as well as the lower demand associated with the macroeconomic crisis of 2000 and 2001 (Atasoy 2013, 553).

The DPA compensated for only 40 per cent of the net loss in agricultural incomes. Many farmers were not included in the DPA program because they were not formally registered with the Ministry of Food, Agriculture and Livestock (MFAL), even though the WB required the government to set up a national registry of farmers for implementation of the program. In fact, a national registry of farmers (Çiftçi Kayıt Sistemi – ÇKS) only began in 2001 in Turkey with the ARIP-required implementation of the DPA program. Initially, US $35 million of ARIP aid was allocated for instituting the national registry of farmers. In 2005 this was reduced to US $20 million and in 2007 to 11 million. In actual fact, only US $5.7 million of the ARIP budget was used for the registry (MFAL 2014c, 207–8).

According to the official statistical data that I gathered from MFAL's draft *Introduction to Agriculture*,[1] close to 2.77 million farmers out of approximately 4 million were included in the national registry in 2003 – an increase from the 2001 level of 2.1 million farmers. For unknown reasons, this number fell back to approximately 2.3 million farmers in 2011.[2] In other words, only 58 per cent of farmers have been registered by the ministry. The remaining 42 per cent appear to remain outside the government market-oriented policy implementation targets. Nonetheless, this does not mean that unregistered farmers operate outside the general state-led transformative context of agricultural restructuring – the main theme of the next two chapters.

Table 2.1 National Registry of Farmers

Years	Number of Farmers	Lands (Dekar)
2001	2,182,767	121,964,486
2002	2,588,666	164,960,378
2003	2,765,287	167,346,718
2004	2,745,424	167,099,180
2005	2,679,737	165,826,141
2006	2,609,723	164,930,261
2007	2,613,234	167,277,814
2008	2,380,284	157,694,645
2009	2,328,731	154,360,407
2010	2,320,209	151,027,251
2011	2,288,366	156,287,667

Source: MFAL (2014, 209).

The DPA implementation of the ARIP program has affected farmers differently depending on the size of their holdings. Large-scale farmers with lands of 500 dekar in size have been the primary beneficiaries of this program. Small-scale farmers with greater specialization in cereals including wheat and barley suffered the most when the government's support for grain producers fell from over 40 per cent in 1999 to almost zero in 2001 (World Bank 2004, xi). Nevertheless, agricultural restructuring has not resulted in more permanent *de-agrarianization* in Turkey (Keyder and Yenal 2011, 79–81), nor has it diminished the importance of small-scale production. Rather, the DPA policy has enabled the persistence of small-scale farming practices in Turkish agriculture to be sustained largely by the relative poverty of small producers in rural areas, which increased from 19.9 per cent in 2002 to 31 per cent in 2008 (TMMOB 2011, 526).

The restructuring of agricultural subsidies under ARIP has resulted in a steady decline in the area of land sown with cereal. In 2008, the ratio of total sown field area was 42 per cent of all agricultural lands in Turkey, 72.9 per cent of which was allocated to cereal production (TÜİK 2009, 16, 18). The wheat-sown area represents 64.8 per cent of the total area sown with cereals, and wheat constitutes 58.1 per cent of all cereal production in Turkey (TÜİK 2008a). The Central Anatolian region provides more than 50 per cent of lands allocated for cereals in Turkey (TZOB 2005, 5), with Ankara and Konya provinces being the most significant. However, there has been a steady decline in the area of wheat sown, from approximately 93 million dekars in 2004 to approximately 81 million dekars in 2008.

As seen in Figure 2.1, the amount of land cultivated for wheat production only began to decline after 2000, signalling a reversal in gains obtained since 1955 by small-scale farmers. Although wheat-cultivating areas in Turkey have declined since the early 2000s, Figure 2.1 shows that the amount of wheat produced has in fact increased since the 1980s, albeit with some fluctuation. For example, the amount of wheat produced fell from 21 million tons in 2004 to 18 million tons in 2008 (TÜİK 2009, 19–22). Nevertheless, as a whole,

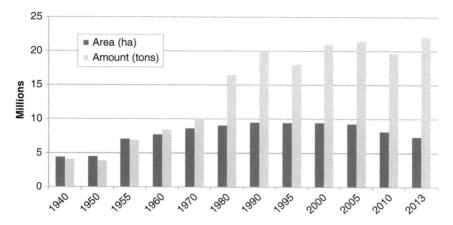

Figure 2.1 Wheat Production in Turkey (1940–2013).
Source: Author, based on data obtained from TMO (2014).

Turkey remained self-sufficient in both cereals and wheat, with a self-sufficiency ratio of 109.7 and 114.8 per cent respectively in 2009-10 (TÜİK 2011). The Turkish Statistical Institute (TÜİK, October 2015) estimated that the production of cereals and other crops would increase from 59.4 million tons in 2014 to 67 million tons in 2015, of which cereals production would constitute 38.6 million tons, an estimated increase of 18.1 per cent. It was estimated that wheat would increase by 18.9 per cent to 22.6 million tons and barley by 27 per cent to 8 million tons in the same time period. The overall increase in the production of cereals is likely due to the use of modern intensive techniques, as wheat cultivation gradually shifts from rain-fed dry agricultural lands in Central Anatolia, including Ankara,[3] to the irrigated lands of the Southeast.[4] However, the outcome is uncertain for Turkey's future self-sufficiency. In fact, self-sufficiency in both cereals and wheat declined to 86.4 and 89.2 per cent respectively in 2014-15 (TÜİK 2016).

The restructuring of agricultural subsidies, which resulted in a reduction in rain-fed agricultural lands in Central Anatolia, where small-scale producers are dominant, diverts extensive dry farming lands away from subsistence and semi-subsistence oriented cereal production to intensive farming on irrigated lands. This is believed to be a more commercially viable use of lands for the production of high value crops such as FFVs. Between 2007 and 2013, according to a report published by the Ministry of Agriculture and Rural Affairs (MARA 2014), intensive farming introduced on fully irrigated lands covered 18 per cent of farming land in Turkey. While the occurrence of semi-intensive farming corresponds to inadequately irrigated lands (2.9 per cent), extensive farming corresponds to dry, rain-fed crop production of cereals – which cover 78.5 per cent of productive agricultural lands (MARA 2014, 8). Figure 2.2 indicates that rain-fed dry wheat-cultivating areas in Ankara have contracted

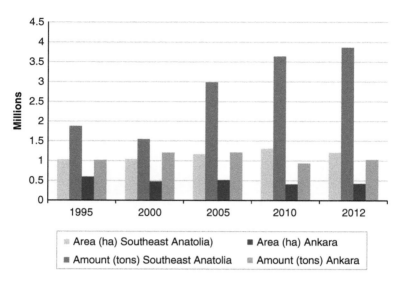

Figure 2.2 Regional Wheat Production (1995–2012).

Source: Author, based on data obtained from TÜİK (2009).

significantly, generating lands for non-agricultural sectors, while irrigation-based areas in Southeast Anatolia have expanded. The government policy of expanding agricultural production in Southeast Anatolia is further supported by the adoption of the 'Prediction of Harvest and Drought Tracing in Agriculture' (TARİT) program of 2008.

The application of modern intensive techniques in agriculture is supported by the TARİT program, which provides much of the required data through satellite imagery and various land-registry and land-mapping technologies. As of 2012, the TARİT program included 100 agricultural and meteorology stations equipped for sophisticated data analysis. Extensive information pertaining to drought and harvest predictions is now gathered through these stations located in the provinces of Şanlıurfa, Diyarbakır, Mardin and Gaziantep in Southeast Anatolia. The stations serve to generate infrastructural data on current land-use patterns and the means of conversion to more commercially effective types. Once irrigation-related infrastructural programs in the region are complete, there will be 1.82 million hectares of irrigated land – a full 20 per cent of all irrigable lands in Turkey (MFAL 2014c, 83–5). Within the larger Southeastern Anatolia Project (GAP), 610 km of irrigation canals were completed by the end of 2012, and over 1.1 million hectares of lands were consolidated in the region (SPO 2014, 121).

At present, the TARİT program in Southeast Anatolia has achieved only a fraction of the planned expansion of irrigable areas. While more than 90 per cent of lands in these provinces were used for dry rain-fed agriculture in the 1980s, more than 370 thousand hectares of lands were opened to irrigated agriculture by the end of 2011 (Oral 2013, 436). Existing government policy aims to harmonize land consolidation and other related land-development programs, while intensive farming on irrigated lands is intended to increase yields and overall productive use of lands. According to the Tenth Development Plan (2014–18) of the State Planning Organization (SPO), the cumulative area opened to irrigation by the General Directorate of State Hydraulic Works (*Devlet Su İşleri*, henceforth DSİ) was increased from 2.53 million hectares in 2006 to 2.81 million hectares in 2012. That area is expected to reach 2.91 million hectares by the end of 2013 and 3.75 million by the end of 2018 (SPO 2014, 99–100).

The shift to irrigation-dependent intensive agricultural production in Turkey, and in Southeast Anatolia in particular, will place heavy stress on underground and aboveground fresh-water sources throughout the country, most notably from the Euphrates and Tiger rivers in the southeast. The SPO's Tenth Development Plan indicates (SPO 2014, 138) that total available water resources in Turkey are 103 billion m^3. Of this amount, 39 per cent is currently used; 32 billion m^3 (73 per cent) in irrigation, 7 billion m^3 (16 per cent) in tap water and 5 billion m^3 (11 per cent) in industrial use. Turkey is now listed among water-scarce countries, with approximately 1,500 m^3 per capita water potential in 2013. By 2030, available water per capita is expected to decrease to 1,100 m^3, and Turkey may be exposed to water scarcity.

According to information that I obtained from the General Directorate of Ankara Agriculture, there are approximately 194 thousand hectares of irrigable lands in Ankara, which constitutes 16 per cent of Ankara's agricultural lands.[5] It is clear that the majority of agricultural lands in Ankara are less suited to irrigated production. Although I do not have official data on irrigation in Ankara, it is fair to assume that a growing emphasis on water-intensive agriculture may be a source of future tension among various groups of water users, given that 73 per cent of all water in use throughout Turkey is for irrigation. Future conflict may also emerge from government concessions of water-use rights and transfer of water management to private commercial interests.

Ultimately, the state owns all water resources in Turkey, which it manages through the DSİ – the main government agency for the development of water and land resources. Since the mid-1990s, the DSİ began to manage these resources through concessions, transforming its state-level management into privately held exclusive water-users' associations (WUAs) formed by commercial farmers as well as into private companies involved in hydroelectricity generation (Svendsen 2001). The organization of farmers into local-level WUAs guarantees their exclusive access to and management of water sources. These associations assume the operational and maintenance responsibility (formerly held by the DSİ) for organizing irrigation at the local level, while the DSİ provides institutional and financial support.

WUAs first formed during the 1950s, but their development was slow. Progress accelerated under the transfer programme for irrigation through ground and spring water funded by the WB in 1993 (Svendsen 2001). The WUAs represent one of the earliest examples of irrigation management transfer in the world through a model based on local groupings of water users for irrigation but without involving extensive community organization at the local level. There are downward links between the DSİ and the local village-level irrigation associations of farmers. An editorial published in *Zaman Gazetesi* on 12 January 1999 described the state transfer of water-use management from the DSİ to private bodies (including public–private partnerships) as Turkey's biggest act of 'hidden privatization' (Altınbilek, *Zaman Gazetesi*, 12 January 1999). Nevertheless, the state maintained its ownership of water sources and irrigation facilities (Svendsen 2001).

Law No. 6171 (enacted on 8 March 2011) is one of the latest regulations on irrigation-management land transfers, designed to facilitate the operation of WUAs as joint stock–like private bodies.[6] According to the law, a WUA can be founded with the participation of at least 15 and at most 100 farmers over an area that may extend beyond one village and operates in a joint-stock company–like structure. Currently, the DSİ transfers approximately 94.6 per cent of its irrigated areas, irrigation operations and related facilities to WUAs to be locally managed (DSİ 2014, 66). According to the DSİ's 2014 report, the total area of irrigated land in Turkey is approximately 6.09 million hectares out of 8.5 million hectares of economically viable irrigable lands. The DSİ developed 3.8 million hectares of these lands (DSİ 2014, 62). Approximately 81 per cent are irrigated from aboveground water sources and 19 per cent from underground sources (DSİ 2014, 64). Out of the total DSİ-managed irrigated lands, 2.5 million hectares have been transferred to WUAs. Currently, there are 393 WUAs in Turkey, holding 89.1 per cent of the state-transferred water-use rights for irrigation in commercial agriculture (DSİ 2014, 66).

Government support for a reduction in rain-fed dry agricultural lands also results in the incorporation of more dry lands into the urban fabric and other artificial areas for real-estate development (Atasoy 2016). In other words, the reduction of rain-fed lands releases more lands that can be consolidated into larger parcels for water/irrigation-intensive commercial FFV farming as well as for real-estate expansion, thereby undermining the economic vitality of small-scale farming in Turkey.

At this juncture a key fact emerges. It is through state policy that the individual actions of agricultural producers are rendered to assume an entrepreneurial quality, turning 'inherently unproductive' small-scale rain-fed dry lands into 'financial assets' by disposing of or selling them for more productive commercial uses (Atasoy 2016). As Polanyi (1944) has noted, the construction of a market economy requires policy making and implementation by the state. State policy is predicated on a 'productivity discourse' (Kumar 2016) that assumes that individuals, in economic terms, can make good use of their 'assets' by engaging in profitable endeavours to obtain and maximize commercial returns. Thus, the neoliberal condition is created through a state policy designed to reorient agriculture, imbuing it with an ontological belief in large-scale commercial intensive agriculture as the sole model for productivity and competitive growth. It is within this context that accelerated land consolidation, land reclamation and expansion of irrigation infrastructure are undertaken to increase the effectiveness of land-development implementation for a commercial economy.

The Neoliberal Condition: Instituting Changes in the Reorientation of Agriculture

As noted earlier, the AKP government has implemented a range of policy reforms to establish new political conditions, change the rules of agriculture and transform relations of production in an effort to institute greater competitiveness in the agricultural sector. There are 15 different laws that have been adopted to sustain a program for structural change and transformation in agriculture (MFAL 2013, 17). The following section provides a critical analysis of several of these programs, including the Land Conservation and Usage Law (No. 5403) of 2005, the 'Documentation and Betterment of Problematic Agricultural Land' (STATİP) project of 2006, and the TARİT program of 2008. This analysis is critical to understanding how the state-led institutionalization of large-scale specialized and input-intensive agriculture has generated, for the first time in Turkish history, the structural possibility of increasingly concentrated landownership.

Land Registration, the Cadastre Modernization Project and Land Consolidation Schemes: A Historical Break with the Ottoman Past

The commercialization of agriculture involves alterations in land use, land access and common property resources. In Turkey, in addition to land consolidation schemes, the state uses land surveys, land registration and cadastral techniques in reconfiguring lands (private and public) to be brokered for commercial use. The implementation of these techniques deepens a process of de-peasantization and de-agrarianization within which livelihoods become increasingly mediated by commercial ties (cf. Marx 1954[1887]; Polanyi 1944).

The land area of Turkey extends across 778,000 km². Forests represent 26 per cent and pasture 12.3 per cent of the total, neither of which can be used for commercial purposes. The remaining 61.7 per cent consists of Turkey's cadastral land (480,000 km² in total), of which 5 per cent is used for residential purposes and 56 per cent is rural lands (Bank and Mataracı 2004, 3). The founding of the General Directorate of Land Registry in 1924 (Law No. 474) initiated cadastral work in Turkey. In 2002, the private sector was also permitted to survey lands and parcel boundaries. In 2008, the government of Turkey signed a loan agreement with the WB for a 'land registry and cadastre modernization project'. Turkey received €135 million to develop a more reliable land register.[7] This loan agreement enabled the government to offer subcontracts to private companies, which use a wide range of modern measurement techniques to develop more precise geodetic infrastructure information on land.

Aerial photography, high-scale photogrammetric and geodetic map production have been used as information technologies to generate nation-wide data and to more accurately appraise, register and re-map 'untitled' common lands. The use of these data collection techniques has revealed the existence of large tracts of 'available' lands recorded as 'public' and owned by the state, effectively masking the customary uses of these lands and the associated livelihood practices of the users. The development of a high technology–based national geodetic infrastructure, then, has provided an effective means for the state to claim greater control and ownership of common lands.

The General Directorate of National Property (GDNP) was founded in 1942 within the Ministry of Finance and has the mandate to manage public lands. There are two types of public lands in Turkey: those registered as 'private immovables of the treasury' and unregistered lands (Atasoy 2016, 6). The amount of registered immovables increased from approximately 95,000 km² in 2002 to 230,000 km² in 2013.[8] Immovables consist of 3,749,420 parcels of land (Maliye Bakanlığı 2014, 8–9). The GDNP also classifies some public lands as 'under state ownership and use', which allows the government to make these lands available for private and public investment projects. The amount of land 'under state ownership and use' has also increased from 69,872 parcels covering approximately 7,578 km² in 2010 to 95,877 parcels covering approximately 9,692 km² in 2014 (Maliye Bakanlığı 2010, 14; 2014, 8–9, 10, 54, 83). This constitutes 3.9 per cent of land surface and 2.4 per cent of parcels of registered immovables (Maliye Bakanlığı 2010, 10). Forests in Turkey are protected areas owned by the state. They cover 171,971 km² of public land, comprise approximately 75 per cent of immovables (Maliye Bakanlığı 2014, 10) and are kept outside of commercial use. However, the development of a high-tech geodetic information system and the use of satellite-based maps, which facilitate more precise measurement of deforested areas, have enabled governments since 2009 to reclassify them as type 2B lands. These deforested areas (resulting from burning or cutting), which cover approximately 3,450 km² of lands, can now be integrated into a commercial property system. The completion of cadastral work over 99 per cent of type 2B land since 2013 has generated a new space use pattern by the state, enabling reallocation for private commercial activities, including agriculture (*Milliyet Newspaper* 2013a). The government sold 1,573 km² of such lands in 2014, which represents almost 50 per cent of all type 2B land (Maliye Bakanlığı 2014, 89).

Unregistered public lands remain under the authority and possession of the state. The government can lease, donate or sell these lands for use in commercial agriculture and real-estate brokerage activities. Law No. 4070 on 'the Sale of Agricultural Public Lands' (1995) has been instrumental in determining the legal status of 'unused' lands in rural areas as 'vacant' and legally owned by the state.[9] The new designation of vacant land, which often refers to unutilized or uncultivated common village lands, generates property rights to the land in question. Once the amount of vacant land is more accurately measured through cadastral work, it can be released for use in commercial agriculture.

Law No. 6292 of 2012 allows the state to sell and lease treasury lands to individuals for commercial agricultural use at up to half their market price (*Hürriyet Newspaper* 2013).

The data presented in Figure 2.3 shows the expansion of registered state-owned public lands. These lands can be released for commercial private use by the state. When this occurs, the ability of small-scale producers to access public lands and derive benefits for their subsistence and livelihood needs diminishes, even though they do not have the property rights to the same lands.[10]

The cadastre modernization and land-registry projects in Turkey align with the WB's general policy model advocated throughout the world. The WB has produced policy papers and advised governments since at least 1975 on the legal titling of common–public lands under state ownership, on the grounds that the land is uncultivated, underused and unproductive (Wily 2012). The state can legislate the conversion of these areas, viewed as 'empty lands', into land for private commercial use. Legislation enacted by governments in Turkey has allowed the expansion of registered state-owned public lands and contracted people's access to common-property resources. However, it is difficult to collect reliable data on the availability, size and sectoral distribution of public lands defined as 'underutilized' and 'uncultivated', as well as their transfer to private usage for more 'productive' commercial activity through selling, leasing or donating (Atasoy 2016; Borras and Franco 2010).

Although leased lands can be re-seized, the state transfers its ownership rights to individual and corporate entities by selling and donating land. There are 11 different laws in Turkey that provide a legal basis for the treasury to lease, sell and donate public lands (Maliye Bakanlığı 2010, 106). The 2010 GDNP Activity Report indicates that in 2010, the total lands leased through Law

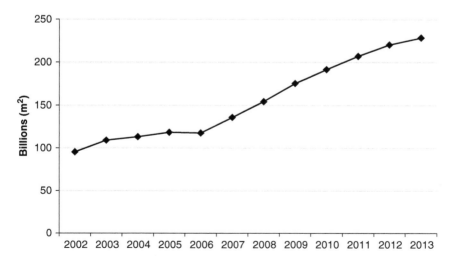

Figure 2.3 Amount of Registered Immovables of the Treasury.

Source: http://www.milliemlak.gov.tr/190 (accessed 30 December 2013).

No. 2886 covered approximately 43 million m² of land surface. This figure was 29.5 million in 2008 (Maliye Bakanlığı 2010, 62). Approximately 73 per cent of this amount (31 million m²) was for agricultural use, which comprises only 24 per cent of the total number of leased parcels (Maliye Bakanlığı 2010, 58).

Government transfer of state-owned public lands for private use did not begin under Erdoğan's AKP government. The practice reflects historical continuity with the Ottoman Empire and early republican land-distribution practices. There is a history in Turkey of viewing appropriation and redistribution of public lands as part of the state's responsibility to support subsistence-based land use by small producers (İnalcık 1994; İslamoğlu 2004). However, the current emphasis given by the government to increasing the availability of lands for *commercial use* represents a historic divergence from that lineage, as does the current tendency for capital concentration of land. This divergence reflects the domestic adoption of a general policy objective established by the WB of 'rational land use' and economic growth through commercialization of agriculture and land titling (World Bank 2007). The 'rational use of land' involves a market-oriented growth regime on large-scale commercial farms, which are believed to be better suited for increasing yields per unit of land under the competitive conditions of the global market economy (White et al. 2012).

During the Ottoman Empire, all cultivated land was state owned. It expanded through military conquest and the reclamation of 'wasteland' – land uncultivated or not in permanent public use (İnalcık 1994). The Ottoman regime of state property follows the example of earlier Muslim states since the time of Prophet Mohammed, which considered conquered land 'the inalienable common property of Muslims' under the trustee of the state (İnalcık 1994, 103). A combination of Islamic jurisprudence and Sultanic law placed these lands under the state's *eminent domain*. Based on the power of eminent domain to appropriate and own the land, the Ottoman land regime established the legal 'right' of peasants to possess and use state land through land titling. Titling guaranteed peasants land possession and use rights but not ownership. The state could also abrogate those rights. The sale, donation, mortgaging, endowment and diversion of land use from food production, as well as inheritance by will, were all prohibited, as these lands could not be privately owned (İnalcık 1994, 110–11). Even after the Anglo-Ottoman Commercial Convention of 1838, which arguably started a process of converting waste lands and state lands to cash-crop production, and subsequent to the 1858 Ottoman land code, which formally recognized private property (albeit with numerous restrictions) (İslamoğlu 2004), the Ottoman land-tenure system continued to enable peasants with a title deed to have legal use rights of state land (Quataert 1994, 856–61).

Ottoman land surveys were crucial in establishing state control over land. They provided detailed information on population, size of arable lands and peasant landholdings, type and amount of products, their potential tax revenues, legal immunities and tax exemptions in the provinces. All of this information was essential for the utility of land as a source of revenue and a means of production and subsistence (İnalcık 1994, 132–9). The surveys represent the establishment of exclusive control over the land by the state and state authority in redistributive justice, which effectively arrested the development of private property relations on land (at least until the nineteenth century) (İslamoğlu 2004, 296). These surveys were distinct from the practice of estate surveying in early modern England, which facilitated and promoted the representation of the land as the lords' own, thus stimulating the legal power of the landholder to assert to 'know one's own' (McRae 1993, 336). The birth of modern surveying occurred in England in the mid-sixteenth century (P. D. A. Harvey 1993, 79–93). It utilized new standards of land information through the use of modern techniques of measurement and advances in geometry, which allowed map-making to supplement or replace written surveys. This process helped create a radically new representation of land as private property, 'to be held, developed or transferred within a dynamic market economy', thereby playing a key role in the rise of agrarian capitalism (McRae 1993, 333). The extremely high concentration of wealth, especially in landholding and farmland, was not only an English experience but was also a general European phenomenon in the eighteenth and nineteenth centuries (Jones 2012; Piketty 2014). The manner in which land was held and cultivated by peasants for their subsistence needs differentiated the dominant pathway of the Ottoman Empire from the highly concentrated private wealth of European societies, which allowed a class of owners to accumulate and transmit wealth to subsequent generations through inheritance.

Since the founding of the republic in 1923, Turkey has experienced a slowly evolving structural transformation from the long-established Ottoman pathway. In large measure, I attribute the republican–era state-led reorganization of land use and ownership to discursive pressure coming from what the state-ruling elite had conceived as 'modern' (Atasoy 2009). This notion of 'modernity', understood as the emulation of European ways, was conceived in productivist terms as surplus generation in agriculture for the purpose of stimulating economic growth.

During the early republican era in Turkey, the adoption of the Swiss Civil Code in 1926 enabled smallholders who had legal use rights over state land to be registered as owners, based on the written boundary descriptions of Ottoman land registers (Gülöksüz 2004, 251–2). In the absence of such registers, the actual users of the land were registered as 'owners' by reference to their continual use and 'possession' of the land. The 1926 civil code required 20 years of demonstrated continuous use in order to be qualified for registered ownership (Demir and Çoruhlu 2006).[11] The early republican process of establishing land ownership slowed during World War II but increased again during the 1950s. Still, the Ottoman legacy of smallholders' land-use rights for subsistence-based production has continued to define Turkish agriculture in subsequent years.

During the developmentalist era, government land-redistribution strategies continued the Ottoman practice of maintaining the centrality of small-scale production in food provisioning and smallholders' access to lands for subsistence. Governments were responsive to the demands of peasants who held little or no land (Pamuk 1988), and they often expanded land under cultivation by carving out additional agricultural areas from state-owned public lands. The government redistributed these newly opened state lands to the landless and least-propertied small producers. In this manner, the amount of land under cultivation during the 1950s increased by approximately 67 per cent (Margulies and Yıldızoğlu 1992, 301). Farm land was also increased through deforestation by burning and from illegal tree-cutting for firewood.[12] This strategy for increasing arable land accounted for 22 per cent of total cultivated land in 1948 (Tekeli 1977, 30). Between 1950 and 1960, the proportion of landless families decreased from 16 to 10 per cent. And between 1950 and 1963, the number of small-producing family farms increased by 30 per cent from 2.3 million to 3.1 million (Keyder 1987, 131).

However, small-scale production rarely sustains the self-sufficiency of rural households, and migration to urban areas frequently becomes the means to secure one's livelihood (Bernstein et al. 1992). In Turkey, the rural population has been in decline since the late 1940s, when 75 per cent of the population inhabited villages; that number fell to 56 per cent by the 1980s and to 35 per cent by 2000 (SPO 2006, 7). According to the latest available figures published by the SPO (SPO 2014, 134–5), Turkey's population increased by 7.1 per cent from 2007 to 2012,[13] but its rural population decreased by 8.8 per cent and fell to 20.9 million from 22.9 million during the same time period.[14] As a result, the rural population had declined from 32.5 per cent of the total population to 22.7 per cent by 2012. This decline was accompanied by an increase in the share of the population 65 years of age and older (from 9.6 per cent) to 11.3 per cent.

Despite the decline and aging of the rural population, labour-force participation in the agricultural sector was still a very high 53.6 per cent in 2012, even registering a 3 per cent increase from 50.8 per cent in 2007 (SPO 2014, 135). This indicates the continuing significance of (semi)subsistence-oriented small-scale farming in Turkey as the dominant form of landholding structure and a major source of subsistence and employment. In 1859, small holdings of 6–8 hectares comprised 82 per cent of all Ottoman cultivable land (Quataert 1994, 863–4). In the Anatolian provinces of the empire, this figure was 82 per cent of Anatolian cultivated lands in 1869, which represented some 80 per cent of all peasant households. Holdings of 4.5 hectares or less continued to include 81 per cent of all Anatolian cultivated land in 1907 (Quataert 1994, 864). At present, holdings of less than 25 hectares constitute 78.9 per cent of all agricultural holdings and operate on 34.3 per cent of total agricultural lands.[15] Holdings of more than 25 hectares represent 21.1 per cent of agricultural holdings in Turkey, but they claim 65.7 per cent of lands (TÜİK 2008b). These figures suggest that although smallholdings continue to be a dominant form in Turkish agriculture, they now claim a smaller amount of land – a clear departure from the old Ottoman and early republican pattern (Atasoy 2016, 8).

The continuing dominance of smallholder agriculture in Turkey demonstrates historical continuity with the Ottoman tradition of state reclamation of public lands for subsistence-based use by farmers. The deeply held ideational relevance of the Ottoman Muslim legacy has established an understanding of public lands as, by definition, *not owned* by anyone. Consequently, people can access them for their subsistence needs. This well-consolidated pattern throughout the developmentalist era contrasts with the dominant policy tool adopted during the same time period by governments in many regions of the global South. For example, land redistribution in Brazil was often carried out through forcible property expropriations. These policies were generally a response to popular demands for agrarian reform mobilized to alter the inequality in landowner-ship remaining from the time of large estates created under Portuguese colonial rule. Still, in Brazil, the current market-oriented redistributive policies, which emphasized the right to property that was defined as 'unproductive', resulted in the privileging of large-scale commercial farmers who furthered their claims to rightful access to land by reference to the market rationality of efficiency and productivity. Simultaneously, this resulted in the de-legitimation of the poor's land-access claims for a family livelihood (Wolford 2005). Thus, at present in Brazil, large-scale agricultural producers, first as plantation owners during the colonial era and now as agribusiness corporations, continue to use 76 per cent of cultivated land, while small-scale family farmers utilize only 24 per cent of agricultural land (Fernandes et al. 2012, 1).

In Turkey, the republican practice of recognizing that long-term land use and possession constitute property rights prevailed in various forms until the 1980s. Since the 1980s, and particularly under the AKP government, Turkey has acted to transform its agricultural land use patterns to fit a market-based development trajectory. In an effort to increase 'effective ownership' (Verdery 2003, 178) of land and extract greater commercial benefit from agriculture, the government passed the Land Conservation and Usage Law (No. 5403) in 2005. This law functions to change people's subsistence-based connections to land and resources and to reorganize the agricultural landscape in the interests of intensive surplus-generating commercial enterprises.

The introduction of the MFAL's draft *Introduction to Agriculture* indicates that there were 2.2 million agricultural holdings in 1950. Divided into shares based on inheritance, this increased to 3.1 million in 2001. As a result, the average size of these holdings fell to 61 dekars in 2001 from 100 dekars in 1960.[16] The MFAL draft indicates that 67 per cent of 1 million land holdings today are less than 50 dekars, or approximately 12 acres, in size. The contraction in size of farm holdings becomes even more pronounced when the fallowing data is considered: agricultural production is carried out on 3 million holdings divided into 40 million shares, but 37 million shareholders are not involved in actual production (MFAL 2014c). In response to this ongoing fragmentation of agri-cultural lands, the Land Conservation and Usage Law now reclassifies mini-mum agricultural land size according to the 'rationalized performance value' of an agricultural business.[17] Minimum land size is set at 2 hectares. Moreover, to prevent the unrestricted break-up of farm lands, the government has pre-pared draft legislation to amend the existing inheritance law, which enables one family member to inherit land by purchasing the inheritance rights of another family member (*Milliyet Newspaper* 2013b). In May 2014, the government temporarily banned the sale of agricultural lands with multiple claim-holders. Institutionalization of an inherently different logic of land ownership and capital accumulation is thus foreseen through a change in the inheritance law, which will likely further the increasing concentration of wealth in Turkish agriculture.

The Land Conservation and Usage Law (No. 5403) of 2005 has required the determination and classification of soil resources and problematic usage of agricultural lands, as well as improvements in land-use planning. The law has also accelerated the implementation of the STATİP project (Documentation and the Betterment of Problematic Agricultural Lands) begun in 2002 (MFAL 2014c, 77–83). STATİP aims to speed up the surveying of agricultural lands within village boundaries and then develop maps based on satellite imaginary and high-scale aerial photography. These maps are designed to enable planners, agricultural producers and investors to have easy access to information on soil resources and reliable data on soil–topography–climate parameters. This is all intended to improve efficiency in land-use patterns and facilitate more economical distribution of agricultural inputs (MFAL 2014c, 77–8). The lands that STATİP maps identify as economically 'unproductive' for agricultural use can then be reallocated for use in other commercial projects, including housing.

The AKP government is also promoting land consolidation in Turkey. The overall strategy includes the consolidation of scattered lands owned by the same person. Cadastral work determines the location and size of these lands through terrain and soil maps, thereby accelerating the conversion of fragmented lands into large-scale parcels for use in commercial agriculture. Once this work is complete and the market value of consolidated lands determined, the original owners will be given the opportunity to purchase the larger parcels, new deeds will be registered and titles will be given to the owners. According to Mehdi Eker (2013), who was Minister of Food, Agriculture and Livestock from 2005 to 2015, there are 30 million parcels of agricultural land in Turkey but only three million farms, indicating an average of 10 parcels per farm. This fragmentation decreases efficient cultivation and economic productivity (Atasoy 2016, 9). As seen from Table 2.2, approximately 3 million hectares were consolidated between 1961 and 2012, with more than 2.5 million hectares of lands concentrated after 2002. The government aims to increase this to 14 million hectares by 2023 (Tarım Reformu Genel Müdürlüğü 2013). Clearly, rather than upholding the long-lasting Ottoman-republican commitment to a 'subsistence ethic' (Scott 1977) of smallholder land-use rights, the government favours large-scale commercial agriculture.

MFAL's *Introduction to Agriculture* (2014c, 51–2) further indicates that land consolidation will lead to savings in labour costs and farm inputs and facilitate farmers' access to road and irrigation networks, increasing both productivity and market integration in agriculture.[18] By preventing further subdivision of small-scale arable land, land-consolidation schemes promote the

Table 2.2 Land Consolidation by Year(s)

Year(s)	Land Surface (ha)
1961–2002	450,000
2003–2007	132,000
2008	430,000
2009	103,000
2010	26,000
2011	601,998
2012	1,210,604
Total	2,953,602

Source: Tarım Reformu Genel Müdürlüğü (2013).

rationalized reorganization of agriculture, a goal advocated by the WB. The land-consolidation policy requires a voluntary *collective* application by producers in villages and towns (MFAL 2014c, 52). However, existing data does not allow us to discern the extent to which already completed land consolidation has actually involved the regrouping of privately owned small-agricultural lands rather than government transfers of state-owned consolidated public lands for private commercial use.

The European Environment Agency (EEA) provides data on land cover and its ongoing changes across 38 countries in Europe, including Turkey. The latest update of EEA data provides information for the period 2000 to 2006. The EEA classifies 'man-made [sic.]' land surfaces of settlement, production and infrastructure as artificial. Artificial areas consist of the general urban fabric, including industrial and commercial lands, road and rail networks and associated lands, port areas, airports, mineral extraction sites, dump sites, construction areas, green urban areas and sport and leisure facilities. The non-artificial 'natural' areas include agricultural lands, pastures, forests, woodlands, scrubs, grasslands, wetlands, open space with little or no vegetation and water bodies. According to EEA data, agricultural zones and, to a lesser extent, forests and semi-natural and natural areas are disappearing throughout Europe in favour of the development of artificial areas. In the case of Turkey, along with a reduction in rain-fed dry agricultural lands and a gradual expansion of lands for irrigated agriculture, land-consolidation schemes have decreased forests, wetlands and semi-natural vegetation, as well as small-scale agricultural lands. Between 2000 and 2006, artificial areas in Turkey increased in size by 37,729 hectares (EEA 2015). The EEA data indicates that in Turkey, 25,952 hectares of forest lands, 13,451 hectares of agricultural land and 1,515 hectares of wetland are now used for urban and other artificial land-development purposes (Atasoy 2016, 10). Approximately 5 per cent of lands were taken from 'open space', compared to an overall European average of 1.3 per cent. 'Open space' refers to unregistered common lands where there are no clearly defined rules for regulating land use and access (Sugden and Punch 2014, 658). Ankara's 4,460-hectare increase in artificial area is the highest in Turkey. İstanbul is second highest with 2,584 hectares (EEA 2015).

Alterations in land ownership, use and access indicate the deepening commodification of the previously core agricultural and natural landscapes. The process has been greatly accelerated by the expansion of state-ownership of 'public' lands and land-consolidation schemes. The various techniques utilized by the state for the identification, classification and reclamation of 'public lands' involves the incorporation of meadows, pastures and/or 'unowned' agricultural lands into artificial land zones and commercial agricultural lands. This shift in land ownership, use and access patterns gradually contracts small-scale rain-fed agriculture and natural areas, converging with the creation of large-scale specialized, capitalized input-intensive commercial farms in FFV production and the opening of more lands for housing. Deepening commodification enlarges the total artificial land-surface area within core natural/semi-natural landscapes and productive agricultural zones. At the same time, increasing urban sprawl contributes to the blurring of an urban–rural distinction. This is a pattern that I have observed first-hand in Güdül in the province of Ankara. Güdül has undergone drastic changes in its rural character, including deepening de-agrarianization and a process of structural change in the conception of livelihood from one based on farmland to one now largely based on real estate and financial transactions. As neoliberal land reconstitution proceeds, agricultural producers in Güdül are more likely to abandon their farming activity and turn their dry farming lands – seen to be 'inherently unproductive' – into 'financial assets' by selling or renting them for more profitable commercial use. In addition to the mushrooming of privately built multi-storey apartment units and single detached houses, I have also observed interesting complications in the changing land-use dynamics of Güdül arising from the government release of state-owned public lands for private commercial use in agriculture (Atasoy 2016). The government reconfiguring of land use through Turkey's Housing Development Administration (TOKİ) is an example of the government-led conversion of dry farming lands into real estate in Güdül.[19]

Concluding Remarks

This chapter has focussed on the ways in which governments in Turkey have worked to reorganize agriculture since the 1980s, especially during the AKP government of Erdoğan. Turkey's quest for full membership in the EU, the WTO's 1995 AOA and the WB's ARIP aid agreement constitute the international context for this reorganization.

In Turkey, the ontological belief in the 'modernity' of market-oriented development is highly determinative. It is reflected in the government adoption of a number of policies for the *contraction* of space used for rain-fed grain production by small-scale farmers and the *expansion* of artificial land surfaces for large-scale, input-intensive commercial agriculture and housing. Significant policies and innovations here include the ARIP, the DPA, the establishment of the national registry of farmers (all adopted in 2001); the TARİT program and the land registry and cadastre modernization project (both adopted in 2008);

land-consolidation schemes; and the STATİP project, as well as changes in inheritance law. The institutionalization and implementation of these projects signal the overall importance attached to the concentration of capital on land, which is a significant departure from long-held Ottoman and early republican approaches to the material and cultural relations of earning a living in agriculture. All of the recent alterations in land access, use and ownership patterns contract small-scale agricultural lands available for food production, expand commodification of land and institutionalize the techno-scientific management of economic growth. This commodification process becomes intensified with the incorporation of state-appropriated public lands and natural areas into wealth accumulation. The *neostatism* (Jessop 2002) of the AKP government is playing a decisive historic role in forcefully and radically reorganizing the landscape towards a *vertically concentrated wealth* by a small group of large-scale commercial farmers. This *historic great turn* marked by AKP government policies signals a new path for Turkey – a path that was once dominant in Europe during the nineteenth century and is again becoming a globally dominant means for the high concentration of wealth (Piketty 2014). While the nature of capital in concentrated wealth has shifted from farmland to the industrial, financial and real-estate sectors in Europe and the US, the re-organization and re-allocation of small-scale farmlands and common public lands (including natural areas) constitute the main source of concentrated capital through commercial agriculture and real-estate dealings in Turkey. Nevertheless, small-scale agricultural holdings continue to prevail in Turkey. This phenomenon is rooted in the past but remains a part of the present-day cohabitation within neoliberal agriculture of various farming styles implemented by different types of farmers.

The following chapter will examine the institutional innovations adopted to advance the entry of techno-scientific expert knowledge into commercial agriculture, including biotechnology and the Good Agricultural Practices act (GAP). This will help us to recognize the diffusion of techno-scientific ways among small-scale as well as large-scale producers, further consolidating neoliberal cohabitation. As small producers adopt new technologies and regulatory mechanisms, they become part of the new configuration of agrifood relationships, although, contrary to Bernstein's (2010) expectation, not as waged workers. They become a dynamic part of neoliberal variegation. Turkey's implementation of neoliberal policies interacts with the cumulative histories of the past Ottoman and republican legacies in generating such a cohabitation.

Notes

1 Taner Ödevci from MFAL allowed me access to the text in draft form.
2 With this decline, the amount of registered agricultural land has also declined from approximately 167 million dekars in 2003 to 156 million dekars in 2011 (MFAL 2014c, 209).
3 There are 16 provinces out of a total of 81 that have more than 4 million dekars of agricultural area in Turkey. Among them, Konya, Şanlıurfa and Ankara have the largest areas of agricultural land, with 14.1, 8.7 and 6.1 million dekars respectively (MARA 2014, 9).
4 http://www.turkstat.gov.tr/PreTablo.do?alt_id=1001 (accessed 11 August 2014).

5 Official Information obtained from Umut Karakuay, Ankara Agriculture, via an email communication (25 June 2014).
6 http://www.ormansu.gov.tr/osb/Libraries/Dokümanlar/6172_sayılı_Sulama_Birlikleri_Kanunu_4.sflb.ashx. (accessed 3 March 2014).
7 http://www.tkgm.gov.tr/tr/icerik/tapu-ve-kadastro-modernizasyon-projesi-tkmp (accessed 15 January 2014).
8 http://www.milliemlak.gov.tr/190 (accessed 30 December 2013).
9 http://www.tarim.gov.tr (accessed 30 December 2013).
10 For a distinction between 'ability to access' and rights, see Ribot and Peluso (2003).
11 The government also appropriated the lands of departing Greek and Armenian Christians at the end of the First World War and sold them to native-born or immigrant Muslims. It is estimated that one-sixth of the cultivable land in Western Anatolia belonged to the departing Greeks (Keyder 1981, 23). It is important to note that, because lands in the public domain, as well as forests and coastal areas, were excluded from private ownership, possessors' rights were not easy to determine.
12 Since 1937, the quantity of illegal wood cut has been approximately 455,000 m³ per year, including 95,000 m³ per year for use in industry and 360,000 m³ per year for use as firewood. This data is limited to fuel and industrial wood and does not provide a comprehensive picture of deforestation in Turkey (Güneş and Elvan 2003).
13 The urbanization rate increased from 67.5 per cent to 72.3 per cent between 2007 and 2012. This is expected to reach 76.4 per cent by 2018 (SPO 2014, 125).
14 Rural–urban migration also resulted in informal *gecekondu* housing as migrants began to build shelters illegally and in haste on private and public lands in cities throughout Turkey, in response to the short supply of formal housing. *Gecekondus* contained 26 per cent of the urban population by the early 1980s. Ankara had the highest percentage of *gecekondus* in Turkey, housing 72.4 per cent of the city's total population in 1995 (Keleş 1984, 351, 357).
15 Smallholdings of 5–12 hectares represent 32.7 per cent of all agricultural holdings in Turkey (TÜİK 2008b).
16 A significant portion of farmers holds approximately 20 dekars of lands or 4.97 acres (TÜİK 2008b).
17 http://www.mevzuat.gov.tr/MevzuatMetin/1.5.5403.pdf (accessed 19 January 2017).
18 For a discussion on land consolidation in eighteenth- and nineteenth-century France, see Jones (2012).
19 TOKİ was founded in 1984 as a government agency for land and housing production in Turkey, operating under the Ministry of Public Works and Settlements. In 2004, it was placed under the Office of the Prime Minister. TOKİ embodies a market conforming but state-sponsored approach to urban renewal and commercial housing – an approach that Jessop (2002, 462) describes as *neostatism*. TOKİ's neostatism involves the restructuring of the land and housing market through a revenue-sharing arrangement with private construction companies. TOKİ acts as a broker of state-owned lands for luxury real-estate developments; its share of the profit is used for funding mass-housing projects for low- and middle-income people, supported by a TOKİ-sponsored mortgage system. TOKİ acquires lands for its housing projects from the treasury and the Urban Land Office (Atasoy 2016, 14–6).

3 GLOBALGAP and Agro-Biotechnology

Syngenta and Rijk Zwaan in Turkish Villages

As explained in previous chapters, efficiency and rationality have become key value considerations in Turkey's state-policy program of expanding land-based spaces for wealth concentration in agriculture. The fundamental criticism of small-scale, subsistence-oriented family farming is its lack of competitiveness in a market economy and its unsuitability for integration into the modern system of food provisioning.

Because agricultural activity is no longer seen as integral to the livelihood of producers and their families but as a private enterprise subject to the entrepreneurial rules of a competitive market economy, it is expected to become integrated into an input-intensive agricultural production system fully coordinated with 'upstream' and 'downstream' supply chains. Bernstein (2013, 318–9) notes that the *upstream* of farming refers to the conditions of production, including the instruments of labour or 'inputs' (tools, seeds, fertilizers) as well as the markets for land, labour and credit. His use of the term *downstream* refers to the marketing, distribution and processing of food produced by farmers. Therefore, the various methods utilized by the AKP government in Turkey (as noted in Chapter 2) to reorganize landscapes constitute a refiguring of the upstream of farming so as to be congruent with the 'rationality' and 'efficiency' requirements of a competitive economy. The growing expectation on the part of government that farmers conform to or adopt agro-industry-led biotechnology innovations and associated information systems constitutes another dimension of refiguring the upstream of farming. Again, this is justified on the grounds of increasing the competitiveness of agriculture within the global market economy, which is also the rationale for ensuring the market integration of farmers through compliance with supermarket-led food standards.

What follows is a detailed account of the biotechnology-led reorganization of the upstream of farming in Turkey. Key factors to be examined include the Good Agricultural Practices (GAP) project of 2004 and development of contract farming, the Agriculture Law (No. 5488) of 2006 and the Seeds Law (No. 5553), also of 2006. Other measures involved in intensifying an agro-industrial input-intensive agriculture in Turkey include the expansion of 'intellectual property rights' and the 'Convention on Biological Diversity' regimes, as well as national biosafety measures. In addition to a contextual analysis of the various policy tools adopted by the government, this chapter draws data from my interviews conducted with the managers and officials of two global biotechnology companies, Syngenta and Rijk Zwaan. I met and interviewed company managers and officials of Syngenta and Rijk Zwaan in Kayabükü, a village within Beypazarı, at an experimental farming day organized by Syngenta. Also present were foreign guest farmers invited by Syngenta to introduce their newly developed biotech seeds for vegetables and salad varieties.

The 'Good Agricultural Practices' (GAP) Project and Contract Farming

In Turkey, the Good Agricultural Practices (GAP) project was first adopted in 2004 (Bylaw No. 25577) and later amended in 2010 (By-law No. 27778) (İyi Tarım Uygulamalarına İlişkin Yönetmelik [İTUİY] 2004; 2010). The Turkish-GAP by-laws embody the EUREPGAP standards. The Euro-Retailer Produce Working Group (EUREP) was founded in 1997. Although the European Union (EU) played no active role in creating EUREPGAP, the Turkish-GAP reflects the belief that EUREPGAP will increase Turkey's competitiveness in EU markets.

GAP refers to a common set of standards for food safety and quality, environmental health, labour and animal welfare. It focuses on the product, the production process and the entire supply chain. GAP also takes into account standards issued by the International Organization for Standardization (ISO), particularly ISO 14000 standards, which focus on good environmental practices to reduce environmental pollution. Compliance with standards is followed through the producers' transmission of information on product quality shown on product labels in ways that are auditable. Quality information may include origin (geographic indication), safety (pesticide residues, levels of toxins) and environmental and socio–economic conditions (Gibbon and Ponte 2005, 2), which in turn affect consumer choices. EUREPGAP lists 47 major and 98 minor quality standards and 65 recommended control points and compliance criteria, along with a broad range of production requirements (Akkaya et al. 2006). 'Compliance with these protocols was expected of all fruit and vegetable growers supplying European retailers that had signed up with EUREPGAP' (Campbell et al. 2006, 70).

The GLOBALGAP (Global Partnership for Good Agricultural Practice) represents the most significant recent change involving the development and enforcement of private standards by supermarket chains. Established in 2007, the GLOBALGAP replaced the EUREPGAP with the aim of harmonizing standards for 'good agricultural practice' worldwide. The GLOBALGAP is a consortium of many of Europe's leading supermarket chains, including Carrefour, Walmart, Royal Ahold, Tesco, Aldi, Safeway, Sysco, Migros, Metro, Kesko, Marks & Spencer and Sainsbury. The GLOBALGAP website lists 15 supermarket chain members. These chains are what Gibbon and Ponte (2005, 99) refer to as 'lead firms' in the GLOBALGAP, which, as a group, dictate the terms of participation among suppliers in the commodity chains. The GLOBALGAP plays an increasingly important role in global commodity chains, particularly in the enforcement of private standards as a market access requirement for producers and suppliers in the EU market (Kleemann et al. 2014; Tennent and Lockie 2011).

The GLOBALGAP functions as a 'third party certification' (TPC) device, assuring consumers of quality standards and safety of food as well as environmental protection and worker's health, safety and protection. TPC is an audit mechanism used by independent auditors for verification of compliance with standards and the grades used to implement them. The GLOBALGAP represents 'retailer-specific audits' of food produced by unfamiliar producers, often in distant places, thereby leading to a further decline in the influence of locally practised relations of quality assurance (Rosin et al. 2008, 64). Currently, there are 130 certification bodies affiliated with the GLOBALGAP.[1]

The GLOBALGAP lists 234 control points for its required audits of FFVs, 117 of which are focussed on food safety, 50 on the environment, 46 on traceability and 21 on workers' welfare.[2] Implementation of standards on these points requires extensive documentation, labelling and input calculation, as well as rigorous third-party certification. The costs related to proving compliance belong to producers (Tennent and Lockie 2011, 35). Research suggests that leading retail firms are able to impose their own private standards *when and if* they are able to shift the cost of standards implementation to producers (Vandemoortele and Deconinck 2014, 156). However, producers are not party to negotiations involved in the development, maintenance and alteration of grades and standards (G&S), which typically requires the technical expertise of professional specialists. The resulting expert knowledge-based grades and standards are thus detached from the locally specific practices of food provisioning systems, although they are always *applied* locally. Supermarket chains do not exert direct control over the operations of production at source, but they often rely on preferred suppliers to achieve compliance with their standards (Gibbon and Ponte 2005, 123).

The GLOBALGAP has now been recognized on more than 112,600 farms in over 100 countries, including Turkey. In total, it has certified 97,361 producers of FFVs in 105 countries. Italy has the highest number of GLOBALGAP certified producers at 19,508. Spain has 15,919, Greece 10,952 and the Netherlands 5,125. Turkey has 2,534 GLOBALGAP certified producers, while Brazil has only 327.[3] These relatively small numbers indicate that a large majority of farmers in the world are not included in GLOBALGAP-certified FFV supply chains. Nevertheless, supermarkets are increasingly demanding that farmers comply with GAP certification so that they can display the certification label on the food in their stores. I have observed this conspicuous trend more often in the last few years on FFVs sold in national supermarkets in Turkey, such as Migros, Altunbilekler and Makromarket.

In order to increase the number of producers involved in certified chains, the GLOBALGAP also recognizes nationally established GAP standards, provided they are equivalent and receive approval. Approved certification is based on the same rules ensured by the GLOBALGAP Integrity Program.[4] This is significant for new competitor regions and producers entering the supply end of European FFV commodity chains. It also expedites the domestication of private retailer–specific standards in the national governance of food systems. Therefore, the world-wide harmonization of private standards as well as competitiveness in pricing by producers determines the market accessibility of growers in relation to quality control, management, traceability and certification.

However, global enforcement of GAP standards may not facilitate trade from countries in the global South. Standards may even result in the exclusion of small producers from GAP-certified FFV production and export chains (Gibbon and Lazaro 2010, 13–4). According to the findings from interviews conducted with quality and safety directors from 16 leading Organisation for Economic Co-operation and Development (OECD) retailers in 2006, only 25 per cent of fruits and vegetables are sourced from 'developing countries' (Fulponi 2006, 7). Poor record keeping, lack of reliable information on variable and often changing standards, the cost of compliance and insufficient infrastructure, skills and technology, as well as time demands and the amount of administrative paperwork required to respond to audit questions, all present a major challenge to the wider implementation of a GAP-required certified production system for producers in global agriculture.

According to Akkaya et al. (2006), there were 326 growers in the Turkish-GAP system in 2006, including 162 cherry, 63 tomato, 24 grape and 22 fig growers. These numbers appear very small, and they are difficult to confirm because the authors do not indicate the source of their information. Given the difficulty of finding reliable information from publicly available official data sources, I contacted the Ministry of Food, Agriculture and Livestock (MFAL) in May 2012 through an official letter. In my letter, I asked a number of questions regarding the current status of Turkish agriculture. An official response came in June 2012 in the form of a report from Mr. Erdal Erol, assistant EU expert in the General Directorate of the EU and Foreign Relations of the Ministry of Food, Agriculture and Livestock.

In regard to the GAP implementation program in Turkey, Mr. Erol indicated in the report that the government had begun a project in 2012 for the Expansion and Inspection of Good Agricultural Practices in Fresh Fruits and Vegetables in order to increase the number of producers participating in GLOBALGAP-certified production and export chains. The project was implemented in 12 different provinces throughout Turkey between 2012 and 2014. Unfortunately, no information has been made available to me regarding the outcome of the project in following years.

Table 3.1 includes the latest official data that I obtained from Mr. Erol in 2012. According to this data, the number of producers participating in the Turkish-GAP project is still low, only 3,047 out of a total of four million producers. The total number of producers participating in the Turkish-GAP program is higher (3,042 producers) than the number of GLOBALGAP-certified producers (2,534) listed on the GLOBALGAP website. There is no available

Table 3.1 GAP Project Implementation in Turkey (2012)

Years	Number of Provinces	Number of Producers	Size of Landholdings (da)
2007	18	651	53,607
2008	19	822	60,231
2009	42	6,020	1,702,804
2010	48	4,540	781,741
2011	49	3,042	499,632

Source: Erdal Erol, MFAL (official correspondence, June 2012).

data that shows how many of these producers in the Turkish-GAP program have also been certified by GLOBALGAP. The average size of land cultivated per farmer within the program is approximately 164 dekars (about 41 acres or 16 hectares). This indicates that the size of farms in the Turkish-GAP program is larger than the average 5-hectare size held by a majority of producers in Turkey. It appears, then, that the implementation of GAP programs requires a shift toward larger-scale agricultural production, in which, as examined in Chapter 2, the government plays a decisive role through re-organizing land-use, access and ownership patterns.

The data presented in Table 3.1 is significant in that it shows a decline in the number of producers in the Turkish-GAP program from its peak level in 2009. This may be due to the fact that many of these producers are not able to comply with Turkish-GAP implementation requirements, which follow GLOBALGAP standards for the approval of national equivalency. Farmers' inability to comply is not specific to Turkey but a general phenomenon observed world-wide.

There is evidence to suggest that small-scale producers cannot easily meet retailers' private standards. These standards are frequently more stringent than their public counterparts set by law (Vandemoortele and Deconinck 2014)[5] and are also increasingly mandatory for access to markets (Dolan and Humphrey 2000). In addition, small-scale producers lack the necessary infrastructure, technology, education and training, as well as the access to credit and capital required for the cooling, storing, sorting, packaging and transporting of produce (Biles et al. 2007). For example, this is the case in Thailand (Kersting and Wollni 2012). Given these constraints, the capacity of small-scale producers to negotiate a locally appropriate application of GAP standards on their holdings appears to be limited. This limitation negatively affects farmers' ability to enter into the certified downstream supply chains increasingly dominated by a small number of large-scale supermarkets. Moreover, these supermarkets require large quantities of steadily flowing food that is produced and packaged in highly specified ways, a condition that cannot easily be met by small producers.

Contract Farming

The complexity of quality content and assurance, and thus the grades and standards-framed governance of supply chains, may serve to strengthen the leading role of supermarkets in the global food-provisioning system. This may in turn encourage a vertical form of integration or 'industrial coordination' (Gibbon and Ponte 2005, 8) where buying and sourcing from a large number of suppliers is controlled centrally through a contractually binding production process. Through vertical arrangements of contract farming, supermarkets, via their preferred suppliers, can maintain control over product qualification from a distance. In this manner, some farmers, food processors and distributors are incorporated into the supply chains, while others are excluded.

Research is not conclusive as to the effects of contract farming. It has been argued that in the case of China, for example, contract farming through a vertically organized institutional structure contributes to agricultural productivity and income increases for producers, thereby furthering national 'economic development', while at the same time contributing to improvements in food quality and safety for consumers (H. H. Wang et al. 2014). This is a questionable argument, however. In the example of Vietnam, research on vegetable producers shows that contracts have less impact on farmers' income than direct sales to consumers (H. Wang et al. 2014). And yet, for Ethiopia (Abede et al. 2013) and Mexico (Echanove-Huacuja 2006), research shows that contract farming offers the possibility for small producers to gain financing, technical assistance and access to quality agricultural inputs, as well as information and marketing arrangements through their integration into vertically coordinated supply chains. These opportunities are often facilitated by 'first-tier' suppliers or other intermediaries involved in sourcing from other smaller-scale suppliers rather than retailers themselves (Gibbon and Ponte 2005, 104).

Small-scale producers' integration into supply chains via contracts generally depends on their compliance with retailers' quality standards (Challies and Murray 2011). Research also suggests that suppliers' support for smallholders' adoption of grades and standards is often sporadic rather than continuous. Therefore, small producers are often unable to maintain their compliance, and, as in the case of FFV farmers in Madagascar (Bignebat and Vagneron 2011) and Thailand (Holzapfel and Wollni 2014), they fail to renew their certification after support ends.

In Turkey, contract farming constitutes a small fraction of commercial farming conducted by small producers. The data in tables 3.2 and 3.3 confirm this. I obtained these tables through Mr. Erol from the MFAL in 2012.

Table 3.2 and Table 3.3 further demonstrate that farmers' integration into supply chains in Turkey does not operate through contract farming arrangements, with the exception of sugar beets, tobacco and ornamental plant production. Sugar-beet and tobacco production has been carried out via contract farming since the sugar and tobacco industry was established under state monopoly during the 1920s (Aydın 2010, 163–9, 171–3; Rehber 2000, 15). Contract farming for international processing companies and domestic exporting firms has only recently begun in sugar, tobacco and seed-oil production with the restructuring of Turkish agriculture in the early 2000s. Producers' unions and cooperatives also play a role in the expansion of contract farming. Trakyabirlik

Table 3.2 Contract Farming in Plant Production[1]

Number of producers*	Number of producers in contract farming	Size of land in contract farming (da)
2,292,380	213,249	4,450,493

1 This table shows the number of producers to be 2,292,380 for the year 2012, which is higher than the figure shown in Table 2.1. Mr. Erol explained this difference in the following way: Data shown in Table 2.1 is based on the number of producers registered in the National Registry (Çiftçi Kayıt Sistemi – ÇKS). The registry is a support-oriented program. Farmers who think that the cost of registration may be higher than the amount of support they would receive from the government may choose not to register for that year or to let their registration expire. Therefore, the number of registered farmers fluctuates over the years. (E-mail communication, 28 September 2014).

Source: Erdal Erol, MFAL. (Official correspondence, June 2012).

and Marmarabirlik are the two main producers' cooperatives that vertically integrate farmers into sunflower, olive and vegetable oil processing in Turkey. The share of contract farming in tomato production is also growing, partly for export but mostly for domestic processing (Ulukan 2009). As confirmed by the most recent data presented in tables 3.2 and 3.3, FFVs are supplied to markets largely without contracts. Although not common, some producers have contractual ties to supermarkets through their own producers' unions (Lemeilleur and Tozanli 2007). As shown in Chapters 5 and 7, 'traditional' wholesale markets continue to be the most important outlet for small producers' market access, as is also observed in France and Italy (Gibbon and Ponte 2005, 106).

Table 3.3 shows the distribution of contract farming in various plant-production areas.

Table 3.3 Plant-Production Areas Under Contract Farming (2011)

Areas in Contract Farming	Total Number of Producers *	Number of Producers in Contract Farming	Land Size and Amount of Production in Contract Farming	
			Land (da)	Amount(ton)
Grain	1,566,098	10,357	1,090,172	448,314
Fruits	976,102	2,750	94,917	112,968
Vegetables	220,838	9,034	232,967	879,697
Legumes	139,925	140	18,378	1,897
Oil seeds	146,334	893	37,369	8,125
Sugar-beet **	118,338	118,338	1,782,682	8,950,721
Tobacco***	56,500	54,314	826,571	67,863
Others	874,264	14,693	364,414	97,316
Ornamental plants	2,730	2,730	3,023	n/a
Total	4,101,129	213,249	4,450,493	10,566,901

Source: Erdal Erol (official correspondence, June 2012).

** indicates the number of farmers contracting with Sugar Factories Ltd of Turkey; *** indicates the number of farmers contracting with the Tobacco- and Alcohol-Market Regulation Institute of Turkey.

In Turkey, small producers' compliance with retailer standards is often addressed through the interpersonal dynamics of wholesale markets based on the perceived trustworthiness of the parties involved. Retailers' ability to impose private standards is frequently the outcome of the cultural complexities of interaction between a range of intermediaries of first- or second-tier suppliers and producers themselves (Vandemoortele and Deconinck 2014). This will be examined further in the following chapter.

The low level of vertical coordination, as evidenced by the small number of producers in contract farming, combined with the lack of industrially certified quality assurance systems, as evidenced by the small number of producers registered in the GLOBALGAP and Turkish-GAP, indicates that in Turkey, different norms, conventions, quality-assurance systems and forms of coordination operate within existing farming scripts and practices. Mercosur countries present a different trajectory.[6] Private standards have become dominant when these countries have individually and collectively lagged in the creation and regional harmonization of public standards – a process consolidated by the rapid expansion of large transnational food-processing corporations, supermarkets and fast-food chains (Farina and Reardon 2000).

The multi-faceted character of global agrifood systems is also observed in the area of agricultural biotechnology.

Global Agricultural Biotechnology: Biodiversity, Patents and Trade in Biotech Seeds

Farmers' compliance with privately established grades and standards, along with product innovation, leads to global homogenization of crop production. The requirement of farmer compliance affects the access, choice and use of seed varieties. Accessibility can be ensured either through open-access and open-variety rights to seeds and biological resources in the public domain (Deibel 2013; Kloppenburg 2010) or through industrial market integration of privately owned, commodified and patented resources governed by intellectual property rights. This is a question of who owns and controls the seeds and plant-genetic resources – the common public domain, which relies on *reciprocity* rather than exclusivity in providing *open-access rights* to farmers for self-provisioning and planting-back; or corporations, which hold *exclusive rights* over genetic materials and impose *restrictions* on the use of patented and high-priced biotech forms. In short, corporate appropriation of seeds and biological resources intensifies the homogenization of crop production, and privately established grades and standards play a pivotal role in this reduced biodiversity.

Gepts (2004, 1295) defines biodiversity as 'the sum of genetic and phenotypic differences existing in living organisms ... at the molecular, individual, population, and ecosystem levels'. Until the 1970s, biodiversity was considered part of the 'common heritage of humankind'. Biological resources and information belonged to the public domain and were not owned by any individual, group, corporation or state (Gepts 2004, 1295). People's access to and use of information and plant resources in the public domain was not considered a question of property and remained outside relations of competition, rights and exclusion. Access to and use of biological resources and information in the public domain was regarded as non-rival '(its use by one person does not compete with its use by another) and nonexcludable (no person can exclude other persons from its use)' (Gepts 2004, 1295). Since the 1970s, there has been a move towards commodification and corporate appropriation of, as well as control over, bio-information and resources through patenting (Deibel 2013). The 1995 Intellectual Property Rights (IPRs) agreement, the 1992 Convention on Biodiversity (CBD) and the 2004 International Treaty on Plant Genetic Resources for Food and Agriculture (ITPGRFA) by the UN Food and Agricultural Organization (henceforth the FAO Treaty) constitute the institutional framework for this new approach. The main drivers of this shift are transnational seed companies, life-sciences industry companies, commercial bio-prospectors specialized in the global collection of biological resources and brokerage companies involved in the creation, renting and licencing of bio-informational resources.

The IPR regime was concluded with the Trade-Related Intellectual Property Rights (TRIPS) agreement of the WTO in 1995, which [itself] was negotiated through the 1986–94 Uruguay Round of the General Agreement on Tariffs and Trade (GATT). The IPR agreement sets the terms and conditions for collecting, transforming and transmitting biological resources, as well as access to plant materials (Parry 2004). IPR-led governance is biotechnology dependent, requiring new biological resources and information for the novelty, inventiveness and utility of patentable products. Novelty and inventiveness are defined as 'non-obvious to someone skilled' in producing varieties by breeding (Gepts 2004, 1296, 1300). This undercuts farmers' right to breed new varieties based on 'the embodied know-how' of generations of farmers and through 'lineage' and 'crop ancestry' (Deibel 2013, 286–7).

IPR governance excludes plants and animals as *whole* biological systems but includes their fragments, components or chemical constituents, involving microorganisms and microbiological and molecular-biological processes (Calvert 2008). According to Calvert (2008), this thoroughly reductionist understanding of biological phenomena, which reduces them to their chemical components – decontextualized and disembodied from their myriad of nuanced, complex networks of biological relationships – fits very well with the conceptualization of life forms as commodities. The notion of disembodiment, reminiscent of what Polanyi (1944) called 'fictitious commodities' and Marx (1954 [1887]) described as 'alienation', makes it possible to transform complex biological entities into 'things' – 'objects outside us'. These fragmented biological processes are then subject to market exchange as tradable commodities within the intellectual property regime.

The CBD, signed in 1992, affirms state jurisdiction over biodiversity (Deibel 2013, 287). It assigns states exclusive property rights over genetic resources within their territorial boundaries, which the FAO Treaty further confirms. The CBD requires governments to facilitate access by other governments and legal persons to the genetic resources within their territories in return for payment. That is, the CBD ties the protection and accessibility of crop varieties to the market-economic principle of 'economic compensation' (Deibel 2013; Gepts 2004). Payments are to be deposited in the Global Crop Diversity Fund first and then used for research on the preservation of plant-based genetic diversity (V. Gill 2010). In its mandate to preserve the genetic diversity of plants, the CBD requires governments to develop a national biodiversity strategy and action plans (NBSAPS).[7] Such plans often focus on the development of national plant germplasm systems through gene/seed banks. These banks are affiliated with the FAO, the world-wide administration that belongs to the Consultative Group on International Agricultural Research (CGIAR).

According to Gepts (2004, 1297), the NBSAPS system of the CBD feeds into increased commodification of biodiversity and commercialization of crops within the IPR regime. Both the CBD and IPR mechanisms and the FAO Treaty substitute open-access and open-variety use rights in the public domain with a private property regime that imposes restrictions on the collection, transformation and transmission of biology (Gepts 2004) – the main vehicles of which are patents, licencing, royalty agreements, material transfer agreements (MTA) and technology use agreements.

The private control and ownership of seeds and genetic resources from crops within the IPR system is reinforced through advancements in biotechnology research – research that continues to evolve through a disciplinary partnership of systems and synthetic biology with engineering, mathematics, statistics and informatics (Allarakhia and Wensley 2005; Brent 2004; Calvert 2008; Parry 2004). Experimental research arising from this partnership helps to further fragment, refine and standardize natural biological 'parts' at the molecular level – to make them 'behave' in predictable and thus controllable ways (Canon et al. 2008). As argued by Calvert (2008), fragmentation, disentanglement and standardization of biological networks into computer-based models is explicitly conducive to the process of commodification. The re-constitution of biological materials 'from a corporeal to an information state' (Parry 2004, 29) has made biological materials amenable to commodification as a form of private property subject to commercial transactions and patenting. '[M]ost synthetic biological parts and devices are produced via a process that starts with the discovery and description of a natural biological function' (Canon et al. 2008, 789). Therefore, locating and utilizing suitable natural 'starting' materials is paramount for biotechnology research, as it connects engineering with the discovery of biological information that extends into *entire* biological systems.

The source of much biological information is often the gene-rich regions of the global South. The genetic richness of these regions, defined in terms of crop diversity, includes not only bred cultivars but also landraces (domestic farmer cultivars, regionally/locally adapted varieties of domesticated plants) and wild varieties in various combinations with domesticated types. Research conducted by Kloppenburg (2005 [1988]) shows that the West Central Asiatic region (including Turkey) has the greatest biodiversity, with a 31 per cent reliance on non-indigenous crops for crop production and improvement, followed by the Indo-Chinese region with a 33 per cent reliance and the Hindustanean region with a 49 per cent reliance. The dependency of Latin America and Chino-Japanese regions on non-indigenous crops is estimated to be approximately 56 and 63 per cent respectively, while North America and Australia are 100 per cent dependent. Euro-Siberia has a 91 per cent dependency and Africa 88 per cent (Kloppenburg 2005 [1988], 178). Thus, the genetically diverse regions of the global South are the main targets of biotechnology and seed companies, while commercial bio-prospectors, often located in the global North, are busily collecting, researching and patenting genetic and biochemical materials.

The corporate-led operation of 'biodiversity markets' requires the pooling of biological information, both from the public domain and private holders of prior patents. Various methods can be employed here, including bio-piracy and market-based purchasing within a 'biodiversity market' (Deibel 2013, 288). The operation of biodiversity markets relies on what I call the *techno-economic management* of bio-information, viewed as a tradable commodity within the corporate-led IPR regime.

Significantly, the global governance of biotechnology research innovation lacks 'transparency' and 'information disclosure' (Gupta 2010). Moreover, the scientific, technical expertise required to undertake the complexities of biotechnology research and governance frequently increases the technocratic-expert power of professionals and specialists within the IPR regime (cf. Vestergaard 2009). The lack of transparency coupled with technical specialization in biotechnology research only serves to deepen the process of commodification of plants and their genetic resources, including bio-information on genes, proteins, cells and other dynamics within the IPR system. Ultimately, it serves to elevate a performance-oriented agro-industrial notion of agriculture to an epistemically dominant position.

Since the 1980s, there has been a proliferation of patents and IPRs registered by both private and public-sector institutions involved in agricultural biotechnology (Graff et al. 2003, 989). It is estimated that only 24 per cent of all agricultural biotechnology patents in the United States (US) are in the public sector; the remaining 74 per cent are in the private sector (Graff et al. 2003, 990–1). In the US, the leading private firms in agricultural biotechnology are Monsanto (St. Louis, MO, US), DuPont (Wilmington, DE, US), Syngenta (Basel, Switzerland) and Bayer (Leverkusen, Germany). Monsanto is the largest patent holder in the US, with a 14 per cent contribution. DuPont is second with 13 per cent, followed by Syngenta with 7 per cent, Bayer with 4 per cent and Dow with 3 per cent. These five companies account for 41 per cent of all patents, with the remaining private-sector patents scattered among various firms. The entire public-sector portfolio represents approximately 22 per cent of the total value of the industry; Monsanto alone represents 19 percent (Graff et al. 2003, 991).

Monsanto, DuPont and Syngenta control approximately 50 per cent of the global proprietary seed market. Monsanto's share of the global market is 23 per cent, DuPont holds 15 per cent and Syngenta 9 per cent (Wield et al. 2010, 347). Between 1990 and 1994, the five largest biotechnology firms accounted for approximately 37 per cent of plant patents. Their share increased to approximately 81 per cent between 2000 and 2004 (Wield et al. 2010, 348).

Since Monsanto introduced genetically modified crops and began buying up smaller seed companies nearly 20 years ago, the seed industry has experienced a faster rate of market concentration than any other farm-input sector. According to a report published in *Heritage Farm Companion* by Hope Shand (2012, 10–5), Monsanto has become the world's largest seed company, holding 27 per cent of global market shares in 2009. It is followed by DuPont, which holds 17 per cent, and Syngenta with 9 per cent. The worldwide market share of the three largest seed firms (Monsanto, DuPont and Syngenta) increased from 20 per cent of the proprietary seed market in 2002 to 53 per cent in 2009. Their market concentration in vegetable seed is even higher. The top four firms controlled 70 per cent of the global market in 2007; the top eight controlled 94 per cent. After acquiring Seminis in 2005, parts of Advanta in 2004 and Aventis/Nunhems in 2002, Monsanto, Syngenta and Bayer, respectively, have emerged as the major players in seeds. This high level of seed-industry concentration is expected to continue in the near future. While a merger between Monsanto and Syngenta appeared a strong possibility in 2015 when Monsanto aggressively pursued a takeover of Syngenta,[8] Bayer, in September 2016, concluded the largest all-cash corporate deal on record to purchase Monsanto (Reuters 2016). *BBC News* (2015) has also reported merger talks between DuPont and Dow. The increasing 'tightness' in seed-industry concentration is also indicative of a lack of competition among global agribusiness firms. These corporations *also* tightly control the global seed markets through cross-licence proprietary germplasm and other technologies as well as consolidated research and development efforts and abstention from costly patent litigation battles. The major corporate players consider farmers who self-provision in seeds as their biggest competitor, particularly given that large numbers of people in the global South remain dependent on farmer-saved seed. Thus, the global seed-industry firms are pushing hard for the introduction of intellectual property rights and biotech-friendly seed laws and agricultural regulations in order to marginalize and ultimately eliminate the practice of seed-saving. In 2007, farmer saved seed represented 21 per cent of total global seed market value. The commercial proprietary seed market comprised 68 per cent and public commercial seed 11 per cent (Shand 2012, 12).

In addition to developing new plant varieties, global seed-industry corporations are constantly working to produce novel agronomic traits and key crop characteristics such as salinity and drought resistance, herbicide and pest resistance and nutritional and flavour enhancement. The end result of their techno-scientific efforts is typically increased genetic uniformity and a reduction in the number of native crops, traditional bred cultivars and landraces grown by farmers.

Together with the supermarket-led imposition of private quality standards, agricultural biotechnology also undermines the 'farming scripts' embedded for generations in the experience-based knowledge of traditional farming practices. At the same time, it creates greater space in the global economy for capitalized farmers to practice biotechnology-intensive, mono-cultural, industrially standardized crop production. The question remains as to what actually happens when countries adopt certain policies that are directed toward a market-oriented, agro-industrial agricultural development model and how such a model is re-worked in practice. It is also important to be aware of the ongoing challenges unfolding on the ground in relation to the norms, practices and objectives of IPR governance of bio-information and genetic resources.

Product Standardization and Global Biotechnology Companies: Open-Field Trial Planting of New Varieties by Syngenta and Rijk Zwaan in Turkey

This section provides a detailed account of how bio-tech driven pressure for standardized differentiation in food varieties and profit-oriented reorganization of farming practices is *brokered* by the upstream and downstream players in food supply chains. The demonstration of open-field trials plays a critical role in the implementation of this brokerage activity by upstream actors of seed-innovation and plant-breeding companies. Syngenta, which holds 20 per cent of the vegetable seed market in Turkey (Mr. Tabur, interview, 28 May 2014), and Rijk Zwaan[9] are actively involved in organizing and participating in food fairs and open-field demonstration days in Turkey.

On 28 and 29 May 2014, Syngenta organized two day-long open-field trial demonstrations in Kayabükü, a village within the Beypazarı region. During this event, I met and interviewed two managers employed by Syngenta who are responsible for vegetable portfolios in Southeast Europe, Europe, Africa and the Middle East (EAME). Tolga Tabur is Turkish in origin and is responsible for Syngenta's vegetable portfolio in 16 countries within Southeast Europe extending from Hungary to Israel; Nicholas Bennett is Australian and is responsible for the leafy, roots and bulbs portfolio in the same EAME region.

Similar to Syngenta's demonstration days in Beypazarı, Rijk Zwaan organized an open-field and greenhouse demonstration day in Antalya, Turkey, from 25 to 28 May in 2014, for the entire region of the Middle East and North Africa. At this event, Rijk Zwaan exhibited lettuce and spinach innovations for sale to seed distributors and growers from Algeria to Iran. Both companies also participated in the 'Fresh Turkey Fair' held in İstanbul in 2015. These fairs have been organized in Turkey since 2011, with the explicit goal of introducing product innovations in FFVs to foreign and domestic purchase managers and sector suppliers. Open-field trial days are held for the same purpose. The Fresh Turkey Fair was supported by many organizations in Turkey, including the Ministry of Food, Agriculture and Livestock, Metropolitan İstanbul, the Vegetable and Fruits Commissioners Federation of Turkey, the İstanbul

Figure 3.1 Tolga Tabur, Syngenta Vegetable Portfolio Manager for Southeast Europe (Kayabükü, Beypazarı, 28 May 2014).

Wholesale Terminal, the Seed Producers Association of Turkey, *pazar* traders, exporters and food processors. Through such fairs and open-field trial days, organizers encourage growers and suppliers in Turkey to become familiar with new varieties of FFVs and other GLOBALGAP-certified products, as well as new developments in infrastructure technologies for calibration, packaging and logistics. These events also provide opportunities to promote FFV products grown in Turkey for export.[10]

Undoubtedly, the fundamental motivation for organizing open-field demonstration days and Fresh Turkey Fairs is the anticipation of greater market demand for the FFV product innovations and seed varieties developed by these corporations. The government adoption of complementary policy changes, as described in the previous chapter, also plays a significant role in facilitating market demand for new innovations linked to increased profitability in agriculture and export earnings. In a letter published on the 'Fresh Turkey Fair' website, then Minister of Food, Agriculture and Livestock, Mehdi Eker, conveyed his support for such fairs and demo days in Turkey:

> [w]e are working harder to extend (our) agriculture with alternative and modern production techniques, strengthen our producers by raising awareness and develop their capacity (for) reaching (new) markets. ... [W]e will be supporting these fair organizations, which we believe will make a great contribution to the sector.[11]

Hundreds of people attended the open-field crops demonstration day organized by Syngenta in Beypazarı. In addition to Syngenta's own managers, participants included growers (Turkish and international), greenhouse seedling growers and seed distributors, professors and students from the Faculty of Agriculture of Ankara University, as well as representatives of rival transnational companies, such as Rijk Zwaan of the Netherlands. My description of Syngenta's activities is based on my interviews with their managers, a representative of Rijk Zwaan-Turkey and a number of local, national and international farmers. The local farmers were from Beypazarı and Güdül in the province of Ankara and from other provinces, including İzmir, Sakarya and Antalya. The international farmers were from Bulgaria, Greece, Holland and Romania. By inviting them to its demonstration day, Syngenta provided these farmers with an opportunity to inspect the soil conditions and plant varieties of the area, as well as to gain information and advice on how to grow these new varieties under locally varied conditions of climate, topography and water availability.

My interviews with Syngenta and Rijk Zwaan officials provide a description of transnationally advocated models of techno-scientific growth along with their supporting ideological foundation. Syngenta promotes its ideational and technical vision of agricultural development via the notion of *optimization of performance value*. This concept, shared by other transnational bio-tech firms, presents a globally integrated ontological perspective of profit-oriented agriculture.

Syngenta's open-field trial-based planting included newly 'innovated' seed varieties and various breeds of lettuce and spinach. These never-before-tried seeds were comprised of 43 different lettuce and 24 different spinach varieties. The varieties were developed in controlled laboratory conditions and planted on 10,000 dekars of open-field farmland. The Turkish farmer who owned the land, Mesut, signed a contract with Syngenta to rent his land for TL 3,000 per dekar.[12] This is far above the average rental price in the area of TL 40 per dekar. Tabur explained that Syngenta knows the area and the farmers in the region very well through direct contact and through seed distributors. He indicated that it wasn't difficult to find a farmer willing to take part in the field-trial planting. Tabur explained that once the open-field demonstration day is over, the farmer can sell the produce (grown with Syngenta trial seeds) on the market the way he would normally. Even if the trial outcome was poor and the farmer was unable to sell the produce, Tabur explained that Syngenta would pay for the farmer's losses.

The 'natural' site selected by Syngenta for its in-soil field experimentation, unlike the artificial conditions of the laboratory, enables the company to determine whether its seed varieties are suitable for planting in the particular soil nutrient and climate conditions of the Mediterranean region. Both Nicholas Bennett, Syngenta portfolio manager for EAME, and Tolga Tabur, Syngenta vegetable portfolio manager for Southeast Europe, informed me that the ecological balance of biological constituents and chemical substances in the soil of the area appears well-suited for growing the particular vegetable/salad varieties designed by Syngenta for the climatic conditions of the Middle East, North Africa and Southeastern Europe. In fact, according to Tabur, the company carefully chose this area to determine whether these crop varieties could be successfully grown under the hot weather conditions of the Middle East and whether Syngenta would be able to successfully create new markets in the region for these innovated varieties.

Andrei, a seed-distributor from Romania who visited the field-site with some of his grower-customers, expressed his surprise at the selection of the site:

> Look at this land and the weather. It is like a desert … too hot; and the soil looks water-deficient; there is no river in close proximity. They planted these vegetables in this desert-like flat plain. Look at the lettuce and spinach in the field … so lush and beautiful – as if they are grown in a fertile river bed.
>
> (Interview, 28 May 2014)

I told the Romanian distributor that the Kirmir River is only 2–3 kilometres away, and that there are underground water reservoirs as well. The Romanian's response was that '[T]he river might be close but look at these high mountains. They are bringing water from a far-away river … I am sure it is very expensive. But the seeds are working wonderfully' (Interview, 28 May 2014).

A farmer from Bulgaria explained:

> We came here to learn from the Turkish experience. We can do the same kind of production in Bulgaria. It is incredible what you see here, and they are growing their produce in such a hot environment and such dry soil.
>
> (Interview, 28 May 2014)

On the issue of finding the best possible match in regard to plant–soil compatibility when developing new varieties, Tolga Tabur offered the following explanation, in which he conveys the importance of locally grown wild varieties for the development of Syngenta's own seeds. Interestingly, in a separately conducted interview, a Rijk Zwaan official, who is also Turkish in origin, expressed the same point of view. Here is Tabur's explanation from Syngenta:

> These seeds are not produced in Turkey. We grow them in countries such as Chile and Thailand where the labour cost is low. We do our plant breeding in six to seven countries; tomato and spinach breeding in Spain, lettuce and cabbage varieties in the Netherlands, watermelon in Hungary, etc. We aim to find the most suitable conditions for our seeds, which we design for high yield. When agricultural lands are decreasing, and the need for more food is increasing, yield becomes more critical for farmers. Unfortunately, we no longer pay much attention to taste and flavour, only to yield and shelf-life. We also have to deal with the problem of fungus

and mildew. Unfortunately, in the process our own local seeds disappear. They are not high-yielding ... but, local wild seeds are important for us. When a plant breeder comes to a field, the first thing he does is to look at the weeds growing wild on the side of the field or side of the road. Among these weeds are also local lettuce varieties. They look as if they are [wild] weeds. But, the plant breeder knows that they are wild varieties and collects them to use as a breeding parent (mother or father) for new high-yielding varieties. You need to have natural materials to develop new varieties. If you want to grow varieties that are appropriate for such hot climatic conditions, you must have wild varieties from this region. Breeding is a long and expensive process. It takes at least six or seven years to develop an F1 variety. That is why we need to carefully discover the wild varieties to invent new seeds and produce marketable products.

(Interview, 28 May 2014)

Yağmur Toprak, the Rijk Zwaan official whom I met and interviewed at the Bey Fide greenhouses in the village of Fasıl in Beypazarı on 27 May 2014, explains further:

Technical infrastructural investment, agricultural research and development, and seed improvement only began in the 1980s in Turkey. Rijk Zwaan began to improve seeds and plant breeding in 1923. We are rich in terms of wild seeds; but we are way behind in terms of agriculturally usable, improved seeds. There is a gene bank recently established in the Aegean region. But, it is for preserving existing seeds rather than improving them for agricultural use. At the moment Rijk Zwaan has ready-to-use varieties belonging to 1,128 races. We don't use a variety for more than three years in the market. We constantly improve and develop new seeds, just as we regularly change cell phones. This year we marketed disease resistant varieties for 31 races. After three years, these seeds lose their insect resistance and herbicide tolerance capabilities. Therefore, we have to move on to the 32nd race and develop new seed varieties.

I also interviewed Saffet Soykan, the owner of Bey Fide greenhouses, in his on-site office on 27 May 2014. He explained:

Just as Rijk Zwaan or Syngenta has to develop new climate appropriate seeds, they must also collect naturally existing wild varieties from all over the world. For example, in our village in Beypazarı, you see wild plants on the road sides. You may think that they are just weeds. In reality they are lettuces, containing male seeds. The companies gather these seeds from us after we send them the plants, and then use them for seed improvement. Since they use our own natural plants, their newly invented plants are suitable for a hot climate. They may also go to village *pazars* where they see local crops. They buy them and immediately send them to their labs (before washing them) for improvement. Once they improve the local seeds, they patent them, but only after stealing the original seeds ...

Although the owner of Bey Fide is fully aware of this corporate process of accessing local seeds in order to steal bioinformation, he is also aware that these seeds, once developed, come back to growers as a means or *service* for generating profits. Similarly, Tolga Tabur from Syngenta is focused on finding the best soil–plant matches for developing new seed and plant varieties. For him, this reflects an 'optimization of performance value' approach, by targeting low-cost areas to produce high-yield seeds for profit. Both views express the calculative logic of optimization that governs all aspects of seed production within profit-driven markets. Germination rates, high yields and disease control are the most important considerations in this value orientation, which drives corporate innovation toward uniform, standardized and 'efficient' seed varieties. Nicholas Bennett from Syngenta spells out the significance of this value orientation for profitability in competitive business. He states:

> We are part of a value chain which produces for seed providers, who in turn provide for young plant raisers, who then sell for growers. Young plant producers are under great pressure to provide cheaper seedlings for plant growers. So you have to give them the best, [with the] highest germination level possible. Out of 100 seeds, we expect 96 seeds to germinate. Every seed is money for the young plant growers. They expect high quality germination to make money. Our view is that we have to find the best possible places to produce [those] optimal quality seeds ... We are a multinational company [operating for profit], producing high quality seeds with high germination rates and good resistance to disease. ... If seeds can't be produced at a particular price, this discourages companies from investing. ... One of the key traits of a new product is disease resistance ... Brown fungus [for example] ... proliferates in multiple races. ... It appears on the leaves ... If you don't take protective action against this disease, you can't sell your produce to a top quality supermarket. ... We develop disease-resistant varieties through natural mating and combining different varieties. It is like humans taking a vaccine. This is definitely not genetic modification but rather recombining materials and putting new resistance into the varieties. We produce something to defend the plant against this disease. The turn-over rate is every two to three years for new varieties. This costs a lot of money ... so you have to gain a return on your investment. At the end of the day, multinationals report to shareholders, and they have to make an appropriate level of profit on that investment. The reason that our company is so strong is that we develop new disease-resistant varieties. If reproduction occurs in those diseases we do not have the ability to invest in new products, [which will] put the company back substantially. At the end of the day you will have the same varieties you had 20 years ago if you don't innovate with new varieties.
>
> (Interview, 28 May 2014)

Nicholas Bennett of Syngenta emphasizes that growers in Turkey must think of their farming activities as a business investment and collaborate with multinational corporations when deciding what and how to grow.

> It is critical, I think, that we make sure the approach of growers is to continue to invest in their business and enjoy partnerships with multinational organizations ... these organizations can support their growth and their businesses. It is a big business for growers too ... they need to plant 80,000 young plants per hectare. Combined with [the] cost of labour, machinery, inputs and transportation, it is an expensive business. We have to provide the growers with advice and optimal quality products so that they can make [a] profit.
>
> (Interview, 28 May 2014)

Given that Syngenta displayed over 70 new varieties of lettuce and spinach in Beypazarı, I asked Nicholas Bennett how a grower can decide what to choose for the market. His answer was as follows:

> When the vegetable growing markets get more professional, producers will segment their production and fragment perfect, optimal varieties for those segments. At the moment, rotation for growing these varieties could be six weeks or less. Growers can change varieties in accordance with those growing rotations. The rate of turn-over for us to develop new products is every two to three years. Professional growers can deal with this; they can respond to a variety of market factors to make profits.
>
> (Interview, 28 May 2014)

It is evident from Nickolas Bennett's response that he considers the decisions that farmers make regarding what particular food variety to grow a matter of professionalism. For him, farmers should be responsive to the technical innovation of new varieties, to the market metric of growth measured by financial return and to new production methods that allow for the growing of many new varieties within the same crop area.[13] Mr. Bennett believes that 'upstream' players involved in seed and plant breeding must be connected to the 'downstream' actors in supermarket chains through professional growers who are able to adapt their production methods to the 2 or 3-year innovation turnover rate. In response to profit-driven private investment in agricultural research and innovation, professional growers are expected to work with seed-innovating companies and supermarket chains. To quote Mr. Bennett again:

> Supermarkets are part of the food-value chain. And the core driver for supermarkets is profitability and providing quality products. Consumers must enjoy the experience [as well]. So we have to be engaged in the value chain from the field to the supermarket shelves. We try to deliver the best, highest quality product for consumers; we must meet their expectations.

> Turkey is an exporting country. Growers must provide quality produce and variety for the consumers; we have to support them. The local growing conditions in Beypazarı are fantastic. Product quality is fantastic. You see the same thing in various places in Europe. It is not behind Europe. We have Romanian colleagues here. They are looking for butter head lettuce. That is not a product grown here in Beypazarı. Growers must respond to consumer demand for different varieties and tastes. I think that the Turkish industry will continue to improve the quality of its produce and they will expand their business.
>
> (Interview, 28 May 2014)

Again, the focus is on farming as a thoroughly professionalized business venture. And the professionalism of farmers is to be determined by their responsiveness to product innovation turn-over rates, compliance with the 'need' to grow new food varieties and the ability to achieve greater profits.

For Nicholas Bennett, seed innovation and plant breeding are key functions that play a crucial role in determining the supply of food varieties through strategic product-line planning. A question arises here as to the meaning of *variety*. For Syngenta, it refers to the development of new products. New varieties are devised and developed by biotech firms in response to supermarket demands for particular food quality standards. The varieties, therefore, are uniform, *standardized* products developed as a response to the *optimal performance-value* requirements of a profit-driven competitive market logic. The characteristics of uniformity and standardization also differentiate products as food varieties. This is aptly expressed in the subtitle of the book *Standards* by Busch (2011, 151) – 'From Standardization to Standardized Differentiation'. Busch argues that 'all standards standardize and all differentiate. After all, they attempt to make beings the same in some way, but in doing so they distinguish those beings from others that are differentiated in some other way'.

Thus, although consumer demand for food variety and a 'joyful' experience in supermarkets is frequently mentioned, the corporate-led supply of food variety does not imply that these firms actually respond to consumers' preference for *dietary variety* in food. Tolga Tabur from Syngenta explains how he selects new varieties for innovation:

> I choose products by visual examination to determine whether or not they would be marketable in certain countries. I pay attention to the climatic conditions of the countries and the consumption habits. Through friendly conversation, and by socializing with growers during my travels in these countries, I gather information and learn what they want. I prepare tables, and insert my observations in the tables regarding what they wish to see in a new product. The plant breeder draws a computerized picture containing the regionally desired characteristics of a plant based on my criteria. I also need to know the food culture in these places. For example, in

Turkey people prefer red cabbage in an oval shape, rather than rounded. Round cabbage does not make money in Turkey. It is just a matter of visual preference for an oval shape.[14] It has nothing to do with taste and the nutritional content of the cabbage. I pay attention to how a product is going to look visually. Is it going to be attractive on the shelf? ... Is it going to be appealing to the eye? These are important criteria for designing new varieties.

(Interview, 28 May 2014)

This method of designing food varieties indicates that product differentiation through standardization is largely a matter of cosmetic appeal, which becomes integrated into a research and development investment function. By offering consumers greater choice from more visually attractive 'varieties' *within* the same food group and by differentiating their products from competitors, seed and plant-breeding companies can maintain an advantageous position on pricing in the market. This approach is highly compatible with 'industrial organization theory' (Weiss 2011, 673–4), which asserts that a requirement for increasing production and productivity is recognizing that consumers have a culturally specific 'drive for sensory variety' (Prescott 2012, 90), together with certain *visual* preferences for product characteristics and food attributes. For Tolga Tabur, the assumed visual preference for oval red cabbage by Turkish consumers is carefully played out through a computerized graphic design that depicts the 'ideal' red cabbage.

The standardized differentiation of food based on computerized design is very different from the millennia-long process of differentiation based on the practice of plant breeding by farmers (Anderson 1969; Polan 2002). In the latter case, locally diverse food cultures, diet, flavour and various soil-forming processes have affected the development of significantly different varieties. The plant-breeding 'standards' used by individual farmers or a group of farmers in a village were based on highly localized experimentation through trial and error, seasonally variable and dependent on the quality of harvest in a given year. They were hardly formalized (Busch 2013, 38–9). Joop Vegter, the marketing manager of Rijk Zwaan, offers additional information with which to better understand the critical role played by companies in forming *demand* for a *designed* variety. The following material was supplied by Joop Vegter in an interview for *Bereket TV* at the 'Growtech Agriculture Fair' in Antalya in 2013. His explanation for the design of new plant varieties gives emphasis to the colour and shape of a product.

Turkey used to grow only a few varieties of FFVs, but now through such fairs they are exposed to more varieties ... with greater potential for export ... and easy [to market in] high quality packaging. This ... eggplant developed for production in Turkey. [Growers] look at it and ask what kind of eggplant this is. And the question arises as to the taste of these new varieties. We say: take it home, prepare a meal from it, and then tell us how you like the taste. These varieties may be better suited in terms of taste for certain meals and not suitable for others ... Turkish people only like two varieties of peppers: *green*, tall pointed peppers and stuffing peppers. But there are more varieties in the world, which we call California varieties. They come in different colours, red, orange and yellow, which go well in salads ... Turkey has just started to grow them but not enough for exportation. We can develop varieties here for world markets. Now we [have] developed a new variety. Here they give it the name of an old local *çorbacı* variety, but actually it is a new variety, designed for resistance to cold, and grown for winter, not summer ... there is a market for this type of product; it will generate good money for producers ... Similarly, they ... say that [the] Yıldız tomato was more flavourful. True, the old tomato was tastier. ... [b]ut we also need to generate a high-yield tomato with a longer shelf-life. We developed this new *pink* tomato, called TY12, combining the old taste with a new demand for high-yield ... it is grown now in Kumluca, Antalya.[15]

Tolga Tabur's comments on the design of new seed varieties suggests that the development and supply of new varieties is neither a response to consumer demand for taste and flavour, nor an attempt to improve the nutritional content of food. Rather, it is simply an effort to advance a business model capable of increasing production and profits. Tabur continues:

When consumers in Turkey do not like a certain food product, when they find it tasteless, they call it *hormonlu*.[16] Even my own mother calls these new varieties *hormonlu* and does not want to eat them. I don't blame her. I myself know the difference in taste, and can remember all the way back to my childhood. But, the grower wants to produce more to make more money, the retailer does not care about the taste, they want to sell more; same as with the wholesale trader. Unfortunately this is the case everywhere. Thus, we provide ever-new varieties for the market. This is now a never-ending cycle.

(Interview, 28 May 2014)

An emphasis on high-yielding varieties, with their visual appeal, colour coordination, long shelf-life and disease resistance has in fact reduced the diversity of food varieties consumed across regions and countries, including those grown for their dietary, nutritional and taste qualities. It has also increased the standardization of food production and the convergence of common consumption patterns toward innovated food that expresses the colour and shape characteristics of 'designed' meals (Fabiosa 2011). This is expressed well by Jool Vegter (of Rijk Zwaan) in his description of California pepper varieties, whose colours – red, orange and yellow – are designed to 'go well' in a salad. Again, the interest in optimization of performance value conveyed here reflects an ontological orientation that contributes significantly to the manufacture of 'mass diets' (Winson 2013).

Visual standardization of food products for mass diets marginalizes farmers who do not comply with the necessary production requirements and lack the necessary self-investing entrepreneurial spirit. This is exemplified by a grower at the Syngenta demonstration day in Beypazarı, whose non-compliance with required standards for the size of food created a barrier for him in marketing his crop:

> Last year I couldn't sell my iceberg lettuce because they were too big. One iceberg lettuce weighed about 3 kilos, which could last a family one week. It is better for the consumer ... it lasts longer, but the supermarket doesn't want it to be bigger than 800 grams. A small iceberg can only last one or two days. Similarly, supermarkets want spinach to have small leaves ... because it looks nicer on the shelf. Families spend more money for a smaller size and they have to buy more food but supermarkets can make greater profit because they sell more.
>
> (Interview, 28 May 2014)

A home-gardener who attended the demonstration day expressed dismay at supermarkets' demand for smaller sizes in fresh produce. She questioned whether they actually base their position on consumers' preference for smaller varieties:

> I am a working woman ... I don't have time to always go to the markets to shop or clean small leaves of spinach. It takes lots of time for me to wash them. I prefer larger leaves, it takes less time to clean. I have a small garden in front of my house where I grow everything, ranging from herbs, spinach, peppers, cucumbers and tomatoes. I don't spray them. I don't even use fertilizers. My food smells great and is very tasty ... no contamination, no hormones. My veggies are delicious and healthier. And I don't need to spend money at the supermarkets or waste my time cleaning tiny leaves. I economize better that way.
>
> (Interview, 28 May 2014)

In this instance, for the home-gardener, 'diet quality', expressed in relation to smell, taste and flavour, as well as the health attributes of food, was the sole criterion. For the grower, the only criterion was his ability to adapt to the requirements of socio-technical innovation imposed by seed companies and supermarkets so that he could increase the marketability of his food. The grower blamed himself for failing to be entrepreneurial enough and not following instructions provided by the seed company. Pointing to a picture in a Syngenta advertisement of a fertilizer product, the grower said: 'Obviously, these seeds work, once it is fed with this fertilizer. How can you not make money from this product? It was my mistake that I let my lettuce get too big'. Clearly, there are divergent value systems at play here between the home-gardener and the grower in regard to personal preferences for the direction of modern agriculture.

Agricultural Biotechnology in Turkey: The Seeds Law and Agriculture Law

In 2013, 175 million hectares of land in 27 countries were planted with commercialized biotech crops (James 2013).[17] This represents approximately 12 per cent of the total 1.5 billion hectares of crops planted worldwide in 2013. The four major biotech crops include soybean, cotton, maize and canola. Biotech crops have been planted by approximately 18 million farmers, 90 per cent of whom are small, resource poor producers from the 'developing' world. The great majority of biotech crops (95 per cent), including genetically modified (GM) varieties, are grown in the US, Brazil, Argentina, India, Canada and China. Brazil has the second largest cultivated area of GM crops in the world after the US. Its production has increased from an estimated 15.8 million hectares in 2008 to 36.6 million in 2012 and 40.3 million in 2013 (James 2013). Brazil also approved six new GM products in 2011, including a homegrown biotech virus-resistant bean developed in the public sector by the Brazilian Agricultural Research Cooperation (EMBRAPA) (James 2011). According to the Scottish Crop Research Institute, GM crops are planted on 0.119 per cent of agricultural land in Europe (Stephan 2012, 105). Turkey is not listed in James' reports on biotech-crop growing countries.

In Turkey, the policy framework for agricultural biotechnology takes the Cartagena Biosafety Protocol (CBP) and the EU as a reference point. The CBP, which is intended to ensure safe use, handling and trans-boundary movement of living GM organisms (Kivilcim 2011, 268), was signed by Turkey in 2000. In 2010, Turkey approved its National Biosafety Law (Law No. 5977) and a related by-law.[18] Biosafety by-law No. 29014 of 29 May 2014 has assigned a 0.09 per cent level of GM contamination as the labelling threshold for crops/products defined as GM. The by-law allows for the sale of products at or below the 0.09 per cent of GM contamination, provided the government has approved the GM genes for agricultural use.[19] The 0.09 per cent GM contamination level appears to be a very low threshold, yet it is also in accordance with the EU-approved level for GM labelling. The labelling requirement is 1 per cent in Australia and New Zealand and 3 per cent in South Korea (Boyacıoğlu 2014).

Given public reaction to the by-law and concerns that GM food might eventually be allowed, the president of the Biosafety Council, Dr. Masum Burak, announced on CNN Türk television on 30 May 2014 that 'There is no permit for GM organisms in food ... and existing laws do not allow the usage and production of GM seeds in food production, nor do they allow importation of GM food' (Burak 2014). According to Burak, the 0.09 per cent GM-contamination threshold is necessary to fill the legal vacuum created by the sale of GM-contaminated feed crops, given that it is not always technically possible to prevent such contamination. He added that there is zero allowance for the sale of GM-contaminated food for human consumption.

To date, 17 GM genes have been approved for seeds used in corn- and soy-based animal feed production in Turkey (Burak 2014). The government has permitted the importation of 14 different GM genes for corn varieties and three genes for soy varieties used in animal-feed production. If corn and soy feed varieties include 0.09 per cent of GM organisms, they must be labelled GM crops. However, animals that are fed GM crops are not required to be designated as carrying GM genes.[20] Dr. Burak points out that these numbers are still well below the EU level, which allows 51 GM genes in animal feed and crops, including soy, corn, cotton, sugar beets and potatoes.

Turkey made the decision to import biotech crops and allow field trials for them in the late 1990s. The trial results have not been disclosed to the public (Kivilcim 2011, 270–1). Turkey also approved 'biotech' importation in 2011 (James 2011, 227), following the passing of national biosafety legislation in 2010. However, it is not entirely clear what biotech importation includes. According to government sources, Turkey does not import food crops and processed-food products containing GM genes, nor does it import seeds containing GM genes for use in food-crop production. However, because there is no mandatory labelling of GM content in seeds, it is difficult to establish that Turkey does not import GM seeds for food-crop production.

I have no data on the GM gene content of imported seeds. The MFAL website lists 41 government-approved laboratories, most of which are located throughout the country rather than at customs checkpoints.[21] There is no evidence to confirm that imported seeds are tested for GM contamination. The 'National Contamination Follow-Up Plan – 2014 Turkey' lists 13 laboratories in various provinces which test food for residues of chemicals, toxins or bacterial contamination, but the list does not include explicit data on laboratory testing for imported seeds and their GM content (GKGM 2014). GM-gene testing is technically complex and costly; I would not expect many of these laboratories to be equipped for such testing. TÜBİTAK (The Scientific and Technological Research Council of Turkey) is equipped for GM-gene testing yet provides no data on the subject.

The most dramatic aspect of Turkey's integration into global agricultural biotechnology is in the area of seed trade, including F1 hybrid vegetable seeds. The estimated value of Turkey's domestic seed market was US $750 million for the year 2012 (ISF 2013a). According to the International Seed Federation (ISF), the total value of the commercial world seed market in 2012 was approximately US $45 billion. The global value of the seed import market for 2012 is estimated to be over US $10 billion and the total quantity approximately 2.4 billion metric tons (ISF 2013b). In 2013, Turkey imported approximately US $194 million worth of hybrid seeds for planting: approximately US $115 million in vegetable crops, US $68 million in field crops and US $11 million in others including flower seed.[22] That translates to approximately 36,000 metric tonnes of imported seeds, of which approximately 20,000 metric tons were in field crops, 499 tons in hybrid vegetables and 15 tons in others including flower seed.[23] The market value of traded seed is based on seed sale prices and licencing revenues. Turkey also produces native hybrid vegetable seed, which reached 45 per cent of its domestic market by 2012, up from less than 10 per cent in 2004 (MFAL 2013, 78). Turkey also exports seeds, with a market value of nearly US $121 million in 2012 (MFAL 2013, 78).

Turkey's integration into the global biotechnology industry through seed trade coincides with the government's adoption of a new seed law in 2006. Although Turkey began to dismantle the public sector on seeds in the 1980s, a major restructuring began in the mid-2000s. The adoption of a law in 2004 on the Protection of Breeders' Rights for New Plant Varieties, the Agricultural Law of 2006 and the Seed Law of 2006 constitute the most important elements of this restructuring.

The 2004 law on the Protection of Breeders' Rights for New Plant Varieties (No. 5042) falls under the International Union for the Protection of New Varieties of Plants (UPOV) convention. The law considers certification of plant variety protection (PVP) for novel cultivars. Unlike IPR rights, the law recognizes that farmers may continue to save seeds for their own use without registering them, provided they do not sell or barter the seeds. This is known as 'farmers' privilege'. In Turkey, 'farmers' privilege' has not yet been tied to a legal framework to enforce PVP certification for traditional varieties and cultivars created by farmers themselves (Atalan-Helicke and Mansfield 2012, 136-8). Rather than protect farmers' privilege, the 2006 seeds law, in practice, enforces patents within an IPR system. It embodies a process which incorporates wild varieties, native crops, farmers' cultivars and landraces into a biological resource economy under the control of the state and IPR patents, thereby governing access to biodiversity in Turkey.

The Agriculture Law (No. 5488) and Seeds Law (No. 5553) were both enacted in 2006. The Agriculture Law promises support for contract farming (Article 13) and recognizes IPRs on seeds and crops (Article 10) (Aydın 2010, 173–4). The law has also partially reinstituted government support for agriculture, as specified in Article 19. This is largely due to growing criticism from smallholders that the DPA policy favours large farmers (Güven 2009). The current government support policies consist of crop-specific deficiency and compensatory payments, agricultural insurance payments, livestock insurance and rural development support (OECD 2011, 47–9). Market-price support now constitutes approximately 88 per cent of government subsidies (OECD 2011, 11). Government backing of agriculture, albeit partial, indicates that the market model has not followed a linear, prescribed path, and its enactment has been responsive to general criticism. However, it would be an error to suggest that the government has retracted from supporting corporate-driven agrarian transformation.

The 2006 Seeds Law, which replaced the 1963 seed law, became mandatory in late 2011. It requires that all seeds be registered and certified before they are sold on the market. Both the Ministry of Agriculture and Rural Affairs and the Association of Seed Producers, a private corporate institution, act as regulatory bodies for the production and marketing of seeds, registration and certification of varieties and checking for compliance with seedling standards (Tohumculuk Kanunu 2006). The law requires all seed growers to be affiliated with the association. There are currently 500 companies affiliated with this association. With no farmer participation, farmers' customary plant-breeding techniques for traditional varieties are not recognized. Therefore, the 2006 law presents a radical departure from the 1963 law, which had defined varieties developed, exchanged, sold and saved by farmers themselves as part of 'plant varieties' that could be commercially traded, exchanged and distributed. The 2006 law views traditional and local varieties developed by farmers, as well as wild varieties, as plant genetic resources that must be registered and certified by the state. Once they are certified, they can be commercially traded, exchanged and distributed.

The seeds law legally restricts seed growing areas, prohibits the marketing of unregistered seeds and plant genetic resources and reduces producers' ability to self-provision for replanting. Consequently, producers are becoming increasingly dependent on the purchase of patented, high-priced seeds from commercial companies, both Turkish and foreign owned.

MFAL statistics indicate that there were 500 seed companies operating throughout Turkey in 2014. Private companies control 100 per cent of vegetable-seed provisioning and 55 per cent of wheat-seed varieties (MFAL 2014a). Between 2002 and 2011, the use of certified seeds increased from 150,000 tons to 550,000 tons (MFAL 2013, 38). According to information that I gathered from Mr. Erdal Erol from the MFAL, 58 per cent of seeds currently used in agriculture are certified seeds; the usage rate for seeds patented/certified by Turkish owned companies is 34 per cent (Official Communication 2012). In the corn-seed market, Pioneer's share is 25.4 per cent, Monsanto's 25.1 per cent and Syngenta's 8.3 per cent. These three companies control 70 per cent of the sunflower-seed market, while for cotton seed, the combined market share of Bayer, Monsanto and Pioneer is 50 per cent (TMMOB 2011, 513). Since the passing of the seed law, private seed companies have also been active in patenting and copyrighting plant varieties in Turkey.

Turkey is located at the junction of four of the world's 34 global biodiversity hotspots: the Caucasus, Iran-Anatolia, the Mediterranean basin and the Middle East Mountains. Turkey itself has tremendous biodiversity; of the 12,500 known species on the entire continent of Europe, Turkey alone has approximately 12,000 known plant species (MFAL 2013, 80). MFAL has identified one third of these varieties as having economical resource and endemic characteristics. Turkey's endemism rate of 34 per cent is much higher than that of other European countries (İncekara n.d., 13–5). Given the lack of research and documentation, the extent of Turkey's biodiversity in plant species, particularly endemic species, is actually unknown.[24] The 2006 seed law enables the lawful commodification of this rich biodiversity in plant species within the IPR system. The government has opened a Plant Genebank in Ankara with a capacity of 250,000 gene samples. This is the world's third largest gene bank after banks in China and the US. Ankara's gene bank has already gathered 86,000 samples belonging to 2,500 plant varieties for use in biotechnology research (MFAL 2013, 80).

A report published in 2014 by MFAL lists approximately 900 plant varieties under state protection, as well as the names of the companies licenced to conduct research on these varieties (MFAL 2014b). The list shows a high level of concentration by private foreign companies that obtained licences to carry out research on vegetable, fresh fruit and flower varieties. Figures 3.2, 3.3 and 3.4 provide data on the distribution of foreign and Turkish owned companies involved in agro-biotechnology research and seed improvement in plant varieties.

While Figure 3.3 shows the overall dominance of foreign-owned companies in plant biotechnology research in Turkey, Figure 3.2 reveals the dominance of Turkish-owned private and public companies in field crops, pulses

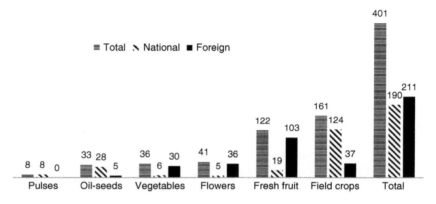

Figure 3.2 Protected Plant Varieties (2014).

Source: Author, Based on Data Obtained from MFAL (2014b).

Figure 3.3 Protected Plant Varieties (2014).

Source: Author, Based on Data Obtained from MFAL (2014b).

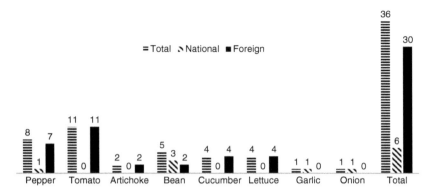

Figure 3.4 Protected Vegetable Varieties (2014).

Source: Author, based on data obtained from MFAL (2014b).

and oil-seed varieties. The field crops, including wheat and barley varieties, form the backbone of semi-subsistence–oriented agricultural production by small-scale farmers who continue to use saved seeds for planting-back grains through 'farmers' privilege'. In contrast, commodification via patenting in plant genetic resources is greater in FFV and flower varieties – varieties that constitute the heart of Turkey's export-oriented agricultural production. It is into these areas of commercialized agriculture that foreign-owned plant bio-technology companies are increasingly entering to develop seeds that possess desired new traits (see Figures 3.2 and 3.4). Due to the 2006 seed law, which restricts producers' ability to self-provision for planting-back and for breeding varieties through seed sharing, farmers are forced to purchase high-priced patented seeds from seed companies.

According to Kloppenburg (2010), farmers' loss of control over their seeds for crop production and the plant genetic resources contained in the wild relatives of crops constitutes a new frontier of what David Harvey (2003) calls 'accumulation by dispossession'. This process embodies multiple and interrelated upstream steps. It includes access to germplasm and related genetic information, production of scientific knowledge, seed development and breeding new crops. This entails nothing less than 'seed enclosures from domesticated to wild' crop varieties (de Wit 2016, 3). Farmers are not only required to purchase seeds on the market but are increasingly unable to reproduce their own germplasm. Therefore, they cannot use the seeds of traditional varieties in production for commercial sales. While common to all agricultural producers, this is especially true for resource-poor, small-scale farmers who typically cannot afford the cost of seed certification, field testing and laboratory controls and also lack information on certification and patent requirements.

On the other hand, a citizen-based opposition movement against the seed law has also developed in defense of farmers' right to save, replant, breed and share seeds. Local producers from small towns in the Aegean region of Turkey have organized local seed-exchange festivals (*Hürriyet Newspaper* 2011), thereby contesting the legal prohibition against seed saving and planting back (Atasoy 2013, 556). These seed-exchange festivals have taken place since 2010 in Torbalı, Seferihisar, Urla, Mordoğan and Karaburun in İzmir province; and in Bayramiçi in Çanakkale.[25] Those involved in seed-exchange projects believe that defying the law is essential for the protection of wild relatives of crops as a common resource to be shared among farmers and for safeguarding farmers' own seed systems. This is also seen as critical for maintaining traditional tastes in local food culture. Although on a small scale, such projects could become part of a larger process that challenges corporate control over seeds and creates a space for the construction of an 'open-source' seed commons to facilitate more culturally appropriate and agro-ecologically suitable food production (cf. Wattnem 2016, 16). Festival organizers have already founded a farmers-owned seed bank (Can Yücel Tohum Bankası) to collect, propagate, save and exchange local seeds. More than 370 local seed varieties have been collected from villages in the region. In 2011, 21,000 seedlings were produced from 224 local seed varieties for distribution to farmers. Organizers of the seed bank hoped to produce 300,000 seedlings in 2012 (Atasoy 2013, 556).

In addition to the founding of a farmers-owned seed bank and the non-profit certification of local seed varieties, producers have become involved in the 'eco-gastronomy' movement as part of the larger Cittaslow and slow food movements. In April 2014, they organized an 'eco-gastronomy' congress in Gökçeada, a small Turkish island at the entrance to the Dardanelles strait in the province of Çanakkale. Gökçeada has been a Cittaslow member for over 10 years. The congress provided a forum for participants to exchange ideas on ways to counter the market logic of industrial food. The congress also referred to the 'Earth Market', which opened in the town of Foça, İzmir, in 2013 as an example of biodiversity protection via the slow-food movement. The Foça Earth Market is a member of the Slow Food Foundation for Biodiversity, a non-profit organization established in 2003. It includes more than 10,000 small-scale food producers in over 50 countries. The market is also a member of a world-wide network of farmers' markets operating under the slow-food philosophy. Participants at the congress identified the Foça Earth Market as more than just another organic market; rather, it represents a significant movement for the protection of local gastronomic traditions and food biodiversity through taste education.

In an event dedicated to the first anniversary of the Foça Earth Market's participation in the international network of earth markets, Gül Girişmen, convivium leader, explained that Slow Food Foça Zeytindalı has become an educational space for biodiversity protection. For Girişmen, taste education is vital for biodiversity. Industrial-input dense food has begun to dictate taste because consumers are increasingly unaware of their own traditions regarding food and plant varieties and are incapable of recognizing the ingredients and culinary techniques in their cuisine (Slow Food Foundation for Biodiversity 2013a). In an attempt to save local biodiversity and food customs, the Foça

Earth Market coordinates the exchange of local seed varieties and organizes taste-education activities directed toward a local sustainable agriculture. The Foça Earth Market focusses on the importance of taste education through the collection and cataloging of plant varieties, animal breeds and food products, as well as the mapping of local biodiversity and diffusion of bio-information. This is in line with the founding philosophy of the Slow Food Foundation for Biodiversity (2013b).

Concluding Remarks

Recent governments in Turkey have instituted numerous programs aimed at 'rational land use' and economic growth. There are two essential threads that stitch these programs together into a comprehensive initiative resulting in the commodification of land, plants and genetic resources: (1) maintenance by the state of *eminent domain* over public lands and the genetic biodiversity within its territorial boundaries and (2) maintenance of the ideationally dominant calculative episteme of *economization* based on the rationality of the market economy model and the optimization of performance values. Together, both threads culminate in the efficient practice of *techno-scientific economic management* of land, plants and bio-information as tradable commodities. Such management relies on the expert knowledge of professional specialists engaged in disentangling, de-contextualizing and isolating land, plants and genetic materials from their biological, ecological and social-relational networks. These materials then become quantified, abstract objects that are entered into standardized, computer-based models of land/soil/plant management for economic valuation and development. At the heart of this entirely reductionist approach, we can discern Marx's concept of alienation and Polanyi's notion of 'fictitious commodities', supported by Weber's instrumental rationality thesis. The process of transforming non-commodities into commodities works through a market-conforming but state-sponsored techno-managerial programme of agro-ecological change, embedded in economization as the dominant episteme.

Based on my interviews with farmers in Central Anatolia, the following two chapters consider the ways in which input-intensive capitalized farming practices are becoming a dominant productivist form. First, I provide data on large-scale farmers.

Notes

1 www.globalgap.org (accessed 25 January 2015).
2 www.globalgap.org (accessed 25 January 2015).
3 www.globalgap.org (accessed 25 January 2015).
4 www.globalgap.org (accessed 25 January 2015).
5 Evidence provided by Vandemoortele and Deconinck (2014) suggests that approximately 70–80 per cent of retailers assess their private standards as higher than public standards.
6 Mercosur, also known as the 'Common Market of the South', is a regional trade organization formed in 1991 to promote the free movement of goods, capital, services and people

among member states. Mercosur member states include Argentina, Brazil, Paraguay and Uruguay. Venezuela's application for full membership is pending ratification. Its associate states are Bolivia, Chile, Peru, Columbia and Ecuador.

7 The Convention on Biological Diversity webpage indicates that Turkey adopted its NBSAPS in 2001, and this was revised in 2007; Brazil adopted its action plan in 2002, and this was revised in 2006 (www.cbd.int/nbsap, accessed 3 March 2014).

8 Monsanto made two attempts to purchase Syngenta. The latest takeover offer of US $47 billion was in 2015 (http://www.reuters.com/article/us-syngenta-m-a-monsanto-idUSKCN0QT1UR20150824, accessed 19 January 2017), which Syngenta rejected by arguing that Monsanto was undervaluing its market worth. Syngenta also rejected an offer of US $42 billion by state-owned China National Chemical Corp in 2015. (http://www.reuters.com/article/deals-day-idUSL3N1383VO20151113, accessed 19 January 2017).

9 Rijk Zwaan, a transnational company based in the Netherlands, specializes in vegetable breeding, seed production and various related research areas including molecular and cell biology, phytopathology, biochemistry and seed technology.

10 www.freshturkiye.com.tr/en/about-fresh-turkiye2/fresh-turkey-t... (accessed 3 March 2015).

11 www.freshturkiye.com.tr. (accessed 3 March 2015).

12 Telephone interview with Tolga Tabur, 3 June 2014.

13 Nickolas Bennett's description of the role of seed and plant-breeding companies and supermarkets in innovating new plant varieties is reminiscent of Schumpeter's conception of innovation. Schumpeter (1934) described innovation as a way of developing new products, new production methods and marketing outlets.

14 I have never met a consumer in Turkey who expressed a preference for oval-shaped red cabbage. Therefore, I am not sure of the source of this information.

15 www.youtube.com/watch??v=a_gqYm7gjU (accessed 3 February 2014).

16 *Hormonlu* is a generic term that people in Turkey often use to refer to food they suspect of containing growth hormones or chemicals. Food that does not taste like 'traditional' varieties is often referred to as *hormonlu*.

17 James (2013) uses the terms 'biotech crops' and 'genetically modified' (GM) crops interchangeably. Biotechnology is more comprehensive and not limited to GM crops. It also includes industrially hybridized seeds, for example. I will use the term *biotech crops*. Terms such as GM crops and agricultural GMOs (genetically modified organisms) will be used where appropriate.

18 http://www.tbbdm.gov.tr/home/regulationshome/nationalregulationsdetails/Biyog%c3%bcvenlik_Kanunu.aspx (accessed 19 January 2017).

19 http://www.resmigazete.gov.tr/eskiler/2014/05/20140529-2.htm. (accessed 3 March 2015).

20 www.tarim.gov.tr/Konular/Gida-Ve-Yem-Hizmetleri/Yem-Hizmetleri/GDOlu-Yemler (accessed 3 March 2015).

21 http://www.tarim.gov.tr/Konular/Gida-Ve-Yem-Hizmetleri/Laboratuvarlar (accessed 3 March 2015).

22 http://www.tarim.gov.tr/BUGEM/Belgeler/Bitkisel%20%C3%9Cretim/Tohumculuk/%C4%B0statistikler/ithalat_miktar_parasal_deger.pdf (accessed 3 March 2015). Field-crop seed includes cereals, industrial crops, potatoes and forages. Vegetable-crop seed includes hybrid seeds for all vegetable varieties with the exception of dry garlic and small onions. MFAL statistics do not provide data on pulses. They may be included in other categories.

23 www.tarim.gov.tr/BUGEM/Belgeler/Bitkisel%20%C3%9Cretim/Tohumculuk/%C4%B0statistikler/ithalat_miktar_parasal_deger.pdf (accessed 3 March 2015).

24 In addition to development projects associated with tourism, housing, road expansion, construction and dam building, capitalized agriculture also poses a threat to this biodiversity.

25 These towns are members of the Cittaslow International Network (founded in 1999), inspired by the Slow Food organization (see http://www.cittaslowturkiye.org/?page_id=523, accessed 27 April 2012).

4 Farming Imaginaries

Convergence, Divergence and Beyond

The shift in Turkey from farming practices of the past to capitalized agriculture has been accompanied by significant social-relational and ideational changes. This chapter examines these changes from the perspective of large-scale farmers in Beypazarı and Güdül in the province of Ankara. It explores how global biotechnology-led agro-scientific innovations and their government-backed implementation foster the transformative context for local agriculture. Several key questions arise: How and why do producers embrace an industrial agriculture that is heavily reliant on input-intensive capitalized farming practices? And what is the nature of the relationship between a capitalized model and the already existing practices and empirical knowledge base of farming? These are crucial methodological questions that bear on the larger issue of people's own active involvement in larger, extra-local institutional processes, structural changes and ontologies. The chapter draws from my interviews with large-scale fresh-vegetable producers to provide an in-depth analysis of how and why techno-economic innovation has become acceptable to farmers, thereby supplanting old customary practices.

To address the significance of farmers' role in the diffusion of industrial agriculture (and inspired by Davis and Burke's [2011] notion of 'environmental imaginaries'), I introduce the concept of *farming imaginaries*. This refers to the ideas, aspirations and evaluations of farmers in relation to the significance and future of their farming practices, livelihood concerns and landscape management, as well as their use of soil/plants/water resources. The concept is distinct from, although related to, Vanclay and Silvasti's (2009) 'farming scripts' and 'style of farming', as discussed in Chapter 2. Vanclay and Silvasti help us to discern differences in the methods/patterns of farming and the persistence of one particular style – 'traditional' peasant farming – in addition to the cultural, emotive and normative aspects of living and farming. My notion of farming imaginaries is different in that it emphasizes the perceptions, evaluations and deliberations not only of traditional ways but also of the new practices and styles that farmers are introduced to and embrace.

Farming imaginaries encompass many issues of interest to farmers, including competitive growth and catch-up developmentalism, techno-scientific progress, modernity and social-economic justice. This chapter, therefore, illustrates farmers' shaping of an affective-evaluative framework for ideas and desires concerning the normative acceptability of techno-scientific ways – ways that substantiate their participation in a particular industrial growth model of agriculture.

Farming imaginaries are also closely bound to the time and place-specific contingencies of a social-change project; they are constitutive of a kind of developmentalist politics that is believed to be attentive to inequalities and social distributive issues. I have formulated the notion specifically in relation to agriculture, but it is closely related to several other concepts, including *knowledge cultures* (Somers 1999), which denotes the complex relationship between individuals' 'cognitive maps' and public networks of meaning-driven schemas; *knowledge structures* (Gill 2000), which refers to certain normative assumptions about the nature of lived reality; and *ideational orientations* (Camic and Gross 2001). All of these signify public narratives and explanatory systems that cognitively embed policy orientations in the thinking and action of people. Moreover, they all convey normative assumptions and meaning-driven schemes as the (background) context for understanding processes of change. I refer to these concepts interchangeably as constitutive of 'background knowledge' in the shaping of farming imaginaries. It is by reference to these normative, ideational orientations that people engage with changing innovation systems and frame their own farming imaginaries to generate economic, social, cultural and agro-ecological 'value' through farming. Value generation through farming imaginaries is relational, containing interpretive assessments, perceptions and emotive accounts which concern the larger histories and narratives of economic growth, development and modernity. Such a process embraces points of tension and ambivalence, as well as attachment, in relation to industrial farming.

Tension and Ambivalence

The producers whom I interviewed are striving to function in harmony with the 'upstream' and 'downstream' of industrial farming. They are increasingly specialized in capitalized, input-intensive fresh vegetable production, growing food for distant consumers rather than for immediate consumption by local and regional residents. Their market linkages do not involve contract farming with supermarket chains and agro-traders; rather, they are independent farmers connected directly to supply chains as traders themselves and/or indirectly through other first-tier traders, wholesale-market commissioners and exporters. They also operate in conformity with the efficiency and performance-enhancing requirements of a high-tech, input-intensive industrial agriculture model, which they believe to be imperative for increasing the productivity of their land as measured by yield per hectare.

These producers are highly critical of transnational biotechnology-company influence and their top-down control over seeds markets, patent ownership of plant genetic information (including plant germplasm, which encases genetic information in the seed) and agrochemical input supply in Turkey. Their concerns include the potentially negative effects of techno-scientific innovation on local and national biodiversity, plant varieties and landscapes – including soil fertility and water resources, as well as locally diverse food customs, food taste and human health.

Farmers believe that the state must take responsibility for the production and dissemination of appropriate technology and knowledge in service of the preservation of local/national biodiversity and plant varieties, prevention of soil and water resource depletion and maintenance of cultures. However, the development of appropriate science and technology must also facilitate farmers' ability to generate income from agriculture. Farmers further agree that state agricultural planning should sustain the institutionalization of knowledge and technology production by Turkish–Muslim owned companies in Turkey. They insist that the state's involvement in the restructuring of food supply chains should be done in such a way as to increase efficiency and output maximization *without* losing control over the very landscapes, natural resources and local food cultures that would place Turkey on a more independent path of economic development. This is the essence of farmers' vision of sustainable growth. Although they are highly critical of the homogenizing effects of supermarket-imposed quality standards, they also blame the state for not institutionalizing alternative ways of knowing and for failing to implement productivity-enhancing innovations that would generate income without jeopardizing the natural integrity of soil fertility and water resources.

In sum, farming imaginaries embody the following beliefs: (1) the control wielded by foreign-owned global biotechnology companies over hybridized seeds and agro-chemical markets jeopardizes Turkey's future ability to sustain its economic independence and feed itself without dependence on external input provisioning; (2) the loss of control over seeds, plant varieties and plant genetic information represents a threat to Turkey's plant biodiversity; (3) foreign control and ownership of seeds and genetic information negatively affects local food customs and taste; (4) unchecked technical innovation in biotech crops and industrial input–intensive agriculture pose a danger for human health and for landscapes (including plants, soil and watercourses) due to chemical residues, hormones and toxins from industrial inputs and industrially hybridized seeds.

A nationalist ideational orientation frames these concerns within Turkey's state polices of economic growth and global competitiveness, providing a foundation for reorienting 'agricultural innovation systems' (Triomphe and Rajalahti 2013, 57). Farmers appreciate the productivity-enhancing innovation, scientific knowledge and technologies produced by biotechnology companies that shape quality and mold taste and markets, as long as they contribute to national economic development and rural incomes. Agricultural growth, then, is the essential component of their imaginary, inextricably tied to achieving higher productivity per hectare. Custom-bound, weather-dependent, trial-and-error-based farming and plant-improvement methods have little place in their farming imaginaries. Nonetheless, these same imaginaries embody considerable *ambivalence*, expressed in an emotional attachment to locally valued food cultures and tastes, but also with a distrust of industrially homogenized food.

The *continuity* with, yet simultaneous ambivalence toward, the transnationally dominant modalities of industrial agriculture highlights the possibility of mixed and contradictory associations, even ruptures, in farming imaginaries. I have identified two strands that express such possibilities: (1) the deepening of farmers' conformity with techno-scientific industrial innovation to increase the competitiveness of Turkish agriculture in global markets and generate increased profit; and (2) the emergence and diffusion of alternative knowledge structures rooted in a heightened awareness of the negative consequences of biotech-intensive farming practices for health and dietary customs, the integrity of landscapes (including plants, soil and watercourses) and the preservation of biodiversity. Various combinations of these strands are expressed in farmers' own assessments of agro-industrial standards and their impacts. The *duality in the assessment* of standards that co-exists in their thinking indicates that the farmers I interviewed have not yet fully conformed to the dictates of industrial agriculture, nor have they established a well-defined critical, political position. Thus, a space remains for contesting and transforming the industrial food system.

The mere existence of ambivalence in an industrial farming imaginary creates the possibility of rethinking an ontological orientation that presents the industrial model as inalterable and inexorable. Farmers frequently verbalize both the desirability and achievability of alternative knowledge structures and agro-ecologically appropriate technologies with the assistance of the state and other players in the field. An additional possibility arising from the *duality of thought* in farmers' imaginaries is that innovation for ecologically friendly agriculture is not necessarily only appropriate for small-scale agricultural operations; it may apply to large commercial producers as well (Reynolds and Nierenberg 2013, 6).

A good starting point to consider the emergence of alternative perspectives is to reflect on farmers' concerns with the currently dominant industrial agriculture. A different type of agriculture stimulates local actors to co-design their food systems, builds bridges between producers and consumers and ensures more agro-ecological production methods (van der Ploeg 2014, 1000–1). A rethinking of these methods takes into account socially inclusive innovation, greater food democracy, locally appreciated taste and quality of food, sustainability and agro-ecologically suitable 'conservation agriculture' (Garcia-Torres et al. 2003). Clearly, industrial agriculture is tied to land and labour productivity issues and economies of scale for increasing technical output per hectare through specialized monoculture-crop production (Rastoin 2009, 15–6). This expresses a mutual cycle of accumulation and a developmentalist project in the global economy (McMichael 2012b). My research shows that the ambivalence expressed by the farmers I interviewed in Turkey cannot be resolved in opposition to a growth-oriented model, largely because that model is deeply embedded in a historical ideational orientation toward the desirability of national economic development dating back to the late Ottoman Empire (Atasoy 2009).

Altieri (1995) and, more recently, Martínez-Torres and Rosset (2014) and Meynard (2013) have argued for the reorientation of innovation and redesign of agricultural systems. I suggest that the existence of ambivalence in farming imaginaries is helpful in this regard. Farmers' ambivalence raises a challenging question as to how to reconnect income generation and concerns with human health, food cultures and the integrity of landscapes. For farmers, farming can no longer be for subsistence only; agricultural innovation must bring together income/profit-generation and nutritional–environmental concerns through systematic and appropriate research on plant and input improvement, knowledge building and the design and development of new farming methods. This is not about going back to the old 'peasant ways' of low-yield subsistence agriculture.

An analysis that focuses on farmers' desires and apprehensions, continuities and ambivalences brings forth points of both conformity and nonconformity with the transnationally advocated techno-scientific knowledge base of agricultural growth. As Dorothy E. Smith (1999) has suggested, the most pressing concern in ethnographic research is to show how individuals encounter the social–political–emotional relations involved in the shaping of a knowledge culture within which they are active. Therefore, the analysis here should speak to broader concerns regarding how an income-generating/profit-driven industrial orientation has gained normative, moral acceptability by those who are also concerned with the negative consequences of that orientation.

The farmers I interviewed frequently emphasize that a potentially class-formative distributional outcome may emerge from their adoption of industrial agriculture. A class-formative outcome has been the research focus in much existing literature on global agriculture and a central theme of the classical agrarian question (Bernstein 1996, 2010; Byres 2009). Weatherspoon and Reardon (2003) show that in Africa, for example, a diversion to industrial input-intensive fresh fruit and vegetable (FFV) production has the potential to marginalize subsistence-oriented small-scale farmers. Gilles et al. (2013) demonstrate that agricultural producers are increasingly abandoning traditional farming knowledge and practices in Bolivia in favour of an innovation system that supports industrial methods of higher yield production. On the other hand, Lemeilleur and Tozanlı (2007) offer the example of the village of Narlıdere in the Bursa province of Turkey as a 'success story'. In Narlıdere, small producers have increased their commercial viability and become integrated into supermarket-led supply chains by organizing producers' unions. A further comparison of existing literature suggests that more nuanced outcomes have emerged that are not easily generalizable – notably in the cases of Madagascar (Minten et al. 2009), Peru and Ghana (Guijt and Walsum 2008). Common to much of the discussion in the literature are the distributional outcomes of changing farming practices and resulting alterations in power dynamics and interest differentiations – to the detriment of small-scale subsistence producers. Bryceson (2010) uses the phrase 'vanishing peasantries' to describe such changes in Sub-Saharan African farming.

My respondents, all of whom are politically nationalist Muslims, adopt a positive moral stance toward industrial agriculture, as expressed in their desire to reposition themselves in the economy through competitive growth. They constitute the agrarian fraction of newly growing capital groups from smaller Anatolian towns and villages (Atasoy 2009, 10–27, 107–36; Atasoy 2013). The main point here is that the adoption of an industrial model is contributing to the reconstitution of an ontology of the social that is intensifying the commercialization of agriculture. A positive valuation of productivity-enhancing industrial standards as integral to wealth creation activity is connected with a concern for feeding 'city folks' and expressed as a 'food ethic' grounded in 'doing good' for society. This is similar to Adam Smith's (1976 [1759]) insistence on the need for moral regulation in the pursuit of capitalist self-interest.

While farmers' conformity with agro-industry expands and deepens the commodification process in land and larger relations of food (Atasoy 2016), non-conformity can also be seen – through a Polanyian prism – as a response to commodification and its destructive effects on landscapes, health, nutrition and culture. However, the picture that emerges from my interviews is more complex and cannot be captured from a binary perspective of convergence and divergence. Even when farmers demonstrate significant conformity to the industrial model, they also reveal divergent narratives. Still, these farmers are not involved in a movement of social transformation, nor are they engaged in an exploration of new alternative products, processes and field-farming practices for re-orientating agriculture. Thus, the future direction of farming remains

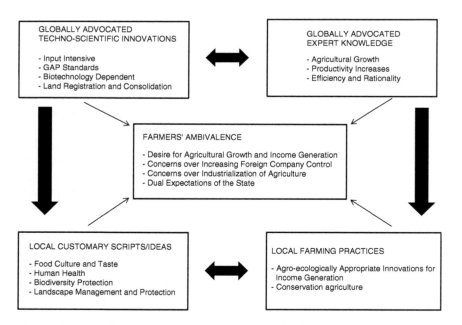

Figure 4.1 Diverse Knowledge Bases and Emerging Ambivalences.

contested in farmers' narratives. Moreover, while the state is expected to act responsibly in the deepening of an industrial model (cf. Polanyi 1944), it is also expected to 'contest' the model by advancing social–ecological–redistributive justice (Atasoy 2016). As noted, the seemingly contradictory expectations are consistent with the *duality of assessments* in farmers' farming imaginaries. These complexities are summarized in Figure 4.1.

Narratives of Conformity and Nonconformity

This section traces the normative judgements, moral valuations and ideational orientations of a multitude of commercialized actors involved in the implementation of industrial agriculture. It will enable us to better understand why they privilege their own thinking over that of others in relation to certain growth-oriented projects. The actors include large-scale commercial farmers, seed distributors and greenhouse seedling growers involved in the production of fresh vegetables.

The existing literature is rather vague on the connections between globally advocated and locally pursued/implemented growth projects. International pressures of coercion, normative emulation and competitive mimicry strongly influence the domestic adoption of a policy model and a vision for acceptance throughout the world (Henisz et al. 2005). Coercion implies external imposition and is implicit in the conditionality agreements of loans, as in the case of loans made by the International Monetary Fund (IMF) and the World Bank (WB) or in membership requirements, as in the case of the European Union (EU). Emulation and mimicry also appear to be crucial in policy transmission. For instance, with the UN-Habitat best/good practices policy, the international awarding of such practices through 'successful' example provides global recognition, generating momentum for policy imitation and encouraging voluntary compliance with norms and policy priorities for the 'proper' organization and regulation of economies (Vestergaard 2009).

This chapter adds a novel dimension to the domestic/local adoption of globally advocated projects – the subjection of agriculturalists own farming imaginaries to reassessment through highly personalized social ties and dynamic interactions with actors in the agribusiness sector. My aim here is to fill an important lacuna in the literature regarding the social–relational and emotive context, which is often detached from considerations of global coercion, emulation or mimicry in the rendering of global ideas and policies at the domestic/local level. This omission results in the exclusion of geo-historically distinct spatial systems of sense-making, making it difficult for us to understand how certain perspectives and models are re-worked on the ground in a way that generates ideational conformity or non-conformity with them. My interviews with various actors in Central Anatolian towns and villages reveal an array of perceptions and moral standpoints that contribute to patterns of conformity with, and/or divergence from, the industrial model of agriculture.

It is a formidable challenge to expose the interconnections between a globally advocated techno-scientific knowledge base, along with its practices – which often reflect a European and North American approach to development issues – and locally embedded knowledge cultures. Brosius (2006) has embraced this challenge in his examination of 'local' knowledge. He is critical of an ideal typical fixation of the 'local' or a generically abstracted sense of locality, and he endeavours to clarify our understanding of local knowledge as it is constituted in global assessments and conventions of development and in relation to the broader contours of power and universalist assumptions. My goal in this chapter is quite different; I intend to provide insight into the changing contours of locally practiced agriculture as they are reflected in farmers' own articulations of industrial farming imaginaries.

These imaginaries do not reflect 'the existence of discursive regularities at work' (Escobar 1995, 155), nor do they represent local conditions of resistance (McMichael 2008). Rather, they reveal points of tension, conformity and non-conformity and ambivalence resulting from an encounter between transnationally advocated innovations and knowledge structures and on-the-ground practices, beliefs and desires (Davis 2005). As noted by Leila Harris (2009) in her analysis of the divergent narratives of environmental change in Southeastern Turkey, an examination of contestation or convergence is not an attempt to add to the discussion on local knowledges, and/or assessments of nationally or globally abstracted growth models, but to recognize the existence of an ideationally dynamic interplay. It is through this dynamism that we can detect how shared and diverging perspectives co-exist for an emergent 'strategic practice of criticism' (Scott 1999, 7) that does not necessarily mean rejecting one model in favour of another. Below is a detailed description of interpretive/evaluative judgements, ideas and desires that shape a position on the acceptability of a corporate-led industrial model.

Future Control of Food and Landscapes: Commercial Farmers, Seed Distributors and Greenhouse Seedling Growers

Commercial Industrial Farmers: Mesut and Hidayet

Mesut and Hidayet are critical of the control wielded by foreign-owned biotechnology companies over agricultural inputs, including seeds and chemicals, and they emphasize the importance of 'national' control over the future of food in Turkey. The preferred alternative for Mesut and Hidayet is infrastructural and financial support from the state for systematic research by nationally owned biotechnology companies on the development of high-yield, commercially viable local/domestic varieties of seeds.

Mesut and Hidayet represent the newly evolving trend of professional farming in the fresh-produce segment of Turkish agriculture. Both are highly specialized in the production and marketing of salad-crop varieties. Mesut was born and raised in Beypazarı and Hidayet in the village of Karacaören in Güdül. Mesut has a high-school education; Hidayet is a university graduate with a degree in business administration. Both are in their late thirties. They are considered large-scale commercial farmers in their towns and villages, where small-scale farming dominates. Each owns approximately 4,000 dekars of farmland under cultivation. In 2015, Mesut purchased an additional 1,000 dekars of land, increasing his production area of self-owned land to more than 5,000 dekars. He farms in the village of Kayabükü in Beypazarı. Hidayet moved his farming operation from Güdül to Beypazarı in 2015. Both men have cold-storage facilities on their farms and both typically expand their area of production by renting additional lands. They employ seasonal Kurdish migrant labour (each employing 150–200 workers on average per day). I met Mesut on 28 May 2014 at Syngenta's open-field demonstration day. I met Hidayet in 2011 in Güdül and have maintained contact with him ever since.

In addition to producing food on his own farm, Mesut procures, processes (sorts and grades) and trades local food produced by smaller-scale farmers. Hidayet combines three different stages of the food chain into his farming activities: production; the procurement, processing and agro-trading of local food; and wholesale commissioning for markets. Together with his older brother, Eyüp, who is a commissioner in the Antalya wholesale market, Hidayet is pioneering a process of commercial concentration under the corporate logo *Eyüp Taş Limited Company*, named after his brother. Through this company, Hidayet has become a central figure in the commodity trade for many small and large-scale producers in Güdül and Beypazarı.

In the virtual absence of contract farming in the province of Ankara, Mesut and Hidayet are the main drivers of increasing commercial concentration of production, procurement, processing–packing and commodity trading for locally produced food by smaller-scale producers. They are stakeholders in the dissemination of a high-technology, input-intensive innovation system in these towns and villages. Mesut and Hidayet are also contributing to the diffusion of a growth-oriented farming imaginary and the gradual marginalization of small-scale, locally produced food for local consumption.

Those two professional farmers represent different dimensions in the vertical diffusion of knowledge in industrial agriculture. Mesut's compliance with industrial agriculture has evolved through his direct working relationship with Syngenta. He rents his farmland to Syngenta for field experiments on Syngenta's newly innovated biotech seeds. He also travels abroad to inspect Syngenta's open-field experimentation with other technologically improved crop varieties. Hidayet, on the other hand, does not have direct vertical linkage with global biotechnology companies. He makes his decisions on seed types and other agrochemical inputs on the basis of advice from seed distributors and seedling growers in Beypazarı with whom he has close friendship ties.

Mesut: Syngenta Seeds and Spatially Sensitive Innovations

Syngenta is a significant player in the introduction of new high-technology based production methods to commercial farmers in the region. Syngenta is careful when selecting its fields for the experimental planting of newly innovated seeds. The company is aware that the diffusion of its innovations into the hot climatic conditions of Southern Europe, the Middle East and North Africa depends on the plant/soil/environment compatibility of those innovations. Syngenta's open-field experiment-based planting on Mesut's farm is designed to demonstrate this 'compatibility' of innovation on the local ecology scale. The emphasis in such demonstrations is often on per-hectare yield and the profit-related advantages of innovation. Significantly, Syngenta's field demonstration of product compatibility parallels the five factors proposed by Mendras and Forse (1983) for the evaluation and general adoptability of product innovation: relative advantage, compatibility with the existing system, complexity, trialability by farmers and observability by others (also discussed by Faure et al. 2013, 23). The commercial farmers I interviewed focus largely on the relative advantage of these innovations for profit generation under their local ecological conditions.

Mesut's introduction to innovation does not occur through information provided directly by experts but through a learning process of farmers exchanging information during field-experimentation demonstration days organized by companies such as Syngenta. Mesut explains:

> Turkey has just started to achieve significant growth in the production and export of fresh produce. Our agricultural growth depends on accessing quality seeds and chemicals. Companies like Syngenta are now becoming more interested in Turkish markets. We don't need to know anything about these companies; they know us very well. These are foreign companies, but they come all the way to our tiny villages and towns to get in touch with us in person. Their scientists who work on seed improvement somewhere in Europe come to our villages to see how their seeds are doing in our fields. As producers we know the soil, climate and water conditions here. Therefore, they come and talk to us about the production conditions of the local landscape. They also take us to the countries where they develop seeds. They have taken me twice to Holland, France and Germany, and once to Spain. There, we not only saw their latest varieties but also how to do modern agriculture. We learn new production techniques to produce 12 tons of carrots from 1 dekar of land. In the past we used to produce 4 tons per dekar. Now, we have learned that with different production and management techniques we can increase that yield.
>
> (Interview, 28 May 2014)

Mesut is attracted to Syngenta's seed innovations because they have a high-yield capacity, greater germination rates and disease resistance. At the same time, Mesut is aware that the very hot summer season and the chalky soils in the area are making the efficient use of these biotech seeds difficult without the intensive use of water and chemicals. The local agro-ecological conditions also generate greater susceptibility to parasitic insects and diseases for the plant

Figure 4.2 Mesut (Kayabükü, Beypazarı, 28 May 2014).

varieties that he grows in Kayabükü. Mesut knows that his farming techniques are not suited to the local climate and landscape, but he finds the higher yields irresistible. To quote Mesut again:

> My farm is at the bottom of the mountain range. It is really hot in summer, reaching over 40 degree Celsius. The Kirmir River is about 3 km away; it is difficult to bring the water here from the river because of the mountains. The soil is calcareous and chalky. Farming needs freshwater which we gather from the wells beneath the mountains. We need lots of water … we cannot sustain our production through digging wells alone … Since the soil is chalky, artesian water brought up from 100–150 meters down is also hard, brackish water. We are in a hot desert-like environment. It helps us to produce more, especially when we increase soil fertility with external inputs; but we are also more susceptible to disease, insects, and hardened soil conditions. We have no choice but to increase our water accessibility and agrochemical inputs, and to cultivate new varieties of seeds … each new variety responding to a particular disease.
>
> (Interview, 28 May 2014)

Mesut describes his farming as commercially productive, but he also questions the suitability of biotech seeds for the *pedogenesis* (locally varied soil-forming processes) in his village. He is ambivalent about the new techno–scientific growth model; he strongly supports it because of its ability to increase productivity and profits, yet he is concerned about its agro-ecological implications for the region.

According to Laliberte et al. (2013, 331–4), pedogenesis refers to a process of soil formation that generally leads to the development of 'soil horizons' – soil layers parallel to the soil surface that have certain physical, chemical and biological characteristics that are important for soil nutrient availability, accumulation of organic matter, formation of clays and metal oxides, changes in pH and so on. There are five major soil-forming factors: parent material (which refers to original material from which a soil is derived), organisms, topography, climate, and time. Laliberte et al. (2013) describes pedogenesis as a central ecological driver of local plant diversity.

The chalky soils on Mesut's farm are directly related to the spatially distinct processes of soil formation that, in ecological terms, integrate the locally diverse conditions of plant-soil suitability for farming. For millennia, such local conditions have been the foundation of farmers' selection, breeding and cultivation of plant varieties (Anderson 1969). The industrial model, which is based on sowing high-tech commercial seeds developed under artificial conditions in the laboratory, measures efficiency and productivity by very different standards than those of plant–soil–water suitability. Mesut is fully aware of the unsuitability of the local landscape for high-technology seeds and the application of their associated chemicals. Nevertheless, he is an ardent supporter of compliance with the standard yield-increasing requirements of industrial farming.

Mesut points out that Syngenta seeds are specifically designed for high yields in the strongly weathered soils of the Middle East, but warmer temperatures in the region also make them highly disease prone, requiring greater dependency on external chemical inputs, which further deplete the fertility of available soil and water resources. There is a mismatch, therefore, between the production and efficiency standards of commercial agriculture and agro-ecologically sensitive farming. Mesut seems to believe that foreign-owned companies may be artificially creating this mismatch in order to create greater dependency on the seeds and agro-chemical inputs that these companies develop. He notes:

> The number of crop-diseases keeps increasing. There are 31 different diseases that have been identified this year alone. If the seeds were suitable for the soil and climate of our lands, we would not have to deal with such a high number of diseases. It looks as if the seed companies are inserting all kinds of diseases into their seeds, eggs from all kinds of louse and insects before they sell them to us. We buy the seeds to deal with the diseases, yet the same seeds introduce us to a new set of diseases. It is a never-ending cycle.
>
> (Interview, 28 May 2014)

Mesut hopes for and expects the government to play a more active role in the development of ecologically adaptive systems and innovations so that commercial agriculture can adjust to regional conditions. He states:

Our government has to support our domestic companies in developing commercial seeds from our own varieties that are suitable for our lands. Our researchers should come to our fields and examine our soil and water conditions, collect seeds from our local lettuce and improve them to be more commercially viable. Our own researchers and seed companies should consult us. We are right here; we know the actual production conditions of our lands. We can help them to develop our own market-ready seeds free of disease and suited to our soil conditions.

(Interview, 28 May 2014)

I asked Mesut if he would be interested in planting local heirloom tomato seeds from the village of Çağa in Güdül, seeds that the mayor of Çağa successfully registered in 2011 under the geographical indication (GI) of Çağa variety tomatoes.[1] Mesut told me:

The heirloom variety is not commercially viable. I am more interested in the commercial improvement of local seeds to increase their durability and strength for transportation and longer shelf-life. In Turkey it takes three extra years to make seeds market-ready after their initial breeding. Europeans are doing it in two months. The lack of attention given to research and development is increasing Turkey's dependency on foreign companies and foreign sources of inputs. These imported seeds are high-yielding no doubt but also extremely expensive. We used to purchase seeds per kilo, but now they are sold individually per seed. This makes me angry.

(Interview, 28 May 2014)

Mesut makes a case for the development of a commercially viable agriculture through the incorporation of local knowledge. It is a call for direct farmer participation in the emergence of 'spatially sensitive innovation' systems (Freeman 1988). As argued by Faure et al. (2013), farmers can play a critical role in such innovation by using their knowledge to address concerns relating to sustainable development. For Mesut, however, this requires government support for research on the preservation and commercial improvement of native varieties, as well as a bottom-up approach based on the knowledge of farmers who are most aware of locally existing landscape conditions. Mesut offers his reasoning for state-sponsored research:

The villages on top of the mountains do not have access to the Kirmir River. Since they are at a higher elevation, they need less water, which they get from artesian wells ... But, we are at the bottom of the mountain in a desert-like environment and need lots of water ... Because of their cooler climate, villages on the mountains do not need to deal with insects and diseases as much as we do here. We produce more because of the heat; but we are also more susceptible to disease and insects, as well as depleted soil conditions. The government must support national companies to develop commercial seeds from local varieties that respond to regionally, locally varied climatic conditions of production in the country. Obviously, they cannot produce different seeds for each village in the country, but we should not be required to use the same seeds everywhere in the country either.

(Interview, 28 May 2014)

Mesut appears to be making an appeal for the local adaptation of corporate-led industrial agriculture through state planning and institutional, financial support for research and development into local plant varieties:

To be honest, I do not want to use imported seeds from Israel, Holland or elsewhere. ... We need to be a bit nationalist. Our government must support our own companies and researchers; scientists must work with us to develop high-yielding native varieties. We should make money from our own seeds, and our companies should make money from us in return. But, I don't see a single national company and their researchers coming to me, talking to me about local varieties and their improvement. However, the foreign companies *are* constantly breeding new varieties, producing new hybrid seeds for the markets, while our companies keep selling the same seeds over and over again with no improvement. The market demands more varieties.

(Interview, 28 May 2014)

Hidayet: Preservation of Water Resources and Soil Fertility

I noted previously that Hidayet's exposure to the industrial innovations of biotech companies is primarily through locally/regionally organized field-experiment demonstration days. He is also introduced to new developments through agricultural trade fairs and personal contact with local seed distributors and seedling growers. He participates regularly in trade fairs organized by corporations such as Start Fuarcılık and in TUYAP Fairs supported by the Ministry of Food, Agriculture and Livestock (MFAL). As a farmer listed in the national registry, Hidayet becomes aware of the fairs through an on-line information exchange facilitated by the MFAL. He attends during the winter months and thus far has visited fairs in Antalya, Adana, İzmir, Kayseri, Konya and Bursa. These agricultural trade fairs introduce farmers to advances in FFV storage and packaging, agricultural machinery and techniques, irrigation and plant nutrition and seed technology and equipment. Hidayet observes:

If you are going to survive in this business, you must grow and renew your know-how, your machinery and other inputs. This is a very expensive field which requires big capital investments. Corporations will soon

Figure 4.3 Hidayet Taş (Karacaören, Güdül, 10 May 2014).

Figure 4.4 Hidayet and His Wife, İlknur Taş (Karacaören, Güdül, 9 July 2016).

be doing agriculture here in our towns and villages. Small producers who produce for their subsistence needs cannot last in this business; they will go bankrupt. They will become labourers on large farms such as mine. That is how it is.

(Interview, 25 June 2011)

Hidayet has mentioned that two associates in Beypazarı, owners of Ayık Tarım and Bey Fide, play a major role in the diffusion of industrial innovations from biotech firms. Both are local seed distributors and seedling growers. In addition to having close friendship ties at the personal and family level, Hidayet shares a religiously oriented worldview with them, as well as a welcoming attitude toward scientifically innovated seeds and agrochemicals.

Hidayet showed me the empty bags and containers for the seeds used on his farm. The Monsanto seed bag has printed on it a 'notice to purchase' warning in English, in large bold letters. It reads:

Do not open this bag or plant this seed until you have read and understand the NOTICE OF PURCHASE. This seed is intended for planting by professional growers who are familiar with this variety or have harvested under their field conditions.

The bag has also an 'Indemnification' warning. It reads:

By accepting this seed, Purchaser agrees to defend and indemnify Seminis from any claim asserted by any transferee of such seed who are notified of the terms and conditions as to LIMITATION OF LIABILITY, DISCLAIMER OF WARRANTY, and NOTICE, in terms similar to those contained herein.[2]

Hidayet does not read or speak English and cannot understand the meaning of the 'notice of purchase' and 'indemnification' warnings listed on the seed bag, which was given to him on a trial basis, free of charge. Such notices are not listed on the seed bags Hidayet showed me produced by Dutch and Israeli companies. I asked him if he had been informed about these notices on the Monsanto seed bag by the seed distributor or an official from Güdül Agriculture. He told me that no one informed him about the notices, but that he has complete confidence in the distributors, whom he believes would not do anything to harm him financially. He is not aware of whether the warning applies to him. Hidayet explains:

I received this bag of seeds from Ayık Tarım in Beypazarı. There are agricultural engineers working together with the store owners. They could have warned me if there was a legally binding situation arising from the use of Monsanto seeds. I am sure they wouldn't have recommended those seeds to me. They were also a gift, given to me to try out. We have an agricultural engineer who regularly comes to our farm on a weekly basis from Beypazarı. He checks our produce, tells us what kind of chemicals and fertilisers to use. We follow a weekly program according to his recommendations, based on what he tells us.

(Interview, 25 June 2011)

Hidayet shares Mesut's view of the problems associated with high-technology, chemically dependent agriculture and scientifically innovated seeds for local soil–water–climate conditions. Nonetheless, he acknowledges that industrial, input-intensive agriculture is now the main driver of profits in farming. He observes:

It is not the way it used to be anymore. The varieties of lettuce I grow are simply not suited to our lands. Think about endive. Since when do people in Güdül know anything about endive? Do they even eat it? Never! But, I am producing it here in Güdül. Another example is carrots. In the past, we didn't grow commercial carrots in Güdül. It all started in 1982 by a French seed company ... They saw this area in Güdül as empty land and gave their carrot seeds for free. My grandfather was the first in the village to begin producing carrots with those free seeds. After seeing my grandfather many of the villagers in Karacaören who had migrated to İstanbul for work came back to produce carrots. But, because they couldn't produce well and couldn't market their crops, they left carrot production and went back to İstanbul. I am the only carrot producer in Güdül ... There is no Turkish-owned commercial carrot seed in Turkey; it all comes from abroad. We currently use seeds from Holland's Royal, Bejo and Nunhems, and Israel's Hazera Genetics companies ... Monsanto creates price incentives for new varieties. One bag of Dutch purple carrots is TL 1,000, as opposed to TL 500 for Monsanto's. This is how they create dependence on their seeds. These are high-yielding seeds; their germination rates are very high: 70 per cent for Bejo's, 82 per cent for Monsanto's, 90 per cent for Hazera's. But, they are also a real source of bugs, pests and all kinds of insects. I sometimes wonder if they implant pests into the seeds before they sell them to us. I honestly question if these chemicals actually proliferate insects rather than eliminate them. Or, are they in fact selling us insect-making chemicals? This is how I think. They sell us these chemicals from Bayer or Banf with the claim that they are a good match for the seeds they sell. But, who knows what is in these chemicals? They are not even cheap ... Seeds don't work without chemicals, but you still cannot get rid of the pests with those chemicals. We couldn't kill the wireworms [agriotes] in carrots, which harm the seeds at germination and damage the roots. We sprayed yesterday, but the worms are still there, alive. I simply don't know what to do. Maybe I should spray again.

(Interview, 15 May 2013)

In addition to disease proliferation, Hidayet is also very concerned about the depletion of water resources. He continues:

> There is more money to be earned from irrigated agriculture. There is no money in rain-fed dry agriculture for wheat or barley. Güdül is blessed with water; there is a river nearby and underground water reservoirs are rich. In Güdül we have a water-users association established for irrigation. Pumping water through the association is almost free. I pay about TL 40 per month for water, which is nothing. The government provides electricity and dynamos to pump the water. I use sprinkler irrigation. One sprinkler distributes 2.5 tons of water per dekar. Seven sprinklers irrigate 1 dekar of land with 15 tons of water per hour. You must provide seven hours of irrigation per dekar for carrots. This means 15 × 7=105 tons of water per dekar for carrots. Carrot fields are irrigated once a week. Lettuce requires less water, 2 or 3 hours are adequate. Because I use a sprinkler system, there is much evaporation. I need perhaps twice as much as 150 tons of water for carrots per dekar because of evaporation. Although it wastes much water, a sprinkler system is more economical for me. One parcel of my carrot fields is approximately 22 dekars. I spent TL 4,000 for a sprinkler system for one parcel only. If it was a drip system I would have to pay TL 8,000, which requires additional labour costs. We rotate three different crops here every three months. That means that I have to implement three different irrigation systems for each crop variety ... I know that our water will be depleted in the next 50 years. When we were kids growing up here, we couldn't cross the river; the water level was above our heads. It is not even at knee level now. In Beypazarı, artesian wells used to be only 30–40 meters deep to reach water; now you need to dig down 200 meters. They also built a dam to divert water for agricultural use in Çamlıdere. In 2007 there was a drought which caused much tension among various village farmers who take water from the same river. I am closer to the river. One villager who is farther from the river took me to court; he believed that I am not releasing enough water for his use ... But let's be clear; our water problem does not emerge from drought alone, it is the irrigation-intensive agriculture itself which depletes our water resources.
>
> (Interview, 15 May 2013)

The effects of irrigation-intensive farming on water supplies are generally difficult to predict. However, Hidayet is aware of the growing problem of water stress at the local level due to increased use of agricultural irrigation, combined with changing climatic conditions and drought. His concern is well supported by official data. The following statistical information provides some indication of the serious implications of agricultural production for water resources.

According to the Organisation for Economic Co-operation and Development (OECD) 'Water Use in Agriculture' report, farming accounts for 70 per cent of freshwater use in the world; approximately 40 per cent of which goes to crop farming and 30 per cent to livestock.[3] In addition to the depletion of water resources, farming is a significant contributor to water pollution from excess nutrients, pesticides and other pollutants.[4] Agriculture accounts for 45 per cent of water withdrawal in OECD countries.[5] It is estimated that up to 5,000 liters of freshwater are needed to produce the daily food for one person (Millstone and Lang 2013, 24). The United States (US) is the world's largest user of groundwater for agriculture.[6] Mexico is the second-largest agricultural groundwater-using OECD country, with agriculture representing over three-quarters of total groundwater withdrawals at the national level.[7] Turkey is the third-largest user.[8] Although Turkey is located in a region with a relative water sufficiency of 3,000 or more cubic meters of available renewable water resources per person per year – about the same level as North America (Millstone and Lang 2013, 25) – decreased water flow in rivers and the greater depth needed to draw water from artesian wells are problems now commonly experienced by producers. According to the State Planning Organization's (SPO) Tenth Development Plan (SPO 2014, 138), Turkey currently uses 39 per cent of its total available water resources, 73 per cent of which is used in irrigation.[9] The SPO plan indicates that Turkey may be exposed to water scarcity by 2030.

Hidayet's farm is located at a relatively high altitude of 735 meters and is therefore cooler than many neighbouring farms. It is also close to the Kirmir River in Güdül. This enables him to continue practicing irrigation-intensive farming, although he is aware of the limited capacity of the river and its watershed. There appears to be a generally low level of awareness among farmers in the region regarding the importance of watershed conservation. They show little indication of adjusting their farming practices by adopting resource-preservation techniques. It has always been a global challenge to draw farmers' attention to the issue of water conservation in agriculture, although there are some indications of progress in this area. Farmers in Costa Rica, for example, are beginning to adopt 'watershed conservation farming' practices as a solution to soil degradation (Solorzano 2003).

Central Anatolia typically receives less than 600 mm of annual precipitation. In Ankara, the average is 383 mm. In addition to the relatively low precipitation, rainfall in Ankara is highly variable; it ranged from 218.1 mm to 612.6 mm between 1926 and 2000 (Çiçek 2003, 1). Given Ankara's location in a semi-arid area, water scarcity is a primary constraint for irrigation-based agriculture in the regional towns of Güdül and Beypazarı. Farms established along the Kirmir River have access to water through village 'water-user associations', which help farmers pump water from the river for irrigation purposes. However, these associations do not play a role in managing the efficient use of water in the agroecosystem of the area. Water conservation can be achieved through various means including such fairly simple techniques as 'water harvesting', and the prolonged retention of moisture in the soil, or storing surface- and subsurface-runoff water for later use (Abdelkadir and Schultz 2005; Yazar et al. 2014). The DSİ (*Devlet Su İşleri*), which is the main government agency responsible for water and land resources, is primarily committed to overseeing the expansion of irrigated lands rather than the implementation of water-conservation methods. Nevertheless, the expression of concern by Hidayet (and Mesut) may be a positive step in the direction of meaningful change.

In addition to his concern for water resources, and closely related to it, Hidayet is worried about soil degradation on his farm resulting from the depletion of primary nutrients in the soil. In my interview with him on 17 May 2013, he said:

> I am going to move my cold storage facility and carrot production to Beypazarı. Güdül has a limited amount of land. It is surrounded by mountains on one side, and the river on the other. There is no room for expansion. Our lands are tired here. Even though lands in Beypazarı are also tired, farmers there can rest the land by expanding into new, previously unused areas. You can only grow carrots in the same field for three years in a row. That means that carrots can be grown in the same field for a maximum of 14 years, as it can only be rotated with other crops seven times. After that, the field needs to be rested for the following seven years. Since the sugar level in carrots is high, they require high levels of nitrogen, which depletes all the minerals and vitamins in the soil. Once nitrogen is depleted, you can no longer grow anything in that field. Lands in Güdül are now completely dead for carrot production. The only thing I can grow in Güdül is lettuce varieties. But, there is no money in lettuce. Since I can no longer grow my own carrots here, I purchase them from small-producers in Beypazarı, bring them to my cold storage in Güdül with trucks and, after sorting and packaging them here, send them in trucks to Antalya markets. Given that Güdül has a labour shortage, I also have to bring workers from Beypazarı for the cleaning, sorting and packaging of carrots. This is not an economical way of doing business.

In my interview with him on 15 June 2015, Hidayet explained, once again, that he is a professional farmer more concerned with making money than with agro-ecological conservation issues. 'We are not concerned with conservation issues. We have so much "idle," unused land around here. We move to other plots of lands to grow our carrots if this plot becomes unproductive'. Hidayet believes that the large tracts of unused, uncultivated land in the area should be incorporated into commercial agriculture.

In 2015, Hidayet moved his operations to the village of Harmancık in Beypazarı, where he built his new cold-storage facility. The facility covers 2,500 m² of land, of which 1,500 m² is used for storage and the rest for cleaning/washing, sorting, grading, packaging and truck-loading. I visited the facility in June 2015. The building consists of three cold-storage chambers, five washing pools, one accounting room, a kitchen and dining room, a prayer room, three bathrooms and a dressing and change room with lockers. The cold chambers are electronically monitored. There is also a very modern

Figure 4.5 Carrot Sorting, Grading and Packaging at Hidayet's Cold Storage Facility (Harmancık, Beypazarı, 17 June 2015).

chrome-plated carrot-washing machine, which cost TL 80,000. It has the capacity to wash 30 tons of carrots a day. From this storage facility, Hidayet transports 300 trucks of vegetables to wholesale markets and supermarkets in Antalya, Samsun, Gaziantep and Kayseri.

The construction of the facility cost TL 2.5 million. Hidayet was successful in securing financial assistance from the Institution of Support for Agricultural and Rural Development (TKDK) through a program called 'Investments for Restructuring the Processing and Marketing of Agricultural and Fishery Products, and for Upgrading to EU standards'.[10] The TKDK provides financial assistance to agricultural projects by paying 50 per cent of their costs through donations pooled from the EU and government budgetary sources.[11] In this particular case, Hidayet's Eyüp Taş Limited Company paid for 50 per cent of the cost through bank credit. The remaining 50 per cent was financed by the TKDK donation. Out of a total donation of TL 1.25 million for this facility, the EU financed 75 per cent and the Turkish government 25 per cent. The Eyüp Taş Limited Company was also rebranded with the marketing tag: 'Discover the Natural Taste, Eat Healthy'.

Although Hidayet's new cold-storage facility in Beypazarı now conforms to EU standards, waste water from his modern carrot-washing machine still contains chemical residues, particularly from nitrogen fertilizers. This waste water is released without treatment into a well nearby. When I spoke to Hidayet on 15 June 2015, he explained that a water-treatment machine will be installed in the near future to decontaminate waste water before it is released into the environment.

Agricultural Bio-Technology Intensification: Ayık Tarım and Bey Fide in Beypazarı

Through Hidayet, I met the owners of Ayık Tarım, a seed-distributing company; and Bey Fide, a greenhouse seedling-growing operation. Hidayet was present during my interviews with the owners. Many of the commercial farmers I interviewed purchase their seeds and chemicals from Ayık Tarım and seedlings from Bey Fide. Ayık Tarım was founded in 1997 and Bey Fide in 2010. They were cofounded by four members of a family: three brothers and a brother-in-law. Later, these operations were consolidated into a joint venture as Bey Fide-Ayık Tarım Gıda İnşaat Nakliyat San. Tic. Ltd. (Bey Fide-Ayık Tarım Food Construction and Transportation Industry Limited). In this family-business partnership, Sadettin Ayık is responsible for the management of Ayık Tarım and Saffet Soykan for Bey Fide. Both are agricultural engineers who met each other as students in the Faculty of Agriculture at Akdeniz University. They are in their late thirties and married each other's sisters. Sadettin Ayık is also the Vice-Chair of the Beypazarı Chamber of Commerce. On 26 May 2014, I interviewed Sadettin Ayık in a restaurant in Beypazarı near the Chamber of Commerce and met with Saffet Soykan in his office at Bey Fide.

Bey Fide is apparently the second largest greenhouse-based seedling-growing company in Turkey. Sadettin Ayık described Bey Fide as having no competitor in the whole of Central Anatolia. According to Yağmur Toprak, a salesperson for Rijk Zwaan, Bey Fide is one of the two largest seedling producers in Turkey. Professional seedling production first started for tomatoes in the province of Antalya in Turkey in 1994. Since then, the number of growers has increased dramatically in the Mediterranean and Aegean regions of Turkey. There are currently 91 registered seedling growers in Turkey, 85 of whom specialize in fresh vegetables (Balkaya and Kandemir 2015). Antalya, with 45 operations, contains 98 per cent of all seedling growers in Turkey, followed by İzmir with 12 operations, Mersin with nine, Bursa five, Adana four and Ankara three.[12] Ankara has two other smaller greenhouse-based seedling companies operating in Beypazarı, named Kırbaşı and Başaran.

The Bey Fide complex covers 38,000 m² of space. The original greenhouse, over 5,000 m² in size, expanded to 22,000 m² in 2013. The complex has four greenhouses for growing seedlings, one water-purification system, one automatic seed-sowing system and three seed-germination rooms – all computerized. The greenhouses contain high-tech, automatically controlled screening installations, heating, cooling, lighting, irrigation and fertilizer application systems. Bey Fide specializes in growing lettuce, cabbage, cauliflower and broccoli seedlings, but during the spring and summer, it grows all varieties of vegetable seedlings. There are approximately 50 people employed in the greenhouse operation.[13]

Bey Fide has the capacity to grow 170 million seedlings per season. It currently produces 80 million seedlings on average, out of an estimated total of 3.2 billion seedlings produced in all of Turkey (Balkaya and Kandemir 2015). Bey Fide uses 50 tons of purified underground artesian water for irrigation per day. Because the underground water of Beypazarı is hard and calcareous, with high pH levels resulting from underground lime deposits, an expensive water-purification system has been installed in the complex. Many of the high-technology inputs, including the seed-planting machine, turf soil and seedling trays, are from abroad. The production process includes the assembly of all ingredients necessary for seedling growing.

Bey Fide has nation-wide marketing connections, and seedling production is based on pre-order purchasing. Farmers involved in specialized crop production often use ready-to-plant seedlings purchased from greenhouse seedling growers.[14] Farmers believe that seedling production is such specialized work that it requires operations to be separated from farming. In fact, 70 per cent of all open-field vegetable production in Turkey begins with seedlings purchased from specialty growers (Balkaya and Kandemir 2015). Mesut notes:

> Seedling production is similar to raising a child, it requires tender care. I am a businessman: I go to İstanbul, Adapazarı and Samsun to sell my products. I am also a second-tier trader of salad varieties produced by small producers, selling them to even larger traders. Everyone should be specialized in a line of work that they know best. I have no time for dealing with seedlings.
>
> (Interview, 28 May 2014)

Bey Fide uses imported and Turkish-produced seeds purchased from its partner company, Ayık Tarım, which in turn procures its seeds from agribusiness firms. Sadettin Ayık explained that Turkish-owned seed growers, especially Bursa Tohumculuk, are becoming increasingly important, having captured approximately 50 per cent of the seed market in tomatoes, eggplants, peppers and cucumbers. According to Sadettin Ayık:

> Foreign seed growers used to think of us in Turkey as seed distributors only. As their market share was shrinking because of the growing market influence of Turkish seed companies, they have begun to establish their own seed breeding stations in Turkey. Seed development is a very lengthy and expensive process. A plant breeder will work for 10 years to develop a new variety; we may or may not like the resulting F1 variety. The plant breeder has to pay a registration fee of TL 7,500 to the government for each of the new improved seeds. This seems like a small amount of money, but the plant breeder is not working on one variety alone. The accumulated cost is high. Foreign-owned corporate seed growers are in an advantageous position here. If they also receive a GI certificate for the new F1 seeds which they develop from our own native varieties,

we will completely lose control over those varieties.[15] Unfortunately, the government is not providing enough financial support for us to improve our own native varieties.

(Interview, 26 May 2014)

Sadettin Ayık's concern with foreign companies receiving patent rights for native seeds rests on Turkey's GI protection legislation of 1995 (No. 555), which harmonizes policy with the Paris Convention and the World Trade Organization's (WTO) Trade-Related Aspects of Intellectual Property Rights (TRIPS) – in relation to intellectual property rights (IPRs) in agriculture (Rai and Mauria 2004).[16] Although GI legislation does not require improvement or invention in products, it does not prevent further innovation through cross-breeding either. Moreover, the use of GI is not restrictive, and all producers in a particular area can use it with their trademarks (Nagarajan 2007, 167). By reference to legislation, foreign companies in Turkey can also register their trademarks for local seeds that originate in the geographical area indicated. However, the legislation is unclear as to whether the companies that use GI with their trademarks can then develop crop varieties in the identified geographical area, including F1 hybrid varieties, from the GI protected seeds. Nevertheless, the F1 varieties of Diyarbakır watermelon[17] and Salihli cherries[18] have been patented under GI regulation. There are now an increasing number of foreign biotechnology companies in Turkey opening seed-improvement and plant-breeding stations in areas where seeds have originated. This is the case for Syngenta's seed-improvement plant for tomatoes and cucumbers in

Figure 4.6 Sadettin Ayık (Beypazarı, 19 May 2014).

Antalya (see Chapter 3). While Yağmur Toprak from Rijk Zwaan, whom I interviewed at the Bey Fide facilities, agrees with Sadettin Ayık's views on the lack of financial support for research and development (R&D) in seed production by Turkish companies, he believes this issue is also related to the business mentality that dominates in Turkish-owned seed companies. He observes:

> Global companies are way ahead in plant-gene pools and in the know-how of seed-improvement technology. Turkish seed growers are more interested in seed-trading rather than improvement and development of new varieties. … There is some investment in seed production, especially in Antalya, for tomatoes, peppers and eggplants, which Antalya produces for export. There is a serious lack of interest in the development of salad varieties and winter vegetables. There is not a single Turkish company in spinach, carrot, lettuce or cabbage … Turkish seed growers concentrate on the export-oriented products which offer greater profit margins. However, there is very strong vegetable seed-development potential in Central Anatolian fields, waiting for Turkish companies to help with improvement.
> (Interview, 26 May 2014)

Both Sadettin Ayık and Saffet Soykan place great emphasis on the competitive growth of Turkish life-science companies in the research and development of agro-industrial inputs. They consider it essential that Turkey shifts its agricultural development away from a long-standing European corporate mooring. Sadettin Ayık compares the current domination of seed markets by foreign companies to colonial-style control over national resources. He elaborates:

> There are many who come to Turkey as tourists, hiking and tracking in the fields and mountains. They have much interest in Turkey's nice smelling, flavourful mountain thymes, oreganos and mints. These so-called tourists are actually bio-prospectors, specialized in stealing seeds. They have been doing this in Turkey since at least the First World War. Many vegetable varieties which European seed growers have monopoly control over are stolen from countries which used to be European colonies. They steal seeds, improve them, breed new varieties, and sell them back to the countries where the original seeds came from. Turkey has never been a formal colony; but the foreign control over our seed markets is creating a similar condition. The only way we can respond to this is by encouraging the competitive growth of our own companies. We have to show that we exist and have no intention of leaving the space to these colonizing powers. Actually, we have already come a long way. Our universities are increasingly emphasizing research in life sciences; researchers are developing new, economically viable, high-yield varieties from our own native seeds. We also have our own organizational infrastructure; we have our own seed-growers union[19] … we can pressure the government to adopt certain policies and support nationally controlled research and technology

development. Bursa Tohumculuk produces good, high quality seeds and has the commercial capacity to sell seeds abroad to the Third World, to Africa and to the former Soviet Turkish republics. Its prices are one third those of European imported seeds.

(Interview, 26 May 2014)

For Saffet Soykan, the growth of national companies in the biotechnology field requires a policy change by the government, starting with a change in educational policy:

From the beginning of the Turkish republic, our educational system has put us villagers to sleep. Our school teachers used to tell us that nothing can come of us ... In contrast, when I was a student at Akdeniz University, our Dean used to tell us that "friends; you are the future of Turkey." If you instil confidence in a kid from the early years in school, that kid can be an achiever. There are some people in Turkey who have been very well educated. These people are the children of the old elite who were educated to be achievers via state financial support. In the past the state deserted the Anatolian rural populations who were believed to be losers. The bitter reality now is that the biggest traitors in this country are the old elite and their children ... the Koç and Sabancı Holdings. The only thing they have done for the Turkish economy is to sell us pieces of tins they assembled as cars. They had no investment for the development of the Turkish auto industry. Same with agriculture, which was totally neglected ...We need strong R&D firms in agriculture ... Turkish seed developers and plant breeders must be able to develop and supply commercially viable seeds to myself and to farmers in order for a well-integrated commercial agriculture to grow in Turkey.

(Interview, 26 May 2014)

In addition to state support for public education and research in universities, Sadettin Ayık also draws attention to the incorporation of local agro-ecological knowledge systems into research. This, for him, requires state 'planning at a landscape scale'. He continues:

Hybrid seeds used in Germany and Turkey display the same standard qualities. But, it is the mineral composition of the soil and sun, and the ecological conditions that enhance the nutritional content of the resulting food. Turkey's farming soils are fertile and rich in vitamins and minerals. Therefore, research in seed development and plant breeding has to take into account the specific ecological and climatic conditions of the area. Government policy must align agricultural production with locally specific ecological conditions, as well as with the globally valid technical requirements of good agricultural practices. Bringing together local conditions and global technical requirements would produce cheaper, tastier and healthier food. It is better to incorporate our own varieties to practice good agriculture under our own landscape conditions ... Under current agricultural practices, it costs 10 times more to produce ecologically suited native varieties of food that have a pleasant aroma, taste and flavour than it does with biotech crops. ... We are now at a crossroads; a choice has to be made.

(Interview, 26 May 2014)

The scientific breeding of hybrid F1 vegetable cultivars has been the basis for the commercial improvement of native varieties. Interestingly, the 'hybrid vigour' (Dutfield 2008, 29) expressed by heightened interest in seed innovation and yield enhancement has undermined native varieties, as hybrids do not lead to true-breeding offspring, thus resulting in the loss of a native variety. Although Saffet Soykan and Sadettin Ayık are aware of this outcome, they regard the scientific separation of hybrid-seed development from the customary practices of plant breeding as an essential component of commercialization. For Yağmur Toprak of Rijk Zwaan, such separation is inevitable:

Everyone has to fulfil their-own responsibilities within the food value chain. The trader has to sell good quality food to consumers; the producer has to produce high quality products; the seed distributor has to sell good quality seeds; and the seed developer has to supply high quality seeds.

(Interview, 26 May 2014)

Bey Fide is highly integrated with the dominant upstream players of the global value chain. Saffet Soykan explains the meaning of seed quality by reference to the value chain:

We visit the fields of new experimental varieties on the open-field demonstration days organized by seed producers. We also inspect the quality of these new crops. The seed producers provide us with relevant literature on new varieties and explain their advantages. The seeds have to produce homogeneous seedlings with high integrity in standards. To achieve the expected standards, farmers must prepare their fields very well; they must provide the irrigation, fertilization and chemical spraying required by these varieties. In the end, the product uniformity we achieve in our seedlings must be reproduced in farmers' fields. Farmers have to grow eight kilograms of lettuce to fit into each produce box ... all the same size and weight ... they must all be uniform. If a farmer plants 6,000 seedlings per dekar, he produces 800 boxes of lettuce. With this level of production he can make a profit. If he cannot obtain product uniformity and achieves only 500 boxes of lettuce, he will lose money. It is very clear ... farmers must employ particular, standardized field practices developed for specific crops in order to reproduce the same uniformity that we produce in our seedlings.

(Interview, 26 May 2014)

Saffet Soykan suggests that 'planning at a landscape level' must integrate local agro-ecological conditions into a vertically designed flow of dominant industrial standards created by upstream players. His reasoning is as follows:

> This is capitalism; but there are other issues to take into consideration: world population is increasing very fast. Food-consumption needs are increasing at a tremendous pace. If we use seed varieties developed 30 years ago, and if a consumer is willing to purchase tomatoes by spending eight lira per kilo, *köylü* [peasant] can produce them based on his customary practices. But if you don't want to pay more than 50 *kuruş*,[20] farming by tradition and with nature is no longer an option.
>
> (Interview, 26 May 2014)

The individuals I interviewed all agree that the hybrid path is necessary to feed the world at a reasonable cost; this includes yield-intensification through genetically modified organisms (GMO). Saffet Soykan explains:

> People exaggerate the effects of GMO. There is a natural order created by Allah. An Ayaş tomato is juicy; a Çanakkale tomato is naturally harder and can remain longer in the market; a Kızılcahamam tomato is higher yielding. These different qualities correspond to locally varied landscapes, soils, climatic conditions … The GMO process is nothing different. Biologists and biotechnology engineers combine these characteristics in a new-crop variety to produce a juicy, higher yielding tomato with a longer shelf life.
>
> (Interview, 26 May 2014)

For Saffet Soykan, small-scale producers cannot effectively implement the standards and practices required by high-tech intensive-agriculture:

> The conditions are too demanding and the expectations too great for small producers to comply with. The government currently provides subsidies but it first wants producers to organize and manage their farms in accordance with European standards. Hidayet can implement these standards, but many small producers do not have enough money to upgrade their farms.
>
> (Interview, 26 May 2014)

Commercial Farmers' View of Small-Scale Production

According to Hidayet and Mesut, specialized, high-tech industrial agriculture forces farmers into a vertically organized value chain that is sectorally driven by agribusiness. It also weeds out those who are unable to comply. Mesut describes the process in the following way:

> The old agriculture – the ways followed by the *köylü* that we learned from our grandfathers – required us to sow seeds by hand-sprinkling them

over the land and then wait for rain. The seeds were our own, saved from the previous harvest. To tell the truth, those seeds were healthier and more resistant to diseases. But, they don't exist anymore now that we have moved to high-tech agriculture. Since the old style seeds are dead, we cannot act like *köylü* either.

(Interview, 28 May 2014)

I asked Mesut what he meant by 'the death of old-style seeds'. He said that new-style farming is a money-making business that cannot achieve success through the customary practices of the *köylü*. Mesut continues:

It is not only a question of whether the old seeds are low-yielding. There are new diseases emerging and proliferating every year; local seeds don't have resistance to them. We also have to deal with supermarket demands that food appeal to consumer taste and have a long life-span on the shelves. These requirements are now like *farz*. If you ask farmers around here, 99.9 per cent of them will say that they are losing money. But I am earning money. That is the difference between the kind of agriculture I do and the old kind they do. I produce standard quality products. I am neither concerned about the taste nor where to sell my products. I can sell them to the highest bidder in the market. I know how the system works: commercial agriculture requires constant mechanization, innovation and renewal. One machine is not enough; if you have a seed-sowing machine, you also need to have a soil-processing machine ... it is not enough to have high yield, you have to be able to process product on the farm. Your farm should be organized like a factory. You have to have the technologies to wash, grade and package your produce. I am not a farmer but a merchant. A farmer must be mentally ready to act as a merchant!

(Interview, 28 May 2014)

Farz means 'duty' in Islam. It refers to the religious rules and Koranic commands that every practicing Muslim must follow. Mesut believes farming behaviour must be completely subordinate to the performance-enhancement requirements of supermarkets. For him, this behavioural subordination is as self-evident as the religious certainty embodied in *farz*, which 'forces' farmers to realize their responsibilities as self-investing, self-marketing and self-enhancing entrepreneurs.

Hidayet echoes these sentiments regarding the market disadvantage of small producers. He states:

There are more than 4 million producers in Turkey who constantly produce surplus at various levels of quality, yet they push the prices down. Their number must be reduced. There must also be a quota system in production; there should be greater government regulation of what crops are to be produced, where and in what quantity. In addition to restrictions on the amount of crops, good-agricultural practices must be enforced and followed by everyone. There are many who are ignorant and unlearned on how to use industrial inputs. They spray lettuce two days before the harvest and sell it at the *pazars* full of cancerous chemical residues. In this high-technology age, farming is a business which must respond to consumer demands for food safety, and farmers must act as responsible business managers. I am a management graduate and I manage my farm as a business. There is nothing that *köylü* can do in this business environment. Unless they are channelled to other employment areas ... perhaps they can receive retirement pensions from the government so they can eat rather than produce food.

(Interview, 8 June 2014)

Hidayet argues that externally driven food-quality standards marginalize small producers and eventually push them out of the sector, which he sees as the inevitable outcome of commercialization in agriculture. To become a certified GAP producer, Hidayet hired a private company on a 5-year contract and paid them TL 20,000[21] to monitor and verify his conformity with GAP standards (Interview, 12 June 2015). This is a very costly process that most small-scale producers simply cannot afford.

Although the existing literature is not entirely clear on how externally driven scientific innovation is implemented at the farm level and what the possible outcomes are for different categories of farmers, the large-scale commercial farmers I interviewed believe that small producers simply cannot sustain themselves under the market demands of new agriculture. The reasons for this are numerous. They include (1) the 'economies of scale' that negatively influence small farmers' ability to meet the high costs of input-intensive, standards-driven production (Dolan and Humphrey 2000); (2) the 'market disadvantage' of small producers in processing, packaging and selling their products (Vorley 2001); (3) the inability of small producers to embody a market rationality and act as 'self-responsible entrepreneurs'; (4) small producers' marginal role in 'national economic growth' projects; (5) a lack of interest on the part of small producers in 'collective capability-building'; and (6) small producers' failure to *optimize the performance value* of their production, which relegates them to the role of unproductive producers in great oversupply. In the thinking of commercial farmers, small producers who are unable to adopt the self-enhancing, entrepreneurial rationality necessary to generate wealth and contribute to national economic growth can only hope to work as wage-earning agricultural labourers.

Hidayet believes that the disappearance of old-style production and farming behaviour is historically tangled up with the Turkish government's pursuit of EU membership. He observes:

The Erdoğan government has been the main driver of agricultural restructuring since 2002. Erdoğan is a smart politician. He restructured the economy under the pretence of preparing Turkey for EU membership. I don't think Erdoğan is really concerned about EU membership, but he used the legitimacy-providing framework of EU membership to deepen commercialization in agriculture. Before 2002, people knew how to stand on their own feet to sustain their families. Farming is big business now. This may not be good for small producers, but overall it is good for the country. Turkey is now one of the most important agricultural countries in the world, superseding many in the EU and catching up with the levels achieved by the US and other big agricultural players. We as a nation are going to become wealthy by growing competitively in the global economy. We will surpass Europe; European economies are dying, anyway.

(Interview, 17 May 2013)

Hidayet views the vanishing of small-scale farming as 'inevitable' because small producers do not act 'responsibly' to build their capabilities and respond more favourably to market realities:

Small production is now dead. Farming lands in Güdül are limited, and parcels are small. Many from Güdül have migrated to cities for work as they cannot sustain their life from the land. Wherever you go in Turkey you find someone from Güdül who often works as a trader. There is a saying around here which goes: "in animal-kind you should be afraid of a donkey, and in humankind a person from Güdül." That is how it is; they are self-interested wheelers and dealers who make money, with no other commitments and responsibilities in life. If they wanted to survive as farmers, they could have formed producers' unions, bring their small parcels of lands together into larger, consolidated units, and then work together. But, this is too much for people in Güdül. Our people are self-centred and self-interested; they resent and envy each other's success. They are very good in neighbourly relations but when it comes down to doing business they won't work together. Even if a cooperative was formed, it would dissolve within one year. Gossip would spread: I have 100 dekars of land, you have only 10; my crop is better quality and I deserve better returns, etc. … Not only could they not work together, they also don't like hard-working people to succeed in farming. For example, most of the land I cultivate is rented. There is 15 dekars of land sitting there idle, which belonged to my grandfather. Since my grandfather died, at least 15 families are claiming inheritance-rights over it. Because they are unable to settle their dispute, no-one has planted the land, which now lies idle. I decided to plant lettuce there last year. You should have seen it … those who had no interest whatsoever in this land until I cultivated it wanted me to pay them rent money for their tiny share. I said never again would I plant anything on that land. This is why people with small plots of land cannot survive in a restructured agriculture.

(Interview, 17 May 2013)

Hidayet knows that Turkey lacks a historical experience of producers' unions and collective farms, which, for example, have been experimented with in most countries of East Central Europe and the former Soviet Union during the Cold War (Mathijs and Swinnen 1998). Nevertheless, he alludes to the lack of a cultural inclination toward building capabilities and participating more responsibly in the transformation of agriculture for the purpose of generating income. This lack of interest in 'collective capability-building' on the part of small producers, coupled with a push by government toward high-tech, input-intensive corporate agriculture, is resulting in the exclusion of small-scale producers. Hidayet notes:

> Approximately 80 per cent of small producers in my village used to be able to sell their products in the *pazar* as independent producers. They now work as salaried grocery workers in supermarkets. Some of them are working here on my farm as temporary wage earners.
>
> (Interview, 17 May 2013)

Hidayet further points out that 'small-scale producers cannot supply produce to supermarkets at a consistently high volume and quality, and at an affordable price. Therefore, they lose out.' In contrast, large-scale farmers have an advantageous market position, which is further strengthened by the current wholesale market law. Hidayet adds:

> There are large tourist hotels, supermarket chains and exporters. The new wholesale market law allows them to buy directly from the producers who can produce large quantities of food. Before this law, producers were required to sell their produce to wholesale traders in the wholesale markets regardless of the amount of food they produce. The wholesale market commissioners would then market a cumulative amount to the hotels, supermarkets, grocers or whomever. Small producers were better off then. Now they have no choice but to wait for a trader to come to their villages to purchase their produce, but he may not come at all. Or, they can sell informally on the streets and at the consumers' doorstep. Many in my village suffer from an inability to sell their crops to a trader.
>
> (Interview, 17 May 2013)

Large-scale commercial farmers understand agricultural marketing in terms of the vertical integration of producers into marketing chains, including upstream actors (involved in purchasing inputs) and downstream players (who market products). Farmers also market their crops directly to corporate intermediaries, retailers, hotels and exporters, eliminating the need for commission agents in wholesale markets. The large-scale farmers I interviewed exemplify a *direct marketing* mechanism that is currently emerging in Turkey. These farmers also act as suppliers for the marginalized small producers who face significant market disadvantages. Mesut explains:

> If there are 100 carrot farmers in this region, 90 of them are small-scale, producing for larger farmers like me. In Beypazarı, approximately 10

farmers are large-scale. In addition to cultivating our own land, we also act as middle-level suppliers, buying crops from small producers and selling them to larger traders. We actually help small producers to survive. Both as producers and suppliers, we have become influential in carrot production across Turkey. And we like to be totally independent as businessmen. Therefore, many of us prefer open markets, rather than having contract ties to supermarkets. After the new wholesale market law was introduced, we no longer had to sell to wholesale markets either. We can sell to whoever gives us the higher price.

(Interview, 28 May 2014)

For large-scale farmers, farming represents a business venture that must be science and technology intensive in order to optimize the performance value of production and maximize profits in open markets. Performance values can also be realized through the utilization of surplus labour, which is abundant in Turkey, according to Mesut. If Turkey is behind in technological innovation and mechanization, it has a population advantage that can be directed toward economic development projects and greater growth. This requires that small producers be released from the land and re-employed as workers:

When I went to these European countries as Syngenta's guest, I realized that they rely on immigrants, but they don't receive immigrants on a large scale anymore either. Since there is no surplus population, they cannot produce cheaply by employing large numbers of people. Rather, they must do so through further mechanization. We have enough of a population. We can produce cheaply and increase our returns. Also, from what I saw, their technologies are not that far advanced beyond ours. We can easily catch up with them. The only thing I expect from our government is to not give money to farmers who operate inefficient farms. Instead of giving them money, which contributes to lingering unproductive farming, the government should support us to grow our businesses; we can hire those former small producers for our farms ... they would make fantastic labourers; they know how to grow things better than anyone.

(Interview, 28 May 2014)

Growth – with a Strong Work Ethic

All of the commercial farmers, seed distributors and seedling growers whom I interviewed are nationalist in their political orientation. They all believe that techno-scientific innovation in farming directed toward the intensification of commercial agriculture will spur national economic development. My respondents frequently invoke nationalist imagery of an east–west divide to highlight the political significance of Turkey's competitive growth through industrial agriculture. Saffet Soykan has expressed this east–west divide in global competition as follows:

Europe is not our culture, but the east is. The east eats the same food as us. The Konya seed-growing company sells to growers in Syria via 'suitcase trading'; they bring money in suitcases and take seeds from the Konya firm back to Syria. We have the weather-soil-sun advantage in Turkey given by Allah. The sword is out of its scabbard now; no one can stop Turkey in the near future. We have to develop hybrid vegetable cultivars from our own native varieties to produce food here and sell abroad to the east. We must stop imitating Europeans and develop our own path. We must be more aware of our potential and strength, and work harder too. We must remember our roots, and turn our eyes to the east.

(Interview, 26 May 2014)

The political and economic significance of redirecting Turkey's economy toward the east is further clarified by Hidayet:

For centuries we have looked to Europe for our direction ... never to our own roots to find strength. ... Europe is getting older, in terms of its population, productivity and soil fertility. The ecology and the climate are not there for agriculture. The centre of the global economy has shifted to the east, soon to be followed by Africa. We have to find our way in the changing dynamics of the world economy and reorganize our production to better suit the tastes of Asians and Africans, not Europeans.

(Interview, 26 May 2014)

For many of my respondents, Europe represents a site of moral degeneration rather than progress (cf. Said 1978). Comments by Saffet Soykan and Hidayet are revealing here. Saffet observes:

There is an ongoing economic crisis in the world. Poor people cannot afford food to eat; they go hungry and die of starvation. If there is a crisis in our country, we will provide social support for our needy. Our customs and traditions, which are deeply rooted in Islam, require us to help people to ensure that they are food secure. But, it is not the same in Europe. I have been in the Netherlands twice for business. I don't like Europe. For Europeans, everything is money and individual gain. They are cold and uncaring; the poor are homeless and hungry. You don't see people homeless and living on the streets in Turkey because of poverty.

(Interview, 26 May 2014)

Hidayet elaborates on the social solidarity at the village level that provides food security and welfare assistance to the poor. He believes that the expansion of commercial agriculture may marginalize and exclude small producers but that it will do so without disrupting the deeply rooted religious and cultural institutions of society. Hidayet notes:

There are many poor people in my village, many of whom are widowed women. These women are not left alone to suffer because everyone in the village who can afford it gives their alms to them. There is no one in the village who cannot afford to live a decent life. Alms-giving is a very important religious duty that strengthens communal social solidarity and provides welfare to the needy.

(Interview, 26 May 2014)

Saffet adds that his seedling firm combines successful commercialization and moral responsibility to reduce the vulnerability and food insecurity of the poor. He states:

We pay our taxes to the state; we also give alms which amount to 2.5 per cent of our firms' profits after expenses. Alms-giving is not tax deductible; we do it on moral grounds. Many Muslim-owned companies in Turkey also give their alms. How can you have hungry and homeless people in such a country? If Sabancı and Koç Holding companies would give their alms, there would be no poverty in Turkey whatsoever.

(Interview, 26 May 2014)

These comments by my respondents about the solidarity-building aspect of normative-religious referents in Turkish culture were repeatedly juxtaposed with the 'moral, cultural decadence' of Europe embodied in the notion of self-interested individualism. This is similar to the binary view of an east–west divide held by Cemil Meriç (2005 [1974]), a well-known Turkish national-ist essayist. He defined the historical lineage of Turkey's modernization from the late Ottoman era as the blind emulation of European practices with-out critically evaluating their applicability to Turkey and without a mean-ingful discussion on the possibility of a synthesis between European and Turkish–Muslim ways.

For my respondents, the discursive east–west divide splits the economic and cultural realms into mutually exclusive domains. Thus far, they have been una-ble to reach a synthesis connecting the two realms – in the form of a different social and technical mode of innovation in agriculture. In the absence of such a synthesis, their thinking oscillates between a high-technology input-intensive 'development' model grounded in Euro-American ways and the desire for preserved landscapes and food cultures. The globally competitive growth of Turkish–Muslim companies along the lines of conventional industrial methods seems to have become the preferred path. Saffet offers the following example:

I went on haj three years ago. There I met with the founder of a firm specializing in fruit juice production. He is from Ankara, a graduate of Middle East Technical University. He borrowed money from his rela-tives in Germany. With that money he purchased a factory and founded

Göknur Gıda in Niğde. Recently he sold 50 per cent of the shares of his factory to an Arab capital group. The firm has a factory in Niğde and a 1,300-dekar pomegranate orchid in Adana. ... He purchased a large tract of land in Mesudiye to establish a tomato-paste factory. The Arab group owns supermarket chains so he doesn't have any problem with the marketing of his produce. He also has large distribution centres in the US and Germany. He doesn't have his own name on his produce. He supplies for Coca-Cola and Pepsi in large barrels. ÜLKER also purchases from Göknur Gıda. He produces for the world market. Is this a bad thing?

(Interview, 26 May 2014)

Concluding Remarks

The farming imaginaries of my respondents reinforce a transnationally advocated industrial agriculture. However, from a cultural standpoint, their comments reflect an 'uneasiness' with Turkey's development projects (Atasoy 2009). This unease is captured by the Turkish novelist Orhan Pamuk in his book *İstanbul* (2006) in the concept of *hüzün* (or melancholy). *Hüzün* is largely the result of a mismatch or dissonance between the desire to 'progress and develop' and the long historical experience of Turkish society. To quote Pamuk:

> Great as the desire to westernize and modernize may have been, the more desperate wish was probably to be rid of all the bitter memories ... as a spurned lover throws away his lost beloved's clothes, possessions, and photographs. But as nothing, western or local, came to fill the void, the great drive to westernize amounted mostly to the erasure of the past; the effect on culture was reductive and stunting .... That which I would later know as pervasive melancholy and mystery ...
>
> (O. Pamuk 2006, 29)

Interestingly, what Pamuk describes in *İstanbul* as the source of *hüzün* has also been a source of great emotional pain and suffering for many in Turkey with an Islamic cultural–political orientation. The Turkish poet Necip Fazıl Kısakürek (1979) conveys this in his poem *Çile* (or suffering). It is almost as if my respondents have internalized Pamuk's notion of *hüzün* and Kısakürek's sense of *çile*. They clearly express such sentiments when they refer to Europe as a source of degradation and a counterpoint to their invocation of a more agro-ecological and culturally sensitive pattern of corporate development. My respondents seem to accept modernity as 'a universal necessity' (Wallerstein 2006) for achieving progress, but only in economic terms – as an institutional foundation for fostering scientific research and innovation. They separate the economic and cultural–political realms, expressing the *commonality* and *desirability* of the transnational industrial model while noting cultural differences in the varied conditions of development. However, they have not fully considered the question of how to synthesize this commonality and difference.

The greatest Turkish novelist of the twentieth century, according to Orhan Pamuk, is Ahmet Hamdi Tanpınar. His two most famous works, *A Mind At Peace* (2008 [1949]) and *The Time Regulation Institute* (2013 [1962]), represent literary accounts of cultural derangement and *hüzün* resulting from the blind emulation of European ways of development – without a creative synthesis that incorporates Turkish society's old temporal order and rhythms of life. In the absence of such a synthesis, Tanpınar's characters suffer eternally, capable of only expressing inarticulate resentment.

In the thinking of my respondents, European individualism and the endless pursuit of self-interest undermine the long-established networks of social solidarity in Turkey needed to support those who suffer from insecurities of livelihood. Their response is to return to the east for inspiration. However, I would argue that the presence and acknowledgement of ambivalence in farmers' farming imaginaries requires an understanding that large-scale industrial farmers aspire to realize a more comprehensive program of growth – a program that would blend socially and ecologically responsible innovation with an *appropriate* science and technology. The following chapter explores this ambivalence in relation to the imaginaries of organic farmers and small-scale producers.

Notes

1 I discuss heirloom tomato production in Çağa in the following chapter.
2 Capital letters are in the original writing.
3 According to a report published by MIT (2014), which offers a different set of data on the world's freshwater withdrawals, agriculture accounts for 69 per cent of the world's freshwater withdrawals, industry accounts for 19 per cent and households and municipalities only 12 per cent.
4 http://www.oecd.org/agriculture/wateruseinagriculture.htm (accessed 12 April 2016).
5 http://www.oecd.org/agriculture/48498988.pdf (accessed 12 April 2016).
6 http://www.oecd.org/tad/sustainable-agriculture/groundwater-country-note-USA-2015%20final.pdf (accessed 12 April 2016).
7 http://www.oecd.org/tad/sustainable-agriculture/groundwater-country-note-MEX-2015%20final.pdf (accessed 12 April 2016).
8 http://www.oecd.org/tad/sustainable-agriculture/groundwater-country-note-TUR-2015%20final.pdf (accessed 12 April 2016).
9 According to FAO statistics, irrigation and livestock accounted for 74 per cent of water withdrawn in Turkey in 2003. (http://www.fao.org/nr/water/aquastat/countries_regions/Profile_segments/TUR-WU_eng.stm, accessed 13 January 2015).
10 The TKDK was founded in 2007 (Law No. 5648) through an agreement between the EU and the Turkish government to establish an Instrument for Pre-Accession Assistance for Rural Development (IPARD). That instrument 'constitutes the legal basis for the provision of financial assistance to candidate countries and potential candidate countries in their efforts to enhance political, economic and institutional reforms with a view to becoming members of the European Union'. (http://www.tkdk.gov.tr/Content/File/Mevzuat/SektorelAnlasmaIngilizce.pdf, accessed 17 August 2015).
11 On 28 July 2015, Mehdi Eker, then Minister of Food, Agriculture and Livestock, explained that since its founding in 2007, the TKDK signed financial-assistance contracts for more than 10,000 projects worth TL 4.7 billion and paid TL 1.6 billion out of its donation share of TL 2.6 billion. According to the minister, the TKDK will continue to provide

TL 3 billion in donations for rural development projects, including renewable energy, within the context of the second phase of the Instrument for Pre-Accession Assistance Rural development (IPARD) programme agreement, which will be implemented as of September 2015 (http://www.tkdk.gov.tr/Duyuru/eker-tkdk-tarim-ve-kirsal-kalkinma-alaninda-ulkemizin-en-guzide-kurumudur-79, accessed 17 August 2015).

12 http://www.fidebirlik.org.tr (accessed 5 March 2016).

13 I will analyze workers' narratives in Chapter 6.

14 Hidayet plants seeds directly into the soil because there are no seedling growers for carrots.

15 Geographical indications (GIs) are place-based names that convey the geographical origin, as well as the cultural and historical identity, of agricultural products. They provide a means of ensuring that control over the production and sale of a product stays within a local area, but they also serve as a link between local production systems and global markets (Bowen 2010).

16 For a detailed analysis of GI patent rights, see Chapter 5.

17 http://www.tpe.gov.tr/TurkPatentEnstitusu/resources/temp/B6501349-C363-4092-928E-9C86CA080B71.pdf (accessed 2 April 2015).

18 http://www.tpe.gov.tr/TurkPatentEnstitusu/resources/temp/E6F027E2-B036-43DF-B46C-ACF77A61AD96.pdf (accessed 2 April 2015).

19 After the Seeds Law of 2006, some 41 seedlings growers founded FİDEBİRLİK (the Seedling-Growers Union) in 2008. By 2016, its membership had increased to 109. (http://www.fidebirlik.org.tr/uyelik/fidebirlikin-yillara-ve-illere-gore-uye-sayisi/, accessed 29 July 2016).

20 The *kuruş* is a Turkish unit of currency. One Turkish Lira (TL) is equal to 100 *kuruş*. On 17 February 2015, one Turkish Lira was equivalent to US$ 0.4084.

21 TL 20,000 is equivalent to US$ 6,850, based on 2 March 2016 exchange rates.

5 The Taste and Smell of Place

The present chapter reveals that *organic* and small-scale producers share the *farming imaginaries* associated with industrial farming and expressed by large-scale, growth-oriented commercial farmers. These imaginaries also reveal a *sense-based* normative 'distrust' of agro-industrial processes. At the epistemological level, this distrust may signal a cultural dissonance in farming concerning the question of how to articulate a history of the senses (Ackerman 1991; Polan 2002), food culture and heritage and the place of food (Bowen and De Master 2014; Carroll and Fahy 2014; Feagan 2007). The normative distrust experienced by farmers emerges from a mindset that requires them to *act/ think-like-a-firm* in commercial farming. Recent literature has identified acting/ thinking-like-a-firm as a manifestation of 'neoliberal rationality', which figures humans as entrepreneurial, self-investing capital seeking to maximize their performance values and competitively reposition themselves in society (Brown 2015; Dardot and Laval 2009). This chapter examines whether 'organic' and small-scale farmers' distrust reflects a distinctive value orientation that appeals to certain quality practices and marketing strategies – specifically situated at the landscape level of the farm – in relation to the smell, taste and texture of food. Distrust, therefore, brings forth spatially valued traditions and practices that co-exist as one of the hybrid forms within agro-cultural diversity. I explore this hybridity by considering the simultaneous co-existence of what I call *participatory certification by consumers* for non-standard local food and corporate-imposed Good Agricultural Practices (GAP) standards for industrially designed food.

In Turkey, it is common for large-scale organic farmers and small-scale farmers to integrate their farming with animal husbandry to produce organic fertiliser. In fact, 96.38 per cent of the farms in Turkey combine field-crop production and animal husbandry (MFAL 2014c, 158). This practice underscores a respect for organic soil matter and exists in tandem with agro-ecological conservation. Farmers define themselves as 'organic' as a means of conveying that they practice customary ways of agriculture in as self-sufficient a manner as possible (Campbell and Liepins 2001). This includes saving seeds for planting local landraces or folk varieties. Practices like these reveal farmers' appreciation for, and interest in, maintaining the agro-ecology and conservation methods that preserve plant genetic resources and crop diversity. Existing literature shows that producers themselves do not need to engage in the development of alternative innovation systems (Warner 2007), but their concern with the negative effects of industrialized farming can be mobilized for the reorientation of agriculture and its market linkages (Kloppenburg 1991; Parrott et al. 2002). Nevertheless, the actually existing realities that farmers face in earning an income and implementing industrial methods, albeit partially, deter us from adopting a binary approach in favour of a greater appreciation of permeability.

Recent scholarship highlights the significance of smallholders (and peasants) from the global South in the local mobilization of efforts against corporate-led global agribusiness and agro-industrial models (McMichael 2008). Farmers in Southern European countries are also often seen as defending their traditional agricultural practices and culinary habits against industrial food production (Miele 2001). Similarly, the development of small-scale organic agriculture in Europe is interpreted as a breakthrough in the struggle against mainstream industrialized agriculture (Michelsen 2001). However, at the same time, there is an expectation that small producers should increasingly abandon traditional farming practices and knowledge in favour of capitalized models; this is the case in Bolivia, for example (Gilles et al. 2013). Based on my research findings in Turkey, I question the usefulness of a binary perspective, particularly given the shared perceptions and concerns among different categories of producers in regard to the expansion and deepening of agro-industrial ways. This highlights the intersection of agro-ecological effects with a development focus in agriculture, revealing commonly experienced conflictual tendencies, 'ambivalent tensions' and cultural dissonance rather than reinforcing dualisms (Escobar 1995; Gupta 1998; Harris 2008). These ambivalent tensions reveal that farmers wish to preserve their customary knowledge systems. They want to be self-sufficient and respectful of natural processes in conservation agriculture and, at the same time, they aspire to increase yields through industrial inputs for income/profit generation.

Definitions of sustainable, conservation agriculture range from a minimalist approach to the conservation of biodiversity to a more holistic approach that includes economic, social and cultural considerations and assessment of productivist projects for land/soil/water/animals/plants (Burgio et al. 2015; Ruttan 1994). The selection of appropriate biological indicators to define sustainable agriculture, including organic, is a complex and highly debated issue (Burgio et al. 2015; Duelli and Obrist 2003). Since 2007, the European Union (EU) has developed various policy positions, commonly known as *agro-environmental measures*, to articulate an understanding of ecological sustainability in organic production (Melozzi 2009, 14). The implementation of these measures is voluntary. Governments provide monetary incentives for farmers to implement less intensive farming methods and grow/raise a specific breed at risk of genetic erosion. Incentives are tied to third-party organic certification of farmers in compliance with standards that are determined by individual governments at the national level and by the International Federation of Organic Agricultural Movements (IFOAM) at the global level (Thiers 2006, 197).

The third-party certification requirement reflects an assumption that formally established standards generate greater trust in the quality and sustainability of the food to be consumed.

In Turkey, there were 42,460 certified organic farmers in 2011 – an increase from 14,798 in 2003 (Balaban 2014, 13). There are only five GAP-certified farmers in Beypazarı, one of whom I interviewed.[1] None of the farmers I interviewed is certified organic. The majority of small-scale producers I interviewed market their produce informally as street vendors and *pazar* merchants. Nevertheless, they often refer to their production as organic, as is the case with GAP-certified large-scale farmers. Once again, the term organic expresses a commonly shared concern with the conservation of ecological integrity at the landscape (soil/plants/watercourses/energy), health, nutrition and cultural level. It also points to the centrality of natural processes in farming perspectives for pollination, disease suppression, nutrient cycling and water and soil-fertility conservation. The term organic is mobilized to advertise the trustworthiness of the food and is often deployed as a marketing strategy. GAP-certification enables large-scale farmers to formally market their products to supermarkets. Small producers seek consumers' endorsement of their product quality within the personally established networks of trust cultivated over the years. I describe this informally established, direct, personal and trust-based relationship as participatory certification by consumers for non-standard food without design.

I will first examine the views expressed by organic producers (small- and large-scale) and then present the perspectives of small producers. There are numerous categories of organic and small-scale producers; hence the multiplicity of divergent narratives.

'Organic' Producers in Beypazarı and Güdül

This section focuses on the views recounted to me by Nuri, Halit and Hamza. Nuri is a large-scale farmer in his sixties from the village of Fasıl in Beypazarı. Hamza and Halit are small-scale producers in the village of Karacaören in Güdül. They are in their forties. Nuri, whom I interviewed on his farm on 26 May 2014, is the only farmer I have met in Turkey who produces for supermarkets through contract farming with first-tier suppliers. I met with Hamza and Halit separately on their farms in Karacaören. I interviewed Hamza on 23 June 2013 and Halit on 2 July 2013 and 10 June 2015. Hamza is a grape grower who sells his produce for cash in the town square of Güdül. He also has access to off-farm income to supplement his earnings. Halit previously produced for a 'niche' heirloom market through the 'Güdül village products' (Güdül *köy ürünleri*) store in Ankara. He co-owned the store with a friend. As the store did not generate enough income for both families, Halit broke the partnership in 2015. He now produces radishes and lettuce varieties on 4 dekars of land, which Hidayet markets in an Antalya wholesale market but not through a contractual relationship. Nuri employs hired labour, while Hamza and Halit rely on the labour of family members.

Nuri has held GAP certification since 2007; Halit and Hamza are uncertified. All agree that traditional agriculture based on local customary knowledge is the most appropriate way of managing the agroecosystem (cf. Holt-Gimenez and Altieri 2013). As a large-scale commercial farmer, Nuri has chosen formal GAP certification for the monitoring and verification of his product quality through quantifiable and replicable factors. This enables Nuri to incorporate his products into a vertically integrated supply chain, supplying 'certified crops' to high-end supermarkets.

GAP-Certified Large-Scale Production for Supermarkets: Nuri in Beypazarı

Nuri specializes in the production of carrot and lettuce varieties, as well as wheat. He cultivates approximately 4,000 dekars of open-field farmland and employs approximately 100 workers, 15 of whom are salaried. The remainder are seasonal migrant workers from Eastern Turkey. Nuri inherited 58 dekars of farmland from his father and later purchased 420 dekars in the surrounding area. He rents a significant portion of his farm lands from local villagers. As a result, Nuri's farming takes place on a number of fragmented plots scattered throughout the area, which he contends increases his production costs for irrigation, electricity and petroleum. Nuri believes that small landowners should leave agriculture to release more lands and make them available for land consolidation. This would allow for more efficient land use by professional farmers.

Figure 5.1 Nuri (Fasıl, Beypazarı, 20 May 2014).

When I met Nuri in the spring of 2014, I noticed an enlarged copy of his GAP certification hanging on the wall of his farm office. His products are sold in wholesale markets in Antalya, Ankara and İstanbul through first-tier organic-food supplier firms such as ÇEKOK and MANGO and by individual wholesale-market traders, including Hidayet. Hidayet is Nuri's link to a commissioner in the Antalya wholesale market who is also Hidayet's brother and business partner in Eyüp Taş Limited Company. Nuri also produces for large supermarket chains including BİM and MİGROS through contract farming with intermediary supplier firms.

Nuri believes that his production methods are ecologically sustainable yet do not compromise yield and productivity. There are myriad indicators of sustainable agriculture within organic production that suggest different bases for assessing particular aspects of sustainability. They include species conservation and species richness for a variety of organism groups in the local environment, ecological resilience and genetic diversity, biological control of potential pest organisms and other related issues such as soil-nutrient conservation, landscape protection and cultural heritage (Duelli and Obrist 2003, 92; Thompson et al. 2007). Each of these areas requires its own assessment indicators. GAP certification does not provide a means for assessment in any of these areas, but it does offer Nuri greater justification for his selection of customary knowledge-based methods. For example, he regards the use of animal manure as a good indicator of 'soil fertility management' (cf. Forge et al. 2016) and respects it as a long-practiced technique of organic farming that enhances habitat. He further believes that the soil's organic structure is restored through crop rotation and home-made organic fertilizer. Nuri describes how he converts animal manure into compost for soil amendment:

> I only use chicken and cow manure, nothing else. They call me a *bokçu* (shit user) around here. I did not know how to use it properly in the beginning; I thought it was a simple matter of spreading manure on the land. But it hardened my soil so badly. I met a professor … and told him that I have all the machinery and tools but still cannot loosen the soil. It is too hard to mix with the manure and too hard to absorb water so the roots can grow. It was like you could plough the concrete road but not my field. After analyzing the soil, he told me that "your use of untreated chicken manure damaged the soil given to you by Allah" … He gave me instructions on how to combine chicken manure with cow manure, hay, sunflower stalks, and some water. I cover this combination with a large plastic sheet and leave it to rest for some time. This process turns the manure into usable organic fertiliser. He also recommended that I add humic acid to the fertilizer to increase soil aeration and water permeability, as well as to neutralize the acidic effects of the chicken manure … I was also told that I should rest my land for three to four years to restore itself. I listened to his advice: I was able to rest the soil because I have access to lots of land around here through renting. I also practice crop rotation on a

3-year basis. Carrots eat up too many nutrients from the soil. I don't need to kill my soil by continuously producing carrots. I have a large open field. I can easily grow different crops on the same field until the nutrients are restored and ready for carrots again.

(Interview, 26 May 2014)

Nuri uses chemical sprays as a means of pest and weed control. Although he insists that he utilizes appropriate weed-management strategies such as crop sequencing, tillage, organic fertilization, biological control and direct harrowing and hoeing, he argues that the problem is just too great to be managed in such a way. He also claims that the sheer size of his field impedes his ability to fully practice local weed-management strategies. He states: 'Look at this field; it is too large. Weeds are everywhere – as if someone spread seeds from the air by plane. I have no choice but use chemicals, although they don't work well either' (Interview, 26 May 2014).

The specialized commercial agriculture Nuri practices relies heavily on store-purchased certified seeds, including hybrid seeds. The use of certified seeds is required by law for GAP certification. For Nuri, the use of hybrid seeds is counter to locally specific, customary weed-management practices. In addition to the size of his farm, Nuri justifies the use of chemicals by referencing the changes in local farming practices brought about by the use of hybrid seeds. Hybrid seeds affect the overall integrity of the local landscape setting and violate landscape-context factors including natural biodiversity, which in turn play a role in weed proliferation (Barberi 2002; Petit et al. 2016). Although the debate over a yield gap between organic and conventional agriculture is ongoing in the literature (de Ponti et al. 2012), Nuri contends that organic farming must be supplemented by genetic engineering in seed innovation in order to control problematic weeds and diseases that reduce yields.

The relationship between organic agriculture and biotechnology is an important consideration in agro-ecology research (Roland and Adamchak 2008; Tomich et al. 2011). Although public opinion on the subject is highly polarized, Nuri does not view biotechnology and organic agriculture as diametrically opposed. His concern is rather with the fact that technologically engineered certified seeds hamper customary weed-management strategies. He doesn't consider local seeds saved by producers themselves, which are generally not certified by producers and not available commercially. Nuri believes that his dependency on agricultural biotechnology firms increases as long as he practices GAP-certified farming, with potentially damaging consequences for customary farming practices, landscapes and food cultures. He states:

I prefer to purchase seeds from open markets produced by farmers like myself. Open-market seeds are much cheaper. I also prefer to save my own seeds, and I have the ability to do so. Two sacks of seeds come close to 100 kilos. It is not that difficult to generate these seeds and keep them for next year's sowing. My crops ought to be traceable from sowing to sale in the market. I have to produce paperwork to prove the origin of the seeds. I cannot do so for the seeds saved by myself or those purchased in open markets from other villagers. I can certify my own saved seeds, but it is a very long and complicated process ... I have no time to deal with the bureaucracy. You cannot tell supermarkets that you use your own seeds or the ones produced by local farmers. Our old ways of reliance on trustworthy farmers are no longer relevant in the economy ... they only trust me if I have the paperwork, receipts, or certification. In the end, you become dependent on foreign seed and chemical producers to eat the very food in this village, food that I produce here in the same village.

(Interview, 26 May 2014)

In addition to the challenges of formal bureaucratic procedure, Nuri highlights the changing relations of trust in relation to food quality. The continued intermingling of both customary and industrial knowledge systems generates tension between what he knows and assumes to be good about local agricultural methods and the external standards required for marketable varieties. The tension arises from his practice of a profit-oriented professional farming that requires greater specialization in market varieties and the intensive use of industrial inputs for weed and disease control. GAP certification allows him to prove to consumers in both local and distant locations that the conduct and management of his food system is ethically sound, something that can no longer be taken at face value based solely on his personal commitment to a good quality product. Nuri continues:

I can take the lettuce and carrots from my fields to my home without hesitation. This is my only criteria in producing for supermarket chains. I don't need certification for that. I began to implement GAP requirements with the recommendation of MANGO ... They told me that if I wasn't certified, they wouldn't sell my products to MİGROS, BİM, or A-101. I now work with ÇEKOK ... MANGO went bankrupt. ÇEKOK analyzes my food before sending it to the supermarkets. They stamp their findings on the box to show that my food is good. MİGROS can do the same in minutes.

(Interview, 26 May 2014)

Nuri, who supplies large supermarkets through ÇEKOK, undertakes his own on-the-farm testing of chemical residues through the use of an agricultural engineer. Testing is done for residues and plant growth regulators to ensure food safety for human consumption. However, transparency in product-quality disclosure is a contested area, as has been argued by Gupta (2010). This is also the case for water conservation, which receives no attention in Turkey's GAP certification. Nuri confirms this and observes:

I have 50 water wells drilled 200 metres down. Water is pumped by electrical dynamos for sprinkler irrigation. I pump 10,000 tons of water to spray 4,000 dekars of land. Each water-spray nozzle discharges 3 tons of water per hour, 1 ton of which evaporates. There is no possibility that the water will dry up. As long as we are here on this earth, Allah bestows his blessings for abundant sustenance. If the water sources do dry up, we will dry up too. There is no reason for changing my irrigation system to drip watering at the moment. It is too expensive.

(Interview, 26 May 2014)

Nuri prides himself on being respectful of natural processes in production; he endeavours to maintain soil nutrient availability through crop rotation, organic-manure compost application and the use of some customary practices in weed-disease management. On the other hand, Nuri loses one-third of his irrigation water to evaporation and has very low 'water productivity' – defined as the ratio of agricultural output to amount of water consumed (Molden et al. 2009, 528). Moreover, his specialized production and its vertical integration into supermarkets, along with a heavy reliance on water/ energy-intensive inputs, *conventionalize* his farming within GAP-oriented industrial agriculture. This is similar to the conventionalization of organic agriculture seen in other examples, including California (Guthman 2004); England (Kings and Ilbery 2014); Burkina Faso (Laurent et al. 2013); and Australia (Lockie and Halpin 2005).

One Hundred Years of Vineyards for Local Food Production and Organic Artisanal Niche Markets: Hamza and Halit in Karacaören, Güdül

Hamza and Halit pride themselves on producing organic food untainted by energy-intensive agrochemicals such as synthetic fertilizers, pesticides and herbicides. Hamza has no desire to have his grapes formally certified as organic; he believes the more than 100-year natural history of village vineyards is sufficient verification. Halit has applied for GAP certification of his vegetable production and is waiting for accreditation.

According to Hava Yıldırım, the mayor of Güdül:

There are very few of this sort of vineyard left in Turkey. A vineyard with 100 years of history does not need chemicals ... They get their nutrients from the soil and the sun, and have their own disease control mechanisms without any external intervention.

(Interview, 23 June 2013)

Hamza and Halit believe their production methods are ecologically sound and free of the food-safety risks associated with agro-industrial production. The food they produce is ready for immediate consumption through direct marketing at local *pazars* and in artisanal 'niche' markets specializing in village products.

There are no clear-cut definitions and production standards that differentiate those who maintain organic values from those who use the term organic as a market-accessing mechanism (Lockie et al. 2000). In accessing high-end markets, codified standards are often employed to provide consumers with quality assurance of food safety and health benefits (Guthman 2004). This is the case with Nuri, who holds GAP certification; and Halit, who is in the process of receiving accreditation. This approach often marginalizes non-codified agro-ecological values, which include biodiversity preservation, water-energy conservation and the centrality of natural processes in maintaining soil nutrient availability and managing pests and diseases (de Ponti et al. 2012). Hamza's farming practices embody these values; his grape production utilizes customary production methods without codification. Because the grapes grown in these 100-year-old vineyards are completely integral to the local landscape and wholly suited to regional soil and climate conditions, and because local farmers are careful to maintain the original genetic structure of their grape varieties, there is no need for chemical spraying or other industrial inputs.

Hamza and Halit are aware that third-party certification formally codifies consumer trust, rationalizing market-exchange relations long mediated by personal ties. They also appreciate the significance of local history and the reputation of producers whose integrity is central in generating consumer confidence and trust in the food they produce. Trust remains a commonly held, key reference point in describing their production methods as organic, even though there is never a definitive basis or conclusive grounds for trust. It always involves some degree of uncertainty, tied to formal and informal relations of confidence (Sztompka 1999). For Hamza and Halit, informally diffused trust in the quality and marketability of their products is at least as valuable as formal rules of codification.

I haven't found a clear demarcation between non-certified small-scale farmers and large-scale GAP-certified producers in terms of one group or the other being more mindful of agro-ecological processes. This is consistent with research findings by Lockie and Halpin (2005) on the transformation of organic agriculture in Australia. Lockie and Halpin show that there is more commonality among producers in terms of production practices, market linkages and normative values than there is clear bifurcation or polarization. The evidence provided in the narratives of Hamza, Halit and Nuri reveals greater commonality than divergence in relation to the significance of customary ways of producing quality food and maintaining local ecology. They also share an ambivalent attitude toward the actual practices and productivist values of modern industrial agriculture, which they believe make them more dependent on corporate agro-industrial inputs.

The mayor of Güdül, Hava Yıldırım, expresses the connection between food quality and natural heritage, but she also notes the ambivalence resulting from marketing for distant consumers. She states:

> These grapes are well-known in the area. As soon as the producer brings them to the town square for sale, they are gone in a few minutes. We also send some as gifts to the prime minister, cabinet members and other

influential politicians and bureaucrats, to advertise our products and gather support for our local economy. These grapes are not resilient and durable enough to transport to distant markets. If farmers wish to be commercially oriented, they cannot choose the native varieties but ought to opt for hybrid ones.

(Interview, 23 June 2013)

In contrast to the mayor's position on hybrid production for distant markets, Hamza and Halit are proponents of direct marketing for local consumption and regionally established niche markets. Hamza describes the quality of his production in relation to the locale of his vineyard:

These vines in my vineyard are native, in contrast to those hybrid varieties across the field which are propagated by the *ziraat* (Ministry of Agriculture). I don't understand why they planted them here because they don't adapt well in this soil. They won't last long here; it is a waste of time and money. It is *günah* (sinful). Our native varieties include *Çavuş* (white sergeant), *Kadın Parmağı* (lady's finger) ... really good for eating, and *Büzgülü* (ruf-fled pleated). We also have other sweeter cultivars which we use to make molasses. My mother-in-law and my wife make the molasses after harvest in the fall, which we sell to neighbours, friends and relatives in the village and in Güdül ... Everybody knows that our product is clean and organic. They spread the word around. I also sell grape leaves for *dolma* (stuffed grape leaves), which I gather at least four or five times per season. They are silky smooth and lemony delicious ... just perfect for *dolma* with yoghurt and garlic sauce. How can you do any better than that?

(Interview, 23 June 2013)

When explaining the taste and quality of his grapes, Hamza makes an impas-sioned appeal to the senses – the sweetness, smoothness, scent and beauty of the fruit. He describes *Kadın Parmağı* (lady's finger) as a variety that is 'slimmer, longer, red, sweet and fragrant like perfume'. By describing the shape, smell, taste and overall sensuality of a woman's finger, Hamza is able to help awaken the strong emotive attachment to the vineyard and its locality. In calling for an emotional, sense-based connection to place, he rejects externally imposed modifications by unnatural chemicals:

I make sure that I don't destroy the soil. There should be enough air cir-culation: you shouldn't go too deep when ploughing it, nor should you allow the soil to become hardened and dehydrated. Nowadays people are using anchor machines for tillage, which go too deep into the soil. The best tools for the right-amount of digging to aerate the soil are hand-operated tools. I don't use power tools. With my *bel* (ploughshare or hoe) I can get through 20–25 cm, which is adequate for aeration and water penetration in winter, and for better weed management in the summer.

After overturning the soil I use a hand rake to level the soil. I have never had a weed problem.

(Interview, 23 June 2013)

Hamza combines the location/origin of production, the production methods themselves, and the history of crop varieties, along with the sensory experience they evoke, to sustain his 'organic' claims. On the other hand, Halit's claim to be practicing organic agriculture appears to be a substitute for the origin and geographical proximity of his production (cf. Gracia et al. 2014) – in the form of the artisanal niche market he serves. His production methods include a limited amount of chemical use, certified hybrid/biotech seeds and greenhouse-grown seedlings purchased from Ayık Tarım and Bey Fide in Beypazarı. Halit, like Nuri, justifies the use of chemicals for pest control and biotech seeds/seedlings on the grounds of increased yield.

Halit showed me the tomatoes growing in his field. Some of the young seedlings were completely destroyed by a pest known locally as *danaburnu* (*gryllotalpa gryllotalpa*). He showed me one of the pests, about 4 cm long, and said:

> *Danaburnu* eats the plant's root, and then the seedling drops dead. A few *danaburnu* can destroy an entire crop. It takes 50 days for one tomato seed to grow into a seedling: 40 days in the greenhouse and 10 days in my field. If I don't get rid of this pest, all my money and effort will be wasted. I have to use chemicals. Actually, there is another way to deal with this pest. You can wrap the roots of the young plant with walnut leaves, and then plant the seedling. But, this is a very time-consuming method. I have only myself and my son working in this field. I could allow chickens into the field to eat these pests, but the chickens would also destroy my tomatoes. I do care about the negative effects of this chemical on the soil, so I try to lessen its impact by combining it with wheat bran, and spreading it only where I grow tomatoes.
>
> (Interview, 2 July 2013)

The cow manure used widely in the village is part of the reason for the proliferation of *danaburnu* in the area. Halit explains:

> I produce my own fertiliser. I gather about 10 trucks of cow manure from the barns in the village, and spread it over the field in spring. *Danaburnu* also loves this manure. As a result, I have to accept the fact that I must apply some chemicals to kill the *danaburnu*.
>
> (Interview, 2 July 2013)

Halit severed his partnership with the 'village products' store in Ankara in 2015 after the store went bankrupt. This signals a break in his production linkages with local/regional markets, tying his production to a vertical linkage through

Figure 5.2 Halit (Karacaören, Güdül, 17 June 2015).

the mediation of Hidayet, who acts as a supplier for the Antalya wholesale market. The newly established vertical supply link forces Halit to pay closer attention to the commercial viability of his products and the dictates of industrial standardization. He explains:

> We save seeds from our own native varieties, as most people do in the village. And we eat village-style food at home; I also used to sell it in my artisan food shop. But, İstanbul and Ankara ladies will not buy this food. It doesn't look attractive at the table. If you want to sell food, you have to produce standardized varieties ... it must look good at the table.
>
> (Interview, 10 June 2015)

According to Halit, farmers purchase biotech seeds and greenhouse-grown seedlings to make sure that their crops conform to the standards expected for mass consumption. This is a new pattern that intensifies the 'tension' Halit experiences due to the disappearance of local customary ways and the increase in vertically integrated commercial production. He explains that the close proximity of his artisanal store to his farm, only 90 km, strengthened the local aspect of his organic production. He said: 'I would collect my crops early in the morning and immediately transport them with my own pick-up truck to the shop in Ankara in about one hour'. An important component of this local connection was his ability to use crop rotation to produce seasonal food, as well as his daily access to fresh raw milk. Halit elaborates:

My small store offered organic food. I used to sell seasonally grown vegetables and fruits. I never tried to sell cherries or eggplants in winter. My customers didn't come to me to buy watermelon in winter, but rather, cauliflower … they knew that it is simply absurd to buy summer crops in winter. I also used to sell organic raw milk, fresh daily in my store. I had 15 cows, which I still have. I would use their manure as fertiliser and sell their milk in my store. I was never a specialized producer. I had customers who would not buy food from supermarkets because they didn't trust supermarket food; but they trusted me … they knew that I was a clean, organic producer … I also worked together with a friend from the village to sell organic raw milk from door to door in Ankara neighbourhoods. I am still doing this. I and my friend have all the necessary equipment to milk the cows in sanitary conditions. We sell approximately 1 ton of milk every day, packaged in plastic 5 litre jars. It works in an informal way. We have the phone numbers and addresses of our customers. In addition to the milk, they buy seasonally grown vegetables and fruits in this door-to-door way. This is how I make my living.

(Interview, 10 June 2015)

Halit's father, whom I interviewed during my latest visit to Halit's farm on 10 June 2015, is convinced that the era of traditional, ecologically sound farming practices is over. For him, this has little to do with being more 'modern' in agriculture per se (cf. Kaltoft 2001); it is necessitated by a specific sectoral shift from subsistence-based food production to commercial fresh fruits and vegetables (FFV) production, which requires intensive, input-dependent farming. He observes:

I am 79 years old. I have never worked for someone else, only for myself and the family. I still work in my son's field every day from 6 am to evening. I am now harvesting radishes here. I have always been my own task master. In the past we would cultivate these fields to grow wheat and barley, using a single iron blade pulled by oxen, which does no harm to the soil. We now have lots of machinery, which allows us to cultivate smaller plots for more food. They call it intensive agriculture … more efficient. Wheat does not make money any longer … people want to make more money by growing fruits and vegetables on small plots of lands. They use more fertilizers and water, machines and store-purchased seeds. I don't like it, but that's how it is now. It is all about how to produce more … To produce more, we use chicken manure. It is really rich in nutrients, but it turns the soil into rock. We use cow manure too, but it generates so many weeds that you cannot even enter the field. So, we use chemicals to kill weeds. It is a vicious circle, but they won't go back to the old ways either … The old ways are over now.

(Interview, 10 June 2015)

In response to his father's complaint that increasing productivity through the use of fertilizers and chemicals turns the soil into a 'rock', Halit reminded him that he 'takes care' of the soil, that he rests it by practicing crop rotation and diverse seasonal production, by combining crop and livestock production and by using organic manure as fertilizer. For Halit, the challenge does not arise from whether he can adhere to agro-ecological values and natural processes; it stems from the 'impossibility' of being completely outside industrial farming, which relies on the appropriation and misuse of nature, energy-intensive chemicals, mechanization and standardization of products. Halit explained, for example, that carrots can be effectively rotated with onions and spinach up to seven times within a 14-year period. After 14 years, production has to move elsewhere as the soil *must* rest for a while. For this to happen, a farmer has to have access to large tracts of land or switch to producing something else. 'Since I don't have 4,000 dekars of land, I can only practice limited rotation. If Hidayet wants carrots from me, the danger I face is that my soil will become nutrient deficient, and I will be doomed' (Interview, 10 June 2015).

Halit's point about his lack of access to large tracts of land raises questions concerning the locational characteristics of customary production and whether they contribute to the integrity of landscape structures and biodiversity. This is an ongoing debate in current scholarship (Bengtsson et al. 2005; Kings and Ilbery 2014; Lockie and Halpin 2005).

The farms worked by the small-scale farmers I interviewed are surrounded by naturally formed heterogeneous landscapes of non-cropped areas made up of field margins, hedge-rows and natural pastures. Farmers associate productive areas with crop production and consider the natural surroundings as surplus lands freely available for crop rotation. Although crop rotation is important for building soil fertility, farmers often use the practice to expand their production into previously uncultivated non-crop areas. This is not consistent with an awareness of naturally existing heterogeneous landscapes as an important component of biodiversity (cf. Belfrage et al. 2015; Duelli and Obrist 2003; Petit et al. 2016). Nuri practices GAP-certified farming on large-scale monoculture plots that extend into a natural area used for crop rotation. While this is not a concern for Hamza, who in fact may be contributing to greater biodiversity in the area, Halit appears to be more anxious about the shifting spatial patterns of his production linkages.

There is considerable heterogeneity and diversity in the narratives of farmers, who both conform to, and diverge from, agro-industrial methods of production. This reduces our ability to make a clear distinction between organic and conventional farmers in relation to the locality, scale and style of farming, as well as the associated value orientations and motivations of farmers (Kings and Ilbery 2014; Lockie and Halpin 2005). Below, I provide an empirical illustration of the diffusion of agro-industrial perspectives among small-scale producers who make no claims to being organic.

Small-Scale Conventional Producers

The control of pests, weeds and disease, and conformity with industrial quality standards, are central to the yield increases and marketability of products associated with the conventional industrial model. The way in which small-scale producers actually embrace techno-scientific innovation and industrial productivist perspectives in agriculture remains an empirical question (Cheyns and Riisgaard 2014; James and Sulemana 2014; Jonsson et al. 2014). In the following section, I detail the range of experiences described by farmers from the villages of Karacaören, Kamanlar and Çağa in the Güdül region of Ankara; and from the village of Savcılı Büyükoba, Kaman, in Kırşehir.

Self-Reliance: Ramiz and Bilal in Karacaören, Güdül

Ramiz is a 50-year-old man who cultivates approximately 100 dekars of land; 35 were inherited from his father and the rest were purchased. He does not rent land, nor does he expand into the surrounding areas for crop rotation. Ramiz owns one of the two cold-storage facilities in the village; Hidayet owns the other. It has two rooms with a 70-ton storage capacity. Ramiz calls Hidayet the *ağa* (translates roughly as the 'landlord') of the village because he is the largest commercial farmer and agro-trader in the area. Ramiz has linkages with the İstanbul wholesale market through a commissioner. He has neither GAP certification nor contract-based direct connections to supermarkets. I met and interviewed Ramiz on his farm on 17 May 2013.

Ramiz has farmed since he was 11 years old, together with his father who, in the past, would take him to İstanbul *pazars* to sell the watermelons that his family grew in the village. He relies completely on the labour of family members, including his wife, and four children who are university students. Self-reliance is the key defining feature of his family's commercial farming activities. Ramiz states:

> We are trying to live solely by our own means [*kendi yağımızla kavruluyoruz*] without any outside help. We do not aim to earn more. What we have achieved so far is enough for us. There is no need to be greedy. There is nothing that we can take with us to the other side when we pass away.
>
> (Interview, 17 May 2013)

Ramiz and his family grow artichokes, beets, red and white cabbage, apples, grapes and quince, in addition to wheat and barley. Their grain production is rain fed, and the water for their fruit and vegetables is pumped from the Kirmir River, 2.5 km away. Ramiz does not describe himself as an organic producer. Still, he is engaged in building soil fertility by rotating the production of vegetables on a yearly basis, without expanding into the surrounding landscape. If he plants vegetables one year, he switches to grains the following year to rest the soil and restore its organic matter. He uses animal manure obtained from friends' barns in the village, and he prefers to manage weeds by hoeing rather than using chemicals. In short, Ramiz' production methods share many of the characteristics of organic agriculture.

Ramiz grows quince varieties that are native to Turkey, but his grapes and apples are hybrid. His brand-name commercial apple varieties include Fuji,

Gala, Jonagold and Golden Delicious; his table grapes include Italian white, Asos and Yalova Pearl. With the exception of artichokes, for which there are no industrially improved hybrid varieties, Ramiz's vegetable production depends entirely on industrial seeds and greenhouse-grown seedlings, which he purchases from Ayık Tarım and Bey Fide in Beypazarı. Ramiz states:

> I can produce native, field-grown tomatoes and sell a few kilos of them locally. Some will sell because they taste very good, but what will happen to the rest? You cannot keep those tomatoes even for two days after harvesting, they will go mushy. F1 bunch-tomato seedlings can keep for at least 15 days on the shelf.
>
> (Interview, 17 May 2013)

Ramiz believes that small producers can no longer survive the ongoing changes in agriculture:

> In the past we had no fear of being unable to sell our products. There were at least three or four commissioning traders who would come to the village and collect our produce for sale in the wholesale markets. Those traders are now producers, traders and wholesale commissioners all at the same time. Hidayet is an example. They don't need to deal with the small amount of produce grown by small farmers. Trader–commissioner–producers also rent land from villagers and continually expand their production. This is resulting in the death of small-scale production in Turkey.
>
> (Interview, 17 May 2013)

According to Ramiz, large-scale producers who combine separate food-provisioning functions play a pivotal role in the current trend toward monopolization of production – a trend that is undermining customary village-based ways. Ramiz suggests that small-scale producers can counter this trend through more direct, contractual relations with supermarkets. However, this is difficult, and as a result, many of these smaller producers become wage labourers in food-related areas:

> Contract farming may guarantee markets for the producer. But, supermarkets don't want to have crops for only four months during the summer; they want to have the same produce 12 months of the year. I can supply markets for up to eight months since I have cold storage. Each type of produce has a maximum storage time: beets can keep for a year, carrots for a very long time, apples can keep for four months, but red cabbage cannot wait. As long as you can afford to pay the electricity costs and build a cold-storage room, you can work with supermarkets. Small producers cannot afford these costs in Turkey. As a result, monopoly control in agriculture by trader-commissioners expands ... The possibility for producers to organize a producers' union is slim ... In my village most small producers

have abandoned agriculture and migrated to İstanbul to work in *pazars*, food processing factories or the grocery department of supermarkets. For example, they can work in an artichoke peeling factory, and earn 10 *kuruş* per artichoke. If someone peels 1,000 artichokes a day, and works 2–3 months in that factory, he can earn approximately TL 8,000, which is probably more than what he would earn as a producer in the village.

(Interview, 17 May 2013)

Bilal is another small producer in Karacaören whom I interviewed on 29 April 2012. Bilal agrees with Ramiz that an approach focusing on *self-reliance* can counter monopolization, provided producers can afford it. Bilal grows hybrid varieties of commercial apples, grapes and watermelon on 55 dekars of land. The trees and vines are grown from certified saplings, which he purchased from Güdül Agriculture. Bilal was a vegetable and grain-producing farmer in the past, rotating crops on a 3–4-year cycle. He has now completely shifted to fruit production because he no longer sees the previous line of production as profitable. For Bilal, small-scale commercial fruit production does not require the intermediary of agro-traders; hence, it offers greater earning opportunities for farmers. Bilal sells most of his produce informally in the Güdül market square because the townfolk know him and trust the safety and quality of his products.

Horizontal Differentiation, Localized Competition: Musa and Mustafa in Kamanlar, Güdül

Musa and Mustafa are brothers whom I interviewed on 2 May and 15 June 2014 in their farmhouse by the Kirmir River in Güdül. Musa is 40 years old and Mustafa 45. They produce lettuce, beans, peppers, cucumbers, tomatoes and eggplants for spring and summer sales; and leaks, spinach, radishes and carrots for winter. They have approximately 300 cherry and mulberry trees and a number of grapevines – each variety ripening in succession. Musa and Mustafa's mother oversees the production of milk, which Mustafa sells daily in the *pazars* alongside their vegetables and fruit. Musa is responsible for production and marketing in Güdül; Mustafa is responsible solely for marketing. He sells the food produced by Musa in *pazars* in Sincan[2] and surrounding neighbourhoods such as Yenikent and Törekent in Ankara. Surplus produce that is not sold in the *pazars* is sold in the Ankara wholesale market through a commissioner. The brothers own a cold-storage facility with a 200-ton capacity in Sincan.

Musa and Mustafa grow vegetables on 80 dekars of land, 20 of which they own. They have access to state-owned public lands by the river at no cost, and in return for their use of privately owned land they give a portion of their crops to the owners – who allow them to cultivate the otherwise untended land. The practice of cultivating state-owned public lands and private lands without cost is common in small towns and villages in Central Anatolia. It is also the case for Zübeyir from the village of Savcılı Büyükoba in Kaman, whom I discuss

Figure 5.3 Musa (Kamanlar, Güdül, 21 May 2014).

later in the chapter. Musa and Mustafa's access to private lands through informal sharecropping arrangements is sometimes conflictual due to the owners'
arbitrary profit-seeking behaviour (Atasoy 2016, 18). The brothers usually give
the owners a few kilos of their produce in exchange for use of the land.

The lands cultivated by the brothers are broken into small plots spread over
3 km², from the lowlands of the Kirmir River uphill approximately 40 meters,
then up another 100 meters in elevation to the scenic caves near the river. The
high elevation and fragmented land plots make irrigation difficult because the
water must be pumped by dynamo from the river through pipes and then onto
the land. Almost 4 km of irrigation pipes were installed over 10 years at a cost
close to TL 20,000. Musa and Mustafa don't have to pay for the water drawn
from the river, but it costs approximately TL 5,000 per season for the electricity used to pump the water.

The brothers use sprinklers rather than drip watering for irrigation. They
have no intention of changing their method of irrigation, even though their
use of sprinklers results in considerable water loss from evaporation. They justify this waste by explaining:

> You must use a sprinkler system for herbaceous plants such as spinach and
> lettuce. For other plants with wider roots such as cucumbers you can use
> drip irrigation. But, it is too expensive to set up two systems for different
> crop varieties.

(Interview, 2 May 2014)

Musa offers an explanation for why his father switched from dry to irrigation-based agriculture some 30 years ago:

> These are drylands, not suitable for vegetable production. My father and grandfather grew wheat and barley here in the past, and raised cows as well. As technology developed and improved, water engines became more widely available to pump water from the river. With the financial help of the water users' co-operative my father purchased a water engine to irrigate the land and then grow sugar-beets. We even sacrificed a sheep to celebrate having the engine, and held a festive dinner for a large group of people whom we invited to the ceremony. It was like a great picnic in the hills. However, the engine was not strong enough to pump water to a higher elevation. But I remember – we were just kids, and so happy that we could irrigate up to 150 meters in elevation.
>
> (Interview, 2 May 2014)

Since the project was successful, the cooperative promoted irrigation-based agriculture in the area, using Musa and Mustafa's father as an example. The co-operative has now been suspended; the membership has dwindled and the remaining members do not want to pay their membership fees. Mustafa notes: 'A Güdüllite does not like to work but would rather sit in the coffee shop in the town square. Why should they be a member of the co-operative?' (Interview, 2 May 2014). Musa adds:

> They invented a variety of reasons for not paying their membership fees. Some said they did not get enough water; others said they never got water; some said the fee is too high ... Initially the co-op had 60 members; it now has only 10 or 15 ... There is now greater technological capacity to pump water from the river to farms that are 500 to 600 meters high in elevation. But people are not interested in farming anymore. They say there is no money in it; in reality people here are lazy and prefer to sit in the coffee shop rather than work. It is only the people from Kamanlar like us who will do agricultural work in Güdül.
>
> (Interview, 2 May 2014)

Mustafa details the local nature of their production and its close connection to the local Güdül produce market as a 'natural' process, which changed after irrigation was introduced:

> Our production began with two donkeys and a horse. We ploughed the land with our horse and carried the crops to the Güdül town square on our donkeys. We produced tomatoes, cucumbers and peppers. I remember the cucumbers we grew then. They were really big and juicy. After the donkeys were loaded, my father used to say: "my son, take the load to Güdül." I wasn't even able to reach the donkey's belly at that time but

I was expected to push the donkey up-hill from the river to an elevation of 500 meters and then make the push down to Güdül. He used to say "Don't worry son. Once you take it to Güdül square, they will help you to unload the crops." The whole crop at that time was two boxes of tomatoes and two or three large bags of cucumbers. I used to cry when the donkeys refused to move. There was no road, just a stony path covered by thorny shrubs. I used to be so embarrassed as a boy coming by donkey from the village to town.

(Interview, 15 June 2014)

The brothers happily recount their daily life during those past times. Their lives were governed by the mundane but were joyfully experienced nonetheless. For Mustafa, the memories so fondly remembered now become a kind of cultural catalyst or tool for awakening what amounts to a 'natural history of the senses':

We used to work in the field during the day and take a load of produce to the Güdül *pazar* the following day at 5 am. We were just sleepy kids. I remember going to the *pazar* on our donkey … I would fall asleep and then fall off the donkey as it was climbing the hill … Those were the days!

(Interview, 15 June 2014)

There is a rich historical sensory experience concealed in the seeds that were saved in the past for the commercial production of local food. Mustafa explains how the purchase of industrially designed seeds forever altered this experience:

We used to harvest our own seeds from the crops we grew. We only began to purchase seeds much later. Everything is calculated now … the germination percentage and the yield percentage. When I was a kid, I could only carry one cucumber in my arms. It was huge, very juicy, fresh and great-smelling. When you slice these new varieties, there is no water dripping; they are like spongy meat. The reason for the switch from good to bad is simply money. Now you can produce much more and earn much more. In the past, you got 1 ton of traditional cucumbers from 1 dekar of land, now you can get 4 or 5 tons. I make a profit for sure, but I also spend more money for chemicals. And the money I spend on these inputs is enough to sustain the livelihood of a poor family.

(Interview, 15 June 2014)

I asked Mustafa why he switched to hybrid seeds if he ended up spending so much of his profit on the purchase of inputs. His explanation is insightful:

It is all about image! Image is indispensable to selling. The vegetables at the stall have to look absolutely fantastic. If I place a traditional style, large cucumber in my vegetable stall at the *pazar* and try to sell it, customers will not even look at it. I remember when my grandfather used to grow those old-style heavy cucumbers. And I remember trying to carry one … It was so heavy … I fell into the ditch and got all muddy. Similarly, the green beans of Kızılcahamam region were known as the Kızılcahamam stick variety, the very best. They've all disappeared. Some villagers from Kızılcahamam still sow them for their own families' consumption. But, you won't find them sold commercially. The same with heirloom tomatoes; in the past you could smell their aroma from far away. They have totally disappeared and been replaced by hybrid seed tomatoes. They *look* good but there is nothing else exciting about them.

(Interview, 15 June 2014)

Musa and Mustafa have a greenhouse in the village, which is used by their mother to grow native varieties of cucumber and tomato. They believe that these varieties, which they grow exclusively for their own consumption, taste much better than their commercial counterparts. The brothers cultivate hybrid varieties for commercial sale only. They generally prefer to plant seedlings purchased from Bey Fide in Beypazarı. Each seedling costs 5 *kuruş*, which is expensive, but the brothers explain that they have no time to grow their own seedlings. As commercial farmers, they are fully integrated into the process of industrial agriculture. Their fundamental operating principle is simple: 'To earn more, you need to produce more'. Still, the brothers often mention their personal preference for the superior taste of local heirloom varieties from their childhood years, not only as a nostalgic memory but as a possibility for contemporary innovation.

Musa and Mustafa give great significance to the combination of soil, climate and water in Güdül, which they believe creates very supportive microclimatic conditions for a strong agriculture. They note that watermelon, which is sometimes currently grafted on to pumpkin plants, is generally considered to be less tasty, aromatic and colourful than the traditional Diyarbakır or Adana varieties. But they grow it nonetheless because the profit margin is higher, due to its heavy weight and the resilience of the fruit in relation to certain viruses. They believe that pumpkin-grafted watermelon can also achieve good taste if it is grown in Güdül. There is no need, they say, to be categorical in choosing between the traditional and hybrid varieties or between the folk varieties or landraces and techno-scientific ways of improving plant varieties. They insist that both varieties can be grown as long as research-based innovation is carried out in a socially and ecologically responsible manner – to ensure that farmers can grow regionally and climatically suitable crops with a significant degree of diversity. For Musa and Mustafa, irresponsible innovation is an assault on the senses of the growers and the landscape itself. For example, they point out that a hybrid variety of cherries known as Agriculture-900 (*Ziraat 900*), which they themselves have planted, has neither the cultural nor the ecological basis to be successfully grown in Güdül. Musa states:

I planted 150 *Ziraat 900* cherry trees 10 years ago … I paid TL 1,000 for them, but I couldn't even harvest 1 ton of cherries from them. Güdül has a native variety known as *Yarımca*, with an amazing taste and incredible aroma, which is also highly productive. But its fruit is too watery and soft; it doesn't last the journey to the *pazar*. Also, it is small and looks pinkish, not a very attractive appearance. You have to pick the cherries from the tree and eat them almost immediately. We keep these trees for ourselves. The *Ziraat 900* fruit is large, has a bright red colour, and looks very attractive in the stall. It might be productive elsewhere, in Manisa maybe, but not here. I am planning to graft something else onto the *Ziraat 900* trees.

(Interview, 15 June 2014)

Interestingly, Musa and Mustafa also contend that local agro-ecological conditions can no longer be relied upon to optimize the yield potential of crops without industrial inputs. Rather than practise 'agro-ecological peasant agriculture' (Holt-Gimenez and Altieri 2013, 93), they prefer to see a better match between biotech varieties and local landscape conditions as a means of increasing yields. Musa declares:

The natural balance has already been destroyed. When we grew those traditional cucumbers in my childhood, we didn't have to deal with these new insects. The pests are already here, introduced by the hybrid seeds. Our native crops cannot resist the new diseases because they were not exposed to them in the past. We should stop pretending; the old-style agriculture is dead.

(Interview, 15 June 2014)

The agro-industrial farming that the brothers now practice confines their choices to technologically defined and differentiated product characteristics, including image appeal. This is typical of what Lancaster (1966) calls 'horizontal differentiation' in conventional production. The brothers choose seeds that exhibit commercially desirable product characteristics that consumers expect to see in vegetable stalls. 'Horizontal differentiation' helps them to sell their crops in *pazars* alongside other commercial varieties that look 'close' to theirs in relation to product characteristics. This is called 'localized competition', according to Merel and Sexton (2011, 261). The brothers typify this commercial marketing pattern, commonly practiced among other conventionally oriented producers, both small and large scale.

My interviews with producers from the village of Çağa in Güdül and Savcılı Büyükoba in Kaman provide examples of small-scale vegetable production with no obvious commercial rivals for localized competition. These producers cultivate heirloom market crops and enter into a marketing pattern without competing against conventional varieties. Nonetheless, they do not entirely refrain from the production of conventional hybrid varieties.

Discovery of Forgotten Heirlooms: Çağa in Güdül and Savcılı Büyükoba in Kaman

In the example of Çağa in Güdül, I examine the geographical indication (GI) patenting of local heirloom tomatoes. This allows me to pose questions concerning shifting relations in the spatiality of rights from the collective local level to individualized patented rights, and whether this shift entails new production linkages between local heirlooms and extra-local supply chains. Emerging tensions are also explored in relation to the livelihood concerns of farmers that may be intensified by such linkages. The village of Savcılı Büyükoba in Kaman provides a comparative example, allowing me to contrast the GI patenting of heirloom tomatoes in Çağa with another path of production in which traditional varieties are grown without GIs. In contrast to the individualization of patent rights in Çağa, farmers in Savcılı Büyükoba are the collective keepers of local heirloom seeds, which they exchange with other farmers. Farmers in both villages produce for urban, street-level niche markets in Ankara, which are created individually and nurtured through an appeal to participatory certification by consumers.

Production is on a small scale in both villages, designed for commercial sale through the informally established urban-consumer networks of street vendors and neighbourhood *pazars*. Producers have intermittent formal marketing connections with agro-traders. Production is also labour intensive and generally relies on hired labour supported by household family members, with the exception of Zübeyir (and Burhan) in Savcılı Büyükoba, who regularly employs hired labour. Much existing literature refers to the use of household labour in small-scale production as a distinguishing characteristic of 'subsistence' (Hall 2009) or 'semi-subsistence' farming (Aliber et al. 2009). My case examples illustrate that small-scale household-labour intensive farming is a commercially oriented type of production specializing in FFVs, which also employs workers. Farmers maintain livestock for commercial milk production and as a source of producing organic fertiliser. They do not reject industrialized agriculture. In actuality, they wish to be better incorporated into its commercial dimension.

Heirloom Tomatoes and Geographical Indications: Çağa, Güdül

On 12 June 2012, I held a meeting in the village of Çağa. Participants included Muzaffer Yalçın, then Mayor of Çağa and current president of the Güdül branch of the AKP; Hava Yıldırım, the current Mayor of Güdül and then-elected official of the Ankara Special Provincial Administration; and four farmers from the village. On a separate occasion (5 May 2011) I interviewed another producer from the village in a coffee shop in Güdül.

A particular heirloom variety known as the 'Çağa tomato' has a special place in the farming history of the village and is now protected under the GI denomination of origin regulation. The Mayor of Çağa has formally patented this variety under his name through Turkey's 'Protection of Geographical

Indications' legislation of 1995 (No. 555).[3] The legislation harmonizes Turkey's GI regulation with the relevant international treaties of intellectual property rights (IPRs) related to agriculture, including the Paris Convention, the Word Trade Organisation's TRIPS, and the EU's GI protection regulation.[4] The GI designation emphasizes the traceability, consistency and enforceability of formally established private product-quality standards as linked to the specificity of a geographical area, as Bowen (2010) explains in the case of GI-designated tequila in Mexico.

The mayor was motivated to patent the Çağa tomato by the new whole-sale market law of 2010, which requires designation of the crop's geographical origin on the product label when sold in wholesale markets. My meeting with the two mayors and the producers allowed me to explore a number of issues: (1) the shifting relations of control over long-held customary knowledge systems in regard to seed-saving of this heirloom variety, as well as the conservation of biodiversity for this particular crop and its production methods; (2) the level of bureaucratic involvement and the private appropriation of plant genetic resources; (3) the compatibility of GI protection for conservation agriculture; and (4) possibilities for enforcing product quality standards through cross-breeding and plant improvement.

At the meeting, farmers and the local political elite expressed interest in expanding commercial production in the village through GI protection of heirloom tomatoes. This prospect seems contrary to a general scholarly expectation that heirloom-seed savers, who are often comprised of independent gardeners and small-scale farmers, serve as an antidote to the mono-cultural production practised by industrial agriculture (Bocci 2009; Bocci and Chable 2009; Nazarea 2005), and that 'peasant farming systems' persist outside of, and/ or as a barrier to, capitalized agriculture (Edelman 2000; McMichael 2008; van der Ploeg 2013). In actual fact, farmers in the village are not driven to preserve 'peasant farming systems'. They are cognizant that the heirloom seeds are planted in their *terroir* (loosely translated as 'land' or territory) (Bowen 2010) and have evolved in ecological harmony with the conditions of the village. The seeds merely need to be improved for commercial use through research in the life sciences, a goal that the mayor strongly supports.

The mayor's political–bureaucratic role is the key institutional and power barrier to the establishment of 'conservation variety' tied to producers' rural innovations (Bocci and Chable 2009, 81) – as distinguished from the industrial seed systems under IPR and GI patents protection. This 'power play' on the part of the mayor reflects the belief, generally supported by research, that small producers who save heirloom seeds and pass along native varieties are often too weak to influence policy and prevent the corporate development of new agricultural technologies (James and Sulemana 2014). The weakness is largely attributed to the marginality of these small producers in the cultural framework of an industrial agriculture (Nazarea 2005) and their generally low socio-economic status and power in society (J. Friedmann 1992), as well as an already existing multitude of political and institutional power barriers that exist in food provisioning systems (Nelson and Tallontire 2014). In Çağa, farmers' marginality and weakness is evident in the GI protection application process, which generally requires substantial bureaucratic and economic resources. Acting on that weakness, the mayor was able to mobilize the required resources through the authority of his office and personal political–bureaucratic connections. Nevertheless, small producers in Çağa persist in maintaining the diversity of their crops, which have no commercial substitute in the markets. They also continue to nurture their informal marketing networks as a protective barrier against the dominant ethos of industrial developmentalism.

Patenting the Çağa Heirloom Tomato: Divergent Approaches to Commercialization

The population of Çağa is approximately 2,000, about half of which works in agriculture. The village contains 100,000 dekars of land; 1,000 are residential and the remainder agricultural. Approximately 10 per cent of agricultural land is irrigated for production of tomatoes, cucumbers, eggplants and beets. The balance is dedicated to rain-fed dry agricultural production of wheat, barley, chickpeas, sunflowers and corn. According to the mayor, both Çağa and Güdül were part of the municipality of Ayaş (a nearby town in Ankara) until 1957. The village's crops came to be commonly known as Ayaş crops, including their heirloom tomato variety. It is in the policy-implementation context of the new wholesale market law, which requires designations of origin for traceability of product quality, that the mayor took the initiative to place the Çağa heirloom tomato under GI protection.

Çağa also grows F1 hybrids from seedlings produced by Bey Fide in Beypazarı. These hybrid varieties are still known and sold as Ayaş tomatoes, although they are not necessarily genetically related to the heirloom variety. For the mayor, GI labelling is most important for the market position and reputation of village crops, particularly in relation to taste and nutritional quality. In localizing the tomatoes, the mayor does not differentiate between the village's own heirloom and commercially available F1 hybrid varieties. The mayor appears to have fallen into the 'local trap' (Brosius 2006; Carroll and Fahy 2014) – flexibly associating the localness of food with spatially defined 'geographical proximity' (Boschma 2005) and the micro-ecological growing conditions of the area. The mayor valorizes the landscape structure and agro-ecological conditions of the village at the expense of cognitive, historical and social aspects of knowledge creation established over generations with the heirloom varieties. For him, the distinctness of product quality is in Çağa's unique micro-climatic conditions and soil structure, factors that require enhancement through further research. He notes:

> Two firms, one from Israel and the other from the Netherlands, examined the climatic conditions here over a 4-year period. They found a unique microclimate over an area of the village which covers about 10,000 dekars.

The village is situated in a valley, walled on both sides by high hills. There is a unique landscape corridor in the middle, connecting the fertile soils of Ankara, all the way from Nallıhan in the north-west and Beypazarı in the west to Güdül and beyond. In addition, Çağa is situated at a point 600 meters in elevation, similar to Beypazarı at 650 meters elevation, much more favourable for agriculture compared to Karacaören, for example, at 1,000 meters elevation. It is also 6–7 degrees warmer in winter and cooler in summer than Ankara in general. The pH level of the soil is very good and rich, with a well-balanced mineral composition that includes potassium and magnesium. The average number of sunny days is 267, according to the meteorology reports of the last 20 years. We are also blessed with water from the nearby İlhan River, a creek and a number of artesian wells. We have thermal hot springs which can be used for greenhouse production as well. In short, we have a perfect climate, excellent soil structure and good water sources for the growth of large-scale commercial agriculture in the village.

(Interview, 12 June 2012)

Economic considerations are foremost in the mayor's valuation of the agro-ecological and landscape conditions of the area, which include his wish to increase the area under irrigation and improve water productivity through precision irrigation techniques.[5] His fervent desire is to see its local crops fully integrated into commercial agriculture. The mayor sees GI protection as a local economic development strategy that would appear to reinforce the power position of the municipal elite in their efforts to expand an industrial farming imaginary (cf. Dupuis and Goodman 2005). The mayor's appropriation of heirloom ownership through GI patent breaks the bundle of collective rights once held by the community and individuates ownership (cf. Kay 2016). This is ignored in the celebratory claims of those who emphasize the locality of heirloom food. The mayor describes the process:

There was this man who inherited a *kerpiç* house[6] in the village from his father who passed away. When the son was demolishing the house about 15 years ago, to build a more modern house, he found a sun-dried pumpkin container in the house, which held some tomato seeds wrapped in newspaper. This man had obviously saved the seeds for future use. We call these pumpkin containers 'salt pumpkins' (*tuz kabağı*) because they are ideal for keeping salt ... they have humidity-absorbing qualities ... so these old seeds kept well in the container. We sowed these seeds, half of which germinated and produced tomatoes. We immediately realized that these were our native tomatoes. I personally applied to the Turkish Patent Institute of the Ministry of Industry, and registered the patent rights of this variety under my name. For registration, you first declare that you are the producer and breeder of the variety. The declaration is then published on the website of the Institute to make sure there is no counter-claim for ownership of the seeds. I now have the name rights for this heirloom Çağa tomato. As a gift I gave some seedlings of this tomato to the heirloom-vegetable garden of the Museum of Anatolian Civilizations in Ankara. … I am planning to distribute potted seedlings of this variety to apartment dwellers in Ankara for balcony gardens. I want people to get accustomed to the smell, aroma and taste of these Çağa tomatoes. I have also met with the minister of agriculture, seeking certification of the seeds as an heirloom variety. I was told that the seeds need to be analyzed in a government-run lab before their inclusion in the global genes bank. This is a very long process which takes 4–5 years. I haven't started the process yet, but I will.

(Interview, 12 June 2012)

Although it is local farmers who originally developed the cultivar, their role in its development is forgotten. The patenting process will result in the 'disappearance of the variety' as a landrace, meaning that the ownership rights of the mayor will last in perpetuity. This undermines open access rights to the seeds and severs the landrace from its local cultural, historical context. In the long run, this process will remove farmers' economic control over their production and seed development. Further, it will valorize the locality dimension of heirloom varieties and foster commercialization in terms of cultural heritage and 'geographical proximity' of ecological resources. It also appeals to extra-local markets and reinforces a context of diminished opportunities for rebuilding local foods through collective enhancement of farmers' capacities (Bowen and De Master 2014; Demossier 2011).

Turkey's GI legislation allows individuals to patent food crops for GI protection through an application to the Turkish Patents Institute, which declares that they are the producers and breeders of the variety (Article 7). However, the legislation does not have a specific provision for farmers' own collective innovations and crop-related skills on the local, village level. Privatization through GI regulation eventually 'dispossesses' villagers from communal ownership and customary use rights over seeds and plant breeding. Interestingly, none of the producers at our discussion table questioned the mayor's role as private owner of their heirloom through GI rights. Their silence suggests an unwillingness to challenge the mayor and a lack of awareness regarding the internet-based certification process, as well as a poor understanding of the future implications of private ownership rights.

I asked the mayor and the producers how they determined that the seeds belonged to an authentic heirloom variety, given that no one has the knowledge of when and how the variety was bred and cultivated in the village. Yaşar, who is a milk producer and livestock farmer, observes:

We know people who still grow this variety in their fields. You need to be here when it ripens to appreciate how different it is from the hybrid varieties in terms of colour, smell and taste. You will immediately know that it is distinct. I myself used to grow this variety until 1995–96. Was there something called a hybrid in the past? No! We had always produced the local variety and sold it in the markets of Ankara. We used to harvest it during the day and take it to Ankara in our own trucks in the evening for sale the following morning. We knew it was our own tomato.

(Interview, 12 June 2012)

Farmers can opt for cultivating both 'hybrid' and heirloom varieties. The local elite support hybrid varieties. According to Güdül mayor, Hava Yıldırım:

If Çağa tomatoes are going to be commercially viable, there must be different conditions for selling them. These tomatoes cannot make their way to the grocery stores and supermarkets, but must be produced for private consumption in the homes of local villagers.

(Interview, 12 June 2012)

The mayors contend that fresh vegetables must be mass produced for mass consumption within the formal channels of the market economy. The mayor of Çağa envisages large industrial greenhouses heated by the hot springs recently found in the immediate vicinity of the village. He believes this is a better way of managing the landscape to increase mass production of produce and increase competition from local tomatoes before the open-field tomato season begins in Ankara. The mayor seems unconcerned with how the industrially defined climatic conditions of a greenhouse may affect his highly praised landscape conditions and ecosystems – so well-suited to heirloom tomatoes – due to increased nutrient stress, water-use issues and pests–disease control. Both mayors believe that the market advantage provided by the use of greenhouses should be further enhanced through contract farming. Such ideas generate space for a new agriculture and turn a privately patented heirloom variety into a mass-produced and distributed crop that is also improved for market resilience (Jordan 2007). The mayor of Çağa is confident that 'the villagers know how to grow tomatoes very well, but they don't earn enough income because they have difficulty with marketing their produce'. Similarly, the Güdül mayor remarks that 'if these farmers acted as *professional* farmers and adopted technological developments in agriculture, they could earn much more money from their work. At the moment, their hard work is not worth much' (Interview, 12 June 2012).

Both mayors note that farmers produce a wide range of crops including fresh fruits and vegetables, grains and legumes, in addition to raising livestock and producing milk. For the mayors, this 'unprofessional' form of diversification currently enables farmers to hold their own in informal markets. Because they have informally established marketing options, they can continue to produce tomatoes in the same way as their fathers and grandfathers. However, according to the mayors, these past practices keep producers at the margins of formal commercial agriculture. The mayor of Çağa contemplates a change in farmers' marketing behaviour through contract farming. He observes:

We have space allocated for a *pazar* in the village. I managed to get an official permit for it to be licenced as a wholesale market space. ... Currently, this space is used intermittently as a meeting place for producers and traders. The traders come from Ankara with their empty vegetable and fruit boxes. They negotiate a price to fill each box. Let's assume that I negotiate to fill 100 boxes with tomatoes for the trader by the following morning. I do that and receive my money from the trader. This is the most formal marketing arrangement we now have in the village. This system is extremely loose; it leaves a farmer with great uncertainty as he waits for a trader to show up and purchase his products. If the merchant doesn't show up, the producer cannot sell. But, a professional grower will know in advance how much and for whom he is going to produce, and for what price. There is a guarantee in contract farming.

(Interview, 12 June 2012)

Although both mayors identify specialized contract farming as a means to solve marketing problems, producers disagree. According to Yaşar, contract farming is not an economically feasible option in the village, where farming lands are small. 'If *Migros* wants to purchase 5–10 tons of tomatoes from here, a producer has to plant 100 dekars of land, which he doesn't have'. The Güdül mayor insists that 'if you don't have the conditions for professionalized farming, you will need to set them up. You can organize a producers' union and enter into contracts with supermarkets'. Yaşar disagrees and suggests that people prefer to work for their own families first and that they won't enter into such collective organizations:

People in the village will not come together to set up a producers' union; they work on very small plots of lands, and they won't trust the bureaucratic types who manage the union. They will think that the managers mistreat them. It won't work. They are more independent as street vendors; they also earn more by selling on the streets than they would earn otherwise from a more organized way. We have the example of milk vendors to learn from. Milk vendors earn more money than those who are part of the milk producers' union. Period!

(Interview, 12 June 2012)

Farmers are convinced that product diversification and informal marketing strategies protect them from the unpredictability of formal market conditions, enabling them to establish a more secure livelihood. In this manner, farmers position themselves independently in the markets, largely outside agro-industrial supply chains. By emphasizing diversity in crop production, their subsistence is also supported. One farmer remarked:

We grow our own grains, chickpeas, beans, lentils, fruits and so on. We have cows for milk, yoghurt, butter and meat. We don't even buy sugar as we also produce sugar beets. We only purchase cleaning materials and rice from the store. We also grew rice in the past, but we had to give it up. Imported rice from China and Vietnam is very cheap anyway.

(Interview, 12 June 2012)

Producers view their marginality in formal markets as an asset that they can use to their advantage, empowering themselves by building alternative marketing networks based on culturally valued relations of trust and without limiting their options. These producers argue that it is the legal–bureaucratic re-making of fresh-produce supply chains that constitutes a built-in deterrent to the formal sale of heirloom cultivars. One producer elaborated during an earlier interview:

In the past, we used to take our produce in our own trucks to *pazars* in Ankara. Each neighbourhood has a weekly *pazar*. In addition to *pazar* merchants who sell produce purchased from wholesale markets, farmers were also allowed to sell village products from specially designated places adjacent to *pazars*. The new wholesale market law no longer allows farmers to do this unless they register their products and have a registered spot in the *pazar*. If you are not a registered farmer, you have only one option: to sell your produce informally on the streets as a street vendor. I used to do that. I would fill up my truck and go to various neighbourhoods in Ankara. I used to have lots of customers. They knew me personally and trusted me. I could easily sell 2 tons of vegetables and fruit in a day. I am too old for this sort of work now. I am 60 years old.

(Interview, 5 May 2011)

Producers insist that because Ankara is only 70–80 km away from the village, their heirloom tomatoes are well-suited for a short journey to the neighbourhood *pazars* in Ankara. For them, it is the law's 'wholesale registration system' that restricts farmers' options and forces them to adopt hybrid cultivars. These cultivars are fully registered all the way from the development of the seeds and seedlings to the market place. The law excludes their cultivar from sale not only in supermarkets but also in traditional *pazars* because the seeds and other locally available inputs, such as animal manure, are not registered. The 2012 *By-law on Pazars* (No. 28351) reserves approximately 20 per cent of spots in *pazars* for producers to sell their crops,[7] provided they are registered in the National Registry of Farmers. It is by reference to the by-law that farmers who are outside the national registry system are excluded from selling their products in the *pazars*.

As a response to their exclusion, unregistered farmers 'rebuild' the status and strength of local foods, developing informal marketing networks for unregistered local food varieties that can be sold directly to consumers through street vending. Although illegal, this rebuilding effort supports urban niche markets and is culturally sustained through a nuanced understanding of product quality by reference to the trustworthiness of producers, and a rich, sensory-based history and knowledge of produce. Moreover, the process of rebuilding local food receives consumer approval through direct, participatory certification by consumers. There can be no quantitative data, but it is well-known that these informal, illegally organized food marketing networks are extensive in Turkey, ranging from 70 to 80 per cent of FFV sales (see Chapter 7), a fact that supports the strength of participatory certification by consumers as it applies to product quality of non-standard, unregistered food.

In relation to the informal marketing of their food, producers often collaborate with village-based milk vendors who illegally sell unpasteurized raw milk on a daily basis in Ankara neighbourhoods. This type of informally functioning direct marketing is organized alongside the formal arrangement of traditional neighbourhood *pazars*, wholesale markets and supermarkets. Milk vendors are an important element in participatory certification, as many people in the city prefer to purchase raw rather than pasteurized milk. They also trust the product quality of their vendors. Industrially produced pasteurized milk with a shelf life of up to six months does not generate consumer trust, but unregistered village products do, which again reflects the time-tested interpersonal relations of trust between producers and consumers.

There are close to 50 livestock farmers and milk producers in the village who also work as informal milk vendors. They own their own pick-up trucks equipped with coolers to transport raw milk daily to Ankara neighbourhoods for door-to-door sale on the streets. In addition to selling close to 5 tons of fresh milk daily, they sell vegetables on behalf of farmers for a small commission. These milk vendors operate outside the formal channels of the Milk Producers Association (MPA) in the village.

Yaşar, a dairy and livestock farmer who is also president of the water users' association in the village, explained that the Çağa MPA was founded in 1996 as an administratively and financially autonomous joint stock–like private organization for marketing milk. The Ankara Provincial Special Administration provided the financial and infrastructural assistance for the MPA to purchase the milk tanks and build the cold-storage facility in the village. It has 200 members who produce approximately 12 tons of milk daily, which is then sold to large corporations such as ÜLKER. The MPA facilitates producers' market integration while acting as a link between the producers and the state in the distribution of state subsidies. Farmers explained to me that the MPA price per kilo of milk is often lower than the price a milk vendor earns for informally selling on the streets. In addition, MPA payments and the distribution of state subsidies are often late. Therefore, a significant number of milk producers prefer to sell their milk as vendors.

The foregoing discussion offers insight into divergent approaches to commercial agriculture. Although the mayors are keen on integrating GI protection of local varieties into the official developmentalist account of industrial agriculture, small-scale producers present an opposing position to the homogenizing monoculture effects of formally organized commercial agriculture.

This position is backed by informal marketing networks and trust-based alternative 'participatory certification by consumers' for local varieties.

Farmers as Keepers of Heirloom Seeds: The Village of Savcılı Büyükoba in Kaman, Kırşehir

As illustrated in the examples of Zübeyir and Mualla, Savcılı Büyükoba farmers have a commonality with, yet also diverge from, farmers in Karacaören, Çağa and Kamanlar. They share a reliance on industrially produced pesticides, insecticides, fungicides and herbicides, which they believe are necessary for weed, pest and disease control. They also integrate their vegetable production with livestock to produce milk for sale and manure for organic fertiliser. The key point of divergence is their utilization of both hybrid and farmers' own saved seeds. In addition to store-purchased hybrid seeds, Zübeyir plants farmers' seeds obtained from his own village and neighbouring villages. Mualla only sows seeds that she saves from village varieties. These villagers don't purchase seedlings from commercial greenhouses but grow them in their own greenhouses. In fact, Savcılı Büyükoba is the only village I have visited where producers operate self-owned greenhouses to raise seedlings from both store-purchased hybrid and locally saved farmers' seeds, which will then be transplanted into open fields.

The producers of Savcılı Büyükoba combine formal and informal marketing arrangements in their commercialization path. It is similar to the one adopted by producers in Çağa, with one significant difference. Savcılı Büyükoba farmers are both producers and merchants without the third-party intermediation of traders, wholesale commissioners or milk vendors. Both Zübeyir and Mualla epitomize this pattern in their own differentiated ways. The local specificity of this village broadens our understanding of the meaning of *hybridity* in small-scale farming. I interviewed Zübeyir and Mualla on 18 May 2013, separately, on their farms.

Zübeyir

Zübeyir has three greenhouses of different sizes: the smallest is 80 m², another is 100 m² and the largest is 120 m². His farm contains 60 dekars of land. He owns only 16 dekars and uses the rest informally without paying a rental fee in cash or in kind to the legal owners of the plots. He gives the owners vegetables as a gift at the end of his harvest. Although Zübeyir is a small-scale producer, he is the largest producer in the village and can generate six pick-up trucks full of vegetables in a week, equalling 30–40 tons of crops. He does not grow grains and does not use crop rotation.

Zübeyir grows tomatoes, cucumbers, eggplants, peppers, garlic and melon.[8] He explained that hybrid seeds constitute 90 per cent of his planting, which he purchases from Antalya-based firms and has home-delivered by cargo. He rarely uses seeds developed by Turkish companies because, as he says:

> they don't germinate well and I can't obtain the yield I want. You end up losing lots of seeds. They are also not resistant to disease … there are

no chemicals suitable for them on the market. When you use chemicals developed for other varieties, vegetables grown from these seeds get burned and die away … The imported seeds are high yielding and also taste fine.

(Interview, 18 May 2013)

Zübeyir also noted the poor resiliency of farmers' native varieties when transporting them to market: 'they are very tasty for immediate daily eating, but are very watery. You pick them today; they will turn to mush by tomorrow. You cannot take them to the market'. His wife said: 'If a tomato gets watery when you cut it with a knife, you know that it is a native tomato. This is a very good way to test. Native tomatoes also have thinner skins'. Zübeyir added:

You cannot find native seeds at the markets. I found these native tomato seeds somewhere in Nevşehir. A very dear friend of mine gave me 2,000 seeds as a gift. I haven't paid any money for them. He does not give them to everyone but only to trusted friends because it has been illegal since the 2006 seed law to exchange them for commercial planting. I also save my own seeds. I don't care about these silly laws.

(Interview, 18 May 2013)

For Zübeyir, good taste is local and locally varied. Taste differentiation affects the marketability of products. Since not all consumers are familiar with the specific taste of local food, they will not purchase the native varieties from his village. However, Zübeyir believes it is only a matter of educating tastes to develop greater appreciation for local products. He notes:

I grow this purple eggplant variety from my own self-saved seeds. I take 3 tons of the eggplant to Kaman and sell it in one day. It isn't known outside of Kaman. Since I have also been selling my crops in Kulu, in Konya province, for the last 10 years, they've gotten used to the taste and have begun to purchase my eggplants. People who like the taste then recommend it to others. So the market has begun to pick up in other places as well.

(Interview, 18 May 2013)

When the season for his locally grown crops is over, Zübeyir sells crops grown by his friends who farm in other provinces that have warmer climates and later harvests, such as Kahramanmaraş. Zübeyir earns more money from selling local varieties.

If hybrids sell for 50 *kuruş*, native tomatoes sell for TL 2 per kilo. In fact, native varieties sell for as much as TL 5 per kilo at the beginning of the season. People who purchase and eat these varieties do not want to give them up, believe me. They are tasty, and people are willing to pay a higher price for the taste. Some hybrid varieties also taste good, but my customers

do not like to eat them. Also, as a farmer I cannot use their seeds the following year. I will be forced to spend more money each year to buy seeds.
I prefer to have both taste and the ability to save my own seeds.

(Interview, 18 May 2013)

Zübeyir sells his products at *pazars* in towns such as Kaman in Kırşehir,
Şereflikoçhisar in Ankara and Kulu in Konya. All are geographically close to
the village, so the durability of crops is not an issue. He transports the produce
in his own large pick-up truck, carrying 5–6 tons of vegetables per load. He
pays TL 60–70 for a spot in the Kırşehir *pazar* and TL 5 in Kaman. Zübeyir also
sells informally as a street vendor in Ankara neighbourhoods such as Akdere,
where migrants from the village of Savcılı Büyükoba are known to reside and
are familiar with local tastes. Zübeyir does not sell to supermarkets because
supermarket consumers do not care much about the taste of local foods. He
also avoids wholesale markets because he is required to pay a commission to
traders, which he contends reduces his earnings.

Although he recognizes the importance of local taste and appreciates the
greater earning potential of local varieties, Zübeyir also plants hybrid seeds for
certain crops to increase his yield. However, compared to traditional crops and
landraces, hybrid varieties require significant industrial inputs such as inorganic
fertilizers and pesticides, which in turn hinder an integrated soil and water
management strategy (Thompson et al. 2007). The way in which Zübeyir
implements a more industrially amalgamated production method for hybrid
varieties has a direct impact on water use and soil degradation.

The village of Savcılı Büyükoba is 16 km away from Hirfanlı dam on the
Kızılırmak River. The dam supports nine ponds for agricultural irrigation,
including the Savcılı Büyükoba pond. Zübeyir pumps his irrigation water from
the pond with an electrical motor. To conserve water, he has adopted a drip-
watering system rather than use sprinklers. But the water Zübeyir delivers to
the plants is already combined with inorganic fertilizers and pesticides at the
pump. This process can build up dangerous residues in the soil, water table,
pond and river. A focus on yield also raises questions about depleted soil fertility, which can result in the overuse of synthetic fertilizers. Zübeyir feeds
the soil with inorganic fertilizers for seed germination and seedling growing
because they are complete with minerals and vitamins. He continues to use
inorganic fertilizers after the plants are transferred to the open field and before
they flower. Later, after the plants flower, he supplements soil nutrients with
organic fertilizer in the form of manure obtained from his cows.[9] But, there
are drawbacks that he is well aware of; the inorganic DAB (Diamonyum phos-
phate) fertilizer creates an increased dependency in the soil, whereas, Zübeyir
adds, 'cow manure was adequate in the past. The US gave us these fertilisers
and created a dependency problem in our soil. Now, the soil itself wants to
have it. Without it, you cannot have the yield' (Interview, 18 May 2013).

Although Zübeyir spends half of his earnings on input-related expenses,
including hybrid seeds, petroleum, chemicals, fertilizers and labour, he feels

that his earnings are good – because he is able to increase his yields.[10] As long as he uses the required inputs for controlling weeds and disease and building soil fertility, he can grow up to 200 tons of vegetables and earn TL 80,000–100,000 per season.

Mualla

Mualla's farming practices come closer to a 'peasant-style' subsistence type of family farming.[11] Her produce is for the family's subsistence needs and for sale in the Kaman *pazar*. Mualla's husband is responsible for the production of barley on more than 400 dekars of land; Mualla takes care of the greenhouse seedlings and field vegetable production on 6 dekars of land. Her husband helps her to plough the land, apply fertilizers and chemicals and attend to other work. They hire between three and four migrant Kurdish workers per season to help with planting, weeding and harvesting. She wants her children to complete their education and 'make their life from something else'. She adds: 'We are sick and tired of working the land. I don't want them to be farmers' (Interview, 18 May 2013).

Mualla also makes molasses from her own grapes and obtains milk, butter, cheese and yoghurt from one cow, which the family owns and uses for its own consumption and for sales in the Kaman *pazar*. She earns between TL 15,000 and 17,000 per season, half of which goes toward hired labour. She declares: 'Allah gives blessings. This is enough of a contribution by me to the family. I don't know how much my husband earns from barley' (Interview, 18 May 2013).

Mualla has two greenhouses, one 10 m² and the other 20 m² in size, which she uses to grow seedlings of eggplant, tomatoes, cucumbers, peppers, onions and beans. She produces 600–700 bunches of seedlings for each variety, totalling nearly 2,000 individual seedlings. She obtains approximately 1 ton of vegetables for each variety.

Mualla does not use industrially produced hybrid seeds but plants her own self-saved seeds from the crops grown in her field. Once the plant flowers turn to seed, she collects and stores the seeds in newspaper wrapping to absorb humidity. She saves approximately 1 kilo of seeds from each variety to replant the following year. Mualla first sows the seeds in large trays in the greenhouse in March, where they germinate quickly after only two waterings. Following germination, she places the small seedlings into (greenhouse) seeding pouches, which she purchases from the greenhouse equipment store. These pouches help the small seedlings grow faster in the field. Once the seedlings are ready, they are transplanted in their pouches with the help of hired labour for open-field growing.

Mualla is aware of the value of organic matter for restoring and enhancing soil nutrient availability. She uses sheep manure from her own sheep to use in the greenhouses. She uses a drip watering system to irrigate her vegetables, with water pumped from the Hirfanlı dam lake. Mualla also relies on insecticides, which she refers to as 'poison', to fight against fungal diseases. She uses chemicals despite the fact that she defines them as 'poison' and recognizes that they are harmful to human and soil health. She explains that she is not knowledgeable on other ways of keeping pests under control. She also adds that the Kaman Agricultural Sales co-operative recommends them. Since the co-operative is a state-run organization,[12] she has complete trust in the products it sells. Further, although Mualla uses chemicals, she defines her production method as organic. She explains:

> There is a rumour that producers in Savcılı Büyükoba use growth hormones. It may be true that some people use them to increase their yield, but I don't. I produce four to five tons of crops, equaling roughly 10 bags of eggplants, and 10 bags of beans. If each bag is 50 kilo, you can only produce half a ton of eggplant. This is not much. We don't have the capacity to produce more. We don't need to use hormones.
>
> (Interview, 18 May 2013)

Mualla is self-sufficient for her family's needs in relation to vegetables and dairy products. She only uses supermarkets to purchase meat, rice, lentils and cleaning products. Mualla sells her special home-made cheese made with raw milk in the Kaman *pazar*. The milk is filtered through cheese cloth, pressed in a bag made of animal skin and fermented at a temperature of 27–41 degrees Celsius. The cheese is highly admired for its taste and very valuable, selling for TL 17 per kilo. However, she is afraid of feeding her family with this cheese since it is made with raw milk and may cause brucella disease. Therefore, for her own family, she purchases cheese made from pasteurized milk at the market.

Concluding Remarks

Scholars such as Buck et al. (1997) have questioned the ability of small-scale producers to counter globally advocated agro-industrial processes. As argued by Guthman (2000) and as demonstrated in this chapter, small-scale and 'organic' farming in Turkey does not represent an alternative path; its transformative potential is limited. However, as explained in the many examples provided, farmers present an element of ambiguity in relation to the deepening of industrial 'standardization'. This ambiguity holds true for both GAP-certified large-scale producers and small-scale growers engaged in a multiplicity of production and marketing strategies.

My analysis of various farming pathways shows that there is no linear trajectory. Divergent scripts and commercial engagements continue to frame the ambivalent attitudes of producers toward the globally harmonizing processes of corporate agriculture. Many of the farmers use hybrid seeds to achieve greater yields, chemicals to control pests and disease and synthetic fertilizers to increase soil productivity. Nevertheless, they all highlight the importance of agro-ecological considerations in maintaining landscape structure, restoring soil nutrient availability and increasing water productivity (although water conservation receives less attention). Cultural heritage and the locality of ecological resources are also repeatedly mentioned by farmers as part of their commitment to grow nutritious, tasty and culturally appropriate food, *in part* through planting traditional varieties from locally saved seeds and *often* through the use of organic manure and crop rotation. These considerations are not intrinsic to a particular farming practice or to a distinct category of farmers. Rather, they express a convergence of narratives and farming imaginaries circulating in the villages and towns of Central Anatolian provinces. All play a significant role in restructuring commercialization in agriculture through rebuilding the locality of foods.

Although there are commonalities, there are also significant divergences that account for the vibrancy in the persistence of small-scale farming in local traditional crop varieties. The co-existence of vegetable production and animal husbandry at the local village level creates possibilities for the emergence of alternative marketing strategies for non-standard crops. Such strategies are embedded in the trust-based interpersonal relations of collaboration found with raw-milk producers, especially those who lack direct marketing connections to urban niche markets and *pazars*. Farmers sell their crops via a mixture of formal and informal marketing strategies, some as *pazar* merchants, without the intermediary of traders and commissioners, and others as vegetable vendors selling door-to-door on the streets of urban neighbourhoods. Still others enhance their marketing ability by collaborating with milk producers and vendors. The enhanced ability of farmers to produce and sell local varieties on their own as *pazar* merchants and street vendors, and in collaboration with milk vendors, presents a *partial* counter response to the intensification of industrial monoculture and standardization. This response is rooted in the participatory certification by consumers for non-standard local crops produced by small-scale growers. Chapter 7 will focus on the different ways in which an agriculture reflecting ambivalent attitudes and simultaneously co-existing alternative systems of food quality standards interacts with the expansion of supermarkets in Turkey. The following chapter focuses on labour issues in agriculture.

Notes

1 For GAP practices in the province of Ankara, see Table 1.2 in Chapter 1.
2 Sincan is a large suburban town within the province of Ankara, 27 km from the city of Ankara and approximately 60 km from Güdül.
3 http://www.mevzuat.gov.tr/MevzuatMetin/4.5.555.pdf. (accessed 19 March 2016). The legislation was modified in 2008 (No. 5805).
4 The EU's GI protection regulation consists of a concise definition of geographical area as clearly linked to the specificity, quality or characteristics of the product (European Union 2006).
5 The mayor notes that the village manages its ground watercourses for irrigation through the Water User's Association (WUA), founded in 1996. The total irrigated area under WUA regulation is 10,000 dekars, 7,500 of which is in Çağa and the remainder in three villages within Ayaş. The WUA has a total membership of 600 individual farmers.

The WUA water-management system channels river water into the ditches, which, according to the mayor, results in approximately 50 per cent water loss (Interview, 12 June 2012).

6 A *kerpiç* house is a type of a village house built with the use of sun-dried adobe clay soil, mixed with water and straw.

7 For details, see Chapter 7.

8 Zübeyir's family subsistence depends on market purchases. While the family eat fresh vegetables from the farm in summer and make tomato-paste and vegetable preserves by drying and canning for winter consumption, they purchase grain, lentils, beans, chick-peas, fruits and wheat flour, in addition to other materials, for household use.

9 Zübeyir owns 17 cows. In addition to using their manure as fertilizer, he sells their milk daily to neighbours in the village and residents in the nearby TOKİ public housing. He does not grow grain to feed the cows but purchases hay and cracked barley from grain-growing farmers in the village.

10 Zübeyir regularly employs approximately 10 migrant Kurdish workers rather than his own family members (see Chapter 6).

11 Mualla also makes filo-dough bread (*yufka ekmeği*) for the family. There is a special oven-house built in the backyard of every house in Kaman, which the women use to make *yufka ekmeği*. The oven-house has a cylindrical metal oven known as tandoor (*tandır*) in which the village women make bread. Women in the village help each other in bread-making. The reciprocity involved is known as *höbül*. It involves dividing the dough into smaller balls, flattening the balls into very thin filo by rolling, and then cooking them. Three women can make enough bread from 100 kilos of wheat flour in one day for one family to eat for four months. Mualla uses store-purchased enriched white flour because her family doesn't produce wheat. Her family also has one walnut tree, which produces 15–20 kilos of walnuts that are consumed by the family.

12 For further details on agricultural sales co-operatives, see Chapter 7.

6 Trust and Trustworthiness

Paternalist Labour Relations in Agriculture

Evidence provided in the previous two chapters indicates that both formal and informal marketing networks co-exist simultaneously in the commercialization of Turkish agriculture. This is due to the fact that both categories of farmers generate consumer trust in the food they produce. Small-scale producers generate *trust* through informally established *participatory certification by consumers*; and larger-scale producers do so by reference to formally established Good Agricultural Practices (GAP) industrial standards of 'good food'.

The present chapter explores another dimension of trust as it relates to labour relations. It elaborates on how a desire to produce 'good food' interacts with labour practices. I raise issues that involve the re-shaping of gender, race/ethnicity and class-related inequalities in the context of the neoliberal restructuring of agriculture. The analysis is based on the narratives of farmers, agro-labour traders and agricultural workers.

Low wages are a characteristic feature of Turkish agriculture. This is despite the fact that there is a labour scarcity resulting from widespread 'de-peasantization' in agriculture. De-peasantization is measured by the declining number of people employed in agriculture. In just under 10 years, from 2004 to 2013, the average rate of agricultural employment in Turkey dropped from 29 per cent to 23.6 per cent (TÜİK n.d: 9). Farmers' easy access to Kurdish migrant workers helps to further undermine wages, effectively countering the potentiality of higher wages that might result from labour scarcity.

Three categories of agricultural labourers are employed by small and larger-scale farmers involved in organic, conventional and locally oriented food production: low-waged Kurdish migrant labourers, local workers and unwaged household members. Large-scale operations do not use household labour. Most commercially involved small operations also use wage labour. Their reliance on family members is rare; they are used only infrequently to supplement labour needs. The occasional use of family labour resembles a 'half-labour form' to some extent (Chayanov 1966, 18–22, 90–1, 108–10). In my examples, an overwhelming majority of smaller-scale operations use wage labour.

Both large and small-scale farmers employ Kurdish migrant labour, while local workers are employed to fill supplemental labour needs. Greenhouse growers in Beypazarı recruit local workers only rather than using Kurdish

Figure 6.1 Agricultural Labour in Turkey.

migrants. Smaller-scale farmers (i.e. Ramiz, Halit and Hamza from the village of Karacaören in Güdül) who rely exclusively on family members are motivated by their moral orientation and their cultural understanding of what constitutes a 'good farmer' and 'good farming practices' (Silvasti 2003). Such practices, for them, require self-involvement in 'hard work', not the use of hired labour. There is extensive coverage in the literature on the use of unwaged family labour in Turkish agriculture (i.e. Aydın 2002; Keyder 1993). In this chapter, I focus on Kurdish migrant and local wage labour.

Kurdish migrants have a major presence in Turkish agriculture due to the internal displacement of the Kurdish population and the ongoing armed struggle between state security forces and various Kurdish groups. Kurdish out-migration from Eastern and Southeastern Turkey due to continuing violence has created opportunities for the expansion of market-oriented agriculture, even into the smallest farming operations, because it generates cheap and easily obtainable agricultural labour. Migrant Kurds are the backbone of a low wage–earning stratum in commercial agriculture, employed informally in both small and large-scale organic, GAP-certified, conventional and locally oriented farming.

Local women represent an additional low-wage category in agriculture. Migrant labour consists of male and female members of entire households and extended families; local labour tends to consist of individual female workers. With the exception of the greenhouse operation that I visited, where no migrant labour is employed, local women typically represent a secondary labour force in agriculture. This observation requires some explanation. Existing research often shows a 'feminization of agriculture', focusing on rural-to-urban migration and its gender effects (Nguyen and Locke 2014; Piotrowski et al. 2013; Radel et al. 2012). The 'feminization of agriculture' is explained in relation to male out-migration to urban areas, which causes more and more women to be engaged in agricultural production in rural areas as farmers and labourers. This is not the pattern I observed in the labour relations of Central Anatolia in Turkey.

My evidence does not support the 'feminization of agriculture' thesis. This is because both Kurdish men and women, as members of an entire household and extended family, leave their homes in Eastern and Southeastern Turkey to seek agricultural employment elsewhere in the country. This is household migration from rural-to-rural areas. The rural-to-rural migration of Kurdish labour consisting of entire households reduces the need for the employment of local women to sustain a 'feminization of agriculture'.

Ethnic segmentation of the agricultural labour force exists between open-field and non-open-field workers; household Kurdish workers are heavily employed as open-field workers, while local women generally choose not to be involved in field work. I met very few local women employed as open-field workers. This was because the season was just beginning and Kurdish migrants had not yet arrived. While the unavailability of local women increases the employment of Kurdish workers in open fields, it also intensifies ethnic and class-based inequality for the Kurds.

There is no gender-based difference in wages between male and female workers of Kurdish origin, who are regarded as undifferentiated, bounded members of entire households. A gendered wage gap *does* prevail among local workers, who are viewed as independent individuals differentiated along gender lines. The following analysis provides a detailed comparative understanding of agricultural wage work in Turkey using information gathered from field work in several villages and small agricultural towns in Ankara and Kırşehir provinces.

This chapter demonstrates that Kurdish migrants and local female labour add a particular 'racialized/ethnicized and gendered twist' to capitalized agriculture in Turkey. My analysis also provides a correction to the widely held thesis that labour-force informalization contributes to the 'feminization of employment' (Standing 1999). The evidence provided complicates a 'unidimensional and overly deterministic' explanation of agricultural labouring (Raynolds 2001), which often results from a singular research concern with the survival of rural households and their gendered effects (Arizpe 2014; de Haan 2002; Palmer 1985).

While important, such a limiting approach can cause us to neglect the possibility that a majority of field workers may be migrant men and women of a particular ethnic origin whose wages are very low – a phenomenon well-illustrated in the case of the United States (Alkon and Agyeman 2011) – but who are not necessarily gendered. Research that focuses exclusively on the gendering effects of rural out-migration also precludes the possibility that labour market segmentation exists between the culturally undifferentiated workers of a racialized/ethnicized group and gendered local workers.

Further, this chapter highlights a complicating factor that emerges from a process within the market-oriented restructuring of agriculture. This process interweaves separate dynamics and meanings of ethnicity and gender into the institutionalization of segmented labour regimes that simultaneously co-exist in Turkish agriculture.

Informally institutionalized labour brokerage by an intermediary category of labour contractors is the key mechanism in the organization of a particular labour regime for migrants (Barrientos 2013). I call these intermediaries *agro-labour traders*, known as *çavuş* in Turkey. Although they are typically men, this is not always the case. *Çavuş* perform a multiplicity of critical tasks. They provide both farmers and workers with vital services; farmers gain access to trustworthy, reliable labour, while migrant labour secures employment and housing for the season. A distinct labour regime unfolds for migrants based on the *horizontally established ties of trust* (Carswell and de Neve 2013) rooted in the labour loyalty and management activated by the *çavuş*. In this labour regime, the *çavuş* supply the labour while the farmers/agro-traders delegate the responsibility of labour supervision and management to the *çavuş*. Thus, the *çavuş* emerges as the principal, informally functioning institutional mechanism facilitating the expansion of a capitalized agriculture. These agro-labour traders are equipped with the full delegated power of labour control and management, as is the case in South Africa (Addison 2014). They manage and direct the performance of labour, but there is no on-the-job training and skill development for workers, who simply learn by experience.

I argue that trust is a key ingredient in connecting labour and farmers within a specific labour regime. Through the notion of trust, we can better understand how labour relations are determined not only by workers' position in the vertically established relations of production but also by the *horizontally* existing social relations of *hemşeri* and kin networks, geographic–regional connections, migration and household livelihood strategies and racial/ethnic ties (Carswell and de Neve 2013). Trust embedded in these horizontally established social relations is a necessary condition for the recruitment, management and disciplining, as well as wage determination, of both Kurdish migrants and local workers. Given that Kurdish migrant workers are friends, close relatives and members of an entire household, they constitute a specific type of self-disciplined agricultural labour and labour-management regime that facilitates a reduction in the cost of production for both large and smaller-scale farms.

To reiterate, I conceptualize the informal labour of migrant workers in terms of the *entire household as a labouring unit*, with little gender effect on wage determination and labour management. I explore the employment of local labour, which *is* heavily gendered, through the *family-wage* ideal. Figure 6.2 offers an illustration of the chapter's essential argument.

Kurdish Out-Migration and Informal Labour in Agriculture

A brief history of the ongoing conflict between the Turkish state and the Kurdish people is important to an understanding of the background culture of Kurdish internal displacement and out-migration, which resulted in the creation of a large pool of reserve labour in agriculture. Strained relations between the state and the Kurdish people have existed for many years and are largely inherited from Ottoman times (Jwaideh 1999). Problems increased significantly after the First World War, initially because of fierce nationalist claims to Kurdish independence and later due to more subtle arguments in defense of Kurds as a culturally and linguistically distinct category of people.

Particularly after the signing of the Lausanne treaty in 1924, which formally ended the First World War for Turkey, relations between the state and the Kurdish people have been shaped by the state's denial of the existence of Kurds

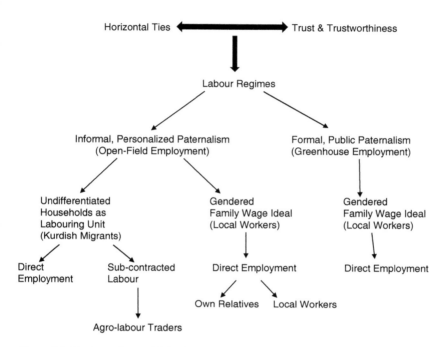

Figure 6.2 Horizontally Established Ties of Trust and Paternalist Labour Regimes.

as a culturally and linguistically distinct people. The Lausanne treaty declared the 'non-Muslim' religious status of people the only distinguishing feature required for their recognition as a minority group. As a result, various Muslim ethnic categories that did not fit into the minority definition designated by the treaty were excluded from minority status (Oran 2004). The Kurds remain unrecognized as a minority group. Their numbers are currently estimated to be between 12 and 15 million, constituting the largest minority living in Eastern and Southeastern Anatolia today.

Since the late 1970s, relations between the state and the Kurdish people have become increasingly violent, a result of the armed conflict between Turkish security forces and the Kurdistan Workers' Party (PKK) – the outlawed Kurdish separatist organization established in 1978. In 2012, the government of Turkey initiated a process to find a solution to the conflict, known as *çözüm süreci*. However, there is still enormous political and bureaucratic resistance to the Kurdish movement out of concern that it is a threat to national security.

The armed conflict that has persisted in Turkey for more than 40 years has resulted in the internal displacement of more than 1.4 million individuals from the Eastern and Southeastern provinces, areas that have a significant Kurdish population.[1] Research conducted by Hacettepe Üniversitesi (2006,

61) has estimated that the number of people who migrated out of the 14 provinces in Eastern and Southeastern Turkey between 1986 and 2005 ranges from 950,000 to 1,200,000. More than 60 per cent of this displacement took place between 1991 and 1995 (A. Sönmez 2008, 384). Approximately 80 per cent of Kurdish migration has originated in the rural areas of these provinces (Hacettepe Üniversitesi 2006, 61), which constitutes nearly 65 per cent of the national total of displaced people from rural settlements (A. Sönmez 2008, 384). There is no hard data to show how many of these displaced people have permanently moved to the villages and towns in Central Anatolia where I conducted my field research, nor is there reliable information on how many are moving back and forth as seasonal workers between their homes in Eastern and Southeastern Turkey and the rural areas of Central Anatolia.

Hacettepe Üniversitesi researchers (2006, 63) estimate that there are between 112,000 and 124,000 returnees. According to A. Sönmez (2008, 371), the return of these displaced people and their re-employment in agriculture in Eastern and Southeastern Turkey is not conducive to the competitive growth of national agriculture. Sönmez argues that it would result in a surplus population of agricultural workers in the region and generate negative effects on the efficiency, productivity and economies of scale for market-oriented agricultural growth. The farms in the East and Southeast provinces of Turkey most affected by armed conflict and displacement tend to be small, below 5 hectares in size. Sönmez (2008, 389–90) further argues that the small size of farms, combined with the large rural-family size of 7.8 in these provinces (the national average for rural households is 4.5), generates significant population pressure on these farms. Still, small farms persist out of the need on the part of individual households to find alternative employment for family members within the region.

A. Sönmez appears to justify Kurdish labour migration to Central and Western Turkey as a means of relieving population pressure on agriculture in Eastern and Southeastern Turkey. The diversion of part of the surplus agricultural population to alternative rural locations creates a cheap labour force for the overall market-oriented transformation of agriculture in Turkey. Agriculture is being reorganized in Southeast Turkey around the *Southeastern Anatolia Development Project* (GAP, the Turkish acronym). The GAP project is a state-led regional development strategy undertaken to bolster the development of large scale irrigation-based capitalized agriculture and agro-industrial projects in the region (Çarkoğlu and Eder 2005, 169, 177). It has been designed to increase productivity in agriculture, alter the habits of the population and change the social structure in the region. The GAP project would further contribute to the release of even more labour from small-scale household agriculture in provinces with a sizeable Kurdish population. I suggest that agricultural commercialization in Central Anatolia, which is labour intensive, continues to absorb surplus Kurdish labour migrating from the region.

M. Sönmez (1998) calculates that one out of three people from the region lives elsewhere in Turkey. In my field research, I observed that all of the Kurdish migrant labour employed in agriculture, without exception, has been informal. In November 2014, a total of 25,874 million people were employed in Turkey (TÜİK February 2015), nearly 5 million in agriculture. In the same year, the national average for informal employment was 33.9 per cent. The rate is 81.7 per cent in agriculture (TÜİK February 2015).[2] The ILO's *Decent Work and the Informal Economy* report of 2002 defines the 'informal economy' as including not only wage employment in unregistered workplaces but also paid work not covered by labour and social security legislation (ILO 2002, 5–9). The statistical data on informal employment in Turkey covers only unregistered employment, regardless of the un/registered status of the workplaces. There is no officially available statistical data that shows the distribution of informal agricultural labour by ethnicity, but it is well known that seasonally employed Kurdish workers constitute a significant majority of the informal agricultural labour force.

There is also a lack of hard data on the distribution of wages by ethnicity. According to TÜİK (March 2015), there is a wage gap between seasonal and permanent agricultural workers, as shown in Table 6.1. The Kurdish workers I interviewed (both male and female) indicated that they earn TL 35 per day, which is below the national average shown in the table. Their work day is usually 13 hours long, from 6 am to 7 pm, which brings their hourly wage to TL 2.7 or US \$1.00.[3]

There is no hard data on unwaged household labour in agriculture. We can assume that female family members employed in agriculture are not waged.

My analysis below underscores the importance of incorporating relations of social exclusion and marginalization (including racism, sexism and lower wages) into an examination of agrifood restructuring. This enables us to move beyond a farmer- and consumer-centred discussion of what constitutes high-quality good food. 'Good food' *must* include good employment and labouring practices (Myers and Sbicca 2015). Even Good Agricultural Practices certification does not ensure good jobs in agriculture. The highly personalized and often arbitrary labour recruitment, management and wage-determination strategies utilized by agro-labour traders are observed in small and large, conventional, GAP-certified and/or organic farms. Commonality resides in the horizontally established relations of trust rooted in regional/local connections, former ties and household livelihood strategies, which secure the bond between a labour

Table 6.1 Average Daily and Monthly Wages of Workers in Agriculture (2013–2014)

	Daily Wages for Seasonal Workers (TL)			Monthly Wages for Permanent Workers (TL)		
	2013	2014	%	2013	2014	%
Average	42	48	13.9	1,232	1,284	4.2
Women	36	41	14.3	1,032	1,118	8.4
Men	48	54	12.1	1,262	1,304	3.4

Source: TÜİK (March 2015).

broker and workers. These horizontal ties shape the personalized dynamics of paternalism in labour relations.

Horizontal Connections and Paternalism on Large-scale Farms: Agro-Labour Traders

The phenomenon of *agro-labour traders* is not new, nor is it unique to Turkey. Agricultural labour brokers emerged in nineteenth-century Europe and Latin America and were often referred to as 'gang masters' in Europe and '*engan-chadores*' in Latin America (Ortiz et al. 2013, 488). They contributed significantly to the development of agrarian capitalism by supplying cheap labour for commercial farms. Labour contractors used various state-sponsored labour-recruitment mechanisms, including slavery, indenture, debt peonage, vagrancy laws and migration arrangements (Ortiz et al. 2013). Nevertheless, labour contracting is not only an arrangement of the past used during the course of early capitalist development in support of primitive accumulation. It also continues to play a role in the recruitment and control of foreign migrant labour employed in the twenty-first century commercial agriculture of Britain, California, Brazil, India and South Africa, among other places (Brass 2011, 199–233). 'The return of the gang master' as described by Brass (2011) notes the continuing role of labour contracting as a fully functioning capitalist method of accumulation adopted to keep labour costs low. On 28 April 2016, the Canadian Broadcasting Corporation reported that labour contractors illegally impose recruitment fees (Can\$ 7,000 per person) and other unlawful charges on Indonesian migrant workers whom they subcontract from Indonesia through a government-sponsored temporary workers program. Without any government oversight, these labour-contracting arrangements have created debt bondage for some foreign migrant labourers, for example, those employed in the greenhouses of Leamington, Ontario, Canada (CBC 2016).

Such forced forms of labour recruitment and use are absent in the agrarian history of the Ottoman Empire, because, historically, subsistence-oriented small-scale farms were the defining feature of agriculture. However, with the expansion of large-scale commercial agriculture, particularly after the early 2000s, labour recruitment and management became important issues. It is in the politically strategic context of armed conflict in the East and Southeast of Turkey that Kurds were displaced from rural areas, resulting in the emergence of agro-labour traders as a culturally and politically significant informal institution connecting migrant Kurds to commercial agriculture. In light of the fact that these traders operate informally, it is not possible to know their exact number.

The labour they broker is composed of informal Kurdish migrants who, together with their families, are tied to unwritten labour contracts brokered for the entire season. They are not party to any negotiations that take place between labour contractors and farmers/agro-traders, and cannot leave their place of work as they are typically not paid until the end of the season. Many of these workers do not know Turkish. The *çavuş* is the primary channel through which workers communicate with agro-traders and farmers. The linguistic barrier further increases workers' vulnerability to labour contractors in the communities where they temporarily live and to farmers and agro-traders in the field. The labour-brokerage activities of contractors are currently outside of governmental labour regulations.

To the best of my knowledge, there is no comprehensive study on the employment of Kurdish migrant workers in the commercialization of agriculture in Turkey, its effects on migrants' livelihood and the various interactions with the rural society in which they live. The working and living conditions of Kurdish migrant labour vis-à-vis the complicated relations between citizenship and the state, as well as the local migrant-receiving community, remain largely unexamined in the literature. My field research and interviews with labour brokers and workers provide much needed ethnographic data on these issues. I have interviewed three *çavuş*: one in the village of Fasıl in Beypazarı, and the other two at the experimental farm-demonstration day organized by Syngenta on Mesut's farm in the village of Kayabükü, Beypazarı. The *çavuş* in Fasıl previously worked as a labour broker for Ömer, an agro-trader who contracted out farm produce from a farmer in Fasıl. This *çavuş* is also a Kurdish migrant. The other two in Kaya Bükü had no direct connection to Syngenta but worked for Mesut, who planted Syngenta's experimental seeds. The two *çavuş* working for Mesut are a married couple from Mardin who migrated to and then settled in Beypazarı.

The delegation of labour recruitment and management responsibilities to labour subcontractors allows farmers, agro-traders and biotech companies to distance themselves from the abusive practices of brokers. Commercial farmers and agro-traders are mainly concerned with a steady supply of reliable, disciplined and low-wage labour. They pay little or no attention to how the labour is recruited, supervised and retained; and how the work itself is organized. Very little attention appears to be paid to the living conditions of these agricultural workers.

Nuri, for example, is a GAP-certified producer subject to certain labour management requirements. He has approximately 100 workers employed on his farm but has delegated all responsibilities related to labour to the *çavuş*. When I spoke with Nuri, he had no idea how the labour on his farm is recruited or treated. He did not even know the exact number of temporary and permanent workers he employed. He estimated that he had 12–15 permanent local workers, with the remainder being seasonal Kurdish migrants.

Hidayet, one of the large-scale farmers whom I interviewed, stated:

> There are a lot of *çavuş* in the region who travel from village to village, and town to town, asking growers if they need workers. They will say "I have 20 or 25 workers. Do you need them?" We negotiate a price per person per day. If we agree on the price and the number of workers we want to hire, the *çavuş* brings them here to the field in his vehicle. This year's price was TL 30 per worker per day. I don't pay the workers directly but through the *çavuş*. I have no clue where these people stay and how they live their lives. I give my list of tasks to the *çavuş* in the morning and expect him to make sure they are completed properly.
>
> (Interview, 17 May 2013)

The contracting of labour through the intermediary of the *çavuş* precludes any possibility of workers independently negotiating a wage and working/living conditions for themselves.

My interviews with Ömer and his *çavuş* (whom I met in Fasıl) contain revealing information on the practice of unfree labour in agriculture. Ömer is an agro-trader who purchases, harvests and markets the entire field of crops grown by a farmer. Once the farmer sells his crops in the field to an agro-trader, the farmer's responsibility for labour ceases and is transferred to an agro-trader. The agro-trader hires his own labour for the harvest through an agro-labour trader. The pattern of labour brokerage activities by agro-labour traders is the same whether the labour is brokered for an agro-trader or a farmer. Ömer explains his use of migrant labour in the following way:

> A *çavuş* brought my workers here from the village of Karadağı in Mazı, Mardin in Southeast Turkey. They came in February and will stay here until November or so. The *çavuş* is also from Mardin. I know him as he has brought people here in the past as well. I also know Durmuş [the farmer who grew crops on his farm for Ömer] from previous years. We often use the same workers. These workers came here with their families and small children. Most of the children are not even of school age but accompany their parents in the field all day long. They sometimes sleep during the day in the van parked over there. The van belongs to the *çavuş*. He transports workers between the field and wherever they're staying in his van.
>
> (Interview, 17 May 2014)

Ömer believes the abundance of Kurdish migrant labour in the area originates from Kurds' 'livelihood response' to poverty. Migration is a survival strategy arising from the need of families to find 'money for the bread they eat' (*ekmek parası*, in Turkish). Ömer asks 'what else can they do? They are extremely poor, with few opportunities to do anything else' (Interview, 17 May 2014).

The Kurdish migrant workers whom I interviewed at Syngenta's open-field demonstration day on Mesut's farm agree with Ömer. One male worker said:

> We are here as a family, far away from home (*gurbetteyiz*, in Turkish). We are five people, including three children. If there was work for me in Diyarbakır, I wouldn't have left my home. We have no choice … we must work here until winter – for about 9 or 10 months.
>
> (Interview, 28 May 2014)

Another male worker added:

> There is no employment possibility for us back home. We have no land to cultivate; and no education to find a job elsewhere, so we must work as labourers. We work here for 13 hours a day, from 6 in the morning to 7 in the evening, and earn TL 35 per day. We are not even paid that money regularly; we have to wait until the end of summer … they give us some allowance for

Figure 6.3 A Kurdish Migrant Worker at Syngenta's Open-field Day (Kayabükü, Beypazarı, 28 May 2014).

the daily necessities. We are crawling here in the fields like worms (*sürünüyo-ruz*, in Turkish). We are on our feet all day long under the sun, hoeing, weeding ... Hopefully, our children will have the opportunity to go to school here in Beypazarı and get some education. That is why we are here.

(Interview, 28 May 2014)

If this worker's hopes for his children's education were realized, it would compensate in part for the suffering experienced working in the field. It is a hope that many other workers expressed during my interviews but one that is rather difficult to fulfill. In Turkey, families wishing to enroll their children in school must provide proof of permanent residence (Erder 1997, 153). Although some of these Kurdish workers have settled in the areas where they work, many others continue working as seasonal migrants, residing in tents set up temporarily in the fields. Those who chose to settle permanently told me that they have done so for their children's education. However, many others who continue to work as temporary seasonal workers often face difficulties in registering their children for school.

According to the narrative provided by Ömer's *çavuş*, the phenomenon of Kurdish labour migration is deeply embedded in the regional and kinship ties between workers and *çavuş*. Ömer's *çavuş* states:

I look after the workers. I make sure that they comply with what the *ağa* says and wants [*ağa* translates as 'master'.]. I recruited the workers directly from my own village of Karadağı. I wasn't doing this work before. I was brought here a long time ago as a labourer by a *çavuş* to work for brother Ömer. Brother Ömer liked me. Later he asked me if I could work for him to bring workers from my village. I brought 20 workers from Karadağı. It is like a chain; initially a relative brings *his* relatives here, which is what happened to me some 10 years ago. Since the *ağa* liked me, I began to bring other sets of relatives ... and it continued in this way. We now have more than 1,000 people working here from my own village and nearby villages, brought by me and others like me.

(Interview, 17 May 2014)

Another *çavuş* I interviewed on Mesut's farm offers a similar perspective. He also describes the harsh working conditions of Kurdish labourers:

I bring people here whom I know and trust. They are families with children from the same village. Men and women do the same kind of work, although men are also doing heavier jobs which require lifting in addition to their regular tasks of weeding, hoeing and so on. I teach them how to do the work. I also teach them during the harvest, how to cut the lettuce and place them in boxes according to their size, and so on. Both men and women earn the same amount of money. By earning TL 35 per day per person, a couple can make TL 2,100 per month. They work every day for 30 days a month. They are not paid for the days they are sick. From their earnings, they spend about TL 250 per month for rent. They spend only a little on their daily food expenses because they bring their staple foods from back home. They try to save as much as possible. The boss does not provide food or tea. They cook their own food in the field. They also give me some money for transporting them to the field in my van.

(Interview, 28 May 2014)

Workers' ability to earn enough to sustain their families depends on their willingness to work collectively as members of an entire family and consolidate their earnings into one family budget. Mesut's *çavuş*, who provides workers to grow crops from experimental seeds innovated by Syngenta, explains:

Most of the families have three or four workers. Children also earn money if they are old enough to work. Each worker earns TL 35 per day. They work 12–13 hours a day, or about TL 3 per hour. That is very low. Therefore, they need to work together as an entire family. If four people from the same family are working, they can earn TL 140 per day, which means TL 4,200 per month. That is sufficient for them to live here in Beypazarı and to even save a little to take back home. However, they also need to spend some money to pay for their housing, electricity, water and food. The employer does not provide anything for them. In the past, they used to stay in the tents for free, which they would set up in the fields where they work. But, the Beypazarı municipality does not allow them to stay in tents anymore. They are now forced to rent a place, which requires them to spend their own money.

(Interview, 28 May 2014)

Although renting allows workers to gain residency and an address, so they can send their children to school, many of those I interviewed continue to stay in tents, which indicates that they want to go back to their villages and towns when the season is over. They also want to save as much money as possible rather than pay rent for a residence. I am not certain exactly how much money a migrant worker or family can save during the season or whether there are additional migration-related costs transferred onto them.

While it does not appear that workers are in a bondage-from-debt situation with the *çavuş*, it is less clear whether the cost of migration is taken out of workers' wages by the *çavuş*. There is evidence to suggest that some earnings are diverted to the *çavuş* as payment for daily transportation between their place of residence (either rental homes in Beypazarı or tents outside of the field) and the worksite. It is also known that workers pay some money to the *çavuş* for recruiting them from their village. However, none of the *çavuş* I interviewed admitted that they receive such money. The workers whom I interviewed denied paying any money to the *çavuş*. The farmers and agro-traders told me that they do not pay contractors for their supply of labour. The only information I have is from Hidayet, who indicated to me that labour contractors in the past were paid by workers for finding them employment. Hidayet asserts:

> I don't know how it used to work exactly, but as far as I know the *çavuş* used to receive a commission from workers for finding them jobs. I know that workers are no longer willing to pay a commission; they have woken up. They have worked long in the area to get to know the producers, and some of them even live here. They are aware that they can find employment on their own. Still, many continue working with a *çavuş*, who makes it easier for them to find a job, and may therefore still be paying a commission. What I know for sure is that a *çavuş* still receives TL 3–5 from each worker per day for his transportation costs. If a *çavuş* transports 100 workers per day in his vehicle, he earns TL 300–500 per day. It is very good money.
>
> (Interview, 17 May 2013)

Farmers such as Hidayet and agro-traders such as Ömer are the legal employers, but they are separated from the employment-related work carried out by labour brokers. The separation of the legal employer from labour is defined in the literature as a *triangular employment relationship* (Theron et al. 2005). For Hidayet, a triangular employment relationship has evolved because he has no reason to employ permanent labour on his farm; the work is seasonal and his farming is mechanized. He only needs labour during certain periods to carry out simple tasks that require no specific skill or training. The most important thing for him is to negotiate a low price, for which the labour-brokering abilities of the *çavuş* are well suited. For Hidayet, a *çavuş* who knows all the tasks and is familiar with how the system works is the best asset to have, rather than skilled labour:

> If I didn't have this much machinery, I would need to employ thousands of workers. If I didn't have this carrot stacking machine, I would need at least 15 people just to stack carrots in the cold storage room. With this machine, I only need one. I use greenhouse-grown seedlings rather than sow seeds in the field. This saves me labour for hoeing, fertilizing, weeding and so on. Plants grown from greenhouse seedlings need to be hoed only twice a season, as they are already hoed once in the greenhouse. Plants grown from seed require hoeing three times. At the moment I have 45 people in the field, whose number goes up to 100–150 during carrot harvesting season. Last year I spent 550,000 lira for the workers ... too expensive. I negotiate workers' wages with the *çavuş*. There are lots of *çavuş* who travel in the area. If I cannot conclude a bargain with one of them, the other will offer a better price for me.
>
> (Interview, 17 May 2013)

Hidayet is clear in pointing out that the mechanization of agriculture and the ready availability of cheap migrant labour allows him to reduce labour costs and free himself from labour management–related responsibilities, including working conditions, wages and labour discipline. He is unlikely to address any concerns that workers may have regarding working or living conditions. Mesut expressed similar disinterest in the working and living conditions of the labour employed on his farm. Both growers exercise their control over the labour process indirectly through the *çavuş*. Therefore, the *çavuş* is beneficial for large-scale commercial farmers not only as a labour broker but also as a labour manager.

Paternalistic relations between Kurdish migrant labour and *çavuş* are established out of the farmers' desire to secure and retain self-disciplined labour. The shortage and high cost of local labour, as well as the seasonality of the work and the lack of government regulation on the agricultural labour force, structurally condition this paternalism. For example, there is a large pool of unemployed women and men in Güdül who could easily be recruited to work on the farms. However, the farmers I interviewed complained that these people are not willing to work as agricultural labourers because they have access to cash and other necessities from the charitable donations of wealthier people in Güdül. As a result, Hidayet explained, he has to hire workers from Beypazarı for the early spring work before Kurdish migrant labour arrives. He transports the labour he employs in March from Beypazarı on a daily basis, which is 35 km from Güdül.

Once the Kurdish migrants arrive from Eastern and Southeastern Turkey, Hidayet no longer hires workers from Beypazarı. The *çavuş* takes over the responsibility of transporting workers between the worksite and their place of residence. The unavailability of local labour from Güdül for direct hiring is the reason Hidayet enters into a labour brokering relationship with a *çavuş*. This sort of 'triangular labour recruitment' arrangement through an agro-labour trader keeps wages low and helps to maintain a disciplined, reliable labour force. Although Hidayet applied for GAP certification in 2015, he explained that GAP does not require him to make any alterations in his employment and wage-determination practices (Interview, 15 June 2015).

A Paternalistic Labour Regime

The labour issues and labour contracting practices on large-scale farms have not been widely discussed in the literature on Turkey. There is also no study, to the best of my knowledge, on the personalized social relations mobilized between labour brokers and workers that enter into the institutionalization of a particular form of labour regime for migrant workers. Based on the evidence gathered from my own field research, I argue that the concept of *paternalism* best explains the institutionalization of various labour regimes in the restructuring of Turkey's agriculture. This concept is discussed in a series of articles published in a special issue of the *Journal of Agrarian Change* (2014) under the theme 'Agrarian Lineages of Paternalism'. Although the concept is difficult to define (Gibbon et al. 2014), I use it to refer to the work ethos, 'protective' oversight and moral basis found in the labour recruitment and management strategy of commercial farms. It is the kin ties and village-neighbourhood networks that are pivotal in the development of highly structured paternalistic relations in agriculture's informal labour markets. I have observed elements of agrarian paternalism used by agro-labour traders in my field work in Turkey.

All of the large-scale farmers and traders I interviewed, including Hidayet, Mesut, Ömer and Nuri, have employed Kurdish migrant labour in the form of kin-based groups recruited by labour contractors. Horizontally established ties among local persons from the same village or town are also an important element in migrant workers search for jobs, as described by Hidayet's worker from Beypazarı (Interview, 17 June 2012). These ties are significant in labour recruitment, whether for direct hiring or through a labour contractor, and help to keep wages low. Low wages are typically accepted by workers because they view themselves and their employment in relation to their contribution to the *family income*. They don't regard themselves as individuals but as members of an entire household unit. This type of thinking, common to workers and farmers, is the ideational basis for paternalism in labour relations and a significant contributing factor to wealth generation and accumulation in agriculture.

The paternalistic dimension of accumulation in Turkish agriculture conflicts with the notion of *wage labour* conceptualized by Karl Marx (1954 [1887]) as independent and free. I believe that paternalism compels us to conceptualize labour in a different way. The meaning of the concept should be shifted away from that of an independent wage labourer to that of an entire household as

Figure 6.4 Tents of Kurdish Migrant Workers (Beypazarı, 20 May 2014).

Figure 6.5 Ömer, a Farmer and a Kurdish Migrant Family (Fasıl, Beypazarı, 20 May 2014).

Figure 6.6 Male Members of the Kurdish Migrant Family Working for Ömer (Fasıl, Beypazarı, 20 May 2014).

Figure 6.7 Female Members of the Kurdish Migrant Family Working for Ömer (Fasıl, Beypazarı, 20 May 2014).

Figure 6.8 Children of the Kurdish Migrant Family Working for Ömer (Fasıl, Beypazarı, 20 May 2014).

a labouring unit. In response to household survival and livelihood needs, the entire household as a labouring unit adjusts itself to become a family budgeting strategy based on income pooling and shared accommodation – in this case, a tent. I observed many cases of an entire migrant household living in a tent with no bathroom or kitchen. Living together in this way, workers endure low wages, long working hours and the withholding of earnings by employers until the end of the season.

Tamer, a large-scale farmer from the Beypazarı area who relies on contractors to recruit his labour, clarifies the significance of viewing labour as an entire household. He employs approximately 120 workers during the peak of the season and pays TL 40 per day for each worker. Tamer also rents 10 vans for TL 100 each to transport workers from their place of residence to the field. Altogether, he spends TL 5,800 per day for workers. Tamer believes that a wage of TL 40 per day is too low for a worker; nonetheless, it represents a considerable amount of money for him. He justifies these low wages on the normative grounds that the workers are members of a larger economic family unit. He states:

> If a worker earns TL 40 per day, she makes approximately TL 1,200 per month. Her spouse is also working and earns about the same amount of money. Between the two of them, they earn TL 2,400. The children also work in Kurdish migrant families. So, I think that a labouring family earns

good enough money ... a retired public employee earns less than that amount in Turkey.

(Interview, 12 June 2013)

The notion of the entire household as a labouring unit can be better understood from a Polanyian (1944) perspective of culture and culturally significant horizontal connections. These connections normatively ground, discipline and regulate behaviour (Sahlins 1976; A. Smith 1976 [1759]; Thompson 1963), and are reflected in the values and sentiments that tie migrants' labouring activity to the survival of the family as a whole (Arizpe 2014).

Trust and trustworthiness are indispensable cultural values in the institutionalization of paternalism within a triangular employment relationship. The *çavuş* are intermediary labour brokers, but they also work alongside farm workers. The ability to elevate their status to the level of a broker is due to the fact that they are long trusted by the farmer and agro-trader after having come to the area as workers themselves years before. The well-established trust enjoyed by the *çavuş* on the part of farmers/agro-traders means that they can be relied upon to continue providing a steady supply of disciplined labour. Given the economic hardship, unemployment and deprivation in their home towns, trust networks invoke a cultural consensus: the *çavuş* expects *hemşeri* to work for lower wages without social-security provision, and labour is willing to do so, but only in return for the necessary shelter, care and support when needed.[4]

To recruit labour, the *çavuş* generally utilizes the informal channels of his/her own community and family-kinship networks. Workers are typically recruited from the same towns/villages that the *çavuş* are from. Horizontal ties between workers and the *çavuş* are based on kin, *hemşeri* (persons from the same region, village and town), *eş-dost* (friends), *tanıdık* (contacts) and *kivre kardeşliği* (fictive kin). These networks remain highly significant in Turkish society today in translating feelings of *dürüst* (trust) and *dürüstlük* (trustworthiness) into a labour commitment.[5] *Dürüstlük* underpins mutual reciprocity by symbolizing the importance of moral integrity and ethical solidarity. It is not only migrant labour and the poor who are integrated into the highly personalized cultural networks of paternalism but also the farmers/agro-traders who seek *dürüst* in the form of reliable workers. The *çavuş* prefers to hire *hemşeri* as they are highly trusted, and workers find jobs by informally mobilizing *hemşeri*, *eş-dost*, *tanıdık* and kin. These ties are also mobilized by the *çavuş* who brokers the employment of former migrants who have settled in an area. For example, the female *çavuş* I met at Syngenta's open-field demonstration day on Mesut's farm in Beypazarı organizes female *hemşeri* who migrated from Mardin and settled in Beypazarı; her husband organizes the male *hemşeri* as labourers.

Gibbon et al. (2014) have also found paternalistic labour relations across South-East Asia and Africa but in a less directly integrated and dispersed form. My field research in Turkey indicates a more widespread and directly integrated implementation of paternalistic labour practices, regardless of the scale of farm, type of farmers or method of production.

Service provisioning by labour brokers underpins the implementation of paternalistic relations in agriculture. The *çavuş* provides various services to migrant workers. He brings them from Eastern Turkey and immediately finds them work. He uses his own vehicle to transport workers between the farm and their place of residence. He helps them find a form of shelter and offers access to health-care facilities and other infrastructural necessities. Since some of these migrants do not know Turkish, the *çavuş* also facilitates communication within the workplace and with the wider community. These are important services that migrant workers gain access to under the tutelage of the *çavuş*. This service provisioning and tutelage also enable the *çavuş* to gain loyalty from workers, thereby contributing to a more self-disciplined work force. The omnipresent possibility of the *çavuş* withdrawing his tutelage further strengthens workers' self-discipline. Thus, the *çavuş* act as an institution and *agent of labour discipline and management* in commercial agriculture. Once the loyalty of workers is secured, the *çavuş* can gain access to the same pool of workers in following years. The potential offer of renewed employment then strengthens the social context in which labour loyalty to the *çavuş* and self-imposed work discipline is further reinforced.

Horizontal Connections and Paternalism on Small-scale Farms: Direct Employment with or without Personal Trust in Güdül and Kaman

Small-scale operations follow a different migrant-labour recruitment pattern than large-scale farms. Rather than rely exclusively on labour contractors, the farmers themselves are more directly involved in hiring migrants based on previous relationships. Migrants also find work based on contacts that they have cultivated during previous employment in the region – employment initially organized by a *çavuş*. They are aware that they can find work on their own without a *çavuş* by informally mobilizing previous contacts of *eş-dost* and *tanıdık* (friends) and kin who have settled in the area. These workers are often surplus labour, which the *çavuş* can easily discard. In this pattern of direct employment without the intermediary brokerage of a *çavuş*, personal confidence in the trustworthiness of the workers becomes even more important for the employer. A lack of personal trust, for example, may worsen workers' living conditions, relegating them to the extreme margins of farm work.

Abdullah from the village of Karacaören in Güdül employed a family of eight people directly from Şanlıurfa through his personal contacts with another farmer in Konya. His friend had employed a Kurdish family on his vegetable farm for four years. He recommended to Abdullah another family that had kin ties with his own workers. The recommendation was based solely on his conviction that these people were trustworthy. For Abdullah:

> If you find the right kind of Kurds who are trustworthy, you don't have to have 'your eyes staying behind' [*gözün arkada kalmaz*, in Turkish].

Figure 6.9 Members of a Labouring Kurdish Migrant Family (Güdül, 13 June 2015).

> These Kurds on my farm are Muslims; they believe in God and are afraid
> of committing a sin. I trust the entire family even in money matters. The
> husband deals with my accounting.
>
> (Interview, 1 June 2014)

The female worker in the family explains how they were hired by Abdullah
and why they like to work there despite the low wages:

> We have been here for three years. My sister was working on a farm
> in Konya together with her family. Her boss knew our boss, brother
> Abdullah. Brother Abdullah was most concerned that there would be no
> thievery on his farm. With my sister's boss' recommendation, brother
> Abdullah himself hired us. We start our work at about 5:30 or 6 am, and
> work until 7 or 8 pm. We are paid a monthly salary of TL 2,000. This
> is the total amount of money paid to myself and my husband. We didn't
> have regular employment back home in Şanlıurfa. We have six children,
> all school-aged. Here there are schools with teachers who regularly hold
> classes. There is a school in my village back home for the children, but
> teachers do not stay there long because it is a region of high deprivation
> even for the basic necessities of life. We cannot settle here for good as we
> cannot afford to purchase a home with such a meager salary, but we want
> to stay until the children's basic schooling is complete.
>
> (Interview, 1 June 2014)

Zübeyir, from the village of Savcılı Büyükoba, Kaman in Kırşehir, expresses a very negative, distrustful view of migrant Kurds. His distrust has resulted in a reduced standard in the living conditions for workers on his farm. In contrast to Abdullah's workers, who were given a one-story house in which to stay without rent, Zübeyir's migrant workers are discouraged from renting accommodation in the village altogether. They are even prohibited from setting up their tents in the fields and are forced to live in make-shift tents on the outskirts of the village. When I asked Zübeyir why the tents were set up so far from the village, he said:

> You cannot trust them with your property, your life or your children's safety. They are thieves and drug dealers. They will corrupt the moral life in the village. There was a Kurdish worker from Diyarbakır who purchased a small plot of land in the past. I guess he liked the village and wanted to settle. We pressured the village administration to make sure that he sells the land back to us. They are not clean people. They do not even wash themselves. The other day I happened to share the same car with one of them. He smelled like animal shit. I asked him the reason. He said that he cleaned a barn three days ago. Clearly he had not washed himself in the last three days. How can you have such people close to your family and children in the village? This soil-tillage machine cost me TL 3,000. If you let these people settle here, the machine will be stolen for sure.
>
> (Interview, 18 May 2013)

There are 70–80 seasonally employed Kurdish migrant workers in Savcılı Büyükoba; many are from Siverek, Şanlıurfa and villages in Diyarbakır and Mardin. They come as families on their own, settle into tents and are then hired on a temporary basis by farmers who need extra labour for various tasks. Zübeyir employs 10 of these migrants. He claims that local workers are either unavailable or too expensive. Therefore, he feels compelled to hire Kurdish migrants even though he distrusts them. Zübeyir explained that while a migrant worker costs him TL 30 to 35 per day, a local worker expects up to TL 110, which he finds unaffordable.

I did not meet any migrant workers on Zübeyir's farm, but I had an opportunity to interview a group of Kurdish migrant workers from Diyarbakır on Burhan's farm. There were seven workers in total: Lütfettin, his three siblings and three cousins. (Their narratives are examined in detail below.) All were employed by Burhan directly without use of a *çavuş*. Burhan allowed them to set up their tents in his field, which is close to Zübeyir's farm. Apparently, Zübeyir was unable to pressure Burhan to move the migrants to the outskirts of the village. They brought their own mattresses, quilts, pillows and bed covers from their village, as well as their own pots and pans for cooking. The farmer gave them the tents only. There was no electricity, running water, toilet, washroom or kitchen in the field where they set up their tents to live for the next 9 or 10 months. They brought some food from their village with them in plastic jars and burlap sacks. This included cheese, pickles, olives, bulgur (cracked wheat) and home-made macaroni. They dug small pits in the ground and buried their perishable food in jars. These workers had no kitchen or stove to cook their food, so they gathered tree branches for fuel and cooked their meals over an open fire. They also built a tandoori-style oven in the field to make their own bread. For a toilet, they just opened a pit in the ground and used a simple curtain for privacy. They are required to travel to a *hamam* (Turkish public bath) in the village to clean themselves properly. But they work for 12–13 hours a day, which makes traveling to the *hamam* very difficult. So they go to the *hamam* only once a week.

While Zübeyir is openly hostile toward Kurdish migrant workers, this cannot be generalized to the entire migrant-labour hiring community of farmers. Nonetheless, Kurdish migrant workers at the farm level are subject to anti-Kurdish sentiments and a tense political environment. This is undoubtedly related to the ongoing conflict in Eastern and Southeastern Anatolia at the national level (Çelik (2005). My interviews reveal that these workers are forced to endure deplorable living conditions, social isolation and segregation from local towns and villages. They are also frequently perceived as potential criminals and thereby exposed to further discrimination.

Even if migrant workers take up permanent residency, as can be seen in Beypazarı and Güdül, their Kurdish identity continues to shape the social isolation and marginalization that continually check the workers' trustworthiness. When a horizontal trust-setting cultural context is absent, as is the case with the village of Savcılı Büyükoba, workers are left to deal with their own concerns without an intermediating institutional mechanism operating either informally through a *çavuş* or formally by the state. The pervasive distrust of Kurds often compels workers to accept the paternalist tutelage of a *çavuş*. The *çavuş* serves as a kind of insurance that workers will not betray farmers' trust.

My interviews show that household, kin and *hemşeri*–regional connections are more important than vertically linked relations of production in generating a horizontal context of trust for workers' integration into the process of agrarian change in Turkey. However, horizontal trust is a two-edged sword: workers find employment and gain solidarity through these connections, but they are also subject to further subordination and exploitation within and through them.

The narratives of Lütfettin and his relatives further illustrate the argument.

A Case Study of Horizontal Trust and Paternalism: Lütfettin and his Relatives in Savcılı Büyükoba

Lütfettin, his three siblings and three cousins are seasonal migrants from Diyarbakır who travelled together to Savcılı Büyükoba as seasonal workers. They have other relatives and *hemşeri* working for different farmers in the village, who also stay in tents set up in the hills outside the village. Lütfettin's siblings include two sisters and one brother, and his cousins include one woman and two men. The men are in their late teens and twenties and the women range from 13 to 15. All know Turkish, which they learned in school, where Turkish is obligatory. The women preferred not to speak with me, although they listened to my conversations and allowed me to take their pictures. Therefore, I only spoke with the men. Lütfettin attributed the women's refusal to speak with me to their shyness. I interviewed the men on 18 May 2013 outside their tents in the field on Burhan's farm.

Lütfettin is a university student studying history. His cousin, Özcan, has a primary school diploma. He is married and has a daughter. Lütfettin's brother, Onur, has never attended school. He cannot read or write. When Onur was school-aged, the village school was often closed, and he did not have the means to travel 60–70 km every day to attend a school in central Diyarbakır. While the least educated in the family had no choice but to work as seasonal farm workers, Lütfettin was doing so to pay for his university education.

Onur noted:

> It would of course be better to work back in Diyarbakır and be together with the entire family. We have about 20 *dekars* of land and only a few cows back home. You cannot rely on that land and those cows to sustain the family. My family has nine members: seven children and my mother and father. You have to find an additional source of income. Therefore, I am here together with my cousins. I will earn about TL 10,000 during this 10-month period, which is about TL 1,000 per month. That is not enough for the family, but what else can I do? It's still better than no money at all.

Özcan stated:

> I don't know exactly how much money I am going to earn by the end of the season. If I could work every day without getting sick or something, I could earn 8,000 to 10,000 lira. I don't purchase anything with the money I earn here for myself or buy gifts to take back home. My family needs the money, not the gifts.

I reminded these men that there is a widespread belief that Kurds in Eastern Anatolia are provided with various social services by the government, including free coal and green cards for free health care. I asked them why they need more money if this is true. Onur explained:

> It is true that the government has begun to provide some services in recent years, but you still need access to cash to buy shoes, clothes, food … You have to live like a human being. You need more than coal to burn. My family lives in a mud-house full of cracks and holes. The coal that you get from the government does not heat the house during winter in the East. It is very difficult to live there when it rains; everything gets muddy. If we had enough money, I would have built a better house for my family.

While the work day for these workers is 12 hours long, from 7 am to 6 pm, they continue working until 7 pm without extra pay if there is additional work to be done. They rest for about 10 minutes in late morning and have a one hour lunch break. Farmer Burhan's wife told me that '6 pm is too early for them to stop working in summer, but the workers get tired and can no longer work. There is not much we can do about it' (Interview, 18 May 2013).

Although their wages are calculated on a daily basis (Özcan told me they are paid TL 30 per day), Lütfettin explained that they are generally paid at the end of the season after all work is completed. Özcan added that 'the boss gives us some money; we are given an allowance from time to time when we need it. But, our actual earnings are not paid until the end of the season'. When given a small allowance for daily spending, Özcan reports that he feels like a child rather than an adult who works for a living. Özcan also said that if they get sick, the farmer may take them to the hospital in his car if he is available, but they are not paid for missed work days due to illness. If the farmer is not around, they have to call a taxi when ill and pay for it from their own allowance.

I asked the workers about their preferred method of payment; whether it might be better to receive a large sum of money at the end of the season, given the possibility that regular small sums can be easily spent if they are received on a weekly or monthly basis. Lütfettin's answer was as follows, with which the others agreed:

> You have no choice in the matter. It does not matter how and when you would like to be paid. He simply does not pay before the season is over. You just have to wait until he feels like paying you. He will say "the crops have not been harvested yet; I don't have money at the moment until I sell my produce at the market, etc." These are the kinds of things you keep hearing as excuses even when he has the money. I guess he is afraid that we may not work for the entire season if we are paid earlier.

The workers believe that farmers simply choose arbitrarily not to pay them until the end of the season. They are often not even paid for the whole amount they have earned. I was told that the farmer may arbitrarily reduce their earnings by TL 500 or TL 1,000 by inventing, according to the workers, some bogus reason. Onur said that they cannot complain against such abuses because they are seasonal, temporary workers without any governmental or trade-union protection. For Lütfettin, it is not only because of the temporary, seasonal nature of the work but also because workers have no protection against the arbitrary, impulsive decisions of farmers. Lütfettin states:

> Such work does not provide any protection and security from abuse and arbitrary action. You have no choice but are obligated to accept the conditions imposed on you by the farmer. These conditions are often unpredictable. You never know when he wants to pay you, or what kind of work he wants you to do and when. You do not have the luxury of negotiating

payment methods or sick leave. Once you leave your home and come here to work, you are completely dependent on him. It is you who are searching for work and it is you who need to persuade him that you are a good worker. If you begin to make a fuss about your payment or whatever, he can easily kick you out and you won't even get what you earned by that time. The only choice you have is not to come next year. But, you cannot do that either because you have a family back home which needs you to earn money. It is as simple as that! Period!

The refrain frequently heard from workers is: 'Even of you are not happy, you are obliged to work for your bread money (*ekmek parası*, in Turkish)'. One farmer in Savcılı Büyükoba bluntly explained his reasons for postponing payment to his workers:

> They are ignorant, primitive, vulgar, unrefined, brutish people. There is a huge difference in people's behaviour, culture and mannerisms in the eastern and western regions of Turkey. They don't know much about anything ... If you pay them weekly or monthly, they wouldn't know what to do with that money. And as soon as they get the money they will leave. They don't know much about a work ethic. They act on their feelings rather than according to work requirements and ethics. There is a student here. I actually prefer to pay his university expenses rather than give him the money. That way he can at least graduate with my help.
>
> (Interview, 25 June 2013)

In another interview conducted on 29 May 2013, a farmer indicated to me that 'we count the number of days workers actually work and calculate payment on the basis of TL 30 per day. But, we give our workers TL 300 or 500 as an allowance if they ask for it'.

This farmer justifies his practice of withholding workers' payment until the end of the season by saying that it is for the good of workers – their need for greater education, personal growth and cultural development. This is a form of paternalism that Mitchell (2005) has defined in relation to the notion of *edification*. Edification here refers to the treatment of workers as children, in the context of a parent–child relationship in the workplace. The farmer's reference to the east–west cultural divide in Turkey conveys the notion that Kurdish migrant workers need to be raised to a higher level of cultural maturity before they can be treated as responsible individuals.

The combination of migrants' horizontal relations and vertically applied farm-level paternalism shapes the conditions for the recruitment, management and discipline of labour through an emphasis on workers' need for protection and improvement. The combination of the two (horizontal ties of trust and vertical paternalism) flourishes in the political context of Kurdish out-migration from the East and Southeast of Turkey, which continues to feed a large pool of reserve labour.

An Example of Wage Differentiation: Paternalistic Wages for Migrants and Gendered Wages for Relatives in Güdül

Musa and Mustafa, the brothers whom I interviewed in May and June 2014, regularly employ seven or eight workers in their field. Many are informally employed women, earning TL 40 per day. These women are close relatives and family friends, including relatives of Musa's wife from Karacaören. Musa transports them daily from the village to his field by the Kirmir River in Güdül in his own vehicle.

There was a tent in Musa's backyard that looked like a labourers' tent, so I asked the brothers if they also employ Kurdish migrant workers. Musa said the tent was currently unused as he did not have migrant labour at that time, but in previous years he employed a migrant family from Adıyaman. Although he generally relies on his own relatives, he also hires migrant labour to supplement his labour needs. He explained:

> This Kurdish family had seven members, four of whom were working. Those not working included the mother, who did the housework in the tent, and two young children. One of the children was school age, whom I took to school in Güdül in my vehicle together with my own children. The other child was only one and half years old. The working members of the family consisted of the father, two daughters and one daughter-in-law. I hired these four as salaried workers and paid them TL 1,000 per person per month. They earned TL 4,000 per month as a whole family, which is good money.
>
> (Interview, 15 June 2014)

Musa was aware that farmers typically pay migrant workers at the end of the season, but this wasn't his practice. He paid them regularly each month. Musa also brought electricity to the labourers' tent (just behind his house) by extending a cable from his house. The tent had lighting, a fridge and a TV. Musa also built a section into the tent to be used as a kitchen. The brothers provided workers with some staple foods, including dry beans, lentils and bulgur, as well as access to running water, but no bathing facilities, just the nearby river. The brothers determined workers' wages based on a standard budget calculation, taking into account the provisioning of the migrant family with infrastructural facilities, staple foods and accommodation.

This form of wage determination is similar to that practiced in the past on colonial plantations for foreign migrant workers in Malaysia, as described by Amarjit Kaur (2014) in relation to Indian workers. According to Ramasamy (1994, 32, quoted in Kaur 2014, 199), a standard wage in a plantation labour regime was to be sufficient to maintain the plantation worker 'in a tolerable state of comfort'. This form of wage determination remains influential in Malaysia's contemporary commercial agricultural sector. It also corresponds to the personalized paternalistic practices of wage determination for migrant Kurdish labour illustrated in my example.

Musa's brother, Mustafa, indicated that they were expecting a Kurdish family to be brought by a *çavuş* from Mardin to work for them. The brothers already knew this *çavuş*, who often brought workers to Beypazarı. If the number of workers exceeds the demand in Beypazarı, the surplus labour is distributed to smaller farms in the surrounding villages. The migrants normally stay in tents. Abdullah is the only farmer I met who provided a house for the migrant workers on his farm. Musa explained that in the previous year, a migrant family from Adıyaman did not want to stay in a single-room tent. They built their own unit with separate compartments for children and parents.

During my interview, the *çavuş* with whom the brothers had previously established a connection telephoned Mustafa and informed him that he had seven extra workers if the brothers wanted to employ them. Mustafa told him that seven workers were too many, but they could take four. The brothers only needed a few migrant workers as they prefer to employ their own relatives. These newly arriving migrant workers were part of a larger extended family of 15 relatives brought to Karacaören from Mardin by the *çavuş*. A farmer in Karacaören wanted to take eight of them, and the *çavuş* was trying to find employment for the remaining seven. Mustafa told me that these new workers did not want to stay in the tent set up in Musa's backyard, separated from the rest of the family. They wished to have a daily transportation arrangement between Karacaören and Kamanlar so they could continue to live in the same location as an entire household. Mustafa said:

> It is understandable that they don't want to be separated from each other. But, it makes life difficult for us because we need to move them back and forth in the morning and evening every day in our vehicle. It will take lots of time and will also be expensive since we have to pay for the gas. Still, we have to accept their conditions as we need extra labour.
>
> (Interview, 15 June 2014)

This narrative shows that the migrants do have some agency of their own. It is mobilized within the horizontally established context of extended family ties and connections with relatives, and negotiated via the intermediation of the *çavuş*. The family refused to stay in an on-site tent, thereby requiring the brothers Musa and Mustafa to transport them daily between the village where they stay and the field where they work.

As mentioned above, the brothers pay TL 1,000 per month for each migrant worker. If they work close to 12 hours every day, we can assume that they work close to 360 hours per month. Calculated on the basis of TL 1,000 per month, they earn approximately TL 2.8 per hour or TL 33.5 per day. This is much lower than the official average wage in Turkey for the years 2013 and 2014. These wages are also lower than the wages paid by the brothers to their own relatives. Significantly, female relatives earn TL 40 per day, while male relatives are paid TL 50–55. Musa's response to the gender-based difference in earnings is as follows:

I don't know why we pay local men more than women. They do exactly the same work. I don't necessarily want to pay the men more than the women who do the same work. Actually, women work even more and harder ... There should be no wage difference between men and women; but men demand a higher wage, they won't work otherwise. It seems to be a traditional requirement.

(Interview, 15 June 2014)

I asked Musa if he pays more to migrant Kurdish men than migrant Kurdish women. His answer was 'no'; the migrants were paid a fixed monthly amount. He explained that the fixed amount of TL 1,000 per month was normal because, according to him, their work capacity and performance in the field was almost 50 per cent lower than that of the locals. Although they did the same kind of work, he still believed that there was a difference in their performance. He did not believe there was a difference in the work performance of local men and women. For Musa, it was only because of a widely practised tradition in Güdül that local men are paid higher wages than local women – a tradition that he does not apply to migrant workers.

I asked Musa if he would accept his own daughter earning less than his son for doing the same work. His answer was: 'of course not. It is simply not possible that I would accept such a thing. We don't make any difference between our daughters and sons' (Interview, 15 June 2014). Clearly, the absence of a gender-based wage gap for migrant Kurdish labour reflects a 'paternalistic notion' of wage determination, which does not consider migrants as individual men and women but as a unified category comprising an entire household.

Musa's justification of the wage differential between migrant and local workers reflects his personal paternalism based on the perceived capacity of Kurds' work performance. For him, if the capacity of Kurdish migrants was elevated to the same level as locals through education and training, they would earn the same amount of money. This cultural perspective of human development and capacity enhancement disguises the economic exploitation of migrants, making Kurds themselves responsible for their own exploitation. Given their limited capacity to perform effectively at work, it is argued that they deserve lower wages.

The emphasis on capacity building to improve performance reveals continuities in the paternalistic labour management and supervision strategies adopted by both large-scale farms and small-scale operations (cf. Gibbon et al. 2014). The only difference between these operations lies in the delegation of paternalism by large-scale farmers/agro-traders to labour brokers. The farmers in small-scale operations generally practice it directly and personally. Vertical paternalism in labour regimes and wage determination is intertwined with horizontal relations of trust in the recruitment and maintenance of informal migrant labour, either subcontracted by labour brokers or hired directly by farmers. These paternalistic labour management and supervision strategies allow employers to maintain, discipline and dispose of workers at low cost.

The Gendering of Formal Employment: Local Workers in the *Bey Fide* Greenhouse in Beypazarı

I have argued that horizontal and paternalistic relations produce a transformative effect in rural livelihoods that allows us to reconceptualize labour as an entire household labouring unit rather than an independent wage-earning individual. This is not a transformation that generates better working and living conditions for migrants but one that confines them to arbitrary, personally organized and managed labour conditions. The key strategic institution here is the labour contractor. The household as labouring unit also activates a form of agency within a triangular employment arrangement of paternalism. This is a form of agency rooted in labourers' struggle to turn migration and paternalism into a family survival and livelihood strategy.

The following section allows us to contrast the paternalistic labour regime instituted for Kurdish migrant workers in open-field agricultural employment with another labour regime implemented for local workers in the Bey Fide greenhouse in Beypazarı. Based on my interviews with workers, I have identified three main areas that contrast sharply with the paternalistic labour regime. Interviews were conducted on 26 May 2014.

First, the greenhouse does not employ migrant workers but only local men and women. It implements a formal, registered employment pattern. Second, the formal employment of local workers adds a 'gender twist' to the horizontal trust and vertical paternalism in labour relations. While the informal labouring of migrant workers generates little or no gender effect on wage determination, the formal employment of local labour is heavily gendered. Third, while paternalism turns the entire household of migrants into a labouring unit in open-field employment, local greenhouse workers are treated as individual wage labourers. They are formally employed, registered for government social security and paid regularly according to government-approved wage schemes.

This section demonstrates a different kind of paternalism which takes on the more public, state-approved form of *human resource management*. The public form of paternalism is a key ingredient in the institution of a gendered labour regime. The common perception of migrant workers as a household labouring unit in need of capacity building and cultural enhancement protects them from gender-based discrimination, even though all members of the family (men, women and children) are discriminated against equally and reduced to the racialized status of marginal people. On the other hand, a conception of labour as *individual workers* subjects these people to a 'modernist', gendered notion of the 'family wage' (Barrett and McIntosh 1980) that favours men. Musa and Mustafa in Güdül refer to the modernism of the family wage as a 'tradition', which gives cultural approval to higher wages for men. Kurdish migrant men are excluded from this 'tradition' and are paid the same wages as women and children. The following section expands on the 'gender twist' of paternalism.

Labour Force Segmentation and the Gendered
Division of Labour: the Bey Fide Greenhouse

There are approximately 20 men and 50 women employed in the Bey Fide greenhouse. There are four male professionals: one agricultural engineer and three accountants. The cook is a woman. Here I will focus on workers' narratives only, rather than those of professionals, in order to demonstrate the gendered division of labour among workers themselves, whose educational levels are about the same.

The division of labour among workers in the Bey Fide greenhouse is clearly gendered. The lifting and carrying of bags of soils, seeds and fertilizer is men's responsibility. Men operate the machines to lift and move these bags from the trucks to the seed-sowing room. They also move the seedling trays from the germination room to the greenhouses and the packaged seedlings from the greenhouses to the trucks. And men are responsible for transporting the seedlings to customers. The operator of the seed-sowing machine and water-purifying machine is a man as well.

Ali, the machine operator, is a 28-year-old high-school graduate who also studied accounting at university for two years before dropping out because of financial difficulties. He worked for eight years at the Ayık Tarım, which is partly owned by Bey Fide, before working at Bey Fide for the last four years. While at the Ayık Tarım, Ali performed all kinds of work: handling fertilizers and chemicals; visiting customers' fields with the engineers to determine the needs of growers and improve their production; and shipping and delivering necessary materials to their fields. At the Bey Fide, he is mainly responsible for operating the machines that sow seeds into seedling vials, and water purification, both of which are computerized. His work day is approximately 11 hours long. After deducting his lunch and tea breaks, he actually works nine hours a day. Ali is a salaried employee with social security, earning TL 1,500 per month. This is above the average wage for men in Turkey (see Table 6.1 in this chapter). Ali also earns extra pay for overtime work. He said that he loves his work and is satisfied with his income. He added that if he had the opportunity to continue his education he would study agricultural engineering and then work at Bey Fide as an engineer.

The seed-sowing machine Ali operates is imported from Italy. He received basic training from the distributor of the machine and then trained himself further on the job. When operating the water-purification machine, Ali also adds fertilizer to the water. The company uses artesian water for irrigation in the greenhouses, but the underground artesian water in Beypazarı is chalky. Therefore, its pH level needs to be regulated to better suit the growing of seedlings. Ali appears proud of his work and believes his job is important.

Most of the seed varieties used at Bey Fide are imported biotech seeds, chemically treated for weeds before they are packaged. Consequently, they do not need further chemical treatment before they are sown into vials. Ali does not deal with chemicals but focuses on soil preparation. He combines the soil mulch with a layer of perlite and fertilizer consisting of nitrogen, phosphorus and potassium. The exact formula is determined by the engineer. This mulched soil–fertilizer mixture is electronically distributed into the vials by the machine, after which the seeds are sown.

If the seeds are produced in Turkey, they are not chemically treated before packaging. Some customers demand that only Turkish-grown seeds be used for the seedlings they purchase from Bey Fide. If Turkish seeds are used, Ali also applies herbicides to the soil when preparing the soil–fertilizer mix. Since Bey Fide also has GAP-registered customers, Ali follows the required procedures listed in the guidelines for the application of chemicals and fertilizers when preparing soil and sowing seeds. The company engineer has trained Ali in GAP procedures. This information is also available on the government website.

Although Ali believes that his work is skilled because it requires some technical knowledge, he adds that anyone with some interest in the job can perform it. He told me that he believes women are actually more careful and pay more attention to detail than men, so there is no reason for machine operators to only be men.

I observed a more clearly demarcated gender division of labour among greenhouse workers. The men are responsible for non-technical aspects of greenhouse work, including lifting, carrying, repair and transportation. They consider their work to be strictly male and view the actual care of plants in the greenhouses as female work. Women do not share this perspective.

Women's tasks in the greenhouse include the general care, irrigation and on-site sorting, grading and packaging of seedlings, as well as overall cleaning. In terms of plant care, their work consists of operating automatic watering and fertilizing machines, grading and sorting of seedlings to maintain standard quality in height and size, thinning and transplanting of seedlings to ensure there is only one seedling per vial, pruning, de-leafing, operating ventilators for climate control and opening and closing windows. This work requires long hours of standing in front of tunnels of seedling trays and a great deal of walking, stooping and bending. This is repetitive manual work, which the female workers do not find difficult but highly monotonous. The greenhouse operates essentially as an assembly line with assembly-line workers who, after doing this work for a while, feel they can perform their tasks automatically with little thought.

Because the seeds are sown electronically into vials and have already been treated with fungicides and herbicides, workers are not expected to have an educational background in horticulture, nor are they given additional training in the technical requirements of growing new seed varieties. The biotechnological information is already inserted into the seeds, so the workers are merely expected to follow the guidelines for applying pesticides and watering seedlings with a ready-made solution of fertilizer.

There is no on-the-job training; the only basic training they receive is through personal observation of co-workers. One female worker describes her job:

> My job is to water plants. They give us a list of things to do every morning. The engineer writes up the list. We simply carry out whatever is written

by pressing certain buttons on the control panel. The list includes tasks to be completed for each tunnel of seedling trays. The tasks are itemized according to the date of planting, the growth period and shipping date. The list also includes information on how to manage the water sprinkler system. The sprinklers are completely automated. By entering the engineer's instructions on the sprinkler's controller panel, and pressing the necessary buttons, we can implement the instructions on how many times the sprinkler needs to move over the seedlings to spray water mixed with fertilizer, and how many times to spray with sweet water after the fertilizer application. Sweet water must be applied after the fertilizer to prevent the seedlings from being burned. I have no idea what sort of fertilizer is used or whether or not there is any chemical or growth hormone contained in the water. This sort of information is not given to us.

(Interview, 26 May 2014)

This woman's behaviour at work is entirely routinized. She has no insight into the technical complexities of her work. Another woman who appeared to be more senior explained that the water also includes root-forming and growth-regulating hormones in addition to fertilizer. She knew that they spray pesticides separately early in the morning whenever there appears to be a need to control insect growth in the greenhouse. However, she was not at all familiar with the type of hormones and chemicals used in the greenhouse, as this information was not released to the workers.

Figure 6.10 A Group of Female Greenhouse Workers at Bey Fide (Fasıl, Beypazarı, 20 May 2014).

Figure 6.11 Saniye (Fasıl, Beypazarı, 20 May 2014).

Figure 6.12 Women's *Kaşıklama* (Spooning) Work (Fasıl, Beypazarı, 20 May 2014).

Another group of women was engaged with the task of grading and sorting seedlings. One woman described her work with seedling grading and sorting as *kaşıklama* (spooning). Workers do not actually use a spoon to do the work, but the task itself is defined as spooning. If there is more than one seedling in a vial, extra seedlings need to be lifted out and transplanted into an empty vial. This task includes dipping a stick-like tool into the soil to lift the extra seedling and transplant it into an empty vial. This is an important task for maintaining standard quality in height and size of seedlings.

I was told that the workers responsible for operating the water-sprinkler system are paid more because their work is considered more technical. Saniye told me that that the *kaşıklama* work is valued less because it is seen as non-technical and easy, although it requires more attention and dexterity to lift and transplant seedlings. Saniye, a 37-year-old woman, has worked in the greenhouse for four years as a *kaşıklama* worker. She doesn't find her work difficult but acknowledges that it is repetitive and monotonous. Nevertheless, she prefers to continue with the same work until her retirement. Saniye is very happy about her job because it is permanent and salaried. She is also registered in a state-governed social security institution. She used to work as a daily waged, open-field worker, but that was temporary, seasonal work with no social-security provisioning. Saniye explains:

> In the past the only employment possibility for a woman with no or lit-tle education was open-field agricultural work. But the local people of Beypazarı do not want to work as open-field workers. Places like Bey Fide have just begun to operate and provide regular employment opportunities for us. We can now have a more permanent job and a decent life. Open-field work is tough as you are under the sun for 12 or 13 hours a day, with no regular breaks or social security. Since we work in the closed environ-ment of a greenhouse ... we are protected from the sun and rain ..., Kurds can still work in open fields. They can now have a job which they didn't have before and earn some money.
>
> (Interview, 26 May 2014)

For Saniye, labour-force segmentation between locals and migrants is accept-able – a view commonly shared by other greenhouse workers. Its acceptability is rooted in the emergence of another labour regime in agriculture that local work-ers have only recently begun to enjoy. This regime includes a formalized system of human resource management, as implemented at the Bey Fide greenhouse for both workers and owners alike. What stands out is that there are no employment opportunities for migrant workers within this human resource–management sys-tem. Migrants' subordination to personalized paternalism as open-field workers continues to be justified by greenhouse workers on the grounds that migrants at least have jobs and the opportunity to earn some money.

My field work demonstrates that personalized paternalism and a human resource–management system co-exist in agriculture as employment has become segmented between informal open-field work for migrants and formal employment for local workers. These are complementary labour forms, integrated into the development of commercial agriculture in Turkey alongside a segmented system of labour exploitation.

Saniye elaborates on how the human resource–management system works in her particular case:

> In Turkey the government-required minimum monthly salary is TL 846. Our daily waged colleagues earn TL 38 per day, which is higher than the wages paid to permanent workers. The Bey Fide also employs daily waged labourers during the height of the season. Most workers are permanent, though. I am a monthly salaried worker. I have had social security for the last two years. I earn TL 1,050 per month, which works out to TL 35 per day. The daily wage may be higher than my earning level, but a daily worker is not on the permanent payroll and has no social security. If I was the only income earner in my family, my salary would not be adequate. I have two children who are high-school students. And children's education is expensive. My husband also earns about the same amount of money. As a family we are okay. But there are other considerations beyond wages. Regular-salaried employment with social security is more important for my future than a little more income. Regular work is always better. You start your work at a regular hour in the morning and end it at a regular fixed hour in the evening ... You are paid for overtime work. I start at 7:30 in the morning and end at 6 pm, with an hour lunch break between 12:30 and 1:30, and a 25-minute tea break between 3 and 3.25 pm. I am happy at my work.
>
> (Interview, 26 May 2014)

Saniye expanded on the benefits of permanent employment in relation to the working environment and facilities, which contrast sharply with the working conditions of the migrant open-field workers in their make-shift tents:

> We have a beautiful work environment here. We have modern toilets, lavatories, a change room, and a very nice kitchen and dining room. Our food is really good, home-made, cooked by a woman who prepares it as if she is cooking for her own family. We don't pay for the food we eat or the tea we drink. We also have a *mescid* [a small mosque]. Our work environment is well suited to the needs of the women. They also provide us with a company van to collect us and drop us off at our homes for free. The kind of work we do here is not like open-field work. Everything is so well-organized and managed. Everyone knows their job in advance; no one is subjected to the whimsical demands of a *çavuş* as always happens in open-field work. If we get sick, they take us to the hospital. No one loses wages for sick days. What else could we ask for?
>
> (Interview, 26 May 2014)

In regard to the level of heat in the greenhouse, none of the workers complained. They mentioned that the heat may become difficult to handle when the humidity increases later in the season and the temperature increases from a reasonable 29° C in the spring to the high 40s in summer. However, they explained that the greenhouses are equipped with strong fans to circulate fresh air and they also have windows that open. All the workers mentioned that if the greenhouses get too hot and stifling, the workers can have a rest in the dining room, and if they get sick they are taken to hospital, with no loss in wages.

During my interviews, I observed that many of the women were wearing traditional-style sleeveless wool or cotton-knitted vests (*yelek*) over their blouses, and traditional-style baggy pants (*şalvar*). While the loose-fitting *şalvar* pants are suited for working in a high-heat environment, the vests are not. I asked if the vests did not bother them in the greenhouses. They answered by saying that it is the cultural norm for women from the Beypazarı region to wear the vests over their blouses or dresses when they go out. They all said they felt naked without them.

I visited the kitchen and dining room and interviewed the cook, Yasemin. She is a 46-year-old woman responsible for cleaning, cooking and tidying up the kitchen and the dining room. Accountants do the shopping on a daily basis from a menu prepared by company managers. Yasemin prepares breakfast for the accountants and provides lunch, cookies and tea for everyone working at the company. The managers and owners eat together with the workers. No dinner is served. Yasemin used to be a greenhouse worker who specialized in spooning. She has just moved to the kitchen as a cook. She said that 'I cook as if I am cooking at home. We eat good food here' (Interview, 26 May 2014). She is married with two sons in their twenties. She works every day except Sundays and earns TL 1,100 per month. She said:

> My income is not adequate for a 12 and a half hour work day. I work more than 300 hours per month. If my wages were calculated on an hourly basis, I could earn more. But my work is certainly better than open-field work. I have total control over the kitchen. No one tells me what to do and how to do it. Still, my income is not adequate for this kind of work or to support a family. My husband has a retirement pension. He still works to supplement his pension as a night watchman. So we combine our incomes to get by as a family.
>
> (Interview, 26 May 2014)

The narratives of local workers indicate that they prefer formal, permanent employment to open-field work, even if they earn less.

The acceptability of segmented labour regimes is closely tied to the dominance of certain cultural norms that govern a gendered division of labour. These norms are engrained in what Wallerstein (2006) has called 'European modernity', existing across space and time. Although men and women are theoretically conceived as independent individuals within that modernity (Wallerstein 1995), women are still identified as wife–mothers, reduced to 'unfree' status (Werlhof 1988) and subjected to a family-wage ideology (Barrett and McIntosh 1980). The family-wage ideology, a central component in the historical development of capitalism in Europe and North America since Victorian times (Ewen 1976), considers women primarily in terms of their position in the family as homemakers and mothers, while men are viewed as heads of the family who *ought to* earn an income high enough to support a wife and children (Barrett and McIntosh 1980). Even though working class men have never earned a wage high enough to support the family, family-wage ideology has long justified their higher wages. The level of women's wages is determined as a supplement to men's family wage – merely a contribution to the family income as whole.

The women I interviewed 'contribute' to family income by working more than 10 hours a day, which allows them little time for themselves and to fulfill their roles as wives and mothers. The long working hours clearly undercut the use of the family-wage ideal in the determination of women's wages. These women often delegate domestic work to their daughters. Many explained that their daughters are students who do not have much time for domestic work either, but they have no choice. Because their daughters can only do a limited amount of housework during school days, the women do much of the domestic work on the weekend together with their daughters. A 'double shift' is then experienced by both working women and their student daughters.

The 'family wage' has been a divisive political issue in the past (Land 1980), often opposed by feminists and favoured by male-dominated labour unions. My interviews show that family survival is predominant in women's beliefs concerning the acceptability of their lower wages. They are most interested in increasing their family's total income by pooling the wages of family members. The total income of the family is then budgeted for children's education, food and shelter. None of the women remarked on the need for money for their own personal spending or their husbands'.

The European Ideology of a Family Wage as an Embodied Practice of Local Tradition

All of the women I interviewed at the Bey Fide greenhouses reported that male workers earn more than they do, although they had no idea exactly how much. The men I interviewed did not disclose the amount of their earnings with the exception of Ali, the seed-sowing machine operator, who earns more than the national average for men in Turkey. Male workers justify women's lower wages on the basis of a division of labour in the workplace, which designates different jobs for men and women. Men said that women should be paid the same amount of money if they do the same kind of work, but they are not. They argued that women are culturally better suited to do the kinds of work they are currently doing in the greenhouse. A male worker, Osman, stated:

> Spooning is women's work. It is not appropriate for men. Men's hands are not suited for that kind of work. They have different tasks to do; they wouldn't waste their time spooning. Men are better suited for carrying and lifting things and for transportation.
>
> (Interview, 26 May 2014)

Another man, Ahmet, added:

> We are hired to ship and deliver the seedlings. We place the trays of seedlings into boxes, carry them outside the greenhouse, load the boxes into trucks and transport them for delivery to customers. We ship three to four trucks full of seedlings each day. We have three trucks, each of which takes 2,000 boxes of seedlings ... Spooning is intricate, fine work. Only women can do it. I actually tried it once but couldn't do it. For me, it is a really boring job. It is not the same for women. Women can spend hours sitting in one spot all day long making lace or doing embroidery. It is in their nature. I cannot sit like that! Women are more suited for that kind of job by creation. They are created like that!
>
> (Interview, 26 May 2014)

Saniye then claimed that

> Spooning requires more patience and endurance, and men are not willing to stand in one spot by the tunnel long enough to do the job. [She asked Ahmet] What happens if you don't show enough patience during spooning? Do you lose your head?
>
> (Interview, 26 May 2014)

Ahmet responded: 'Nothing happens to my nerves, but I simply do not like that kind of work.' Another man entered the conversation and said 'I did not try it before. I could try to see how it is done. But I wouldn't do it to earn my income because I know it is a boring job' (Interviews, 26 May 2014).

I asked the men if they believe that only women should be doing the tedious, boring jobs. The men did not feel this way, but they still argued that women are by nature better suited for spooning rather than lifting boxes, loading trucks and shipping. For Saniye, however, women can do anything and everything, including lifting and loading of the trucks. She added that 'we often lift trays to place them into boxes, and then carry them to the trucks when men are not around. It is not as if we don't do that work at all' (Interview, 26 May 2014). A male worker, Mehmet, responded:

> Spooning is like lace-making, sewing, embroidering, knitting and crocheting. I know nothing about this kind of stuff! ... Men do not involve

themselves with sewing and embroidering. I have never occupied myself with these kinds of things. But, women are doing these sorts of things from the age of six or seven. They learn how to do such intricate work.

(Interview, 26 May 2014)

The male greenhouse workers in Beypazarı made an argument similar to the one expressed by Musa and Mustafa in Güdül to explain the lower wages of women. They share the brothers' reference to *tradition* in relation to the *cultural suitability* of women for certain jobs, and the God-given *innate qualities* of women that predispose them to specific kinds of work. According to Mehmet, the socialization process for girls and young women in the household prepares them for such tedious work in the greenhouse when they begin waged employment. For the men, this learning is embedded in the traditions practiced by women as a way of life in local communities. These traditions, it is believed, enable women to develop the endurance and patience for fine work and to attain the skills necessary for paid employment that are best suited to them (Elson and Pearson 1997).

These arguments raise questions concerning how 'tradition' and 'cultural suitability' are understood to guide cognitive orientation, aptitude and sensibility and how they play a role in naturalizing certain practices as unchangeable certainties of life. What is often taken as a certainty of tradition is in fact an 'embodied practice' (Asad 2015) of 'European modernity', which has reshaped social life through gendered meanings of the family-wage ideal.

According to Wallerstein (2006, 33), modernity is by definition 'the incarnation of the true universal values' and therefore not merely conceived as 'a moral good but a historical necessity'. Modernity presented as a historical necessity requires that certain developments in European history be elevated to a level of universality. European modernity embodies dominant norms of Western liberal thought, which define people as the sum of free, independent individuals holding equal rights (Wallerstein 1995, 78). These norms provide a direction for the capitalist economy (Bell 1979; Marx 1954 [1887]; Weber 1984 [1930]). The free, independent individuals who are elevated to the status of a sovereign as the historic subjects of capitalism become foundational to the cultural constitution of European modernity.

This understanding of modernity has been a dominant paradigm in much social science literature, shared by such thinkers as Karl Marx, Max Weber, Emile Durkheim and Daniel Bell, among others. According to this view, despite claims to its universality, modernity upholds dominant European normative standards. It blends European capitalism with key norms from Western liberal thought relating to the independence of individuals, but with a gendered and ethnicized/racialized cultural orientation to the notion of the family that refigures men's and women's roles in fundamentally new ways.

This modernity contains a mode of knowledge that describes particularities of European cultural practices in universal terms, presented as metanarratives in comparative research (Somers 1992). An embodiment of, and a cultural adherence to, this metanarrative is re-imagined as a local tradition in everyday practices of life (Anderson 1987; Asad 2015). Musa and Mustafa's reference to tradition exemplifies this argument, as does the conversation I had with greenhouse workers.

Concluding Remarks

This chapter has demonstrated the time and space-specific constitution of various labour regimes in agriculture. While it has been long discredited in social science literature, modernity's cultural pretentions continue to be built into the narratives of prevailing relations of labour regimes, as seen in this chapter.

Unpacking these narratives has revealed dynamic, gendered and ethnicized/racialized relations of labour exploitation that are justified within the institution of personalized and public paternalism. Its sustaining ideas are drawn from a naturalistic rendering of the family and gender relations and the universalised normative pretensions of modernity regarding human behaviour. Such notions are engrained in paternalistic labour regimes designed to recruit and manage workers in ways favourable to wealth creation and capital accumulation by both small and large-scale commercial farms engaged in Turkish agriculture. These paternalistic relations and their justifying ideas are mobilized in re-embedding the constitution and regulation of labour into a 'capitalist synthesis' between a cultural construction of interpretive meanings and the material reorganization of labour regimes. The interpretive meanings have been drawn from the dominant norms of 'European modernity' that have been unfolding in Turkey from Ottoman times (Atasoy 2009), only to be reinstalled in a neoliberal restructuring of agriculture.

The adherence to European modernity, although unconscious, prevails as the norm-setting context for a gendered division of labour that supports the family-wage ideal. It also fosters a paternalistic outlook in relation to Kurdish migrant workers. Paternalism in informal labour regimes treats migrants as undifferentiated members of households and extended families. Hence, they are unsuited to modernity and in need of cultural development. Raising them to 'maturity' through edification (Mitchell 2005) involves capacity building for individual autonomy and self-realization outside of horizontally established cultural ties or connections (Bell 1979, 13–4). Kurds are assumed to be lacking these personal capacities to act and operate efficiently and rationally as independent, mature individuals – capacities that are alleged to be 'necessary virtues' for succeeding in a capitalist economy (Hanson 1998). Rather, the Kurdish migrant workers considered here are seen to be bound to horizontally established relations of household and kin and regional–cultural connections that constitute the basic social organization of migrant existence. It is this kind of thinking that justifies personalized paternalism in the institution of a labour regime for migrant workers and defines them as a culturally bounded and socially unified category – that of the entire household as a labouring unit.

Notes

1 There is also a long history in Turkey of forced migration of Kurds from the Eastern provinces. For example, during the implementation of the Settlement Law of 1934 (Law No. 2510) alone, a total of 25,831 Kurds from 5,074 households in the east were forced to resettle in Western Anatolia (Tekeli 1990, 64). These Kurds were not given the opportunity to return to their homes. In 1994, the Turkish government initiated a policy known as the *Return to Village and Rehabilitation Project* to facilitate the return and rehabilitation of displaced people following the armed conflicts of the post-1980s. The outcome of this project is unknown.

2 Given the difficulty of collecting data on the informal economy, these figures should only be taken as an estimate.

3 US $1 was equal to TL 2.7 on 16 April 2015.

4 To the best of my knowledge, there is no scholarly work on the importance of trust networks for labour relations in agriculture. For a comparative perspective on factory organization in Turkey, see Dubetsky (1976); and for the importance of religious trust networks in the neoliberal reorganization of class alliances, see Atasoy (2007).

5 Amongst the unemployed in Turkey, 31.5 per cent look for jobs within informal networks of friends/kin/community (TÜİK May 2007).

7 Supermarkets and *Pazars*

Divergent Paths

Chapters 4 and 5 of this volume examine the different pathways of commercialization adopted by large and small-scale producers, including a mixture of conventional, GAP-certified, organic and customary production methods. Large-scale producers frequently point out that they are mindful of the food safety standards expected from GAP and organic certification, although many of them are not certified GAP and organic producers. GAP referencing generates what I call *commercialized trust* for the quality of their food. It is expressed in globally and nationally institutionalized industrial food standards. For farmers, GAP standards represent 'the ascendancy of institutional trust-producing structures' for profit-oriented growth in agriculture (cf. Zucker 1986).

On the other hand, small-scale producers often rely on a process-based and personalized form of trust that they cultivate with their customers in commercial activities. This form of trust is based on perceptions of the reliability of customary methods and traditional farming knowledge in terms of respect for local agro-ecological processes, food taste and culture. Judgements concerning the reliability and trustworthiness of producers also constitute a central axis of trust that small-scale producers rely upon for their commercialization.

In their appeal to the institutionalization of food-quality standards for generating a commercialized form of trust, large-scale farmers resemble Schumpeter's (1934) entrepreneurs, but with a twist. They gradually break away from the long-established customary methods and experiential knowledge of farming. These farmers progressively adopt techno-scientifically driven agro-industrial innovations and increasingly adhere to a commercially organized food provisioning system. Smaller-scale farmers also *partially* combine techno-scientific methods and globally advocated agro-industrial innovation systems into their production. Nevertheless, the partial adoption of these innovations does not represent a complete break from the past. The enduring reliance on a personalized mode of trust production is integral to the continuing significance of street-level informal markets and neighbourhood *pazars* in the traditional food-provisioning system. Its persistence also effectively impedes the expansion of supermarkets.

The co-existence of various forms of production, commercialization paths and food-quality assurance mechanisms complicates the expansion and deepening of corporate rule in agrifood provisioning in Turkey. Formal, institutional-based commercialized trust tied to globally and nationally established private and public food-quality standards *and* informal, experience-based, personalized trust tied to *participatory certification by consumers* are central to the differentiated pathways of commercialization – but without binary polarization between different production methods. The simultaneous co-existence of the two modes of trust production engenders two forms of commercialization in food supply chains: supermarket food produced by unknown, distant groups of both large and small-scale producers *and* local food produced by personally known and trusted small-scale farmers whose produce is sold in traditional *pazars* and through street vending. They are incorporated, in their own distinct ways, into the restructuring of food provisioning in Turkey – within which supermarket chains are melded.

This chapter shows how, and whether, this melding works to facilitate supermarkets taking hold in Turkey's food relationships. It takes into account the reality that ongoing changes in food provisioning bring together *the old* and *new* ways: one way concerns the historical centrality of small-scale production directed toward local-regional consumers; the other way relates to the increasingly dominant role played by supermarkets in changing the conditions of subsistence.

Moreover, both small and large-scale farmers commonly share ambivalent attitudes toward the new ways. Their *farming imaginary* is mixed with a desire to maintain the old ways within the modernity of the new, to generate growth and income. The implications of a melding of old and new, and the ambivalent attitudes deeply engrained in farmers' farming imaginaries, are significant for understanding the complex ways in which supermarkets are expanding into food supply chains. In this melding, we can certainly expect the power of supermarkets to assume a non-linear form.

In a context where smallholder agriculture dominates, varied trust mechanisms operate, ambivalent attitudes prevail and written contracts with supermarkets and agro-traders are of limited value, the state continues to play a greater role in 'encouraging' the food provisioning system to be more conducive to commercialization. The market-modifying policies of the state include the restructuring of 'traditional' wholesale markets and *pazars* and the privatization of formerly state-led agricultural cooperatives and producers' unions.

The growth of inter-capitalist competition is also important for the expanding role of supermarkets in food provisioning in Turkey. Islamically oriented small, medium and large-scale capital groups are seeking to achieve competitive growth alongside large retailers owned by old Turkish-holding companies and transnational corporations (TNCs). The key point here is that the adoption of a supermarket model by Islamic groups is contributing to the reconstitution of an ontology of the social. This is intensifying market relations in agriculture as these groups increasingly converge into transnationally advocated development models, but with a *difference* in terms of the culturally varied conditions of development. Rather than consider the question of what might result from this entanglement, farmers and retailers focus on capacity building in order to competitively engage with joint-venture holding companies and transnational corporations.

In what follows, I provide an in-depth analysis of the state restructuring of wholesale markets, neighbourhood *pazars* and producers' unions. The final section of the chapter analyzes the particular domestic appeal of a supermarket model to various groups in Turkey, including Islamic capitalists.

The Wholesale-Markets Law, Commissioners and Agro-traders

The Regulation of Fresh Vegetable and Fruit Trade and Wholesale Markets Law of 27 June 1995 (No. 552) has been the key piece of legislation in the state's re-creation of formal markets in fresh fruits and vegetables (FFV) production. This law required all FFV-growing farmers to sell their products through wholesale-market terminals via the intermediary of commissioners. The terminals are operated by city municipalities, and the commissioners are key agents in the traditional value chains that connect producers to retailers via wholesale markets. Retailers include *pazar* merchants, street vendors, small shopkeepers and restaurant and hotel keepers as well as supermarkets. Commissioners, who pay taxes to the municipality, receive a 3–8 per cent commission on total sales for brokering FFV sales on behalf of producers (Lemeilleur and Codron 2011). The wholesale-market law also allows wholesale traders, producers and producers' unions to retail FFVs through the intermediation of wholesale terminals. While commissioners sell produce on behalf of producers without taking ownership of produce, traders purchase produce from the growers and sell as owners; producers and producers' unions sell their own products in wholesale terminals. Traders, producers and producers' unions do not pay a commission to the municipality.

In 2010, there were 203 wholesale terminals in Turkey, two of which were in Ankara. There are 11,823 offices in wholesale terminals throughout Turkey, 9,864 of which are rented or leased out by commissioners, traders, producers and producers' unions. In 2010, there were 7,974 commissioners, 1,815 wholesale traders, 65 individual producers and 21 producers' unions renting these offices (Canik and Alparslan 2010, 3).

Yüksel Tavşan, president of the Vegetable and Fruits Commissioners Federation of Turkey (whom I interviewed on 18 June 2011 in his office at the Ankara Wholesale Terminal), explains the relative absence of producers from terminals in the following way:

Agriculture in Turkey is done by *köylü*-type small producers ... The small scale of their operation poses the greatest challenge for them to market their produce. A majority of FFVs need to be marketed on a daily basis ... Strawberries, cherries, cucumbers, and tomatoes must be brought to the dinner table very fast. They are not durable and cannot be stored. This is the first difficulty for *köylü* marketing their own produce. The second difficulty is that FFVs are not [situated] within a category whose prices are determined in advance. *Köylü* cannot cost his/her cherries based on production expenses. You can price bottled water based on production cost and market circumstances, with an added profit margin ... If the bottled water cannot be sold at a desirable price, it can be withdrawn from the market and stored until prices rise ... This can also be done for cereals, but not for FFVs ... [FFV] prices are determined on a daily demand and supply basis. And, for this, a large number of producers who want to sell should be meeting with a large number of buyers. There is a need for wholesale terminals.

(Interview, 18 June 2011. Quoted in Atasoy 2013, 557–8)

For Tavşan, wholesale markets are the most significant marketing outlet for small-scale growers, and they continue to work through interpersonal relations based on trust:

The Ankara terminal is in close proximity to the producing villages and towns. It can be reached within an hour's drive at the most. This proximity enables both growers and commissioners to develop closer personal ties with each other. They are most likely from the same village ... Commissioners provide advance cash payments to the growers with no interest charges and in return they have an established portfolio with them. These sorts of financial interactions are more attractive to the *köylü* than banks, which require many formalities. ... [I]n return, commissioners ensure a regular flow of produce ... After a while, personal trust-based relations are developed.

(Interview, 18 June 2011. Quoted in Atasoy 2013, 558)

In 2009, approximately 10 million tons of FFVs were sold to retailers through wholesale terminals (Canik and Alparslan 2010, 1). Supermarkets, which require a large and constant flow of FFVs of consistent quality, tend to establish contractual relationships with traders in wholesale terminals, who procure FFVs from various types of growers. Taner Bey, a trader at the Ankara terminal, purchases cherries from many small producers scattered throughout different villages in Ankara and then sells them to a private company for size and quality-based sorting and packaging (Interview, 18 June 2011). These companies give their own names to the produce. If the size of vegetables and fruits is relatively large, as is the case with tomatoes, stickers showing the name of the company are placed on the produce. For smaller products such as cherries, the name of the company is identified on the box (Atasoy 2013, 558). In addition to selling to traditional retailers in the wholesale terminal, Taner Bey also acts as a distributor and transports cherries sorted and packaged by private companies to supermarkets in his own trucks. Emine Ünal, general manager of Altunbilekler supermarkets for the Dikmen district of Ankara, explained that

Altunbilekler contracts with traders (via its procurement managers) rather than producers themselves for the sorting, packaging and transportation of FFVs (Interview, 27 June 2011). When supermarkets contract directly with traders, it also reduces the role of wholesale commissioners.

There are many private sorting and packaging companies whose names are given to packaged goods. For example, cherries sorted by the company that Taner Bey deals with are named Ümit Cherries. Supermarkets buy these 'privatized' goods from traders (Atasoy 2013, 558–9). According to a report published by AMPD (Shopping Centres and Retailers Union), the share of wholesale markets in FFV retailing through wholesale commissioners in İstanbul, for example, has fallen to 30 per cent (AMPD 2010, 4). This is largely because of the growing influence of agro-traders in FFV provisioning for supermarkets. Recent research by Ebru Seçkin (2015, 72) reveals that 40 per cent of producers in the Gürsu region of Bursa province market their FFVs through agro-traders, in contrast to the 20 per cent who sell via wholesale commissioners. The other 20 per cent sell directly to supermarkets.[1] While the cases of İstanbul and Bursa cannot be generalized across Turkey, it shows a tendency in large urban areas for supermarkets to bypass wholesale markets through direct FFV provisioning by agro-traders. Large-scale farmers such as Hidayet and Mesut reflect this trend, acting as both producers and agro-traders.

Supermarkets also buy FFVs from wholesale commissioners if there is a shortfall of FFVs supplied by traders. According to Yüksel Tavşan, the rapid increase in the number of supermarkets in all types of neighbourhoods necessitates a new wholesale-market law. For Tavşan, the new law should accommodate supermarkets' FFV procurement requirements for quality, consistency and volume as well as the sorting and packaging of food. Tavşan hopes that the new law facilitates the diffusion of EUREPGAP/GLOBALGAP standards into small-scale FFV production, which, according to him, is essential for small producers to increase their market viability in the supermarket-led corporate agriculture of Turkey (Interview, 18 June 2011).

A new wholesale-market law was legislated in 2010 (No. 5957) and began to be implemented on 1 January 2012.[2] The new law emphasizes the protection of free-trade conditions in FFVs, in addition to product registration, standardization and traceability of quality and origin of produce (Article 6). To achieve this requires that wholesale markets build cold-storage depots and laboratories for preserving, testing and inspecting produce (Article 16) and that they register the characteristics of products on packaging boxes (*PERDER* Kasım–Aralık 2011, 14). The law aims to ensure industrial certainty concerning local quality at the level of wholesale markets. Information related to product characteristics, according to the law, must be placed on packaging boxes to confirm 'product identity'. The law prohibits unregistered FFVs that lack this product identification from being sold in supermarkets, traditional *pazars* and other traditional marketing outlets such as *manav* (greengrocers).

There has been a general discussion on the benefits of the new wholesale-markets law in *Retail Türkiye* (2012), a magazine widely circulated in the agribusiness sector. The discussion includes various perspectives expressed by people who are influential in the sector. According to Selamet Aygün, president of the Retailers Federation of Turkey, the law will expand formalization in the FFV sector and prevent the unregistered, untraceable sale of FFVs. In relation to traceability, Mehmet Yayla, general director of the supplier chain Mango, indicates that the law will allow consumers to have access to information not only on producers and the origin of production, but also on the seeds, chemicals and fertilizers used at the time of production. According to him, the availability of this type of information on product-identity labels is important to prevent the uninformed use of industrial inputs by unprofessional family-type producers.

The law is intended to upgrade wholesale markets as a principal means of improving the quality and safety of food. It requires the use of cold-storage, inspection and laboratory facilities in wholesale markets to ensure FFV safety standards in relation to pests, microbial pathogens and residues from pesticides and other agricultural inputs and toxins, as well as rot and mildew that can occur during transportation. Although the law foresees the registration of agricultural input use, the discussion in *Retail Türkiye* focuses mostly on food waste resulting from rot and mildew, problems often related to storage, packaging and transportation.

Selamet Aygün, president of the Retailers Federation of Turkey, indicates that in 2010, the total amount of FFV production was approximately 45 million tons.[3] While 5 per cent of this amount was exported, the remaining 95 per cent of FFVs was for domestic consumption. According to the Ministry of Customs and Trade statistics (2013, 17), between the years 2007 and 2012, 94 per cent of production was for domestic consumption and 6 per cent for export. According to Mahmut Celal Seyrek, purchasing director of FFV for the supply chain Mopaş, 25 per cent of the FFVs currently produced in Turkey is dumped into garbage sites and wasted due to inadequate storage and distribution (*Retail Türkiye* 2012). The State Planning Organization estimates a 15 per cent post-harvest loss in tomatoes alone (Buyukbay et al. 2011, 1657). According to Seyrek, the new wholesale law, with its emphasis on product quality and registration, would prevent waste and broaden the formal marketization of FFVs in Turkey (*Retail Türkiye* 2012). According to the Minister of Customs and Trade, Hayati Yazıcı, the amount of FFVs that is wasted is equal to TL 15–16 billion. The minister expects that the law will help prevent such waste in FFVs while ensuring industrial certainty of food quality within the wholesale registration system (*Retail Türkiye* 2012).

With the aim of preventing waste and providing food-quality assurance, the law introduces a 'notification model' (*bildirim modeli*) as a condition for formal distribution of FFVs. It works through an electronically operating 'wholesale registration system' within the Ministry of Customs and Trade. All FFVs produced for wholesale through traditional–customary, conventional, GAP-certified and organic methods must be included within the notification system. The law restricts the definition of wholesale to at least 150 pieces of produce, 50 bunches or 100 kilograms. Food supplied to markets below these amounts is not subject to registration. According to Yüksel Tavşan, this definition excludes the registration of FFVs sold to restaurants, catering companies and schools, thereby keeping them outside the documentation system for the verification of quality (*Retail Türkiye* 2012). FFVs that are not subject to commercialized consumption are also exempt from registration.

Electronic notification centralizes information within the wholesale registration system. Declaration occurs when the FFVs are loaded into trucks in the production area before their transportation to markets. There are three methods specified for the declaration: it can be done through direct application by filling out a declaration form at a wholesale market closest to the production area, through electronic data entry on the ministry's internet page at www.hal. gov.tr or through telephone call-centre registration at 444-0-425.

Individual producers are not required to declare such information if they themselves are transporting the goods to distributors, sorting and packaging facilities and wholesale markets in the production area before these goods are actually traded through formal marketing channels. However, agro-traders are required to declare the information before they transport goods from the field of production. According to the Minister of Trade, Hayati Yazıcı, the electronic product identification kept in the wholesale registration system is based on information provided by FFV-trading individuals rather than producers, who are themselves registered within the wholesale registration system. According to the minister, product identification ensures the traceability of quality and generates consumer confidence in the products presented on supermarket shelves and in *pazars* (*Retail Türkiye* 2014).

The system works in the following way: agro-traders procure FFVs from the farmers and enter the required information into the system by following one of the three methods of registration. Once the information is registered, the system electronically generates an identity for the product within the wholesale-registration system. After registration is complete, the agro-trader can sell the produce directly to retailers without the intermediation of commissioners in wholesale terminals.

The 'Wholesale Registration Declaration Form' available on the Ministry of Customs and Trade's internet page lists the type of information to be provided by FFV traders.[4] It includes the amount of product, the name of the producer and trader who declared the information and the origin of production and the place of distribution, as well as general information on the characteristics of the food in a section titled 'explanations'. This final section is very vague, and the kind of information to be entered is not specified. There is no requirement that agricultural inputs and labour conditions be declared.

The declaration form does not have a section on GAP and organic-certified FFVs. I assume that traders themselves enter this information in the 'explanations' section on the form to differentiate their products from others. There is always a label on the packaging boxes of FFVs that specifies the product as GAP and organic certified. For example, I saw a label placed on a box for tomatoes traded by a company named *Naturagreen-Doğal Tarım* (Natural green – Natural Agriculture). *Naturagreen-Doğal Tarım* is a GAP-oriented supplier chain that procures food produced by an agribusiness firm called the YDA, located in the Aegean region of Western Turkey. The company label on the box indicates that 'this product is produced by *YDA Agriculture and Food Ltd* under good-agricultural-practices certification'. The product identity placed on the box also includes the size, TS (Turkish standard) number and classification of the product, as well as the mailing, e-mail and internet address of the company, in addition to the date and number of the production permit that the company received from the Ministry of Food, Agriculture and Livestock (MFAL). Conventionally produced food is also labelled on packaging boxes but only contains information on the name of the producer, supplier and date of declaration in the system. These labels present no specific information on the production methods. The absence of such information on the boxes seems to indicate that traders do not enter the necessary data in the 'explanations' section of the declaration forms.

During the entire duration of my field research in 2011 and 2015 in the towns and villages of Ankara and Kırşehir, I have not encountered an agribusiness firm or a corporate supplier chain. In addition to the farmers themselves, it is the individually operating agro-traders who buy produce from the farmers (while it is still growing in the field), contract out agricultural workers (often with the intermediation of *çavuş*) and formally market the produce. These field-based individual agro-traders intermediate between producers and markets. For this to happen, they are required to document that they have electronically entered product and producer information in the wholesale registration system at the time trucks are loaded in the field, before they transport the produce (Kök 2010; *Retail Türkiye* 2012).

The new wholesale-market law expands the role of agro-traders in the formal distribution of FFVs produced by small-scale farmers and *gradually* institutionalizes commercialized trust in agro-industrial processes, replacing the personalized trust relied upon by farmers. The expansion of commodification through a product and producer-registration system turns FFV agriculture into a professionalized agribusiness under the business authority of agro-traders. This supports the emergence of agro-trader-led distribution and supply channels for the formal marketing of FFVs, which bypass wholesale markets. While the law generally embraces the wholesale marketing of FFVs through wholesale markets, agro-traders can now supply FFVs procured from a number of small and large-scale producers directly to supermarket chains and exporters. In a context where written contracts are not widely used and a large number of small-scale producers dominate, agro-traders play a significant role in the vertical linkage of producers to fresh-food supermarkets.

The law does not engage with the farm-level production process and business practices of producers and agro-traders in the supply chain. Therefore, many important issues are left out of the registration system, including workplace conditions, labour standards, environmental issues and health and safety.

Ömer, whom I interviewed on 17 May 2014, is an agro-trader who contracts out the produce grown on the farm of a medium-scale producer in the village of Fasıl in Beypazarı – while the plants are still growing in the field. As discussed in Chapter 6, he employs Kurdish labour informally on a temporary basis, which is contracted through a labour broker. These workers, required to work 12–13 hours per day for a daily wage of TL 35, live in make-shift tents in the field during the season. Since Ömer makes his labour-employment arrangements through a labour contractor, he does not feel accountable for the living and working conditions of these workers. He provides information to the wholesale registration system on the general product characteristics and the producer, but he is not required to declare any information that addresses the process of production at the farm level.

Ömer explained that he enters information into the system electronically via his smartphone and distributes his produce to supermarkets, exporters and wholesale markets. He had no idea how this information was being used to make sure that quality standards were monitored and verified. Ömer said that his trucks might be stopped and he might be prevented from delivering the produce to markets if he failed to notify the wholesale registration system, but he had no idea if the information he provides to the system is actually being checked (Interview, 17 May 2014). This suggests a number of unresolved issues regarding the verification of electronic information entered via smartphones and the monitoring of quality standards through spot checks and periodic audits. The law leaves it to consumers to check the information available in the wholesale-registration system. However, the electronic traceability of quality and verification of information is very problematic. One reason is that traders are allowed to register products and producers in the system via the wholesale market that is closest to the area of production. Wholesale markets in Turkey have not fully adopted a computerized system, and the information does not appear to be uploaded regularly to become readily available for consumer use. For example, I was not able to find information in the wholesale-registration system on products produced in the area of my field research, even by the large-scale farmers whom I interviewed, such as Hidayet, Mesut and Nuri.

Ömer offered me no insight into how he actually checks food quality and provides quality-inspection certification when he enters product-identity information and electronic data into the wholesale registration system. The system does not require verification of quality standards by traders. Given that the rate of farmer registration in the national farmers' registration system is low and that GAP certification has very limited application in Turkish agriculture, simple electronic notification by traders does not seem to expand the registration, monitoring and verification of product quality and safety in the supply chain, nor in the business practices of farmers and traders or the processes of production.

Informally established marketing networks handle 70 per cent of FFV sales in Turkey yet continue to be outside the wholesale notification system.[5] Therefore, it is fair to conclude that supermarkets and urban-neighbourhood *pazars* are only responsible for the remaining 30 per cent of formally distributed

FFVs, in competition with the informally functioning street-level sales and village and town *pazars* in rural areas. As discussed in Chapter 5, a significant segment of small-scale farmers continues to rely on informal marketing through local street-level food vendors and *pazars* in rural areas. This is mainly because agro-traders who emerged as the main intermediaries in the implementation of the new wholesale-markets law have little interest in dealing with them. Small-scale producers, then, continue to market their own food informally as street vendors. This is accomplished through traditional marketing networks and by creatively organizing sales outlets, as well as generating trust for the locality of village products without need for formal registration.

Traditional Pazars and Street Hawking: Local Food

Pazars have maintained a long historical presence in the commercial and social life of Turkish society since at least the period of the Anatolian Seljuk State in the eleventh century (Faroqhi 2004). They continue to play a vital role in FFV retailing in Turkey. *Pazars* can be organized in open or closed spaces, convened on a weekly basis in municipally designated places at a set time and day in urban neighbourhoods or held in small towns that sell FFVs and other food items. According to statistics published by the Ministry of Customs and Trade (2014, 3, 6), there are more than 1.5 million small-scale traders and craftspeople in Turkey. *Pazar* traders constitute the sixth largest category out of 60 groupings of traders and craftspeople noted on the ministry's list, with 56,245 registered individuals. No data is available on unregistered, informal *pazar* traders.

According to a report published by AMPD (Shopping Centres and Retailers Union), there were approximately 4,000 weekly *pazars* convened in urban centres alone in 2010, not including *pazars* in towns and other rural areas. There are approximately 570 *pazars* convened each day in these centres. As shown in Table 7.1, there were 165 weekly *pazars* organized in the province of Ankara in 2015, including those in all 24 of the towns belonging to the municipality of Ankara. The *pazar* tradespeople have leased allotments, allowing them to set up their stalls in different *pazars* throughout the week. Among the farmers I interviewed, Musa and Mustafa have *pazar* spaces in Güdül and various neighbourhoods in Sincan in Ankara, as well as Zübeyir in Kaman in Kırşehir, Şereflikoçhisar in Ankara and Kulu in Konya.

Neighbourhood *pazars* are formally regulated by the Ministry of Customs and Trade, which also regulates wholesale markets. The By-law on Pazars (No. 28351) was published on 12 July 2012 in the *Official Gazette*.[6] The by-law is based on the new wholesale markets law legislated in 2010. It defines *pazars* as marketplaces where producers and professional *pazar* merchants retail legally permitted food items directly to consumers (Article 4: f, 1, ö). Article 1 specifies that the goal of the by-law is to

> modernize neighbourhood and producers' *pazars*, to ensure the trading
> of vegetables and fruits and other food items permitted for trade by the

municipalities in accordance with the food quality, standards and safety rules and within the free-competition conditions of the markets, to protect the rights and interests of consumers, and to organize relations between producers and *pazar* merchants.

There are neighbourhood and producers' *pazars* in Turkey. The AMPD report does not differentiate between the two types, nor does the Ministry of Customs and Trade webpage. Producers' *pazars* resemble 'farmers' markets', which are one of the central pillars of short supply chains for local and direct marketing food systems in Canada and the United States (US) (Newman et al. 2013; Wittman et al. 2012). The number of neighbourhood *pazars* permitted in an urban neighbourhood depends on the consumer-population size, transportation facilities and the number of established *pazars* and their proximity to one another, as well as the challenges they may impose on infrastructure, the flow of traffic and security risks that may arise in certain places (Article 5: 3). Municipal permission for producers' *pazars* takes into account the amount and variety of FFVs produced in that locality, the production

Table 7.1 Weekly *Pazars* in the Province of Ankara (2013–2015)

Name of the Towns in Ankara	Number of Pazars
Altındağ	13
Çankaya	23
Keçiören	39
Mamak	22
Sincan	11
Yenimahalle	23
Elmadağ	5
Evren	1
Gölbaşı	2
Güdül	1
Haymana	1
Kalecik	1
Kazan	1
Kızılcahamam	1
Nallıhan	1
Polatlı	1
Şereflikoçhisar	2
Etimesgut	11
Akyurt	1
Ayaş	1
Bala	1
Beypazarı	1
Çamlıdere	1
Çubuk	1
Ankara Total	165

Sources: Based on information gathered from the webpages of town municipalities and from personal visits to neighbourhood *pazars* convened in these towns.

season and consumer demand for locally produced FFVs (Article 5: 4). The by-law makes sure that neighbourhood and producers' *pazars* are not set up on the same day and in the same location (Article 5: 5). Given that many small-scale producers are not registered farmers, producers' *pazars* also aim to facilitate registration and formalization in the market trading of food by producers themselves.

The by-law requires that producers, *pazar* merchants and the food they sell must be registered within the wholesale registration system. The food is required to have easily discernable identification labels on the packaging boxes (Article 18) to ensure the traceability of safety and quality and to maintain the technical and hygienic conditions of the product (Article 19). Producers and merchants are required to wear a uniform and identification card so that consumers can recognize their registered status (Articles 28 and 29). To obtain a retail space in the *pazar*, producers and merchants must receive a municipal permit.

The required information (on the application form) for a permit includes the name and signature of the applicant, citizenship number, tax-identification number and the name of the taxation office where s/he is registered, as well as the type of food s/he intends to retail in the *pazar*. Documentation of membership in a relevant profession and listing with the national farmers' registration system within the MFAL is also required (Appendix 1 of the By-Law).[7] While working in the *pazar*, an identification badge must be worn indicating name, personal qualification (producer, merchant or sales assistant), citizenship number, type of retailed food, number of the retail stall in the *pazar* and location of the *pazar*. The badge also includes a picture of the person as well as a municipal stamp (Appendix 5 of the By-Law).

Unregistered producers cannot market their products in producers' *pazars*, nor can they sell directly to *pazar* merchants. The producers I interviewed in the village of Çağa in Güdül complained that the new wholesale market law and the by-law for *pazars* restrict their ability to market their produce in *pazars*. This is because both producers and their products must be registered before setting up a stall in the *pazar*. The by-law also specifies the amount of food required for a producer to have a space in the *pazar*. That amount cannot be less than 300 pieces, 100 bunches or 200 kilograms by weight for FFVs (Article 19: 2). These amounts are twice as much as those required for registration in the wholesale distribution system. Therefore, unregistered farmers can only opt to create alternative marketing channels for their unregistered food, most notably as street vendors. This spirit of entrepreneurship among small producers functions informally, personally and competitively, outside the registered economy.

Pazars are vital for the direct marketing of food by producers. They are also crucial within the wholesale-retail supply chain of the traditional food provisioning system. There is very limited scholarly research in Turkey on currently operating producers' and neighbourhood *pazars* (i.e. Tunçel 2009). The significance of *pazars* for the continuing relevance of small producers in

Turkey's agrifood system and the development of *local* fresh-food networks is a long-neglected subject of research, although there *is* considerable research on such networks in Denmark (Eriksen and Sundbo 2015), Italy (Sonnino 2007), the United Kingdom, and the US (Hinrichs and Charles 2012).

Pazars provide consumers with easy access to fresh produce in urban neighbourhoods that is supplied by wholesale markets and producers themselves. Products are sold on the same day the *pazars* is convened. This ensures much greater freshness of produce compared to supermarkets. The *pazars* also provide producers with a direct market-entrance opportunity for their products in the area of production, especially in smaller towns, as is the case with Mustafa and Musa in Güdül, and Zübeyir and Mualla in Kaman.

The term *local food* is used in different ways by different researchers (i.e. Eriksen and Sundbo 2015; Feagan 2007; Mandelblatt 2012). My use of the term is based on the way producers themselves understand it. For the producers I interviewed, local food generally refers to food produced in the same geographical area as the neighbouring urban centres and towns where it is sold. This is also the definition used by Eriksen and Sundbo (2015) in their research on local-food networks in rural Denmark. In my examples, producers in the villages and towns of Ankara and Kırşehir sell their products in the same general geographical area, immediately after harvesting. They harvest the food early in the morning and market it by the late morning of the same day in nearby neighbourhoods. Alternatively, they may harvest in the evening prior to marketing their produce the following morning. This ensures the freshness of food, as the distance between place of production and point of sale is often less than an hour's transportation time by pick-up truck.

The 'localness' of local food is more complicated and nuanced than can be understood simply by reference to 'geographical proximity'. Eriksen (2013) has elaborated on the various domains of proximity, which include the proximity of area of production, direct relations with consumers and the generally positive values associated with local production. In addition to these domains, all of the small-scale farmers I interviewed emphasized agro-ecological integrity at the local landscape level – the structures and climate conditions that determine the particularity of local taste. For some of the producers, the 'localness' of their food also reflects specific product characteristics, which they attribute to local and intra-regional exchange mechanisms of self-reliance, particularly in relation to inputs in seeds and fertilizers (cf. Kloppenburg et al. 1996). Producers in the Savcılı Büyükoba village of Kaman utilize local-seed varieties to produce food with a specific, locally valued taste. Similarly, producers in the village of Çağa in Güdül market their 'heirloom' tomatoes by reference to geographical identification and specific taste. This marketing strategy is also practised, for example, by Wisconsin-based artisanal cheese producers, who reframe 'taste' in terms of a territorialized commitment to specific quality practices and agricultural knowledge (Bowen and De Master 2014). The production of local varieties through locally/regionally saved seeds connects taste and spatiality to meet consumer market demands for local taste, as illustrated in the case of Ireland by

Carroll and Fahy (2014). In addition, many other producers, including Musa and Mustafa, emphasize the importance of local landscape and climate conditions in contributing to tasty food, even when they use biotech hybrid seeds. These producers often combine the geographical proximity of production, direct interactions with consumers, the origin of native food variety and food taste to define the locality of food, often with the explicit aim of generating a market niche for their FFVs in neighbouring urban centres and towns.

The production methods adopted by some of the producers I interviewed closely match what is implied by the concept of *foodshed*. Recent literature that elaborates on the notion defines it as an analogue to the *watershed* concept, connecting the cultural (food) and the natural (shed) for a spatial understanding of the flow of food in the food system and food-system sustainability. The idea of foodshed ties local producers and consumers within the natural and social unity of geographical place, offering insights into ecological impacts as well (Kloppenburg et al. 1996; Newman et al. 2013). However, given the varied levels of integration with agro-industrial methods, the localness of food produced by the farmers I interviewed is not entirely disconnected from the longer chain of industrial and trade-based systems. An understanding of localness by reference to the 'geographical proximity' of production and sale (Eriksen 2013) and shorter transport and time chains does not take into account the 'geographical distance' of high-technology inputs and the fossil fuel–operated pick-up trucks that producers use in their farming. Moreover, a heavy reliance on the culturally bounded, racialized labour of Kurdish migrants is not considered in this emphasis on the 'localness' of local food.

There is great variation among small-scale producers: some wish to increase yields by means of industrial inputs and others care about saving their own seeds and using locally exchanged seeds for plant varieties which are valued for local taste; many produce their own fertilizer and use a minimal amount of high-tech industrial inputs; and a few make an effort to increase their self-reliance in relation to inputs while decreasing their dependency on external corporate bodies. Despite variation in their production methods, all have a well-grounded claim to the localness of their food in terms of the unique agro–ecological and climate conditions of their area of production, and the fact that they transport the food themselves a short distance to be marketed in *pazars* or at the doorsteps of urban consumers. This claim supports a form of marketing that is deeply embedded in the cultural trust-producing mechanisms of personal interaction with consumers and reflects the local specificity of valued taste.

My research confirms that *pazars* are significant for small-scale producers who market their FFV products in short transport and time chains and through direct face-to-face relations with consumers. They often sell their food in neighbourhood *pazars* (not necessarily in producers' *pazars*) convened in closer proximity to their production area. The traceability of origin and quality standards of the food they sell are confirmed through informally established personalized relations of trust that the producers have with consumers in urban settings. Nonetheless, they do also enter the larger food chain through wholesale commissioners and agro-traders who distribute to distant geographies, as is the case with Halit in Güdül who markets his food through Hidayet. Thus, claims to the localness of food are complicated; producers are simultaneously engaged with both formal and informal, direct and indirect and short and long supply chains in marketing their food.

There is no official data in Turkey on informally functioning food-supply chains via *pazars* or on the role of street vending in the food supply. The lack of data in other contexts has also been confirmed by researchers such as Bromley (2000). My research suggests that *pazars* often operate as sites of intersection between the formal and informal in food provisioning by small-scale producers. Although registration is required by *pazar* by-laws, *pazars* are spaces for both formal retailing – ensured through registered producers who sell their own food and *pazar* traders who provision from wholesale markets – and informal retailing of unregistered food by unregistered producers. Because municipal checks and monitoring in *pazars* tend to be poorly done, particularly in smaller towns, unregistered producers are able to sell informally in the *pazars* and cultivate personal trust connections with consumers. Hence, they deepen a claim for the localness of their products at the intersection of formal and informal in *pazars*.

At present, *pazars* are uniquely positioned in relation to the growing influence of supermarkets. As supermarkets gain ground in the supply chain, *pazars* maintain their importance in supplying low-income urban families with their weekly FFV needs. They also attract urbanites who seek access to 'local food' produced by personally known and trusted producers as an alternative to the standard bulk food associated with supermarkets. With a well-established historical and cultural presence in Turkey's traditional food provisioning, *pazars* have always created opportunities for small producers to interact directly with markets and consumers. The location of *pazars* at the intersection of formal and informal networks of food provisioning, expressing both commercialized and personalized relations of trust, enables consumers to circumvent supermarkets in the fresh food chain of local food.

While *pazars* allow small producers to play a significant role in Turkey's food relationships, in parts of the global South there are other examples of market-creation initiatives by governments that support smallholders. These initiatives include the Purchase for Progress project operating in 21 countries throughout Africa, Asia and Latin America since 2008; and the Food Acquisition Program of Brazil, created in 2003 (Chmielewska and Souza 2010, 2). The Brazilian initiative, in 2008, had only 2.5 per cent of farmers participating in the program out of a total of 4.3 million establishments. This represents relatively minor coverage with uncertain results for the future of small-scale production in Brazil (Chmielewska and Souza 2010). Nevertheless, such initiatives are significant. They point to the importance of rethinking possibilities for direct food provisioning for local consumption by small producers. Local governments can encourage public procurement of locally produced FFVs for consumption in publicly run institutions such as schools, hospitals and prisons (Morgan and Sannino 2010). These initiatives can facilitate sustainable linkages between small production and local economies. I have explored this possibility in Güdül.

Güdül, including its villages, contains a total of 13 schools with 1,166 students and 130 teachers.[8] The town has one hospital with a 15-bed capacity and 77 personnel.[9] It also has one high-security prison with 46 prisoners and eight personnel.[10] Three of the schools are residential senior high schools, known as lise (lycée) in Turkey. Fen Lisesi (Science Lycée) has 22 teachers and approximately 284 students; Anadolu Lisesi (Anatolian Lycée) has 23 teachers, five staff and 200 students. There is no available information on the number of students and personnel at Anadolu Öğretmen Lisesi (Teacher's Lycée). There are also two privately run dormitories for high-school students, one for male and the other for female students. The prison consists of four wards, each having 11 or 12 prisoners. Among these institutions, elementary schools (10 in number) and the hospital purchase pre-cooked, ready-to-eat packaged meals from various catering companies in Ankara. High schools, dormitories and the prison administration procure fresh vegetables and fruits from local producers based on competitive price bidding, and the government provides the dried food. Prisoners in each ward organize their own cooking.

In 2014, as part of its job creation program, the municipal government of Güdül hired 150 local women for temporary employment in various public institutions in town. However, these women are underutilized, employed largely to make tea and clean up. The municipality has also paid for the professional cooking education of 60 local women through the publicly funded People's Education Institute. Güdül, therefore, has the skills needed to cook local food and serve it on the 'public plate' of all students, patients and public employees. These women could be fully integrated into a locally organized school and hospital food-supply chain. This reorganization would also create formal marketing opportunities for seasonally grown food by local producers. According to the mayor, the goal is to enable these women to secure professional cooking certificates so they can cook local cuisine for various tourism-related activities. The mayor believes this initiative would stimulate rural development. With underutilization of available food-supply potential in public institutions, small producers in the area continue to rely chiefly on informally organized marketing networks in close-by urban neighbourhoods and *pazars*.

'Agricultural Sales Cooperatives and Unions' and Producers' Unions

Agricultural Sales Cooperatives and Unions (TSKBs) were founded in 1935 in Turkey. These state-led organizations regulated by the Ministry of Industry and Trade are intended to promote small growers' market integration via the state purchase of agricultural products. In June 2000, these cooperatives and unions were transformed into administratively, financially autonomous joint-stock like private organizations (Law No. 4572). A minimum of 30 farmer members were required to form an agricultural sales cooperative, and at least three agricultural sales cooperatives were needed to organize an agricultural sales cooperative union (T.C. MAVA 2000). In 2000, there were 331 TSKBs with a membership of 744,303 farmers, across 54 provinces and comprising 23 different produce lines (Aysu 2002, 270).

With Law No. 5200 of 2004, the government also re-organized the agricultural producers' unions into 'joint-stock company' like formations. Producers' unions are designed to be marketing channels for small producers to large retailers, which require compliance with industrial norms and quality standards. Since 2009, at least 50 farmer members are required to form a producers' union. Producers' unions are also expected to support producers in technical matters regarding production, harvest, storage, sorting and packaging. This is crucial to the expansion of agro-industrial ways into small-scale agriculture and the inclusion of supermarket-imposed private standards in the procurement system (Atasoy 2013, 559). As stated in Article 'N', one of the most important aspects of the law is that producers' unions are envisaged as vehicles for the institutionalization of contract farming among small producers – their executive committee is expected to prepare sample contracts and coordinate contractual relations on behalf of members, who receive a 0.2 per cent commission for its services in return (T.C. MAVA 2004).

While in operation, the agricultural reform implementation project (ARIP) aid agreement signed with the World Bank (WB) in 2001 enabled the government to provide assistance to agricultural cooperatives and producers' unions for preparing their members to increase productivity and responsiveness to supermarket standards in relation to quality and volume. ARIP aid was allocated to train 443 cooperatives, 15 unions and approximately 5,500 individuals, including managers, employees, cooperative members and delegates (ARIP Project Brief 2007, 4). In addition to individual farmers and agribusiness firms, the cooperatives and producers' unions have been included in the government Investment Support Program for Rural Development, which entitles them to receive government financial assistance for the purchase of high-technology agricultural machinery and equipment. The program, which began in 2006 within the ARIP project and existed until 2015, provided approximately TL 719 billion toward the purchase of 181,059 pieces of agricultural machinery (MFAL 2014c, 120). A government draft report titled *Introduction to Agriculture* (MFAL 2014c) was provided to me by Taner Ödevci from the MFAL. The report does not indicate the government's actual distribution of monies among potential recipients. Therefore, I cannot determine the share received by cooperatives and unions.

In 2012, according to an official table provided to me as an excel file by Mr. Erdal Erol, assistant European Union (EU) expert in the General Directorate of EU and Foreign Relations of the MFAL, there were 781 producers' unions in Turkey with a membership of 146,841 farmers.[11] This includes 151 fresh fruit–producing farmers' unions with a membership of 10,542, and 66 vegetable and decorative plants–producing farmers' unions with a membership of 7,476.[12]

There are also 21 organic-producing farmers' unions with a membership of 776. Only 21 of these producers' unions have office space in wholesale markets. Others have begun to market their members' produce to supermarkets either directly or via wholesale traders. Overall, membership in these organizations is low, which is indicative that FFV growers remain independent and family run. Small-scale growers continue to rely on commissioners, agro-traders or themselves to market their produce. There are no FFV-based producers' unions in the villages and towns where I conducted my field research, and none of the farmers indicated a desire to form one. They prefer to market their own produce informally or through wholesale commissioners or traders.

A survey was conducted in 2007 by Bignebat et al. (2009) of 183 fresh-tomato producers and 198 commissioners in the Mediterranean (Antalya and Mersin), Aegean (İzmir) and Marmara (Çanakkale) regions of Turkey. The survey shows that 93 per cent of producers rely on commissioners to sell in wholesale markets. Although there is an agricultural cooperative in their village, many of the producers are not members. The long-lasting working relationship between producers and commissioners is the result of the reputation and trustworthiness of both parties established over many years. The advance payments and credits provided by commissioners further strengthen the relationship.

Both TSKB and producers' unions are frequently subject to political patronage and vulnerable to the manipulation of managers. Small producers, who do not trust the managers of cooperatives and producers' unions, find it difficult to influence decisions regarding the price for their produce, infrastructural investments and the selection and price of inputs. In general, TSKB and producers' unions have functioned as state-imposed institutional mechanisms without significant linkages to local, rural actors. However, supermarkets have recently become actively involved in organizing small producers into producers' unions at the village level. For example, Migros played a key role in the establishment of the Narlıdere producers' union in Bursa in 1995 (Lemeilleur and Tozanlı 2007). The Narlıdere producers' union serves as an alternative marketing instrument with implicit contractual linkages to Migros in order to bypass wholesalers. There has been no written contract between the union and Migros, but the union was placed on the preferred-supplier list of Bursa Migros on the basis of an oral agreement (Atasoy 2013, 560). This exemplifies a market-based institutional form of coordination in value chains through the direct intervention of supermarkets.

Commissioners, agro-traders, cooperatives and producers' unions are key agents in a particular reformulation of formal governance in the FFV-marketing system of Turkey. Private sorting and packaging companies also represent the commercial integration of a market-based procurement system into the supermarket model. Both producers' unions and cooperatives have begun to establish a direct farm produce–sourcing system via private contractual ties with supermarkets. This represents a shift from a traditional, local store-based procurement system to a supermarket-led vertical coordination of food relations indicative of a 'market-industrial' system. Nonetheless, both producers' unions and cooperatives remain secondary in the food provisioning system of Turkey, and commissioners and agro-traders remain dominant in FFV procurement from small producers. Although commissioners operate mainly through the trust-based grading of quality, the new wholesale-market law links quality questions to GAP standards. However, the implementation outcomes of the 2012 law are too recent to discern, particularly in regard to how the law might transform the interpersonal relations of market coordination where no written contracts exist. My interviews with farmers, agro-traders and commissioners confirm that personally established trust relations continue to be significant in the commercialization of agriculture.

Supermarket Expansion in Food Provisioning

According to GAIN (the Global Agricultural Information Network of the US Department of Agriculture), the retail sector includes 'organized' and 'unorganized' retailers. GAIN's criterion in differentiating between 'organized' and 'unorganized' retailing is based on whether the retailers are corporate chain entities. GAIN (2011, 4) defines organized retailers as chain stores, supermarkets, discount retailers and gas-station stores. Unorganized retailers include open-air traditional *pazars*;[13] individual *bakkal* (small neighbourhood convenience stores with less than 50 m² of sales area); *manav* (green grocers); *büfe* (tiny shops selling newspapers, magazines, cigarettes, beverages and ready-to-eat packaged foods); street shops; and other forms of convenience stores or stalls. In Turkey, the share of organized retailing is between 40 and 42 per cent, while traditional unorganized retailing maintains a stronger presence in the sector with a market share of 58 to 60 per cent (Sevilmiş 2014, 20). *Fortune Türkiye* (2015) offers a figure of 48 per cent for the presence of organized retailing within the sector.

In terms of revenue value generated by the sector, a report published by Deloitte (2014, 3) estimates that the total value of the entire retail sector in Turkey was US $303 billion in 2013. According to GAIN (2014), the size of the sector is US $311 billion (GAIN 2014).[14] Sevilmiş (2014, 20) estimates that the retail sector will grow by 10 per cent by 2016. *Fortune Türkiye* expects the value of organized retailing within the overall sector to be US $120 billion in 2015. This indicates a 9 per cent increase from the previous year.[15] According to *Fortune Türkiye*, the increase in organized retailing is higher than the 4 per cent increase achieved overall in the Turkish economy, which also indicates that traditional unorganized retailers are gradually losing ground in the sector.

This growth is consistent with the increasing number of supermarkets and shopping centres steadily displacing traditional retail outlets in Turkey. According to Mehmet Nane, president of the AMPD, there were 310 shopping centres in Turkey in 2012 (Küçük 2013). The president of All Shopping Centres and Retailers Federation of Turkey, Vahap Küçük, indicated that in 2015, 20 new shopping centres would be opened in Turkey (*Fortune Türkiye* 2015). In Ankara alone, 28 shopping centres were built by 2010. Based on these figures, Turkey is now the seventh largest retail market in Europe. The retail market in Turkey is now larger than that of the Greek, Czech Republic and Portuguese markets combined (GAIN 2014).

By the end of 2011, the organized retail sector in Turkey included a total of 11,588 chain stores and supermarkets (GAIN 2011). The rate of increase was 35 per cent in 2010 but slowed to 9 per cent in 2013. As of October 2014, there were 149 supermarket chains with 10 or more outlets. These supermarkets have a total of 18,959 outlets, 66 per cent of which are discount stores (GAIN 2014, 3, 4, 5). The share of food within the total retail sector is 60 per cent, and the food retail sector is expected to grow by 8 per cent annually from 2014 to 2018 (GAIN 2014). The share of 'organized' retail in the retail food sector was 54 per cent in 2011 (GAIN 2011) and reached 57 per cent in 2013, whereas the share of small retailers and *bakkal* within 'unorganized' retailing has decreased to 33 per cent (GAIN 2014).[16] Discount stores have become the main drivers of growth in organized food retailing, as they increasingly replace the market share of *bakkals*.

Among the organized food retailers, discount chains have become highly dynamic. They have increased the number of outlets opened throughout the country, focusing on private-label product sales against branded names. Hard discounters such as BİM and A-101 are the main players here. BİM achieved 7 per cent of revenues in 2014, with the greatest share of outlets and private-label products in organized food retailing in Turkey (Euromonitor International 2015). Private labels constitute more than 60 per cent of total sales and 67 per cent of BİM's total revenue (GAIN 2014, 5). Its nearest competition, A-101, receives 35 per cent of its revenue from private-label sales (GAIN 2014, 7). Private-label products represent approximately 40 per cent of A-101 sales.[17]

The Federation of Retailers of Turkey (PERDER) differentiates between supermarkets based on size and degree of national expansion. Large supermarkets that have established a nation-wide presence are defined as *national (ulusal)* retailers. These retailers are generally joint ventures owned by TNCs and Turkish holding companies. Wholly Turkish-owned, small and medium-sized food retailers are defined as *local (yerel)*. Among the large national retailers are BİM, A-101, ÜLKER, Migros, CarrefourSA, Tesco-Kipa and Metro, which operate markets of all sizes, including hypermarkets, supermarkets and discount stores.[18] While European investors have played a significant role in Migros, CarrefourSA, Tesco-Kipa and Metro, Saudi finance is significant in the case of BİM. A-101 and ÜLKER are owned by Turkish holding companies. BİM, A-101 and ÜLKER are notable examples of national discount format retailers owned by Islamically oriented individuals. These chains have established themselves competitively in poorer urban neighbourhoods. This contrasts with the expansion strategy of joint-venture chains that have European investors. They have consolidated their market share primarily in upper-class urban neighbourhoods and in ex-urban areas.

Local supermarkets, typically in smaller cities, are viewed as representing Anatolian capitalists' success against TNCs and Turkish holding companies.

Local supermarkets are increasing in number and in turnover volume. The growth of local chains is largely due to a conversion of traditional retailers within 'unorganized' retailing, such as *bakkal* converting into chain stores within 'organized' retailing. The owners of the Akyurt supermarket chains, for example, have their background in traditional *bakkal* retailing in Ankara.

In 2011, there were 3,303 local supermarket chains in Turkey employing 62,757 workers (GAIN 2011, 7). In 2010–2011, local supermarkets grew by 43 per cent in relation to the number of outlets opened and by 24 per cent in terms of total sales area (Rekabet Kurumu 2012, 6). As a result, since 2010, some local supermarkets have been transformed into a category of national supermarkets. Examples include Makromarket, Altunbilekler, Killer and Adese, originally founded in Ankara.

Large Foreign Joint Ventures vs Islamic Hard Discounters

Food retailing in Turkey is subject to fierce competition between European-owned joint-venture chains (with Turkish holding companies) and Turkish-Muslim owned chains which dominate the discount sector. The joint-venture chains are often referred to as 'multi-format retailers', which provide options for fast shopping and gourmet and boutique stores. Migros utilizes six formats, CarrefourSA four formats and Tesco-Kipa five. Perhaps with the exception of Migros, these foreign-owned and joint venture retailers are currently losing ground to competition from nationally organized discount chains and local supermarkets.

The joint-venture chains have a larger number of hypermarkets; they require a lot size that is large enough to accommodate the hypermarket format. Given that lands are scarce in urban neighbourhoods, these chains need to be located in distant locations far from neighbourhoods. As a result, they require consumers to drive or take public transit to shop. In contrast, smaller-scale discount stores and local supermarkets are conveniently located in neighbourhoods within easy walking distance. In addition, the gourmet-food option provided by CarrefourSA, for example, with speciality cellars that sell wine, imported cheese and delicatessen products, only appeals to a small segment of consumers with high income levels.

In general, the high-priced imported items and brand names (Turkish or foreign) that often appear in nationally operated joint-venture supermarkets and hypermarkets, such as Migros, Metro and CarrefourSA, represent a 'trading-up' phenomena for higher-income consumers (Fabiosa 2011). This 'trading up' involves competition between supermarkets based on food varieties. The competition is between gourmet food and other high-priced imported products, including brand names sold in joint-venture chains *and* discount-store private labels. The challenge that joint-venture supermarkets/hypermarkets face is to establish 'habit formation' and 'habit persistence' in the general consumption of the product varieties they offer, as well as meeting the price competition from discount chains (cf. Daunfeldt et al. 2011).[19] Private-label

Table 7.2 National Supermarkets, Turkey (2015)

Largest (based on # of stores)	Supermarket Chain	Owners	# of Stores & type of outlet	# of Employees*	Founding Year
1	BİM (Turkish and Saudi)	Turkish citizens Mustafa Latif Topbaş, Fatih Saraç, the Zapsu brothers, Ekrem Pakdemirli, and Saudi citizen Abdulrahman El Khereiji	4,502 Hard discount	28,000	1995
2	A-101 (Turkish)	Aydın Holding (78%) and Azizler Holding	2,694 Hard discount	18,000	2008
3	ŞOK (Turkish)	Yıldız Holding/ÜLKER	2,542 Discount (ŞOK, DiaSA, Onurex) Wholesale (Bizim Toptan)	12,500**	1944 (ÜLKER) 1989 (Yıldız Holding)
4	Migros (Turkish)	KOÇ Holding	1,272 Hyper (5M & 3M), Super (2M & M, M-Jet, Tansaş), Macro Centre, Ramstore, e-trading	10,000	1954 (Swiss Migros) 1975 (Migros–Turk)
5	CarrefourSA (Turkish and French)	Sabancı Holding (50.8%) Carrefour France (46.2%)	333 Hyper, super, gourmet, mini	n.a.	1997
6	Makromarket (Turkish)	Songör Family	192 Supermarket	n.a.	1991
7	Tesco-Kipa (UK)	Tesco-UK (93%) Turkish– KİPA (7%)	189 Hyper, super and express	9,600	2003
8	Metro (German)	German Metro Group & Turkish citizen Galip Öztürk, (25% of shares)	41 Wholesale (Metro) Supermarket (Real)	n.a.	1990 (Metro) 1998 (Real)
Total			11,765	78,100	

Source: The firms' websites and press releases. * Some of the supermarket chains do not provide information on their number of employees. ** Includes only the targeted number of employees at ŞOK supermarkets in 2015.

products in discount stores account for 8 per cent of total sales in Turkey and are generally priced 30 per cent below the well-known brands (GAIN 2014, 5). Moreover, local supermarkets and discount stores provide consumers with more traditional and culturally appealing food categories and product varieties. Discount-store food often reflects long-persisting taste habits, religious considerations and lower-priced private-label products.

A combination of food taste in specific food categories and product varieties, lower prices associated with private labels and convenient locations within walking distance gives a competitive edge to discount chains over larger-scale supermarkets and hypermarkets. For example, TESCO announced in 2013 that its half-year profits had fallen by a third (Dombey and Felsted 2013). Similarly, Carrefour ceded majority control and management of CarrefourSA to its Turkish partner Sabancı Holding, and Sabancı sold its DiaSA discount stores (in which it had partnered with Spanish DIA) to Turkish-owned ÜLKER. Meanwhile, Praktiker, the German DIY chain, closed its nine stores in Turkey (Dombey and Felsted 2013). In this competitive environment, Migros holds a rather unique position.

Migros and GAP Standards

Migros began as a joint venture in 1954 between Turkish-owned Koç Holding and Swiss-owned Migros. It has been under Koç Holding's ownership since 1975. With 1,277 stores operating in 74 provinces in seven geographical regions across Turkey, as well as abroad, Migros is the fourth largest national chain in Turkey and the 199th largest food retailer in the world. It registered TL 7.1 billion in revenues in 2013[20] and receives fierce competition from national discount chains and local supermarkets. In response to this competition, and particularly since selling its ŞOK discount stores to ÜLKER, Migros began to operate M-Jet stores in 2011 as a gas-station market in collaboration with Petrol Ofisi.[21] Although relatively small, M-Jet stores are not discount stores. Whereas discount stores provide approximately 700 product varieties, M-Jet stores sell nearly 3,200 product varieties and maintain a supermarket mode of operation (GAIN 2014, 7). What is believed to give Migros a competitive edge is their convenient location in gas stations rather than the price of M-Jet products, which are the same as Migros' prices in its other store formats.

In addition to establishing M-Jet stores, Migros has responded to local and discount-store competition by supplying products with specific characteristics reflected in GLOBALGAP standards. The GAP-certified food categories that Migros sells include fresh fruits and vegetables, chicken and meat. Migros, together with Mehdi Eker – then Minister of Food, Agriculture and Livestock – announced in 2010 that it would procure FFVs only from GAP-certified farmers through contract farming. With the assistance of the ministry, Migros signed with 2,000 GAP-certified farmers out of a total of 2,534 GLOBALGAP certified producers in Turkey[22] to supply Migros exclusively (*Hürriyet Newspaper* 2015).[23] These farmers who implement binding GAP standards have now been commercially integrated into the vertical value chain dominated by Migros. This is an example of the 'trading-up' phenomenon in the consumption patterns of consumers with higher incomes. This move also helps to expand the standardization process in FFV production in Turkey, appealing to consumers to have trust in the commercially established industrial standards of supermarket food. This expansion is now part of the general competition among supermarket chains.

Migros currently procures food exclusively from GAP-certified producers. On its webpage, Migros indicates that quality management and food safety are guaranteed through the ISO 9001:2000 Quality management System and the ISO 22000-2005 Food Safety Management System.[24] However, Migros does not provide data on who undertakes audits of suppliers that conform with GAP standards, how the audits are done or what the outcomes are. GLOBALGAP standards establish requirements for the cultivation and safety of food, workers' occupational health and safety and environmental protection. GLOBALGAP also requires the implementation of GLOBALGAP-GRASP standards[25] in the areas of good social practices and adequate working conditions. The only information available on Migros' website under the 'Good Agricultural Practices' section is that Migros provides producers with accessibility to its B2B System Migros Traceability Portal, and that it has facilitated the GAP training of 168 of its employees in six different regions of Turkey by GAP representatives in FFVs. The website also indicates that in 2013, Migros renewed the GAP Controllers licences, approved by the Turkish Standards Institute (TSE), of its personnel responsible for GAP implementation. There is no indication that Migros requires its suppliers to fulfil GAP-GRASP standards, and no information is provided on how FFV suppliers will conform to GLOBALGAP-GRASP requirements. The highly exploitative use of informal labour through labour contractors and the poor working conditions of Kurdish migrants are commonplace in Turkish agriculture, including among GAP-certified producers.

GAP-certified standards apply to all fresh fruits and vegetables sold in Migros stores. Migros places a GAP logo on the FFVs marketed on its store shelves to indicate its compliance with GAP-required food quality standards and good agricultural practices. In 2013, the number of GAP-certified products sold in Migros stores reached 288,000 tons, procured from 132 GAP-certified producers through contract farming and with the assistance of agro-traders and supplier firms.[26] ÇEKOK is one of those firms, and it is listed as the 500th largest ISO firm in Turkey. It operates under the registered trademark of 'Professional Product' and provides product guarantees of traceable agriculture with the implementation of food-safety standards adopted by EUREP-GAP, GLOBALGAP, HACCP, the TSE and ISO 9001 – ISO 22000.[27] FFVs sold in Migros combine GAP certification and 'professional product' branding. This is an appeal to commercialized trust for FFVs in Migros by higher income consumers who seek to 'trade-up' in their food consumption. Migros' food branding, therefore, is a competitive strategy for gaining an edge over other supermarket and hypermarket chains that serve a similar demographic of high-income consumers. This strategy, particularly after the sale of its discount-store format ŞOK chains to ÜLKER in 2011, enabled Migros to move out of direct competition with national discount chains and local supermarkets.

In the context of such intense competition, FFV supply chains are highly fragmented between commercialzed trust generation through GAP-based quality assurance of professional food, and other forms of trust formation. The fragmentation is between the organized retailers of corporate chains and the unorganized mechanisms of traditional food provisioning. Migros' move to GAP standards intensifies this fragmentation, as other national chains and local supermarkets increasingly adopt GAP standards. The fragmented structure in FFV value chains is further complicated by strong competition from the Islamically oriented capital groups active in national discount and local chains.

BİM, A-101 and ÜLKER: *Hard Discount Stores*

The expansion of national hard-discount format chains, including BİM and A-101, is a result of the economic crisis of 2001. The crisis enabled discount markets to achieve a 17 per cent growth rate by 2010 (*PERDER* Ocak–Şubat 2011, 39), as hard-discount stores became more attractive to cash-constrained consumers. As mentioned above, discount stores at present constitute 66 per cent of supermarket outlets in Turkey. The popularization of credit-card use by poorer segments of the population has also helped their expansion.[28] Significantly, BİM initiated its credit-card sales in 2002, immediately after the 2001 economic crisis, when it opened 87 new stores despite, and benefitting from, the crisis.[29]

BİM is now the largest chain in Turkey, with a network of 4,502 hard-discount stores by the end of 2014. This represents a 13 per cent increase in one year. BİM offers 600 different varieties of product. A TL 11.8 billion turnover in sales revenue in 2013 represents a 20 per cent increase.[30] BİM procures its FFV mainly from ÇEKOK, in packaged form. With 1,500 tons of packaging capacity a day, ÇEKOK is the largest GLOBALGAP/EUREPGAP-certified food-processing, packaging and exporting company of FFVs in Turkey. It also has ISO-9001 and ISO-22000 certifications.[31] BİM has also moved into international markets, operating 223 stores in Morocco and 81 stores in Egypt by 2014. It opened its first store in Egypt in 2013.[32]

The second largest chain in Turkey is A-101, with a network of 2,694 hard discount stores in 2014 and TL 3.2 billion in revenue registered in 2013. BİM is expected to further consolidate its market share in food retailing in a hard-discount store format as it achieves further competitive growth against Migros and CarrefourSA. This is particularly the case after ÜLKER's purchase of Migros' ŞOK discount stores in 2011 and Sabancı's DiaSA in 2013.

ÜLKER is a newcomer in the supermarket retailing of food. It is the largest confectioner in Turkey, founded in 1944. ÜLKER-brand name companies are housed within Yıldız Holding, founded in 1989 as the parent company of ÜLKER. Yıldız Holding is known by its ÜLKER brand name. With its purchase of ŞOK in 2011, DiaSA and Onurex in 2013 and Turkey's largest cash-and-carry wholesale store, Bizim Toptan, in 2002, the number of ÜLKER-owned discount stores rose to 2,542 by 2014. ÜLKER is currently converting its DiaSA and Onurex stores to ŞOK. ÜLKER has now become the third largest player in the discount-store format of food retail chains, after BİM and A-101. It registered TL 2.2 billion in revenue in 2013.

Yıldız Holding/ÜLKER has also begun procuring FFVs directly from producers through its ŞOK-led *tarım platformları* campaign. The ŞOK market began the *tarım platformları* (agricultural platforms) in Antalya first and then in Bursa in 2013. The Bursa platform was established over a 9,000 m² enclosed area built on 22,000 m² of open field. ŞOK's aim is to buy FFVs from the producers operating in these platforms without the use of intermediary suppliers.

According to Mustafa Altındağ, president of ŞOK markets, FFVs constitute only 4 per cent of ŞOK's food supply, but direct procurement reduces the FFV-provisioning costs by 10 per cent. ŞOK engages with approximately 500 producers in these agricultural platforms. From its Antalya *tarım platformu* alone, ŞOK procures 400 tons of FFVs a day. These FFVs go from the fields to ŞOK's regional distribution centres (17 in total), and then to retail stores, in its 30 refrigeration-equipped 18-wheeler trucks – all within 24 hours. According to the president, ŞOK obtains 95 per cent of its FFVs from local producers, and the future expansion of *tarım platformları* will ensure the standardization of food production sold in ŞOK's retail stores. ŞOK conducts its own field inspection of food according to *its* quality standards. Altındağ has said that ŞOK severs its ties with those producers who do not comply with company standards (Yıldız 2014). However, no specific information is available on these private standards and how they are implemented, nor is there information on the organization of production and labour relations in these agricultural platforms.

Since ÜLKER is a large transnational corporation involved in food manufacturing, supply and packaging, its strong presence in discount-format food retailing can challenge the market position of local chains, which also sell ÜLKER brand-name products. ÜLKER's ownership of Turkey's leading cash-and-carry wholesale retail store, Bizim Toptan, allows the corporation to penetrate both organized and unorganized traditional markets. A report published by Bloomberg in 2011 shows that Bizim Toptan, with 109 stores, held a 35 per cent share of organized wholesale-store markets compared to 48 per cent held by the German-owned Metro.[33] As of 2014, Bizim Toptan had 155 tores in 65 cities throughout Turkey. Bizim Toptan increased its market share to over one million registered and 650,000 active customers purchasing more than 7,000 food varieties.[34] The customers of Bizim Toptan include traditional wholesalers, traders, *bakkal*, small markets, supermarkets, hotels, restaurants and cafés.[35]

Bizim Toptan supplies all ÜLKER-owned stores; ÜLKER also provides its own brand-name food to other food retailers. According to PERDER-İstanbul president İhsan Biçen, ÜLKER's increasing control over supply networks may not be easy for smaller-scale local firms to accept. Nonetheless, according to Reşat Narman, the general director of a local chain, MOPAŞ and the current vice president of PERDER, it is better for a Turkish-owned company to grow and curb the expansion of foreign-capital groups in the Turkish economy. He also does not believe that ÜLKER would create unfair competition for local firms (Tatlı 2013), a belief that reflects an ideational affinity between the vice president of PERDER and ÜLKER.

Small and Medium-Sized Local Food Retailers: Islamic Competition and PERDER

Since the 1990s, and particularly after the 2001 economic crisis, there has been a substantial increase in the number of wholly Turkish-owned medium and small-sized local chains. According to PERDER (2015, 11), the number of PERDER-member local firms rose to 369 in 2015, with 3,680 local outlets and 68,962 employees throughout Turkey. The former president of PERDER, Selamet Aygün, has indicated that local chains such as Makromarket, Akyurt, Başgimpa and Altunbilekler have taken important steps toward becoming national chains (Küçük et al. 2013). Makromarket, now the sixth largest national chain in Turkey, has 192 stores operating in 13 cities throughout six different regions of Turkey.[36] It procures its FFV through FİBA Gıda, headquartered in Beypazarı, which specializes in the production and marketing of carrots, radishes, lettuce, spinach, cabbage and onions in the Beypazarı region. FİBA Gıda is a GAP-certified company.

Similar to BİM, A-101 and ÜLKER's ŞOK, Makromarket, Başgimpa and Akyurt are owned by Islamically oriented individuals. BİM, A-101, ÜLKER, Makromarket and Akyurt [37] are members of the Islamically oriented Independent Industrialists' and Businessmen's Association (MÜSİAD).[38] In my earlier book, *Islam's Marriage with Neoliberalism* (2009, 10–27, 107–36), I explained that an Islamic orientation cannot necessarily be associated with class size and region – for example, with 'small and medium-scale' or newly growing capital groups from smaller Anatolian cities and towns – as opposed to the secularly oriented large bourgeoisie concentrated in the İstanbul region. Still, the political legacy of state-led 'developmentalism' continues to have a profound ideological effect on the creation and reproduction of cultural differences between smaller-scale Anatolian businesspeople and large-scale İstanbul capitalists. Islamic capitalists question the class and region-based biases of developmentalism and regard Anatolian groups as 'victims' of social injustice. They claim that developmentalism as a historically specific 'state project' has marginalized small-scale Anatolian capitalists because of their Muslim beliefs and rural family backgrounds. While these smaller capitalists feel they are perceived as culturally backward and thus unsuitable for 'modernity', larger, secularly oriented business groups from İstanbul are seen as 'modern' and provided with patronage, financial support and other opportunities. MÜSİAD and other Islamically oriented business associations are a significant factor in the realignment of Anatolian groups in the economy as a culturally specific capital fraction; they blend adherence to a market model with an Islamic normative orientation toward 'fair competition' and 'social justice' (Atasoy 2013, 562–4). It is because of this normative orientation that ÜLKER's increasing monopoly over the wholesale food supply is not viewed as undermining the growth of local chains.

In an effort to successfully compete with large national retailers, the owners of local chains established *Türkiye Perakendeciler Federasyonu* (the Federation of Retailers of Turkey – PERDER) in Ankara on 12 September 2006. It was founded to create organizational unity among smaller-sized markets. Its headquarters moved to İstanbul in 2008. Makromarket owner Şeref Songör, together with Akyurt, was influential in the founding of PERDER. Songör was president of Ankara-PERDER until 2010 and is the current chair of the Ankara-PERDER Consultation Committee, which further demonstrates his long-term commitment to the development of local markets. Başgimpa owner Mehmet Başdurak is the current chair of Ankara-PERDER and a member of the board of directors of PERDER-*Türkiye*. Ankara-based Başgimpa is among the 10 fastest growing local chains in Turkey (See Table 7.3), and has opened new stores in the provinces of Bolu and Zonguldak since 2013.

The federation is currently composed of 17 regional retailers' associations (PERDER) distributed throughout Turkey. Its current president is Mustafa Altunbilek, head of the board of directors of the Altunbilekler Supermarket Chain. The previous president was Selamat Aygün, head of the board of directors of the Hatipoğlu supermarket chain based in İstanbul. Aygün is a founding member of the Ümraniye municipal branch of the AKP.

Table 7.3 Fastest Growing PERDER-Member Local Supermarkets, Turkey (2015)

Largest	Supermarket Chain	Number of Stores (March 2015)	Number of Stores (January 2014)	Difference	Growth Rate (%)
1	Hakmar Express (İstanbul discount)	300	295	5	10.63
2	Çağrı Semt (İstanbul discount)	162	150	12	25.53
3	Mopaş (İstanbul)	100	100	0	0
4	Pakdemir (Denizli)	89	87	2	4.35
5	Çağdaş (Ankara)	86	84	2	4.35
6	Yunus (Ankara)	74	73	1	2.12
7	Altunbilekler (Ankara)	71	70	1	2.12
8	Peynirci Baba (Kocaeli)	58	55	3	6.38
9	Seyhan Express (Bursa discount)	57	55	2	4.35
10	Başgimpa (Ankara)	54	54	0	0
Total		1,051	1,023	28	58.57

Source: Adapted from PERDER (2015, 131).

In his opening address published on the federation's website, Mustafa Altunbilek explained that the primary goal of the federation is to systematically develop the food-retail sector of Turkey in accordance with the principles of product quality, registration and institutionalized rules and sustainability in value chains. According to Altunbilek, in instituting these principles in the sector, PERDER 'encourages dialogue and collaboration among member firms in order to share experience, develop original models and methods, and demonstrate their distinctiveness so they can attain a competitive edge in the sector'.[39]

In 2011, PERDER had 264 member retail chains, with 2,344 stores, 48,357 employees and 1,909,384 m² of sales area (*PERDER* Mart–Nisan 2011, 67). According to Mustafa Altunbilek, in 2013, PERDER members increased their number of stores by 12 per cent, the number of cashiers by 10 per cent, their sales area by 10 per cent and their number of employees by 11 per cent. This translates, according to him, to a total of 2,555 stores, 8,349 cashiers, 1,619,850 m² of sales area and 46,069 employees (*PERDER* 2014, 9).[40] By 2015, these numbers had changed significantly. According to the latest figures listed on the PERDER website, PERDER now has 377 member retail chains[41] with 3,714 stores, 70,273 employees and 2,450,749 m² of sales area.[42] As seen in Table 7.3, discount-format stores have achieved the fastest growth. Some of these PERDER members have now joined the group of national supermarkets while maintaining their membership within PERDER.

In 2011, the regional association of Ankara-PERDER had 20 member retail chains with 593 stores, 14,111 employees and 400,779 m² of sales area (PERDER excel file 2011). As of March 2015, this number had increased to 23 member firms, with 588 new stores opened.[43] Although local retailers achieved large growth rates, many PERDER-member chains are medium and small-sized, and their growth strategy is based on expansion into urban neighbourhood locations that are within walking distance.

Among PERDER member firms in Ankara, Makromarket, Yunus, Altunbilekler, Başgimpa and Çağdaş have been the fastest-growing chains since 2011 (*PERDER* Mart–Nisan 2011, 65–6). All are family firms. Makromarket was founded in 1991 by four brothers – Şeref, Mustafa, Mehmet and Uğur Songör. In 2009, *Fortune Magazine* listed Makromarket as the 95th largest firm among all private and public companies in Turkey and the 39th largest employer. Makromarket's sales revenue was TL 790 million in 2010 (Atasoy 2013, 565). Based on the high growth rates it has achieved, Makromarket has now moved into the category of national chains, with 192 stores operating in Turkey. It is currently the sixth largest national retailer in Turkey. Makromarket aims to be Turkey's largest retailer by 2023 (*Retail Türkiye* 2011, 40). Similarly, Yunus, another family firm, has been operating stores in nine cities in Turkey since 2008 (its website indicates that in 2008, Yunus had 22 nationally operating stores in Turkey). With seven new stores opened in one year between August 2013 and August 2014, Yunus was the fastest growing local chain in Ankara (*PERDER* 2014, 32). Table 7.4 shows the

Table 7.4 Local Supermarkets, Ankara (2015)

Largest	Supermarket Chain	Number of Stores	Number of Employees	Size m²	Founding Year
1	Çağdaş	86	n/a	171,129	1991
2	Yunus	74	2,000	58,600	1995
3	Altunbilekler	71	2,000	31,130	1994
4	Başgimpa	54	n/a	n/a	1991
5	Soykan	46	580	22,643	1993
6	Akyurt	45	861	23,962	1996
7	Öztürk	23	n/a	29,305	1995
8	Çelikler	21	402	14,930	1996
9	Erdemler	16	n/a	8,100	n/a
10	Halciler	14	n/a	8,200	2008
Total		450	11,311	328,682	

Source: Adapted from PERDER (2015, 128–30).

10 largest medium-sized chains from the Ankara region. It includes PERDER members only.

The PERDER website declares that its mission is to be actively involved in the legal, institutional reorganization of the retail sector in Turkey in order to 'ensure fairness in competition' and to support its members competitive growth by sharing information and experience.[44] Since 2009, PERDER has organized annual nation-wide conferences under the name '*the Meeting of Local Chains*'. The seventh conference was held in April 2015. Each of these conferences focuses on a different theme. The first conference organized in 2009 was titled 'Opportunities will be Discussed: Don't Miss Them'; the subject of the second was 'Discover Your Power: Let Us Write the Rules of the Game'; the subject of the third was 'Now is the Perfect Time: Continuous Growth'; the subject of the fourth was 'Institutionalization'; the subject of the fifth was 'Start the Transformation, Earn the Future: Humans, Brand Name, Technology'; the subject of the sixth was 'Brand Names'; and the subject of the seventh, organized in 2015, was again 'Start the Transformation and Earn the Future'.

These conferences have repeatedly emphasized the importance of competitive growth by local chains against joint ventures and transnational retailers. According to Selamet Aygün, PERDER aims to achieve a 15 per cent annual growth rate, which means that its member firms will reach more than 70 billion in sales revenues by 2023 – the 100th anniversary of the founding of the Republic of Turkey. Aygün believes that this kind of growth will enable the 10 largest local firms to be at least nationally active in the retail food sector (*PERDER* 2012, 12). Aygün's commitment to PERDER is based on his conviction that the federation helps local firms institutionalize the articulation of national cultural values and establish social dynamism in its profit-oriented market principles (*Perakende* 2011, 12).

Yılmaz Pekmezcan, a scholar who writes for *PERDER* magazine, believes this articulation is important for continuous growth (*PERDER* 2012, 15).

Because many of these chains are family operations with a long-standing background in the unorganized retail sector of traditional *bakkals*, it is believed that the owners need to learn how to embody a profit-driven mentality and an entrepreneurial orientation in their activities. The conferences organized by PERDER are dedicated to creating an opportunity for such learning to take place.

Metin Yılmaz, general director of Düzey Marketing, attributes the competitive growth of local chains to their ability to create a 'unique concept of competition' (*PERDER* Mart–Nisan 2011, 12). It includes a synthesis of two elements: 'universality' in quality, standards and project rationality; and 'locality' in ethics and values (Atasoy 2013, 566). Selamet Aygün stresses the importance of this synthesis for local chains that wish to realize success in market relations through mutual respect, cooperation and unity. According to Aygün, such an approach helps local chains stand up to the transnationals that compete against each other through mergers and acquisitions (*Perakende* 2011, 12). İstanbul-PERDER expresses this sentiment under the banner 'Stronger Together'. The slogan is also aimed at connecting supermarket chains to local producers and agro-traders through a series of panels to be organized every three months (*PERDER* 2016, 10). The first of these panels was held in March 2016 under the name 'Local-Market Week'. It is believed that this kind of collaboration will enable local chains to respond more effectively to consumer demand for food with culturally valued local taste – thereby enhancing the chains' competitive market advantage.

PERDER's pathway to competitive growth ties culturally established relations of personalized trust for local producers and agro-traders to commercialized trust in industrial food-quality standards. PERDER-member firms rely heavily for their fresh-produce procurement on wholesale markets, which often market FFVs produced by smaller-scale farmers. For improved quality assurance, PERDER also supports closer market coordination between small-scale producers and its member supermarket chains through agro-traders within a GAP-driven certification system. Therefore, it has welcomed the new wholesale market law. It is now common to see the GAP logo on FFV shelves in Altunbilekler and Makromarket stores. This also indicates that these stores are willing to meet the competitive challenge of Migros, not through contract farming with GAP-certified producers but through wholesale terminals and independent agro-traders who frequently supply food from smaller-scale producers.

Concluding Remarks

The restructuring of agrifood supply chains in Turkey cannot be understood in terms of a binary opposition between small-scale producers on one side and large-scale commercial farmers and powerful corporations on the other. Turkish agriculture is best described as a 'muddy terrain' into which agricultural production dominated by an extensive number of small producers is integrated, mainly through looser market-coordination arrangements with retailers.

Small-scale producers who rely on diverse production methods cannot readily meet the quality, consistency, volume and sorting–packaging–transportation requirements of supermarkets. In order to facilitate smallholders' participation in the supply chains, the state has actively participated in the restructuring of wholesale markets, traditional *pazars* and formerly state-led agricultural sales cooperatives and producers' unions into joint-stock company–like private organizations. Cooperatives and producers' unions have been redesigned to become market-coordination agents in direct farm produce sourcing for supermarkets through contract farming. They also act as enforcers of industrial quality standards for the production and supply of food. Nonetheless, they remain secondary in Turkish agriculture. Retailers procure from an extensive range of suppliers, and relatively low levels of vertical coordination characterize smallholders' integration into transformed markets.

Wholesale markets maintain a dominant position in food provisioning where smallholders' market access is coordinated without written contracts – through interpersonal dynamics based on trust and reputation for quality assurance, expressing rather imprecise grading and looser marketing arrangements. Compliance with quality standards has now been addressed as wholesale markets are institutionally realigned within a GAP-driven food-quality assurance system. Although it is too soon to predict, I expect that the new wholesale-market law will engender a form of connectivity between 'trust/reputation-based' market coordination of small-scale production by agro-traders and industrial certainty over, as well as commercialized trust in, the quality required by supermarkets. This connectivity underscores a more context-specific path of supermarket expansion in rural Turkey. The reorganization of wholesale markets expands the intermediary role of agro-traders and gradually institutionalizes commercialized trust in GAP-certified industrial standards for food quality. The re-organization of *pazars* is also an attempt to institutionalize food-quality standardization and traceability assured by agro-traders within the wholesale registration system. Still, different forms of commercialization simultaneously co-exist in food supply chains: supermarket food produced by unknown, distant groups of both large and small-scale producers; *and* local food produced by personally known and trusted small-scale farmers whose produce is sold in *pazars* and through street vending. What we observe is a diversification in food provisioning, whereby different types of farmers operate through their own differentiated but also unevenly converging pathways within the process of commodification. The restructuring of food-provisioning is entangled with the fiercely competitive growth of supermarkets, which is also expressed in the political reconfiguring of class relations. The competitive growth of Islamically oriented small, medium and large-sized capital groups alongside large transnationally owned and joint-venture retailers can only deepen the commodification process and expand commercialized trust in industrial standards. The adherence of these groups to a market-economy principle of competition and their staunch support of local capital strengthens a corporate-driven model as an organizing episteme of supermarket expansion.

Notes

1 Seçkin provides information on only 80 per cent of the producers in her research area, with no explanation for the remaining 20 per cent. Further, no information is provided on the role of unorganized and unregistered markets in FFV retailing by producers, which includes street vending. This omission in research allows us to consider the possibility that the remaining 20 per cent of producers in the Gürsu region of Bursa may be involved in unregistered trading of their produce.

2 www.resmigazete.gov.tr/eskiler/2010/03/20100326-1.htm (accessed 20 January 2013).

3 According to the latest figures provided by TÜİK, the total amount of FFV production in Turkey in 2014 was 45.7 million tons: 28.6 million tons of vegetables and 17.1 million tons of fruits. For 2015, TÜİK projected an estimated 47.7 million tons of FFV production. Out of this total amount, vegetable production is estimated to be 29.5 million tons and fruits 18.2 million tons (TÜİK, May 2015).

4 SEBZE VE MEYVE TİCARETİ VE TOPTANCI HALLERİ HAKKINDA YÖNETMELİK EK-5 (Hal Kayıt Sistemi Bildirim Formu) (http://www.hal.gov.tr/Sayfalar/MatbuFormlar.aspx, accessed 19 January 2017).

5 *Retail Türkiye* (2009) reports that in 2009, consumption of unregistered FFVs constituted 80 per cent of FFVs produced in Turkey.

6 http://www.resmigazete.gov.tr/eskiler/2012/07/20120712-13.htm (accessed 30 May 2015).

7 The by-law of 2012 was modified in 2013. The modified by-law (No. 28706) requires producers to be registered within MFAL and *pazar* merchants to be registered within the Union of Small Tradesmen and Craftsmen (*Esnaf ve Sanatkârlar Odası*) (Article 12 of the modified by-law) (http://www.resmigazete.gov.tr/eskiler/2013/07/20130713-4.htm, accessed 3 March 2013).

8 http://gudul.meb.gov.tr/ (accessed 20 May 2015).

9 http://www.gudul.gov.tr/ilce-saglik-mudurlugu (accessed 19 January 2017).

10 I obtained information on the prison from a personal visit.

11 There are differences in the figures in official government reports provided to me by different experts from the MFAL. An MFAL (2014c) report provided by Taner Ödevci indicates the total number of producers' unions in Turkey to be 801 with a membership of 221,446 farmers.

12 According to the report provided by Mr. Erol, there are 443 producers' unions in animal husbandry with a membership of 120,137, and 29 unions in water products with a membership of 978. The report provided by Taner Ödevci indicates 471 unions with a membership of 194,344 farmers in animal husbandry. Regardless of the differing numbers, both reports indicate high numbers of producers' unions in animal husbandry. This may be related to government efforts to institute a commercial specialization in animal husbandry through farmers' organizations. Given the fact that only 3.62 per cent of the farms in Turkey are specialized in animal husbandry while 96.38 per cent combine field-crop production with animal husbandry (MFAL 2014c, 158), it seems fair to say that commercial livestock production at present lacks specialization.

13 The designation of *unorganized* is misleading in relation to traditional *pazars* in Turkey. Although *pazars* continue to combine formal and informal marketing activities, they are increasingly organized and regulated through the government by laws under the Ministry of Customs and Trade.

14 According to *PERDER* (Mart-Nisan 2011, 15, 22), the entire retail sector generated TL 130 billion annually by 2011. Food retailing was responsible for TL 80 billion, TL 40 billion of which was generated by organized supermarket retailing. The share of wholly Turkish-owned local supermarkets within overall supermarket retailing is TL 20.5 billion. Traditional food retailers generate 50 per cent of the total TL 80 billion.

15 http://www.fortuneturkey.com/perakende-sektorunde-2015te-yuzde-9-buyume-bekle niyor-7217 (accessed 2 August 2015).

16 Different sources provide different figures for the distribution of organized and traditional retailing within the food sector. According to TAMPF (n.d., 20), the share of food within the total retail sector is 62 per cent. The share of traditional retail in the retail food sector is close to 80 per cent, while 23 per cent belongs to organized retailing. The TAMPF figures are not entirely clear.

17 http://aydin.com/a101/ (accessed 3 July 2015).

18 Hypermarkets are defined as stores with a sales area greater than 3,500 m² and having more than eight cash registers. Large supermarkets are between 1,000 and 3,500 m² with more than four cash registers, and medium-sized supermarkets are between 400 and 1,000 m² with more than two cash registers. *Bakkal* have less than 50 m² of sales area, and a hard-discount format typically has a sales area size between that of a *bakkal* and a supermarket (Codron et al. 2004, 591; GAIN 2014, 3). The average size of discount stores varies between 200 m² and 400 m². They often provide approximately 700 product varieties, whereas local retailers provide 2,000–2,500 different varieties of products (GAIN 2014, 5).

19 To the best of my knowledge, there is no research in Turkey on habit formation in food consumption, particularly in regard to gourmet food and brand names.

20 https://www.migroskurumsal.com/Icerik.aspx?IcerikID=457 (accessed 19 January 2017).

21 Petrol Ofisi is a Turkish company that sells fuel products and lubricants. It has 3,000 fuelling stations in Turkey.

22 www.globalgap.org (accessed 25 January 2015).

23 http://www.migroskurumsal.com/EN/Basin-Aciklamasi.aspx?BasinAciklamasiID=45 &height=500&width=600. (accessed 13 December 2015).

24 www.MİGROSkurumsal.com (accessed 15 December 2015).

25 GLOBALGAP-GRASP refers to GLOBALGAP Risk Assessment on Social Practice. It ensures good social practices and adequate working conditions in agricultural production. (For additional details, see 'Production Conditions/Migros at http://m14.migros.ch/media/2015/02/production-conditions.pdf (accessed 15 December 2015).

26 https://www.migroskurumsal.com/en/Icerik.aspx?IcerikID=408 (accessed 15 December 2015).

27 www.cekok.com.tr (accessed 14 December 2015).

28 Although the history of credit cards in Turkey dates to 1968, their use for consumer purchases paid by instalments began in 1999 (see Kaya 2009).

29 http://www.bim.com.tr/Categories/626/tarihce.aspx (accessed 20 February 2011).

30 http://www.bim.com.tr/hakkimizda/basin-odasi.html (accessed 15 January 2015).

31 ISO 500 lists ÇEKOK among the 300 largest companies in Turkey (http://cekok.com.tr/turkce/hakkimizda.html, accessed 15 January 2015).

32 http://www.bim.com.tr/Categories/108/hakkimizda.aspx (accessed 15 January 2015).

33 http://www.isyatirim.com.tr/WebMailer/files_att/2_20110418091616468_1.pdf (accessed 2 June 2015).

34 https://www.yildizholding.com.tr/uretiyoruz/toptan-ve-perakende-satis/ (accessed 2 June 2015).

35 http://www.biziminvestorrelations.com/en/view-to-bizim-toptan/about.aspx (accessed 2 June 2015).

36 http://www.makromarket.com.tr/Kurumsal/Hakkimizda (accessed 2 June 2015).

37 http://emusiad.com/hakkimizda (accessed 19 January 2017).

38 Founded in 1990, MÜSİAD in general represents small and medium-sized Muslim business groups with strong family ties to small Anatolian towns and villages. Some of its member companies are now large and located in İstanbul. MÜSİAD's membership exceeds 4,000 firms (Atasoy 2009, 117–22).

39 http://www.tpf.com.tr/baskannin-mesaji/ (accessed 19 January 2017).

40 Although Altunbilek indicates a 10 per cent increase in sales area and an 11 per cent increase in employment, the numbers he provides in relation to sales area and employment are lower than the 2011 figures.

41 The *Türkiye Perakendeciler Federasyonu* (the Federation of Retailers of Turkey – PERDER) website lists 377 firms as PERDER-member local firms for the year 2015. This is higher than the 369 firms published in the PERDER magazine (2015, 11). The difference may be due to the fact that the website includes the latest statistics.

42 http://www.tpf.com.tr/ (accessed 19 January 2017).

43 http://www.perakende.org/dernekler/ankara-perder-ailesi-genisliyor-1342799929h.html) (accessed 2 June 2015).

44 http://www.tpf.com.tr/misyon-vizyon/ (accessed 19 January 2017).

8 A Discussion on Diversity

This book has examined structural transformations in Turkey's food-provisioning system through case examples chosen from Ankara and Kırşehir provinces. It has brought to light the historically and culturally complicated processes of convergence and divergence, conformity and nonconformity, that simultaneously interact with the global conditions of agrifood commodification. Moreover, it has shown that place-specific 'diversity' happens *together with* the expansion and deepening of globalized standards and normative practices of commodification. Small-scale, traditional production and marketing strategies are also a dynamic part of a complicated plurality and diversity within the commodification process. The co-existence of multiple scales of production, types of farmers and marketing methods, as well as divergent manifestations of commodification, suggest that research must move beyond a linear developmentalist perspective that anticipates a gradual disappearance of small-scale and peasant-style farming as an inexorable, self-evident tendency within capitalist modernity.

Diversity is constitutive of the emergent dynamics – simultaneously both complementary and conflictual – within a global process of commodification. This view of diversity need not be confined to epistemologically binary hierarchies of large-scale, corporate-led commercial versus small-scale, peasant-style subsistence farming. Our task is to address the multiple ways of farming along with their locally varied conditions and combinations. The multiplicity of farming practices is in part a reflection both of concern with corporate appropriation and control of nature and biological processes *and* of enthusiasm for an agro-industrial notion of agriculture. Farmers in Turkey, as well as seedling growers and seed distributors, share a *normatively grounded ambivalence* with regard to commodification. They also share an awareness of the potential negative consequences of techno-scientific innovation and knowledge structures for the integrity of landscapes, human health and the locally valued taste and smell of food. Recognition of this shared ambivalence and consciousness should cause future researchers to question the uniformity expected from the discursive logic of *economization*. However, this does not necessarily mean that farmers' ambivalence becomes manifested in contestation and resistance.

My notion of *farming imaginaries* privileges 'diversity' in research. It not only emphasizes the perceptions and deliberations of farmers in relation to the preservation of customary ways but also facilitates the adoption of new practices and styles. These deliberations are normatively grounded and extend over a wide range of farmers' concerns: livelihood and aspirations for income generation and profit making; appropriate landscape-management strategies (including soil, plants and water resources); preservation of plant biodiversity and control over genetic information; and desire for techno-scientific enhancement of agriculture's market-economic performance as a means to contribute to national economic development. The multiplicity of concerns and aspirations bourgeons as farmers encounter corporate agro-industry-led technical innovation and knowledge systems, while also experiencing their own hopes and desires. There is a dynamic ideational interplay in farmers' normative ambivalence regarding the acceptability of an industrial model. The specific challenge in future research, I suggest, is to unveil the significance of farmers' own farming imaginaries, as fused with *diversity* in the continual reconfiguring of commodification in land, labour and food – a fusion that occurs through state mediation and at the intersection of familial, local/regional and national conditions and global dynamics.

The cases I have examined in Turkey show that there is significant conformity to, as well as divergence from, the industrial model among all types of farmers. Most importantly, farmers' farming imaginaries, which embody the co-existence of commonly shared and simultaneously diverging perspectives, are *internal* to a global process of commodification. (The only exception, out of the 51 Turkish farmers I interviewed, is Hamza – the grower who produces artisanal grapes from a 100-year-old village vineyard.) Consequently, a binary perspective of convergence and divergence does not constitute a counter narrative and is therefore not meaningful in reorienting agrifood systems away from a corporate-led industrial model. The *duality of assessments* and mixed associations in wide-ranging imaginaries are not necessarily reflective of contradictory expectations and ruptures. Rather, they are profoundly consistent with the diversity that enters into the commodification process in reshaping future paths and emergent patterns in farming, as well as with its contestability.

A discussion on diversity requires that we delve into the histories of places, landscapes and peoples, as well as the natural histories of species, in interaction with larger structures, processes and normative framings of global projects. Rather than demonstrate a methodological concern with diversity in terms of multilateral *regime maintenance* (Ruggie 1982), I explore these diversities as conjunctural locations of simultaneously occurring ambiguities, tensions and accommodations. These sites of ambivalence constitute a 'strategic practice of criticism' within the neoliberal remaking of agriculture and its ecological relations. They influence farmers' reinterpretation of 'the present with a view to determining whether [and how] to continue with it in the future' (Scott 1999, 7), as well as in relation to the past. This is a form of diversity that entails judiciousness in sense-making based on a mix of desires, hopes and hesitations in farmers' farming imaginaries that oscillate between preferences for market and non-market values, often with varied combinations.

Research that brings farmers' imaginaries to the forefront must question the notion of *agency* in connection to structural, externally operating prescriptions, innovations and impositions. The role of the state in the reorganization of land–property–food relations is also crucial to this research. These considerations are central to a discussion on diversity's relevance to problematizing global mobility and the diffusion of a single, monolithic regulatory framework for restructuring global agricultures and ecologies. The co-existence of multiple sensory experiences in farming imaginaries implies that farmers' consciousness embodies continual reflections and deliberative interpretive/evaluative judgements. The effects on the commodification process are complex, extending market relations into new domains, including biological processes. In addition, new political possibilities and new spaces of resistance are created.

The idea of interpretive judgement assigns an 'intentional explanation' to farmers in their encounters with global prescriptions and impositions. As shown throughout the book, farmers' thinking and actions comprise combinations rather than a single, goal-directed orientation. These combinations result from the concurrent practices of adoption and non-adoption of a market morality in farming, as well as farmers' normatively grounded agency in making choices that reflect elements of knowledge systems rooted in long-tested local histories and structural impositions.

Emerging complexities within the general commodification process cannot be fully appreciated from a Weberian-style 'methodological individualism' of purposive, goal-oriented behaviour (Weber 1947, 87–123, 158–71) that assumes individuals to be key players in decision-making processes and agents of social change. This assumption poses the risk of turning social reality into an abstraction and neglects the highly variable geo-historical, political, cultural specificity of context. On the other hand, Marx interprets human agency ambiguously (Callinicos 2006), not as immutable but historical – contained in the relationship of the present to past. In *The Eighteenth Brumaire of Louis Bonaparte*, Marx (1982 [1885], 96) wrote: 'Men make their own history, but they do not make it just as they please; they do not make it under circumstances chosen by themselves, but under circumstances directly encountered, given and transmitted from the past'. This suggests that historically rooted structural, material and cultural circumstances constrain the agency of humans in pursuit of their conscious aspirations. Further, this suggestion has important consequences for comprehending the significance of the ambivalence found in farmers' farming imaginaries and addressing how this ambivalence permits farmers to resist commodification sometimes and accord with it at other times, bringing together market and non-market values, often at the same time.

Perry Anderson (1980) provides an explanation of the Marxian understanding of mutability and ambiguity in human agency. Action does not stem, he suggests, from inexorable, externally determined impositions but from humans converting structural, historical conditions into subjective, consciously sought projects through systematic, cognitive efforts to understand the past and present and to produce a desired future. Through their 'conscious, goal-directed activity', according to Anderson (1980, 19–20), individuals pursue three goals: (1) private goals in conformity with existing social relations (For the farmers covered in this book, these include cultivating a plot, making a living and generating income and profits.); (2) public goals, again in conformity with existing relations (These include sustainable agriculture, conservation of landscapes, improvements in health and nutrition, and preservation of local food cultures and taste.); and (3) collective pursuit of change, aimed at creating new, alternative structures that do not conform with existing structures. (Farmers seldom, if ever, invoke this goal.) It is the third form of agency in Anderson's thinking that assumes the potential for self-determination in history. In relation to farmers' encounter with the larger processes of commodification of ecology and agrifood systems, it seems that all three 'goals' interact to engender ambivalence in farmers' consciously undertaken and normatively grounded deliberations. It is the *cognitive* dimensions of human agency that enable farmers to deliberate and seek a balance between the viability of certain farming practices for income generation and profit making and the conservation of natural environments, maintaining a sense of place and taste of food and fostering a more holistic worldview. This worldview considers nature *alive* and meaningful, not in abstract terms of moral laws but in terms of shared histories with humans.

Despite the aforementioned heterogeneity that dominates Turkish agriculture, all categories of farmers possess a common Turkish–Muslim nationalistic orientation to the role of the state. They expect the state to play a primary role in initiating different kinds of relationships to agriculture and food, and to assume responsibility for social–economic and technical innovation. State-mediated farmer–scientist collaboration is desired for the integration of local agro-ecological conditions and concerns into the enhancement of performance values as applied to native, traditional crop varieties in commercial agriculture. Farmers believe that producers' knowledge of local landscape conditions pertaining to soil, plants, climate and water should be utilized in the development of high-yielding native crop varieties by nationally owned biotechnology research companies. They are critical of the control wielded by foreign-owned global biotechnology companies over seeds and agro-chemical markets. For farmers, foreign biotech company control leads to a loss in national plant-crop varieties and their wild relatives, food customs and food tastes. Given that the cultural and technological appropriateness of these biotech innovations remain unchecked nationally, farmers are concerned about their potential negative consequences for human health, integrity of landscape structures and biological processes. This is not a call for an end to biotechnology research but an appeal for the increased involvement of the state in public-service provisioning and other policy domains, including techno-scientific development, innovation and programme design.

There are two distinct, though related, aspirations here for income/wealth generation and a more agro-ecological and culturally sensitive pattern of national economic development. Although logically distinct, these aspirations connect the private and public goals within farmers' farming imaginaries. They are joined through an appeal to state-backed research collaboration between farmers and scientists for the purpose of increasing the competitive growth of Turkish–Muslim-owned biotechnology companies. This appeal is two-fold: on the one hand, the state is seen as a source of broad social, political and economic change through the institution of new practices and beliefs (cf. Polanyi 1944); and, on the other, the state is believed to have the capacity to re-orient Turkey's developmentalist path onto a more nationally inspired one. The two are combined in farmers' critical reassessment of Turkey's moderniza-tion trajectory, which is seen as historically moored in the 'blind' emulation of European practices since the late Ottoman and early republican periods. For farmers, the outcome of this long lineage is the institutionalization of certain material and normative practices that have been detrimental to the flourishing of social and economic creativity in farming and the design of more effective innovations on the local and national level.

Farmers' repeated emphasis on the state's role in innovation is a plea for a more nationalist stance in Turkey's changing agrifood relations. It is also a position with far-reaching implications. It recognizes the fact that farmers of all types wish to be more respectful of agro-ecological processes, human health and food quality, but it also acknowledges that they are engaged in an entrepreneurial enterprise that is entangled with state-brokered expansion and the deepening of commodity relations. Farmers behaving as business operators require that the state achieve a balance between a science and technology-intensive modernity that optimizes performance values in agriculture and the conservation of cultural and agro-ecological conditions of development.

What is absent in this consideration is that the primacy attributed to the state in technical and industrial innovation may help some farmers enhance their profit-making capacity, but it may also foreclose on the possibilities for 'diverse economies' to emerge with agro-culturally and ecologically distinct relations. Without social–economic innovation that facilitates the emergence of diverse economies, the state actually opens a larger space for change in the direction of greater *continuity with*, rather than a shift *away from*, market-based value genera-tion. The seeming irreconcilability between economic aspirations and cultural, agro-ecological sensitivities continues to generate mixed associations in farm-ers' thinking and their production and marketing strategies. Farmers are aware that state-led integration of local agro-ecological domains and cultural realms into the commodification process would result in uncertain outcomes. I think it is this consciousness of uncertain outcomes that is significant if 'diversity' matters in imagining economies outside of agro-industrially standardized ways.

The apparent contradictory expectations in farmers' farming imaginaries reflect the incoherence within a knowledge culture of 'neoliberalization' that does not necessarily eliminate the role of the state (Jessop 2002; Storper 2016), contrary to much scholarly assertion. Farmers envisage strong state intervention through policy and regulatory arrangements to extend market mechanisms in favour of an outcome that competitively repositions Muslim capital groups in the economy (including farmers, biotechnology companies and supermarkets). Nevertheless, farming practices and imaginaries are far from forming a single consistent, core narrative; rather, they comprise a diverse range of narratives and 'immanent desires'. Farmers' normative oscillation between market and non-market values, as well as their expectation that the state enhance its regulatory powers, is congruent with the very diversity expressed across and within the heterogeneous economies engaged in the commodification process. It is this normative oscillation and conflicting expectations of the state that, I believe, foster a public ethos for emergent, yet state-mediated, possibilities in refiguring futures. However, the outcome cannot be discerned through an abstract polarity between commodification and counter movements, and it is certainly without guarantees. Still, the existence of incongruous expectations in farmers' imaginaries opens a potentially important discussion for researchers on how the dual nature of the state as an idea and an apparatus holds together (Abrams 1988) – how the long-held belief in the 'idea of the state' as a responsible agent for realizing the common good can prevail when the state is the political site of contested processes and conflictual interests. We would also do well to question rival, one-sided interpretations of the state – as a monolithic, uniform regulatory power; or as a downwardly re-scaled rule within political practice – and begin to consider the state as a fundamentally ambiguous idea and practice.

The reconfiguring of relationships among the state, farmers, agro-capital groups, landscapes and various agro-ecological ensembles is crucial to life itself. These relations cannot be limited to a singular realm of the social involved in the remaking of markets, citizenship and class relations. The refiguring of these relations is more comprehensive, extending into fundamental ontological transformations in the connections between the social and ecological. In short, it is normative, and thus it allows for the acceptability of expanding commodity relations into new areas in the web of life. Such expansion results in wealth accumulation by some and dispossession of livelihoods by others in simultaneously occurring combinations, in addition to intensifying the appropriation of nature. The yielding to commodification is also relational, reflecting heterogeneity in peoples' commitments, hesitations and hopes for the future. Such an understanding affirms the importance and plausibility of spatial imaginaries and knowledge systems, as well as material practices and changes, for the *cognitive remaking* of agro-ecological spaces and the creation of diverse economies. This sort of cognitive remaking is far from being based on utilitarian assessments made by individuals in relation to their private goals. Rather, it is closely associated with the *structural capacities* of humans (Wright 2010) to mobilize their interpretive, 'creative potentialities, with no presupposition other than (the) previous historic development' (Marx 1973 [1857], 488). This perspective emphasizes historically rooted interactions between subjective and material relations in refiguring human connections to the ecology.

There are significant implications arising from the possibilities of emergent diversities, including differing production and marketing strategies, labour employment patterns and agribusiness practices. These should not be summarily dissolved into a context-specific variant form of global commodification. It is equally important that we avoid associating the mere existence of varied practices and expectations with transformative potential and oppositional mobilization. As shown throughout the book, there are multiple assessments that enter into viewing the persistence of traditional methods as representing an outdated past in need of eradication, and the commencement of new, capitalized ways as representing the future. Hopes for the dynamism of the new are sought in state-led elimination of the old through a sustained break from the influence of Turkey's modernity project since Ottoman times. This consideration runs affectively across the east-west discursive divide and amplifies Turkey's geo-historical differences within the disunity of capitalist modernity – a disunity thought to be rooted in the West-centred techno-scientific management of capitalist economic growth, on the one hand; and the sense of continuity and/or rupture with the past, on the other.

Disunity finds its expression in the duality of assessments in farmers' farming imaginaries, between the universality of global standards and the locality of experience and values. It is a duality that has become the most enduring discursive concern over the nature of capitalist modernity in Turkey. As farmers wander between the two worlds, they are uncertain how to reach a synthesis between them, but they are not willing to 'let one die and the other be born' in conditions of powerlessness and dispossession.

The pursuit of a synthesis between what is perceived as 'universal' and what is local constitutes the cultural conditions of *Islam's Marriage with Neoliberalism*, the title of my 2009 book (Atasoy 2009). That marriage re-signifies some of Islam's moral–ethical and cultural dimensions in conjunction with Euro-American normative categories, articulated as part of a social transformation project. It describes the ruling AKP's political economy approach based on the state's policy commitment to 'the reproduction of our own *authentic* value systems on the basis of our deeply rooted ideational tradition, along with *universal standards*' (Akdoğan 2004, 12–3, quoted in Atasoy 2009, 10). This description further conveys modernity's fragmentation into a techno-scientifically driven economic order with unquestionable global dominance of market values, on the one hand; *and* the knowledge culture and affective sentiments associated with a Turkish–Islamic outlook on non-market values, on the other. The fragmentation does not impugn the assumed universality of techno-scientific progress ideology but aims to conceptually wed Turkey's 'authentic' value systems to that ideology and its market economic values and standards.

Such a viewpoint has been embodied by large-scale capitalized farmers and agribusinesses, including seedling growers and seed distributors, who long for the state-activated institution of a context for Turkish–Muslim owned corporate agribusiness control over a process of competitive growth. They view the predominance of market-economic values and techno-scientific reorientation of agrifood relations as categorical expressions of universal standards in which local/national cultural ways should be anchored. This approach solidifies economization as a normative project of neoliberalism, with the ontological backing of non-market moral, normative, cultural commitments that cognitively expand and deepen entrepreneurialism among farmers. It is a cognitive reorientation that enables large farmers to view themselves as self-investing, responsible individuals seeking to maximize their performance values in agriculture for the purpose of generating income.

What does this cognitive reorientation say about a possible remaking of the social and re-establishing congruence between two sets of knowledge systems to achieve market–economic growth? It suggests that a normative reconfiguration is underway to create greater spatial diversity within neoliberalism's economization. Resonant with Adam Smith's (1759/1976) insistence on the need for moral regulation in the pursuit of income/wealth generation, *homo economicus* is reimagined with an Islamic twist, which I have called *homo Islameconomicus* in another work (Atasoy forthcoming). *Homo Islameconomicus* signifies a mentality for correcting the 'historical distortions' inherited from past practices of 'blind emulation of Western ways' in order that Muslim individuals can take part in economic growth and accumulation. *Homo Islameconomicus* ties the present wealth-creation of Muslim individuals to a supporting normative, historical structure. It upholds the Weberian thesis in regard to the renewed unity of modernity, between techno-scientific progress ideology infused with market values *and* the ethically grounded behaviour of 'doing good' for society. In such a formulation, the agency of the state would be re-conceptualized in terms of its managerial and regulatory policy in coordinating technical-industrial innovation by Turkish–Muslim individuals and companies, the reconfiguring of land–property–food dynamics as space-making for commodification and engineering the diffusion of a market ethos and discipline for the entrepreneurial remaking of farmers. This involves state-led breaking of the long-existing cultural connections with old-style farming as well as its resource, land access and property dynamics.

Said (1978) and Wallerstein (2006) would argue that this is a 'distorted representation' of universalism by describing the *particularities* of European achievements in universal terms. The Turkish government's appeal to the universal is a call for categorical meanings to reconstruct a norm-setting context for a particular viewpoint. Globalized techno-scientific ways thus become incorporated into a nationalist and Islamic reframing of interpretive meanings for a social change model. However, the translatability of globalized agribusiness practices to a norm-setting position is not a trans-historical phenomenon but a historical process that prevails in bracketing farmers' behaviour from the hitherto existing ways of living and farming.

Diversity acquires a different meaning in relation to the formation of ontologically distinct material arrangements and cognitive orientations at the general national level than the complexities that emerge at the local level of farming, as discussed earlier. Still, the state reconstruction of a norm-setting context insinuates the possibility of a distinct form of commodification and accumulation that must be analyzed as such in its historical specificity. It is also subject to contestation and negotiation within the state and at different levels of social relations.

Rather than 'diverse economies' flourishing at the local level (Gibson-Graham 2008), diversity now includes the redefinition of a 'knowledge structure' that provides a *homogenizing* background context for various types of farmers and farming practices to be integrated into a global condition of commodification as culturally different fractions of capital. State policy is reoriented to generate competitive growth, which, in purely economic terms, is associated with increased efficiency in labour and capital use. It includes state control over, and appropriation of, common public lands; reconfiguring of land-use and access patterns through land titling and land consolidation schemes; diversion of underground and aboveground fresh water into irrigation-intensive agriculture; and the intensified use of high-technology inputs. State-brokered deepening of commodification runs contrary to a general expectation among scholars that the state withdraw from public-sector involvement under neoliberalization, although the belief in the 'idea of the state' as a responsible agent for securing the common public good might manifest itself differently in the public eye.

Farmers continue to imagine food relationships in normatively different ways. Respect for agro-ecological integrity, recognition of local taste and food cultures, reinstitution of trust between farmers and consumers and renegotiation of food-quality standards are all considerations that enter into farmers' consciousness. Does this consciousness open a space for disrupting the deepening of commodification? And is it a matter of reconfiguring farmers' farming imaginaries to provide normative reorientations to diverse economies that contest neoliberalism?

There is substantive local heterogeneity in Turkey's agrifood provisioning system, as demonstrated throughout this book. Is heterogeneity a reflection of neoliberalism's contextual variegation (Brenner et al. 2010) and further conformity to its global convergence and dominance? Or, is the term *neoliberalization* used in a totalizing way to over-identify different sets of practices, styles and normative imaginings (Pinson and Journel 2016) – such that research is deterred from paying closer attention to the co-existence of diverse orientations, narratives and contexts?

The heterogeneity of farming in Turkey contains experiences of convergence and divergence. It is a complicated, multi-faceted narrative in which small-scale farmers are active participants. With few exceptions, the small-scale farmers I interviewed are not subsistence oriented; they participate in processes of commercialization with the goal of generating income and profits through increasing efficiency of production. They also participate in the use of biotechnology inputs. Further, they partake in the intensification of highly exploitative, paternalistic relations of waged labour. Nevertheless, these farmers *also* attribute normative, subjective judgements to their commercialization, including many different elements of divergence that inhibit further agro-industry penetration into agriculture and food. The mere co-existence of these multiplicities highlights the importance of thinking through the cracks and inconsistencies in the edifice of neoliberalization – inconsistencies that cannot be fully appreciated through a binary understanding of diminishing roles or potentialities for resistance.

There is *visible* heterogeneity *cohabitating* within the deepening agro-industrial model. The heterogeneity is not scale specific; smaller-scale farmers also constitute a heterogeneous category that includes those groups who adopt conventional-industrial, self-declared organic and customary ways of heirloom production and mixed marketing strategies. Nevertheless, these groups share a sense-based distrust of agro-industrial processes and continue to cherish non-market values and customary knowledge systems. They collaborate with other producers, including milk vendors, in the creation of new marketing channels and in the modification of older, traditional forms. They also generate ideas concerning the trustworthiness of their food through interpersonally established trust networks with other farmers – expressed in the exchange of local seed varieties and the cultivation of close ties with their long-established customers. All farmers share a concern with the conservation of local agro-ecological integrity at the landscape, health, nutrition and cultural levels. They mobilize their informally established interpersonal, trust-based connections to generate *participatory certification by consumers* for non-standard food without design and as an alternative to industrial knowledge systems and corporate-led GAP standards for food quality assurance. These interpersonal connections rooted in trust are also manifested in farmers' multiple roles as street vendors, traditional *pazar* merchants, door-to-door suppliers and business partners in trendy, boutique-style 'village products' stores.

The cohabitation of these often informally functioning activities is not sustained by a 'view from nowhere' (Nagel 1986); it relies on the activation of ideas for the maintenance of local landscape structures and agro-ecological history, the personal trustworthiness of farmers and farmer-varied customary production vis-à-vis impersonal, codification-dependent industrial methods. The significance of farmer-based personal variance in the trustworthiness of non-standard food, which is assured by reference to customary production methods, confirms the cohabitation of conflicting and contradictory tendencies and uneven subjective judgements within the global diffusion of agro-industrial ways, although not to the exclusion of complementarities as well.

Heterogeneity and mobilization of ideas concerning the 'locality' of food also valorizes a sense of place by embedding economic activity in agro-ecological conditions of geography, as is evident in discussions on the geographical indication (GI) certification of local heirloom varieties. This valorization ties a meaning-giving sense of place to the need for technical, industrial innovation at the local level of the economy. Again, as seen with large-scale capitalized farmers and agribusiness groups, the state is still expected to mobilize its regulatory power to bring together the economic and cultural realms through a market-making and market-conforming emphasis on techno-economic and social innovation for the commercialization of heirloom varieties.

Interestingly, farmers' emphasis on a sense of place is *also* connected to the reactivation of state power to support the emergence of more 'diverse economies' rooted in different sets of nonmarket values. This is the very essence of the *immanent ambivalence* that exists in farmers' farming imaginaries – an ambivalence that compels us to systematically rethink how to reconstruct place-specific heterogeneous economies based on ontologically different processes – in a way that avoids a valorized proliferation of local difference in commodification.

It would be a mistake to think of farmers' ambivalence as signaling the presence of a distinct ontology in their farming imaginaries that may eventually lead to divergent economies. These considerations are process based and accommodated in broader socio-economic, cultural contexts, with deep historical lineages to Ottoman and Islamic cognitive evaluative frames for social–economic realization. This lineage has inflicted a modernist ideational attachment to catch-up developmentalism, expressed in the marriage of Islamic values with European techno-scientific progress ideology (Atasoy 2009). An economic calculative logic and a self-interested view govern the 'rationality' principle of European capitalism, which has been directed toward the growing separation of humans from the web of life since the fifteenth century. This perceived separation enables humans to view nature as only having instrumental value – a commodity to be possessed and harnessed for the purpose of economic growth and wealth generation. Farmers' farming imaginaries reflect the tensions that emerge from such separation.

In the *Discourse on Method* (1952 [1637]), René Descartes clearly articulates this dualistic view of humans and nature.

> As soon … as I had achieved some general notions about physics, and when, testing them in various critical problems, I noticed how far they might lead and how they differed from the principles accepted up to this time … For they satisfied me that it is possible to reach *knowledge that will be of much utility in this life*; … by which knowing the nature and behavior of fire, water, air, stars, the heavens, and all the other bodies which surround us, as well as we now understand the different skills of our workers, we can employ these entities for all the purposes for which they are suited, and *to make ourselves masters and possessors of nature*. This would not only be desirable in bringing about the invention of an infinity of devices to enable us to enjoy the fruits of the earth without labor, but even more so …
>
> (Descartes 1952 [1637], 45, italics mine)

The separation of humanity from nature found in the mechanistic worldview offers license to 'vex' or disturb nature through the application of scientific technology. To quote Francis Bacon from his *New Organon*, published in 1620:

> A natural history which is composed of its own sake … contains the variety of natural species only, and not experiments of mechanical arts. For even as in the business of life a man's disposition and the secret workings of his mind and affections are better discovered when he is in trouble than at

other times, so likewise the secrets of nature reveal themselves more read-ily under the vexations of art than when they go their own way. Good hopes may therefore be conceived of natural philosophy, when natural history, which is the basis and foundation of it, has been drawn up on a better plan; but not till then.

(Bacon 1620, Book 1, Aphorism XCVIII)

The human control over nature advocated here is predicated on the moral guidance of a logic of utility. This generates a potential normative conflict between the market-oriented techno-scientific exploitation of nature *and* the nonmarket values of wholeness and integrity attributed to nature found in the Islamic values to which farmers are ideationally attached.

Nature in the Koran assumes the qualities of a seamless whole: 'a firm, well-knit structure with no gaps, no ruptures, and no dislocations … [as it is considered] one of the handicrafts of Almighty' (Rahman 1980, 3, 79, quoted in Özdemir 2003, 8). This conception is intended to foster in humans the awakening of a higher consciousness that can apprehend the countless inter-relationships within the universe. According to İbrahim Özdemir (2003), the Koranic perspective is one that encourages a distinct way of looking at the world so as to shift people's thinking and practices toward ecological integra-tion and holism. It is a worldview based on both the underlying unity of reality (*tawhid*) and an understanding that nature as a whole is *alive* – a meaningful and purposeful being. Such an outlook establishes humans' position in nature not as 'masters' and 'possessors' but as *vicegerent*, wholly accountable to maintain, use and improve the natural world for the benefit of generations to come, includ-ing the future generations of other species.

In the words of the great Sufi poet Rumi, the *living* universe, including the totality of interrelations of organisms, far from being inert or mechanical, is dynamic, intelligent and intimate, speaking and communicating the 'Word of God' in a system of mutual attraction (Clarke 2003). Rumi writes:

> The thirsty person moans: 'O delicious water!' The water moans too, say-ing, 'Where is the water-drinker?'
>
> Attraction to water causes thirst in our hearts because we are its and it is ours.
>
> The divine wisdom is destiny and decree made us lovers of one another.
>
> Because of that fore-ordainment, all the particles (atoms) of the universe are paired as mates and they are in love with each other.
>
> Every atom of the universe is in search of its mate, just like amber and the blade of straw.
>
> (Book 3/4395–4400, *Mesnevi*, my translation)

This view of nature as possessing its own inherent wisdom and integrity is entirely distinct from the norms and practices of techno-scientific develop-mentalism. The nonmarket value of ecological 'wholeness' seen as 'a bestowed trust' (Foltz et al. 2003) not only has strong affective resonance in the cognitive orientation of devout Muslim farmers; it also bears a deep affinity with many other spiritual traditions. Okanagan native spirituality in British Columbia, Canada, for example, identifies humans as inseparable from other species because of their connection to the land. Jeannette Armstrong explains:

> When we say the Okanagan word for ourselves, we are actually saying 'the ones who are dream and land together.' That is our original identity. Before anything else, we are the living, dreaming earth pieces ... We use a word that translates as *heart*. It is a capacity to form bonds with particular aspects of our surroundings. We say that we as people stay connected to each other, our land, and all things by our hearts.
>
> (Armstrong 1996, 461, 464)

This holistic representation of the earth and all its inhabitants – human and non-human – can be observed in other contexts and legacies, including that of some Mexican indigenous people who envision the world as a house, 'a world in which many worlds fit'. Such examples demonstrate a common connection to the land through ecosystem stewardship.

All of the farmers and agribusiness owners whose narratives appear in this book are devout Muslims. As previously noted, they all care about the health of landscapes, the agro-ecological conditions of farming, local food cultures and health and rural poverty issues. But, they walk the 'thin line' of modernity: they find it very difficult to establish an existentially sustainable synthesis between farming *and* their own Muslim ways – one that emphasizes 'transformative harmony with nature' (Clarke 2003, 54).

Bridging the gap between humans and nature requires a kind of *social–ecological realization* – a move *toward* integration and wholeness, *away from* the logic of commodification that fragments and objectifies natural processes into separate 'things' outside of us. (Notably, this fragmentation and objectification is central to Marx's notion of alienation.) Social–ecological realization entails a profoundly new way of thinking and acting in relation to economic and technological innovation. And it raises important ontological questions regarding the multiplicity of reciprocal relations between humans, nature and other species. The embodied know-how of generations of farmers and their knowledge-intensive farming systems and practices are invaluable here. They are integral to historical and natural cycles at the landscape level (including soil, plants and watercourses) and anathema to processes of commodification leading to vertically concentrated wealth. Re-activation of these knowledge systems and practices involves re-making relationships between humans and nature and the re-contextualization of farming activities and landscape structures within their myriad biological relationships. This re-contextualization must extend social and economic innovation to include an appropriate science and technology that is commensurate with the integrity of landscapes and ecological relationships.

Social–ecological realization is a substantive issue requiring the rehabilitation of human relationships with nature. It cannot be understood by reference to a standard, Weberian-style cause-and-effect analysis of instrumental rationality or a calculative episteme identified with neoliberalism's economization logic. Significant issues remain. As Amartya Sen (2009, 219–21) rightly points out, the relevance of an ontologically consistent evaluative frame of reference lies beyond utilitarian ethics. Sen's emphasis is on social realization. But, there can be no social realization without the ecological, and ethically embedded, agency-relevant decision making on a range of issues concerning personal and public goals and transformative possibilities. All must transcend the fetishism of a growth-oriented modernity understood in purely economic terms. The valuing of social–ecological realization centres decision making on an ethically grounded responsiveness to the demands of the integrity of landscapes, con- servation of agro-ecology and trustworthiness of food in a *conscious* shift from imaginaries to transformational reality. Without critically engaged discussion, and reconnection with the historical and natural rhythms of meaningful agro- ecological relationships, a deeply rooted, psycho-emotive *hüzün* (melancholy) will continue to envelop farmers' farming imaginaries in Turkey.

References

Abak, K., E. Düzyaman, V. Seniz, H. Gülen, A. Pekşen and H. C. Kaymak, 2010. 'Sebze Üretimini Geliştirme Yöntem ve Hedefleri'. In *Ziraat Mühendisliği VII. Teknik Kongresi Bildiriler Kitabı* vol. 1, 477–92. Ankara: TMOBB.

Abdelkadir, A. and R. C. Schultz, 2005. 'Water Harvesting in a "Runoff-Catchment": Agroforestry System in the Dry Lands of Ethiopia'. *Agrofores*, 63: 291–8.

Abede, G. K., J. Bijman, R. Kemp, O. Omta and A. Tsegaye, 2013. 'Contract Farming Configuration'. *Food Policy*, 40(2013): 14–24.

Abrams, P., 1988. 'Notes on the Difficulty of Studying the State'. *Journal of Historical Sociology*, 1(1): 58–89.

Ackerman, D., 1991. *A Natural History of the Senses*. New York: Vintage Books.

Addison, L., 2014. 'Delegated Despotism: Frontiers of Agrarian Labour on a South African Border Farm'. *Journal of Agrarian Change*, 14(2): 286–304.

Akbay, C., I. Boz and W. S. Chern, 2007. 'Household Food Consumption in Turkey'. *European Review of Agricultural Economics*, 34(2): 209–31.

Akkaya, F., R. Yalçın and B. Özkan, 2006. 'Good Agricultural Practices (GAP) and Its Implementation in Turkey'. *Acta Horticulturae*, 699: 47–52.

Aliber, M., M. Baipethi and P. Jacobs, 2009. 'Agricultural Employment Scenarios'. In *Another Countryside,* ed. R. Hall, 121–63. Cape Town: Institute for Poverty, Land and Agrarian Studies, University of the Western Cape.

Alkon, A. H. and J. Agyeman (eds), 2011. *Cultivating Food Justice*, Cambridge: MIT Press.

Allarakhia, M. and A. Wensley, 2005. 'Innovation and Intellectual Property Rights in Systems Biology'. *Nature Biotechnology*, 23(12): 1485–88.

Altınbilek, D., 1999, 'DSİ'de Sessiz Sedasız Özelleştirme', *Zaman Gazetesi*, 12 January, http://arsiv.zaman.com.tr/1999/01/12/ekonomi/2.html (accessed15 March 2013).

Altieri, M., 1995. *Agroecology*. Boulder, CO: Westview Press.

Altieri, A. M. and V. M. Toledo, 2011. 'The Agroecological Revolution in Latin America'. *Journal of Peasant Studies*, 38(3): 587–612.

AMPD, 2010. 'Türkiye Parekende Sektörü Genel Bilgiler', http://www.ampd.org/arastir-malar/default.aspx?SectionId=97 (accessed 10 November 2010 and 28 May 2015).

Anderson, B., 1987. *Imagined Communities*. London: Verso.

Anderson, E., 1969. *Plants, Man and Life*. Berkeley: University of California Press.

Anderson, P., 1980. *Arguments within English Marxism*. London: Verso.

Araghi, F., 2000. 'The Great Enclosure of Our Times'. In *Hungry for Profit*, eds F. Magdoff, J. B. Foster and F. H. Buttel, 145–60. New York: Monthly Review Press.

ARIP Project Brief, 2007. http://siteresources.worldbank.org/TURKEYEXTN/Resources/361711-1206357596243/ARIPprojectBrief-2007-hkray.pdf (accessed 5 October 2010).

Arizpe, L., 2014. 'Relay Migration and the Survival of the Peasant Household'. In *Lourdes Arizpe: A Mexican Pioneer in Anthropology*, ed. L. Arizpe, 71–92. Cham: Springer.

Armstrong, J., 1996. 'Sharing One Skin: Okanagan Community'. In *The Case against the Global Economy*, eds J. Mander and E. Goldsmith, 460–70. San Francisco: Sierra Club Books.

Asad, T., 2015. 'Thinking About Tradition, Religion and Politics in Egypt Today', http://criticalinuiry.uchicago.edu/thinking_about_tradition_religion_and_politics_in_egyp_today (accessed 22 April 2015).

Atalan-Helicke, N. and B. Mansfield, 2012. 'Seed Governance at the Intersection of Multiple Global and Nation-State Priorities: Modernizing Seeds in Turkey'. *Global Environmental Politics*, 12(4): 125–46.

Atasoy, Y., 2007. 'The Islamic Ethic and the Spirit of Turkish Capitalism Today'. In *Socialist Register* 2008, eds L. Panitch and C. Leys, 121–40. London: the Merlin Press.

Atasoy, Y., 2009. *Islam's Marriage with Neoliberalism*. London & New York: Palgrave Macmillan.

Atasoy, Y., 2013. 'Supermarket Expansion in Turkey'. *Journal of Agrarian Change*, 13(4): 547–70.

Atasoy, Y. (ed.), 2014. *Global Economic Crisis and the Politics of Diversity*. London: Palgrave Macmillan.

Atasoy, Y., 2016. 'Repossession, Re-informalization and Dispossession: The 'Muddy Terrain' of Land Commodification in Turkey'. *Journal of Agrarian Change*, doi:10.1111/joac.12182.

Atasoy, Y., Forthcoming. 'Neoliberalization and *Homo Islameconomicus*: The Politics of Women's Veiling in Turkey'. In *The Routledge International Handbook of Veils and Veiling Practices*, eds A.-M. Almila and D. Inglis. London: Routledge.

Aydın, Z., 2002. 'The New Right, Structural Adjustment and Turkish Agriculture'. *The European Journal of Development Research*, 14(2): 183–208.

Aydın, Z., 2010. 'Neo-Liberal Transformation of Turkish Agriculture'. *Journal of Agrarian Change*, 10(2): 149–87.

Aysu, A., 2002. *Tarladan Sofraya Tarım*. İstanbul: Su Yayınları.

Bacon, F., 1620. *The New Organon*, http://www.metaphysicspirit.com/books/The%20New%20Organon.pdf. (accessed 13 October 2016).

Bair, J. (ed.), 2009. *Frontiers of Commodity Chain Research*. Stanford: Stanford University Press.

Bair, J. and P. Hough, 2012. 'The Legacies of Partial Possession: From Agrarian Struggle to Neoliberal Restructuring in Mexico and Colombia'. *International Journal of Comparative Sociology*, 53(5–6): 345–66.

Balaban, Y., 2014. *Organik Tarım*. Ankara: Elma Yayınevi.

Balkaya, A. and D. Kandemir, 2015. 'Türkiye Sebze Fidesi Üretimindeki Son Gelişmeler', https://www.researchgate.net/publication/274719191_TURKIYE_SEBZE_FIDESI_URETIMINDEKI_SON_GELISMELER (accessed 5 March 2016).

Bank, E. and O. Mataracı, 2004. 'Cadastral Data Management System in Turkey'. FIG Athens-Greece, May 22–27, http://www.fig.net/pub/athens/papers/ts28/TS28_3_Bank_Mataraci.pdf (accessed 2 August 2015).

Barberi, P., 2002. 'Weed Management in Organic Agriculture'. *Weed Research*, 42: 177–93.

Barrett, M. and M. McIntosh, 1980. 'The "Family Wage"'. *Capital & Class*, 4(2): 51–72.

Barrientos, S. W., 2013. 'Labour Chains: Analysing the Role of Labour Contractors in Global Production'. *The Journal of Development Studies*, 49(8): 1058–71.

BBC News, 2015. 'Dow and DuPont Confirm Merger Plan', 11 December, http://www.bbc.com/news/business-35069280 (accessed 23 July 2016).

Becker, G. S., 1962. 'Investment in Human Capital'. *Journal of Political Economy*, 70(5): 9–49.

Belfrage, K., J. Björklund and L. Salomonsson, 2015. 'Effects of Farm Size and On-Farm Landscape Heterogeneity on Biodiversity – Case Study of Twelve Farms in a Swedish Landscape'. *Agroecology and Sustainable Food Systems*, 39(2): 170–88.

Bell, D., 1979. *The Cultural Contradictions of Capitalism*. New York: Basic Books.

Bengtsson, J., J. Anhnstrom and A.-C. Weibull, 2005. 'The Effects of Organic Agriculture on Biodiversity and Abundance'. *Journal of Applied Ecology*, 42(2): 261–69.

Bennholdt-Thomsen, V. and M. Mies, 1999. *The Subsistence Perspective*. London: Zed Books.

Berdegue, J. A. and H. M. Ravnborg, 2007. 'Agricultural Development for Poverty Reduction'. Danish Institute for International Studies, April.

Berdegue, J. A. and T. Reardon, 2008. 'The Retail-Led Transformation of Agrifood Systems'. In *Creating Food Futures*, eds. C. R. Farnworth, J. Jiggins and E. V. Thomas, 11–26. Aldershot: Gower.

Berk, A., 2013. 'Processor Driven Integration of Small-Scale Farmers into Value Chains in Turkey'. FAO, http://www.fao.org/3/a-au850e.pdf (accessed 24 May 2016).

Bernstein, H., 1996. 'Agrarian Question Then and Now'. *Journal of Peasant Studies*, 24(1–2): 22–59.

Bernstein, H., 2010. *Class Dynamics of Agrarian Change*. Halifax, NS.: Fernwood.

Bernstein, H., 2013. 'Historical Materialism and Agrarian History'. *Journal of Agrarian Change*, 13(2): 310–29.

Bernstein, H., B. Crow and H. Johnson (eds), 1992. *Rural Livelihoods*. Oxford: Oxford University Press for the Open University.

Bignebat, C., A. A. Koc and S. Lemeilleur, 2009. 'Small Producers, Supermarkets, and the Role of Intermediaries in Turkey's Fresh Fruit and Vegetable Market'. *Agricultural Economics*, 40(Supplement): 807–16.

Bignebat, C. and I. Vagneron, 2011. 'Private Certification in the Madagascar Lychee Export Chain'. Working Paper NTM Impact Project, http://www.bioeconomy-alcue.org/gg/user_files/13712064022.2%29.pdf (accessed 15 April 2013).

Biles, J., K. Brehm, A. Enrico, C. Kiendl, E. Morgan, A. Teachout and K. Vasquez, 2007. 'Globalization of Food Retailing and Transformation of Supply Networks'. *Journal of Latin American Geography*, 6(2): 55–75.

Bocci, R., 2009. 'State Legislation and Agrobiodiversity'. *Journal of Agriculture and Environment for International Development*, 103(1–2): 31–49.

Bocci, R. and V. Chable, 2009. 'Peasant Seeds in Europe'. *Journal of Agriculture and Environment for International Development*, 103(1–2): 81–93.

Borras Jr., S. M., 2003. 'Questioning the Pro-Market Critique of State-Led Agrarian Reforms'. *The European Journal of Development Research*, 15(2): 109–32.

Borras Jr., S. M., 2009. 'Agrarian Change and Peasant Studies: Changes, Continuities and Challenges'. *Journal of Peasant Studies*, (36)1: 5–31.

Borras, S. Jr. and J. Franco, 2010. 'From Threat to Opportunity?' *Yale Human Rights and Development Law Journal*, 13: 507–23.

Borras Jr., S. M., P. McMichael and I. Scoones, 2010. 'The Politics of Biofuels, Land and Agrarian Change'. *Journal of Peasant Studies*, 37(4): 575–92.

Boschma, R. A., 2005. 'Proximity and Innovation'. *Regional Studies*, 39(1): 61–74.

Bowen, S., 2010. 'Embedding Local Places in Global Spaces'. *Rural Sociology*, 75(2): 209–43.

Bowen, S. and K. De Master, 2014. 'Wisconsin's "Happy Cows"?'. *Agricultural Human Values*, 31(2014): 549–62.

Boyacıoğlu, H., 2014. ''Bulaştıran Kurtulacak''. *Hürriyet*, http://www.hurriyet.com.tr/ekonomi/26513622.asp (accessed 17 October 2014).

Brady, D., J. Beckfield and M. Seeleib-Kaiser, 2005. 'Economic Globalization and the Welfare State in Affluent Democracies, 1975–2001'. *American Review of Sociology*, 70(6): 921–48.

Brass, T., 2011. *Labour Regime Change in the Twenty-First Century*. Leiden: Brill.

Brenner, R., 1982. 'Agrarian Roots of European Capitalism'. *Past and Present*, 97: 16–113.

Brenner, N., J. Peck and N. Theodore, 2010. 'Variegated Neoliberalization'. *Global Networks*, 10(2): 182–222.

Brent, R., 2004. 'Partnership between Biology and Engineering'. *Nature Biotechnology*, 22(10): 1211–4.

Bromley, R., 2000. 'Street Vending and Public Policy'. *International Journal of Sociology and Social Policy*, 20(1): 1–28.

Brosius, P., 2006. 'What Counts as Local Knowledge in Global Environmental Assessments and Conventions?' In *Bridging Scales and Knowledge Systems*, eds W. Reid, F. Berkes, D. Capistrano and T. Wilbanks, 129–44. Washington DC.: Island Press.

Brown, W., 2015. *Undoing the Demos*. New York: Zone Books.

Brown L. D. and N. Woods (eds), 2007. *Making Global Self-Regulation Effective in Developing Countries*. Oxford: Oxford University Press.

Bryceson, D. F., 2000. 'Disappearing Peasantries?' In *Disappearing Peasantries*, eds D. F. Bryceson, C. Kay and J. Mooij, 299–326. London: IT Publications.

Bryceson, D. F., 2002. 'The Scramble in Africa'. *World Development*, 30(5): 725–39.

Bryceson, D. F., 2010. 'Sub-Saharan Africa's Vanishing Peasantries and the Spectre of a Global Food Crisis'. In *Agriculture and Food in Crisis*, eds F. Magdoff and B. Tokar, 69–84. New York: Monthly Review Press.

Buck, D., C. Getz and J. Guthman, 1997. 'From Farm to Table: The Organic Vegetable Commodity Chain of Northern California'. *Sociologia Ruralis*, 37(1): 3–19.

Burak, M., 2014. 'Biyogüvenlik Kurulu: "Rahat olun, GDO'ya izin yok', *CNN Türk*, http://www.cnnturk.com/haber/turkiye/biyoguvenlik-kurulu-rahat-olun-gdoya-izin-yok (accessed 17 October 2014).

Burch, D. and G. Lawrence (eds), 2007. *Supermarkets and Agri-food Supply Chains*. Cheltenham, UK: Edward Elgar.

Burch, D. and G. Lawrence, 2009. 'Towards a Third Food Regime'. *Agriculture and Human Values*, 26: 267–79.

Burch, D. and G. Lawrence, 2013. 'Financialization in Agri-Food Supply Chains'. *Agriculture and Human Values*, 30(2): 247–58.

Burch, D., J. Dixon and G. Lawrence, 2013. 'From Seedling to Supermarket'. *Agriculture and Human Values*, 30(2): 215–24.

Burgio, G., G. Campanelli, F. Leteo, F. Ramilli, L. Depalo, R. Fabbri and F. Sgolastra, 2015. 'Ecological Sustainability of an Organic Four-Year Vegetable Rotation System'. *Agroecology and Sustainable Food Systems*, 39(3): 295–316.

Busch, L., 2010. 'Can Fairy Tales Come True?' *Sociologia Ruralis*, 50(4): 331–51.

Busch, L., 2011. *Standards*. Cambridge: The MIT Press.

Busch, L., 2013. 'Standards Governing Agricultural Innovation'. In *Renewing Innovation Systems in Agriculture and Food*, eds E. Coudel, H. Devautor, C. T. Soulard, G. Faure and B. Hubert, 37–55. Wageningen: Wageningen Academic Publishers.

Buyukbay, E. O., M. Uzunoz and H. S. G. Bal, 2011. 'Post-harvest Losses in Tomato and Fresh Bean Production in Tokat Province of Turkey'. *Scientific Research and Essays*, 6(7): 1656–66.

Byres, T. J., 2009. 'The Landlord Class, Peasant Differentiation, Class Struggle and the Transition to Capitalism'. *Journal of Peasant Studies*, 36(1): 33–54.

Callinicos, A., 2006. *Making History*. Chicago: Haymarket Books.

Calvert, J., 2008. 'The Commodification of Emergence'. *Biosocieties*, 3(4): 383–98.

Cameron, A., 2004. *The Imagined Economies of Globalization*. London: Sage.

Camic, C. and N. Gross, 2001. 'The New Sociology of Ideas'. In *The Blackwell Companion to Sociology*, ed. J. R. Blau, 236–49. Malden, MA: Blackwell.

Campbell, H., 2009. 'Breaking New Ground in New Regime Theory: Corporate Environmentalism, Ecological Feedbacks and the 'Food From Nowhere' Regime?' *Agriculture and Human Values*, 26: 309–19.

Campbell, H. and R. Liepins, 2001. 'Naming Organics: Understanding Organic Standards in New Zealand as a Discursive Field'. *Sociologia Ruralis*, 41(1): 21–38.

Campbell, H., G. Lawrence and K. Smith, 2006. 'Audit Cultures and the Antipodes'. In *Between the Local and the Global*, eds T. Marsden and J. Murdoch, 69–93. Amsterdam: Elsevier, JAI.

Canik, F. and Y. Alparslan, 2010. 'Türkiye'de Yaş Sebze-Meyve Pazarlaması ve Toptancı Haller'. Tarımsal Ekonomi Araştırma Enstitüsü – *BAKIŞ*, 11(2): 1–8.

Canon, B., A. Labno and D. Endy, 2008. 'Refinement and Standardization of Synthetic Biological Parts and Devices'. *Nature Biotechnology*, 26(7): 787–93.

Carroll, E. B. and F. Fahy, 2014. 'Locating the Locale of Local Food'. *Renewable Agriculture and Food Systems*, 30: 563–76, doi:10.1017/S1742170514000404.

Carswell, G. and G. De Neve, 2013. 'Labouring for Global Markets'. *Geoforum*, 44(2013): 62–70.

CBC (Canadian Broadcasting Corporation), 2016. '"Migrant Dreams" Broken as Workers Face Exploitation on Ontario Farms', April 28, http://www.cbc.ca/news (accessed 28 April 2016).

Challies, R. T. E. and W. Murray, 2011. 'The Interaction of Global Value Chains and Rural Livelihoods'. *Journal of Agrarian Change*, 11(1): 29–59.

Chayanov, V. A., 1966. *The Theory of Peasant Economy*. Homewood, IL: Richard D. Irwin, Inc.

Cheyns, E. and L. Riisgaard, 2014. 'The Exercise of Power through Multi-stakeholder Initiatives for Sustainable Agriculture and Its Inclusion and Exclusion Outcomes'. *Agriculture and Human Values*, 31(3): 409–23.

Chmielewska, D. and D. Souza, 2010. 'Market Alternatives for Smallholder Farmers in Food Security Initiatives: Lessons for the Brazilian Food Acquisition Programme'. Working Paper, International Policy Centre for Inclusive Growth, No. 64.

Clarke, L., 2003. 'The Universe Alive: Nature in the Masnavi of Jalal al-Din Rumi'. In *Islam and Ecology: A Bestowed Trust*, eds R.C. Foltz, F.M. Denny and A. Baharuddin, 39–65. Cambridge: Harvard University Press.

Codron, J.-M., Z. Bouhsina, F. Ford, E. Coudel and A. Puech, 2004. 'Supermarkets in Low-Income Mediterranean Countries'. *Development Policy Review*, 22(5): 587–602.

Coleman, J. S., 1988. 'Social Capital in the Creation of Human Capital'. *American Journal of Sociology*, 94(Supplement): S95–S120.

Collier, P., 2008. 'The Politics of Hunger'. *Foreign Affairs*, 87(6): 67–79.

Collier, S., 2005. 'The Spatial Forms and Social Norms of 'Actually Existing Neoliberalism''. International Affairs Working Paper 2005-04.

Çarkoğlu, A. and M. Eder, 2005. 'Developmentalism *alla Turca*'. In *Environmentalism in Turkey*, eds F. Adaman and M. Arsel, 167–83. Aldershot: Ashgate.

Çelik, A. B., 2005. 'I Miss My Village'. *New Perspectives on Turkey*, 32(2005): 137–63.

Çiçek, İ., 2003. 'Statistical Analysis of Precipitation in Ankara, Turkey'. *Fırat University Journal of Social Science*, 13(1): 1–20.

Dardot, P. and C. Laval, 2013. *The New Way of the World*. London: Verso.

Dasgupta, P., 2008. 'Common Property Resources'. In *Promise, Trust and Evolution*, eds R. Ghate, N. Jodha and P. Mukhopadhyay, 19–51. Oxford: Oxford University Press.

Daunfeldt, S.-O., J. Nordström and L. Thunström, 2011. 'Habit Formation in Food Consumption'. In *The Oxford Handbook of The Economics of Food Consumption and Policy*, eds J. L. Lusk, J. Roosen and J. F. Shogren, 770–90. New York: Oxford University Press.

Davey, S. S. and C. Richards, 2013. 'Supermarkets and Private Standards'. *Agriculture and Human Values*, 30(2): 271–81.

Davis, D., 2005. 'Indigenous Knowledge and the Desertification Debate: Problematising Expert Knowledge in North Africa'. *Geoforum*, 36(4): 509–24.

Davis, D. K. and E. Burke, 2011. *Environmental Imaginaries of the Middle East and North Africa*. Athens: Ohio University Press.

Davis, M., 2006. *Planet of Slums*. New York: Verso.

De Haan, A., 2002. 'Migration and Livelihoods in Historical Perspective: A Case Study of Bihar, India'. *The Journal of Development Studies*, 38(5): 115–42.

De Noronha Vaz, T., T. Nijkamp and J.-L. Rastoin (eds), 2009. *Traditional Food Production and Rural Sustainable Development*. Farnham, England: Ashgate.

De Ponti, T., B. Rikk and M. K. van Ittersum, 2012. 'The Crop Yield Gap between Organic and Conventional Agriculture'. *Agricultural Systems*, 108(2012): 1–9.

De Wit, M. M., 2016. '"Stealing into the Wild" Conservation Science, Plant Breeding and the Makings of New Seed Enclosures'. *The Journal of Peasant Studies*, doi:10.1080/0306 6150.2016.1168405.

Deibel, E., 2013. 'Open Variety Rights'. *Journal of Agrarian Change*, 13(2): 282–309.

Deloitte, 2014. *Retail Sector Update*, July, http://www2.deloitte.com/content/dam/ Deloitte/tr/Documents/mergers-acqisitions/tr-retail-sector-update.pdf (accessed 4 June 2015).

Demir, O. and Y. E. Çoruhlu, 2006. 'Determining the Land Ownership on Cadastre Works in Turkey', http://www.academia.edu/378703/DETERMINING_THE_LAN DOWNERSHIP_ON_CADASTRE_WORKS_IN_TURKEY (accessed 4 March 2014).

Demossier, M., 2011. 'Beyond Terroir: Territorial Construction, Hegemonic Discourses, and French Wine Culture'. *Journal of the Royal Anthropological Institute*, 17(4): 685–705.

Descartes, R., 1952 [1637]. *Discourse on Method*. Upper Saddle River: Prentice-Hall, Inc.

Dixon, J., 2009. 'From the Imperial to the Empty Calorie'. *Agriculture and Human Values*, 26(4): 321–33.

Dixon, J. and B. Isaacs, 2013. 'There's Certainly a Lot of Hurting Out There'. *Agriculture and Human Values*, 30(2): 283–97.

Dolan, C. and J. Humphrey, 2000. 'Governance and Trade in Fresh Vegetables: The Impact of UK Supermarkets on the African Horticulture Industry'. *The Journal of Development Studies*, 37(2): 147–76.

Dombey, D. and A. Felsted, 2013. 'Turkey's Fragmented Market Frustrates Foreign Retailers', *Retail*, October 11, http://www.ft.com/intl/cms/s/0/709bfa14-31bf-11e3-817c-00144feab7de.html#axzz3cBcvnHdT (accessed 5 June 2015).

DSİ, 2014. *Devlet Su İşleri Genel Müdürlüğü 2014 Yılı Faaliyet Raporu*, http://www.dsi. gov.tr/docs/stratejik-plan/dsi-2014-faaliyet-raporu.pdf?sfvrsn=2#page=62 (accessed 9 December 2015).

Dubetsky, A., 1976. 'Kinship, Primordial Ties, and Factory Organization in Turkey'. *International Journal of Middle East Studies*, 7(3): 433–51.

Duelli, P. and M. K. Obrist, 2003. 'Biodiversity Indicators'. *Agriculture, Ecosystems and Environment*, 98(1–3): 87–98.

Dupuis, E. M. and D. Goodman, 2005. 'Should We Go Home to Eat?' *Journal of Rural Studies*, 21: 359–71.

Dutfield, G., 2008. 'Turning Plant Varieties into Intellectual Property'. In *The Future Control of Food*, eds G. Tansey and T. Rajotte, 27–47. London: Earthscan.

Echanove-Huacuja, F., 2006. 'Contract Farming and Small-Scale Producers'. *Iberoamericana*, XXXVI (1): 83–102.

Edelman, M., 2000. 'The Persistence of the Peasantry'. *North American Congress on Latin America*, 33(5): March–April, New York.

Eder, M., 2003. 'Implementing the Economic Criteria of EU Membership'. *Turkish Studies*, 4(1): 219–44.

EEA, 2015. 'Land Use – Drivers and Pressures (Turkey)', http://www.eea.europa.eu/soer/countries/tr/land-use-drivers-and-pressures-turkey (accessed 3 December 2015).

Eker, M. M., 2013. '2013 Değerlendirme Toplantısı', http://www.tarim.gov.tr/Sayfalar/Anasayfa.aspx (accessed 28 January 2014).

Elson, D. and R. Pearson, 1997. 'The Subordination of Women and the Internationalization of Factory Production'. In *The Women, Development and Gender Reader*, eds N. Visvanathan, L. Duggan, L. Nisonoff and N. Wiegersma, 191–203. London: Zed.

Engels, F., 1872. *The Housing Question*. http://www.marxists.org/archive/marx/works/1872/housing-question/index.htm (accessed 2 February 2014).

Erder, S., 1997. *Kentsel Gerilim*. Ankara: Umağ.

Eriksen, S. N., 2013. 'Defining Local Food'. *Acta Agriculturae Scandinavica Section B: Soil and Plant Science*, 63(1): 47–55.

Eriksen, S. N. and J. A. Silva, 2009. 'The Vulnerability Context of a Savanna Area in Mozambique'. *Environmental Science & Policy*, 12: 33–52.

Eriksen, S. N. and J. Sundbo, 2015. 'Drivers and Barriers to the Development of Local Food Networks in Rural Denmark'. *European Urban and Regional Studies*, pp. 1–15, doi:10.1177/0969776414567971.

Escobar, A., 1995. *Encountering Development*. Princeton: Princeton University Press.

Euromonitor International, 2015. 'Grocery Retailers in Turkey, April 2015', http://www.euromonitor.com/grocery-retailers-in-turkey/report (accessed 4 June 2015).

European Union, 2006. 'Council Regulation [EC] No. 510/2006 on the Protection of Geographical Indications and Designations of Origin for Agricultural Products and Foodstuffs'. *Official Journal of the European Union*, L 93, 31, March 2006, 12–25, http://eur-lex.europa.eu/legal-content/EN/TXTP/PDF/?uri=CELEX (accessed 8 April 2014).

Ewen, S., 1976. *Captains of Consciousness*. New York: McGraw-Hill.

Fabiosa, J. F., 2011. 'Globalization and Trends in World Food Consumption'. In *The Oxford Handbook of The Economics of Food Consumption and Policy*, eds J. L. Lusk, J. Roosen and J. F. Shogren, 591–611. New York: Oxford University Press.

FAO (Food and Agriculture Organization of the United Nations), 2015. *Yield Gap Analysis of Field Crops*, http://www.fao.org/3/a-i4695e.pdf (accessed 3 January 2016).

Farina, E. M. M. Q. and T. Reardon, 2000. 'Agrifood Grades and Standards in the Extended Mercosur'. *American Journal of Agricultural Economics*, 82(5): 1170–6.

Faroqhi, S., 2004. 'İç Ticaretin Örgütlenmesi'. In *Osmanlı İmparatorluğu'nun Ekonomik ve Sosyal Tarihi, 1600-1914, C: 2*, ed. H. İnalcık, 616–20. İstanbul.

Faure, G., E. Coudel, C. T. Soulard and H. Devautour, 2013. 'Reconsidering Innovation to Address Sustainable Development'. In *Renewing Innovation Systems in Agriculture and*

Food, eds E. Coudel, H. Devautour, C. T. Soulard, G. Faure and B. Hubert, 17–33. Wageningen: Wageningen Academic Publishers.

Feagan, R., 2007. 'The Place of Food'. *Progress in Human Geography*, 31(1): 23–42.

Ferguson, J., 2006. *Global Shadows*. Durham and London: Duke University Press.

Fernandes, B. M., C. A. Welch and E. C. Gonçalves, 2012. *Land Governance in Brazil*. International Land Coalition, Land Governance in the 21st Century: Framing the Debates Series, No. 2 ILC, Rome.

Field Crops Research, 2013. *Special Issue: Crop Yield Gap Analysis*, 143(2013): 1–156.

Foltz, R. C., F. M. Denny and A. Baharuddin, 2003. *Islam and Ecology: A Bestowed Trust*. Cambridge: Harvard University Press.

Fonte, M., 2006. 'Slow Food's Presidia'. In *Between the Local and the Global*, eds T. Marsden and J. Murdoch, 203–40. Amsterdam: JIP Press.

Forge, T., E. Kenney, N. Hashimoto, D. Neilsen and B. Zebarth, 2016. 'Compost and Poultry Manure as Preplant Soil Amendments for Red Raspberry'. *Agriculture, Ecosystems and Environment*, 223(2016): 48–58.

Fortune Türkiye, 2015. 'Perakende Sektöründe 2015'te Yüzde 9 Büyüme Bekleniyor', 20 January 2015, http://www.fortuneturkey.com/perakende-sektorunde-2015te-yuzde-9-buyume-bekleniyor-7217 (accessed 4 June 2015).

Foster, J. B., B. Clark and R. York, 2010. *The Ecological Rift*. New York: Monthly Review Press.

Fox, J., 2007. *Accountability Politics: Power and Voice in Rural Mexico*. New York: Oxford University Press.

Freeman, C., 1988. *Japan: A New National System of Innovation?* London: Pinter.

Friedmann, H., 1992. 'Distance and Durability'. *Third World Quarterly*, 13(2): 371–83.

Friedmann, H. and A. McNair, 2008. 'Whose Rules Rule?' *Journal of Agrarian Change*, 8(2–3): 408–34.

Friedmann, H. and P. McMichael, 1989. 'Agriculture and the State System'. *Sociologia Ruralis*, XXIX(2): 93–117.

Friedmann, J., 1992. *Empowerment*. Oxford: Blackwell.

Fulponi, L., 2006. 'Private Voluntary Standards in the Food System: The Perspective of Major Food Retailers in OECD Countries'. *Food Policy*, 31(2006): 1–13.

GAIN (Global Agricultural Information Network), 2011. 'Turkey: Retail Foods, Retail Food Sector', USDA Foreign Agricultural Service, www.gain.fas.usda.gov/../Retail%20Foods_Ankara_Turkey_1-3-2012.pdf (accessed 5 June 2015).

GAIN, 2014. 'Turkey: Retail Food Report, December 1, 2014)', USDA Foreign Agricultural Service, http://www.fas.usda.gov/data/turkey-retail-foods-report. (accessed 5 June 2015).

Garcia-Torres, L., J. Benites, A. Martínez-Vilela and A. Holgado-Cabrera (eds), 2003. *Conservation Agriculture*. Dordrecht/Boston/London: Kluwer Academic Publishers.

Gepts, P., 2004. 'Who Owns the Biodiversity, and How Should the Owners Be Compensated?' *Plant Physiology*, 134: 1295–307.

Gershon, I., 2011. 'Neoliberal Agency'. *Current Anthropology*, 52(4): 537–55.

Gibbon, P. and S. Ponte, 2005. *Trading Down*. Philadelphia: Temple University Press.

Gibbon, P. and E. Lazaro, 2010. 'Agro-Food Standards and Africa'. In *Global Agro-Food Trade and Standards*, eds P. Gibbon, S. Ponte and E. Lazaro, 1–20. Hampshire, UK.: Palgrave Macmillan.

Gibbon, P., B. Daviron and S. Barral, 2014. 'Lineages of Paternalism'. *Journal of Agrarian Change*, 14(2): 165–89.

Gibson-Graham, J. K., 2008. 'Diverse Economies'. *Progress in Human Geography*, 32(5): 613–32.

Gill, S., 1998. 'New Constitutionalism, Democratisation and Global Political Economy'. *Pacifica Review*, 10(1): 23–38.

Gill, S., 2000. 'Knowledge, Politics, and Neo-Liberal Political Economy'. In *Political Economy and the Changing Global Order*, eds R. Stubbs and G.R.D. Underhill, 48–59. Oxford: Oxford University Press.

Gill, V., 2010. 'Wild Food Crop Relatives to be "Rescued"'. *BBC Earth News*, 10 December, www.news.bbc.co.uk/earth/hi/earth_news/newsid_9273000/9273567.stm (accessed 30 September 2014).

Gilles, J. L., J. L. Thomas, C. Valdivia and E. S. Yucra, 2013. 'Laggards or Leaders: Conservers of Traditional Agricultural Knowledge in Bolivia'. *Rural Sociology*, 78(1): 51–74.

GKGM (Gıda ve Kontrol Genel Müdürlüğü), 2014. 'Ulusal Kalıntı İzleme Planı–2014 Türkiye', http://www.tarim.gov.tr/Konular/Gida-Ve-Yem-Hizmetleri/Gida-Hizmetl eri/Kalinti-Izleme (accessed 6 October 2014).

Godden, D., 1999. 'Attenuating Aboriginal Property Rights'. *The Australian Journal of Agricultural and Resource Economics*, 43(1): 1–33.

Goodman, D. and M. Watts (eds), 1997. *Globalising Food*. London: Routledge.

Gracia, A., J. Barreiro-Hurle and B. Lopez-Galan, 2014. 'Are Local and Organic Claims Complements or Substitutes?' *Journal of Agricultural Economics*, 65(1): 49–67.

Graff. G. D., S. E. Cullen, K. J. Bradford, D. Zilberman and A. Bennett, 2003. 'The Public–Private Structure of Intellectual Property Ownership in Agricultural Biotechnology'. *Nature Biotechnology*, 21(9): 989–95.

Guijt, I. and E. V. Walsum, 2008. 'Balancing Business and Empowerment in Fair Fruit Chains'. In *Creating Food Futures*, eds C. R. Farnworth, J. Jiggins and E. V. Thomas, 81–96. Aldershot: Gower.

Gupta, A., 1998. *Postcolonial Developments: Agriculture in the Making of Modern India*. Durham: Duke University Press.

Gupta, A., 2010. 'Transparency as Contested Political Terrain'. *Global Environmental Politics*, 10(3): 32–52.

Guthman, J., 2004. 'The Trouble with "Organic Lite" in California'. *Sociologia Ruralis*, 44(3): 301–16.

Guthman, J., 2000. 'Raising Organic: An Agro-Ecological Assessment or Grower Practices in California'. *Agriculture and Human Values*, 17(3): 257–66.

Gülöksüz, E., 2004. 'Negotiating of Property Rights in Urban Land in Istanbul'. In *Private Property in the East and West*, ed. H. İslamoğlu, 248–75. London and New York: I. B. Tauris.

Güneş, Y. and O. D. Elvan, 2003. 'The Underlying Causes of Illegal Logging Activities in Turkey', http://www.fao.org/docrep/ARTICLE/WFC/XII/0313-B1.HTM (accessed 10 December 2015).

Güven, A. B., 2009. 'Reforming Sticky Institutions'. *Studies in Comparative International Development*, 44: 16–87.

Hacettepe Üniversitesi, 2006. Türkiye Göç ve Yerinden Olmuş Nüfus Araştırması. Ankara: Hacettepe Üniversitesi Nüfus Etütleri Enstitüsü, Yayın No. NEE-HU.06.01.

Hall, R., 2009. 'Land Reform How and for Whom?' In *Another Countryside: Policy Options for Land and Agrarian Reform in South Africa,* ed. R. Hall, 63–91. Cape Town: Institute for Poverty, Land and Agrarian Studies, University of the Western Cape.

Hall, A.P. and D. Soskice (eds), 2001. *Varieties of Capitalism*. Oxford: Oxford University Press.

Hall, D., P. Hirsch and T. Murray Li, 2011. *Powers of Exclusion: Land Dilemmas in Southeast Asia*. Honolulu, HI: University of Hawai'i Press.

Hanson, P. C., 1998. *Necessary Virtue*. Charlottesville: University Press of Virginia.

Harris, L. M., 2008. 'Modernizing the Nation: Postcolonialism, (Post)development, and Ambivalent Spaces of Difference in Southeastern Turkey'. *Geoforum*, 39(5): 1698–708.

Harris, L. M., 2009. 'Contested Sustainabilities: Assessing Narratives of Environmental Change in Southeastern Turkey'. *Local Environment*, 14(8): 699–720.

Harriss-White, B. and S. Garikipati, 2008. 'India's Semi-Arid Rural Economy'. *The European Journal of Development Research*, 20(4): 547–8.

Harvey, P. D. A., 1993. *Maps in Tudor England*. Chicago: University of Chicago Press.

Harvey, D., 2003. *The New Imperialism*. Oxford: Oxford University Press.

Harvey, M., 2007. 'The Rise of Supermarkets and Asymmetries of Economic Power'. In *Supermarkets and Agri-food Supply Chains*, eds D. Burch and G. Lawrence, 51–73. Cheltenham, UK & Northampton, MA, USA: Edward Elgar.

Hawken, P., 2010. *The Ecology of Commerce*. New York: Harper Business.

Henisz, J. W., B. A. Zelner and M. F. Guillen, 2005. 'The Worldwide Diffusion of Market-Oriented Infrastructure Reform, 1977–1999'. *American Review of Sociology*, 70(6): 871–97.

Hinrichs, C. C. and L. Charles, 2012. 'Local Food Systems and Networks in the US and the UK'. In *Rural Transformations and Rural Policies in the UK and US*, eds M. Shucksmith, D. Brown, S. Shortall, M. Warner and J. Vergunst, 156–76. London: Routledge.

Holmes, G., 2014. 'What Is a Land Grab?' *The Journal of Peasant Studies*, 41(4): 547–67.

Holzapfel, S. and M. Wollni, 2014. 'Is GlobalGap Certification of Small-Scale Farmers Sustainable? Evidence from Thailand'. *The Journal of Development Studies*, 50(5): 731–47.

Holt-Gimenez, E. and M. A. Altieri, 2013. 'Agroecology, Food Sovereignty, and the New Green Revolution'. *Agroecology and Sustainable Food Systems*, 37(1): 90–102.

Hueth, B., E. Ligon, S. Wolf and S. Wu, 1999. 'Incentive Instruments in Fruits and Vegetable Contracts'. *Review of Agricultural Economics*, 21(2): 374–89.

Hutchinson, J. A., 2012. 'Surviving, Coping or Thriving? Understanding Coping and Its Impact on Social Well-Being in Mozambique'. *British Journal of Social Work*, doi:10.1093/bjsw/bcs167.

Hürriyet Newspaper, 2011. 'Anadolu'nun Tohumları Sakin Şehirler'de Yeşeriyor', 25 December.

Hürriyet Newspaper, 2013. 'Hazineye Ait Tarım Arazileri Yarı Fiyatına Köylünün Olacak', 28 September, http://www.hurriyet.com.tr/ekonomi/24806130.asp (accessed 21 December 2013).

Hürriyet Newspaper, 2015. '2 Bin Çiftçiyle İyi Tarıma Girdi, Sebze-Meyve İTU'lu oldu', 11 February.

ILO (International Labour Organization), 2002. *International Labour Conference 90th Session 2002, Report VI: Decent Work and Informal Economy*. Geneva: International Labour Office.

İnalcık, H., 1994. 'State, Land and Peasant'. In *An Economic and Social History of the Ottoman Empire: 1300–1600*, vol. I, ed. H. İnalcık, 103–78. Cambridge: Cambridge University Press.

İncekara, Ü., n.d. 'Biological Richness of Eastern Anatolia (Turkey)', http://esruc.atauni.edu.tr/sunu/kutuhane/sunum/umitince.pptx (accessed 28 October 2014).

ISF (International Seed Federation), 2013a. 'Value of the Domestic Market for Seed in Selected Countries', Domestic_Market_Value_2012-1pdf (accessed 30 September 2014).

ISF, 2013b. 'Imports of Seed for Sowing by Country – Calendar Year 2012', Seed_Imports_2012.pdf (accessed 30 September 2014).

İslamoğlu, H., 2004. 'Politics of Administering Property'. In *Private Property in the East and West*, ed. H. İslamoğlu, 276–319. London & New York: I. B. Tauris.

İyi Tarım Uygulamalarına İlişkin Yönetmelik [İTUİY], 2004. http://www.iyi.tarim.gov.tr (accessed 30 January 2012).

İTUİY, 2010. http://www.iyi.tarim.gov.tr (accessed 30 January 2012).

James, C., 2011. *Global Status of Commercialized Biotech/GM Crops: 2011*. ISAAA Briefs, Brief 43. International Service for the Acquisition of Agri-Biotech Applications, isaaa-brief-43-2011.pdf (accessed 10 October 2014).

James, C., 2013. *Global Status of Commercialized Biotech/GM Crops: 2013*. ISAAA Briefs, Brief 46 – 2013 Executive Summary, http://www.isaaa.org/resources/publications/briefs/46/executivesummary/ (accessed 16 October 2014).

James, H. S., Jr. and I. Sulemana, 2014. 'Case Studies on Smallholder Farmer Voice'. *Agriculture and Human Values*, 31(4): 637–41.

Jansen, K. and S. Vellema (eds), 2004. *Agribusiness & Society*. London: Zed Books.

Jessop, B., 2002. 'Liberalism, Neoliberalism, and Urban Governance'. *Antipode*, 34(3): 452–72.

Jones, P. M., 2012. 'The Challenge of Land Reform in Eighteenth- and Nineteenth-Century France'. *Past and Present*, 216 (August): 107–42.

Jonsson, M., R. Bommarco, B. Ekbom, H. G. Smith, J. Bengtsson, B. Caballero-Lopez, C. Winqvist and O. Olsson, 2014. 'Ecological Production Functions for Biological Control Services in Agricultural Landscapes'. *Methods in Ecology and Evolution*, 5(3): 243–52.

Jordan. J., 2007. 'The Heirloom Tomato as Cultural Object'. *Sociologia Ruralis*, 47(1): 20–41.

Journal of Agrarian Change, 2014. Special Issue: *Agrarian Lineages of Paternalism* 14(2): 165–321.

Jwaideh, W., 1999. *Kürt Milliyetçiliğinin Tarihi*. İstanbul: İletişim Yayınları.

Kaltoft, P., 2001. 'Organic Farming in Late Modernity'. *Sociologia Ruralis*, 41(1): 146–58.

Kaur, A., 2014. 'Plantation Systems, Labour Regimes and the State in Malaysia, 1900–2012'. *Journal of Agrarian Change*, 14(2): 190–213.

Kay, K., 2016. 'Breaking the Bundle of Rights'. *Environment and Planning A*, 48(3): 504–22.

Kaya, F., 2009. *Türkiye'de Kredi Kartı Uygulaması*. İstanbul: Türkiye Bankalar Birliği.

Keleş, R., 1984. *Urbanization and Housing Politics*. Ankara: Ankara University Press.

Kersting, S. and M. Wollni, 2012. 'New Institutional Arrangements and Standard Adoption: Evidence from Small-Scale Fruit and Vegetable Farmers in Thailand'. *Food Policy*, 37: 452–62.

Keyder, Ç., 1981. *The Definition of a Peripheral Economy*. Cambridge: Cambridge University Press.

Keyder, Ç., 1987. *State and Class in Turkey*. London: Verso.

Keyder, Ç., 1993. 'The Genesis of Petty Commodity Production in Agriculture. The Case of Turkey'. In *Culture and Economy*, ed. P. Stirling, 171–86. Cambridgeshire: The Eothen Press.

Keyder, Ç. and Z. Yenal, 2011. 'Agrarian Change under Globalization'. *Journal of Agrarian Change*, 11(1): 60–86.

Kısakürek, N. F., 1979. *Çile*. İstanbul: Büyük Doğu Yayınları.

Kings, D. and B. Ilbery, 2014. 'The Lifeworlds of Organic and Conventional Farmers in Central-southern England'. *Sociologia Ruralis*, 55(1): 62–84.

Kivilcim, Z., 2011. 'The Legal Framework for Agrobiotechnology in Turkey'. In *Rethinking Structural Reform in Turkish Agriculture*, eds B. Karapinar, F. Adaman and G. Ozertan, 267–82. New York: Nova Science Publishers.

Kleemann, L., A. Abdulai and M. Buss, 2014. 'Certification and Access to Export Markets: Adoption and Return on Investment of Organic-Certified Pineapple Farming in Ghana'. *World Development*, 64: 79–92.

Kloppenburg, J., 1991. 'Social Theory and the De-Construction of Agricultural Science'. *Rural Sociology*, 56(4): 519–48.

Kloppenburg, J., 2005 [1988]. *First the Seed*. Madison: University of Wisconsin Press.

Kloppenburg, J., 2010. 'Impeding Dispossession, Enabling Repossession'. *Journal of Agrarian Change*, 10(3): 367–88.

Kloppenburg, J. Jr., J. Hendrickson and G. W. Stevenson, 1996. 'Coming in to the Foodshed'. *Agriculture and Human Values*, 13(3): 33–42.

Kök, G., 2010. 'Hal Yasası Değişti, Peki Ya Hallerin Yeri?' *ntvmsnbc*, 25 March.

Kumar, R., 2016. 'The Perils of Productivity: Making 'Good Farmers' in Malwa, India'. *Journal of Agrarian Change*, 16(1): 70–93.

Küçük, M., 2013. '2013'ün Ortak Hedefi: Yatırımlara Devam – 1', 4 April, http://www.perakende.org/guncel/2013un-ortak-hedefi-yatirimlara-devam-1-1342791841h.html (accessed 4 June 2015).

Küçük, M., O. E. Harputoğlu and U. Tatlı, 2013. 'Devler 2012 ve 2013'ü Yorumluyor – 1', 7 February, http://www.perakende.org/guncel/devler-2012-ve-2013u-yorumluyor-1-1342791096h.html (accessed 4 June 2015).

Laliberte, E., J. B. Grace, M. A. Huston, H. Lambers, F. P. Teste, B. L. Turner and D. A. Wardle, 2013. 'How Does Pedogenesis Drive Plant Diversity'. *Trends in Ecology & Evolution*, 28(6): 331–40.

Lancaster, K. J., 1966. 'A New Approach to Consumer Theory'. *Journal of Political Economy*, 74(2): 132–57.

Land, H., 1980. 'The Family Wage'. *Feminist Review*, 6(1980): 55–77.

Lane, C. and G. Wood, 2009. 'Capitalist Diversity and Diversity within Capitalism'. *Economy and Society*, 38(4): 531–51.

Laurent, C. G., A. P. J. Mol and P. Oosterveer, 2013. 'Conventionalization of the Organic Sesame Network from Burkina Faso'. *Agriculture and Human Values*, 30(4): 539–54.

Lee, R., 2014. 'European Food Governance'. In *Sustainable Food Systems*, eds T. Marsden and A. Morley, 62–83. London: Routledge.

Lemeilleur, S. and J. M. Codron, 2011. 'Marketing Cooperative vs. Commission Agent'. *Food Policy*, 36 (2011): 272–9.

Lemeilleur, S. and S. Tozanlı, 2007. 'A Win–Win Relationship between Producer's Union and Supermarket Chains in Turkish Fresh Fruits and Vegetables Sector'. Working Paper, Innovative Practices Series, Regoverning Markets, http://www.globalfoodchainpartnerships.org (accessed 11 May 2011).

Lerner, D., 1958. *The Passing of Traditional Society*. New York: Free Press.

Leys, C., 2007. *Total Capitalism*. London: The Merlin Press.

Li, T. M., 2009. 'Exit from Agriculture'. *The Journal of Peasant Studies*, 36(3): 629–36.

Lockie, S. and D. Halpin, 2005. 'The "Conventionalization" Thesis Reconsidered'. *Sociologia Ruralis*, 45(4): 285–307.

Lockie, S., K. Lyons and G. Lawrence, 2000. 'Constructing "Green Foods": Corporate Capital, Risk and Organic Farming in Australia and New Zealand'. *Agriculture and Human Values*, 17(4): 315–22.

Lund, C., 2009. 'Recategorizing "Public" and "Private" Property in Ghana'. *Development and Change*, 40(1): 131–48.

Magdoff, F., J. B. Foster and F. H. Buttel (eds), 2000. *Hungry for Profit*. New York: Monthly Review Press.

Mainville, Y. D. and H. C. Peterson, 2005. 'Fresh Produce Procurement Strategies in a Constrained Supply Environment: Case Study of Companhia Brasileira de Distribuicao'. *Review of Agricultural Economics*, 27(1): 130–8.

Maliye Bakanlığı, 2010. *Milli Emlak Genel Müdürlüğü 2010 Yılı Faaliyet Raporu*, http://www.milliemlak.gov.tr/documents/10326/212a91e6-6c51-4d9c-8df6-1884b45ac97e (accessed 8 January 2014).

Maliye Bakanlığı, 2014. *Milli Emlak Genel Müdürlüğü 2014 Yılı Faaliyet Raporu*, http://www.milliemlak.gov.tr/Faaliyet%20Raporlar/2014_YILI_MEGEM_FAALIYET_RAPORU.pdf (accessed 1 January 2016).

Mandelblatt, B., 2012. 'Geography of Food'. In *The Oxford Handbook of Food History*, ed. Jeffrey M. Pilcher, 154–71. Oxford: Oxford University Press.

MARA, 2014. Investment for Pre-Accession Assistance Rural Development (IPARD) Programme (2007–2013), IPARD Programme-ENG-2014.pdf (accessed 3 December 2015).

Margulies, R. and E. Yıldızoğlu, 1992. 'Tarımsal Değişim: 1923–1970'. In *Geçiş Sürecinde Türkiye*, eds I. C. Schick and A. Tonak, 285–309. İstanbul: Belge Yayınları.

Marois, T. and A. R. Güngen, 2016. 'Credibility and Class in the Evolution of Public Banks: The Case of Turkey'. *The Journal of Peasant Studies*, http://dx.doi.org/10.1080/03066150.2016.1176023.

Martínez-Torres, M. E. and P. Rosset, 2014. 'Diálogo de Saberes in La Vía Campesina'. *The Journal of Peasant Studies*, 41(6): 979–97.

Marx, K., 1954 [1887]. *Capital*, vol. 1. Moscow: Progress Publishers.

Marx, K., 1973 [1857]. *Grundrisse*. New York: Pelican.

Marx, K., 1982 [1885]. *The Eighteenth Brumaire of Louis Bonaparte*. Moscow: Progress Publishers.

Mathijs, E. and F. M. Swinnen, 1998. 'The Economics of Agricultural Decollectivization in East Central Europe and the Former Soviet Union'. *Economic Development and Cultural Change*, 47(1): 1–26.

McMichael, P., 1990. 'Incorporating Comparison within a World-Historical Perspective'. *American Sociological Review*, 55(3): 385–97.

McMichael, P., 2008. 'Peasants Make Their Own History, But Not Just as They Please'. *Journal of Agrarian Change*, 8(2–3): 205–28.

McMichael, P., 2009. 'Banking on Agriculture: A Review of the World Development Report 2008'. *Journal of Agrarian Change*, 9(2): 235–46.

McMichael, P., 2012a. 'The Land Grab and Corporate Food Regime Restructuring'. *The Journal of Peasant Studies*, 39(3–4): 681–701.

McMichael, P., 2012b. *Development and Social Change*. Thousand Oaks, CA: Sage.

McRae, A., 1993. 'To Know One's Own'. *Huntington Library Quarterly*, 56(4): 333–57.

Melozzi, L., 2009. 'Incentives for Agrobiodiversity within the European Union'. *Journal of Agriculture and Environment for International Development*, 103(1/2): 11–30.

Mendras, H. and M. Forse, 1983. *Le Changement Social*. Paris.

Merel, P. R. and R. J. Sexton, 2011. 'Models of Horizontal Product Differentiation in Food Markets'. In *The Oxford Handbook of The Economics of Food Consumption and Policy*, eds J. L. Lusk, J. Roosen and J. F. Shogren, 260–91. Oxford: Oxford University Press.

Meriç, C., (2005 [1974]). *Bu Ülke*. İstanbul: İletişim Yayınları.

Meynard, J. M., 2013. 'Innovating in Cropping and Farming Systems'. In *Renewing Innovation Systems in Agriculture and Food*, eds E. Coudel, H. Devautour, C. T. Soulard, G. Faure and B. Hubert, 89–108. Wageningen, the Netherlands: Wageningen Academic Publishers.

MFAL (Ministry of Food, Agriculture and Livestock), 2013. *Structural Changes and Reforms on Turkish Agriculture, 2003–2013*, KEY WORK Turkey changes_reforms Agriculture 2013.pdf. (accessed 7 October 2014).

MFAL, 2014a. 'Yetkilendirilmiş Tohumcu Kuruluşları', 26.09.2014/ 14:28', http://www.tarim.gov.tr/Konular/Bitkisel-Uretim/Tohumculuk/Yetkili-Tohumculuk-Kuruluslari (accessed 20 October 2014).

MFAL, 2014b. 'Koruma Altındaki Çeşitler Ve Lisans Alan Kişiler Listesi, 19.09.2014/14:24'. http://www.tarim.gov.tr/BUGEM/TTSM/Belgeler/Kay%C4%B1t%20Listeleri/ Koruma%20Alt%C4%B1na%20Al%C4%B1nan%20%C3%87e%C5%9Fitlerin%20 Listesi%20(Protected%20Plant%20Varieties%20for%20PBR)/Korunan_ CesitList19.09.2014.pdf (accessed 20 October 2014).

MFAL, 2014c. 'Introduction to Agriculture', Draft. Official Communication with Taner Ödevci, MFAL, June 2014.

Michelsen, J., 2001. 'Recent Development and Political Acceptance of Organic Farming in Europe'. *Sociologia Ruralis*, 41(1): 3–20.

Miele, M., 2001. *Creating Sustainability: The Social Construction of Markets for Organic Products.* Wageningen: University of Wageningen.

Milliyet Newspaper, 2013a. 'AK Parti'den Sürpriz 2B Teklifi', 22 February, http:// www.milliyet.com.tr/ak-parti-den-surpriz-2bteklifi/ekonomi/ekonomide- tay/22.02.2013/1672207/default.htm (accessed 15 January 2016).

Milliyet Newspaper, 2013b. 'Miras Toprakta Şirketleşme Adımı', 24 June, http://blog.mil- liyet.com.tr/--miras-toprakta---sirketlesme-adimi/Blog/?BlogNo=420025 (accessed 15 March 2014).

Millstone, E. and T. Lang, 2013. *The Atlas of Food.* Berkeley: University of California Press.

Ministry of Customs and Trade, 2013. *Tarım Sektörü.* Risk Yönetimi ve Kontrol Genel Müdürlüğü Ekonomik Analiz ve Değerlendirme Dairesi, Ankara.

Ministry of Customs and Trade, 2014. *Esnaf ve Sanatkâr İstatistikleri Bülteni*, http://esnaf. gtb.gov.tr/data/5368dd60487c8e09e818147d/Nisan_2014.pdf (accessed 20 May 2015).

Minten, B., L. Randrianarison and J. F. M. Swinnen, 2009. 'Global Retail Chains and Poor Farmers'. *World Development*, 17(11): 1728–41.

MIT, 2014. 'The Future of Global Water Stress: An Integrated Assessment', http://www. globalagriculture.org/report-topics/water.html (accessed 26 February 2016).

Mitchell, G., 2005. 'Libertarian Paternalism is an Oxymoron'. *Northwestern University Law Review*, 99(3): 1245–77.

Molden, D., T. Oweis, P. Steduto, P. Bindraban, M. A. Hanjra and J. Kijne, 2009. 'Improving Agricultural Water Productivity'. *Agricultural Water Management*, 97(2010): 528–35.

Moore. B., Jr., 1966. *Social Origins of Dictatorship and Democracy.* Boston: Beacon Press.

Morgan, K. and R. Sannino, 2010. 'Rethinking School Food'. In *State of the World, 2010: Transforming Cultures*, eds E. Assadourian, L. Starke and L. Mastny, 69–74. New York: WW. Norton & Company.

Morgan, K., T. Marsden and J. Murdock, 2006. *Worlds of Food.* Oxford: Oxford University Press.

Mueller, C. and B. Mueller, 2010. 'The Evolution of Agriculture and Land Reform in Brazil, 1960–2006'. In *Economic Development in Latin America*, eds H. S. Esfahani, G. Facchini and G. J. D. Hewings, 133–62. London and New York: Palgrave Macmillan.

Myers, J. S. and J. Sbicca, 2015. 'Bridging Good Food and Good Jobs'. *Geoforum*, 61(2015): 17–26.

Nagarajan, S., 2007. 'Geographical Indications and Agriculture-Related Intellectual Property Rights Issues'. *Current Science*, 92(2): 167–71.

Nagel, T., 1986. *The View from Nowhere.* New York: Oxford University Press.

Nazarea, V. D., 2005. *Heirloom Seeds and Their Keepers.* Tucson: The University of Arizona Press.

Nelson, V. and A. Tallontire, 2014. 'Battlefields of Ideas'. *Agriculture and Human Values*, 31(3): 481–97.

Newman, L., C. Ling and K. Peters, 2013. 'Between Field and Table'. *International Journal of Sustainable Society*, 5(1): 11–23.

Nguyen, T. N. and C. Locke, 2014. 'Rural–Urban Migration in Vietnam and China'. *The Journal of Peasant Studies*, 41(5): 855–76.

Nuijten, M., 2003. *Power, Community and the State: The Political Anthropology of Organization in Mexico*. London: Pluto Press.

OECD, 2010. *Agricultural Policies in OECD Countries*. Paris: OECD.

OECD, 2011. *Evaluation of Agricultural Policy Reforms in Turkey*. Paris: OECD.

Official Journal of the European Communities, 1998. 'Legislation: L 86', vol. 41, 20 March.

Oral, N., 2013. 'Bitmeyen Masal: Güneydoğu Anadolu Projesi'. In *Türkiye'de Tarımın Ekonomi-Politiği, 1923–2013*, ed. N. Oral, 429–44. Bursa: ZMO.

Oran, B., 2004. *Türkiye'de Azınlıklar*. İstanbul: TESEV Yayınları.

Ortiz, S., S. Aparicio and N. Tadeo, 2013. 'Dynamics of Harvest Subcontracting'. *Journal of Agrarian Change*, 13(4): 488–519.

Otero, G., G. Pechlaner, G. Liberman and E. Gürcan, 2015. 'The Neoliberal Diet and Inequality in the United States'. *Social Science & Medicine*, 142(2015): 47–55.

Özcan, G. B., 2008. 'Surviving through Transplantation and Cloning'. In *Handbook of Administrative Reform*, eds J.Killian and N. Eklund, 181–205. Boca Raton: CRC Press.

Özdemir, İ., 2003. 'Toward an Understanding of Environmental Ethics from a Qur'anic Perspective'. In *Islam and Ecology: A Bestowed Trust*, eds R. C. Foltz, F. M. Denny and A. Baharuddin, 3–37. Cambridge: Harvard University Press.

Özkaya, T., G. Günaydın, M. Bozoğlu, E. Olhan and C. Sayın, 2010. 'Tarım Politikaları ve Tarımsal Yapıdaki Değişimler'. In *Ziraat Mühendisliği VII. Teknik Kongresi Bildiriler Kitabı 1*, 3–22. Ankara: TMOBB.

Palmer, I., 1985. *The Impact of Male-Outmigration on Women in Farming*. West Hartford, CT: Kumarian Press.

Pamuk, O., 2006. *Istanbul*. New York: Vintage.

Pamuk, Ş., 1988. 'War, State Economic Policies, and Resistance by Agricultural Producers in Turkey, 1939–1945'. *New Perspectives on Turkey*, 2(1).

Parrott, N., N. Wilson and J. Murdoch, 2002. 'Spatializing Quality'. *European Urban and Regional Studies*, 9(3): 241–61.

Parry, B., 2004. 'Bodily Transactions'. In *Property in Question*, eds C. Verdery and C. Humphrey, 29–48. Oxford & New York: Berg.

Pechlaner, G. and G. Otero, 2008. 'The Third Food Regime: Neoliberal Globalism and Agricultural Biotechnology in North America'. *Sociologia Ruralis*, 48(4): 351–71.

Perakende, 2011. Nisan–Mayıs, Vol. 14.

PERDER excel file, 28 June 2011. 'Membership profiles'. Provided by Eda Güngör, PERDER Public Relations Ankara Coordinator.

PERDER, 2011. Ocak–Şubat, Vol. 20.

PERDER, 2011. Mart–Nisan, Vol. 21.

PERDER, 2011. Kasım–Aralık, Vol. 25.

PERDER, 2012. Mart–Nisan, Vol. 27.

PERDER, 2014. 'Stok Yönetimi', Vol. 40.

PERDER, 2015. 'Dönüşümü Başlat Geleceği Kazan', Vol. 42.

PERDER, 2016. 'Verimlilik', Vol. 46.

Petit, S., S. Gaba, A-L. Grison, H. Meiss, B. Simmoneau, N. Munier-Jolain and V. Bretagnolle, 2016. 'Landscape Scale Management Affects Weed Richness but not Weed Abundance in Winter Wheat Fields'. *Agriculture, Ecosystems and Environment*, 223(2016): 41–7.

Phillips, N., 2009. 'Migration as Development Strategy?' *Review of International Political Economy*, 16(2): 231–59.

Piketty, T., 2014. *Capital in the Twenty-first Century*. Cambridge and London: The Belknap Press of Harvard University Press.

Pinder, J., 1989. 'The Single Market'. In *The European Community and the Challenge of the Future*, ed. J. Lodge, 94–110. New York: St. Martin's Press.

Pinson, G. and C. M. Journel, 2016. 'The Neoliberal City'. *Territory, Politics, Governance*, 4(2): 137–53.

Piotrowski, M., D. Ghimire and R. Rindfuss, 2013. 'Farming Systems and Rural Out-Migration in Nang Rong, Thailand, and Chitman Valley, Nepal'. *Rural Sociology*, 78(1): 75–108.

Polan, M., 2002. *The Botany of Desire*. New York: Random House.

Polanyi, K., 1944. *The Great Transformation*. Boston: Beacon Press.

Prescott, J., 2012. *Taste Matters*. London: Reaktion Books.

Pritchard, B., 2009. 'The Long Hangover from the Second Food Regime'. *Agriculture and Human Values*, 26: 297–307, doi:10.1007/s10460-009-9216-7.

Pritchard, B., C. P. Gracy and M. Godwin, 2010. 'The Impacts of Supermarket Procurement on Farming Communities in India'. *Development Policy Review*, 28(4): 435–56.

Quataert, D., 1994. 'The Age of Reforms'. In *An Economic and Social History of the Ottoman Empire: 1600–1914*, vol. 2, eds H. İnalcık and D. Quataert, 759–943. Cambridge: Cambridge University Press.

Radel, C., B. Schmook, J. Mcevoy, C. Mendez and P. Petrzelka, 2012. 'Labour Migration and Gendered Agricultural Relations: The Feminization of Agriculture in the Ejidal Sector of Calakmul, Mexico'. *Journal of Agrarian Change*, 12(1): 98–119.

Raghavan, C., 1990. *Recolonization*. London and Penang: Zed Books Ltd.

Rai, M. and S. Mauria, 2004. 'Intellectual Property Rights Related Issues in Plant Breeding'. In *Plant Breeding*, eds H. K. Jain and M. C. Kharkwal, 691–718. New Delhi: Narosa Publishing House.

Rastoin, J-L., 2009. 'Is the World Food System Compatible with Sustainable Development?' In *Traditional Food Production and Rural Sustainable Development*, eds T. de Noronha Vaz, P. Nijkamp and J -L. Rastoin, 13–26. Farnham, England: Ashgate.

Raynolds, L., 2001. 'New Plantations, New Workers: Gender and Production Politics in the Dominican Republic'. *Gender and Society*, 15(1): 7–28.

Reardon, T., P. Timmer and J. Berdegue, 2004. 'The Rapid Rise of Supermarkets in Developing Countries'. *Journal of Agricultural Development Economics*, 1(2): 15–30.

Reardon, T. and C. P. Timmer, 2007. 'Transformation of Markets for Agricultural Outputs in Developing Countries Since 1950'. In *Handbook of Agricultural Economics*, vol. 3, eds. R. E. Evenson and P. Pingali, 2808–55. Amsterdam: Elsevier Press.

Reardon, T., C. B. Barratt, J. A. Berdegue and J. F. M. Swinnen, 2009. 'Agrifood Industry Transformation and Small Farmers in Developing Countries'. *World Development*, 37(11): 1717–27.

Rehber, E., 2000. 'Vertical Coordination in the Agri-Food Industry and Contract Farming'. Food Marketing Policy Center, Research Report No. 52, University of Connecticut.

Rekabet Kurumu, 2012. 'Türkiye Hızlı Tüketim Malları (HTM) Perakendeciliği Sektör İncelemesi Nihai Raporu', sektorrapor7.pdf (accessed 21 May 2014).

Republic of Turkey Ministry of Investment Support and Promotion Agency [RTMISPA], 2014. Food & Agriculture in Turkey, http://www.invest.gov.tr/en-US/infocenter/publications/Documents/FOOD.AND.AGRICULTURE.INDUSTRY.pdf (accessed 27 August 2015).

Retail Türkiye, 2009. 'Sebze-Meyve Üretiminin Yüzde 80'i Kayıt Dışı Tüketiliyor', http://www.retailturkiye.com/kapak-konusu/sebze-meyve-uretiminin-yuzde-80i-kayit-disi-tuketiliyor (accessed 28 July 2016).

Retail Türkiye, 2011. Mayıs, No. 27.

Retail Türkiye, 2012. 'Yeni Hal Yasası, Sektörü Yeniden Yapılandırıyor', February, No. 35.

Retail Türkiye, 2014. 'Sebze ve Meyvede Künye Dönemi', 3 July.

Reuters, 2016. 'Bayer Clinches Monsanto with Improved $66 Billion Bid', 15 September, http://www.reuters.com/article/us-monsanto-m-a-bayer-deal-idUSKCN11K128 (accessed 20 October 2016).

Reynolds, L. and D. Nierenberg, 2013. 'Innovations in Sustainable Agriculture'. *World Watch Report* 188.

Ribot, J. C. and N. L. Peluso, 2003. 'A Theory of Access'. *Rural Sociology*, 68(2): 153–81.

Richards, C., H. Bjorkhaug, G. Lawrence and E. Hickman, 2013. 'Retailer-Driven Agricultural Restructuring – Australia, the UK and Norway in Comparison'. *Agriculture and Human Values*, 30(2): 235–45.

Rodrik, D., 2011. *The Globalization Paradox*. New York & London: W. W. Norton & Company.

Roland, P. C. and R. W. Adamchak, 2008. *Tomorrow's Table*. Oxford: Oxford University Press.

Rosin, C., H. Campbell and L. Hunt, 2008. 'Audit Me This! Kiwifruit Producer Uptake of the EurepGap Audit System in New Zealand'. In *Agri-Food Commodity Chains and Globalising Networks*, eds C. Stringer and R. Le Heron, 61–73. Aldershot: Ashgate.

Rosset, M. P., 2006. *Food Is Different*. London: Zed Books.

Rostow, W. W., 1960. *The Stages of Economic Growth*. Cambridge: Cambridge University Press.

Ruggie, G.J., 1982. 'International Regimes, Transactions, and Change'. *International Organization*, 36(2): 379–415.

Rumi, J.a-D., 2008 [n.d.]. *Mesnevi*, translated by A. Karaismailoğlu. Ankara: Akçağ.

Ruttan, V. W., 1994. 'Constraints on the Design of Sustainable Systems of Agricultural Production'. *Ecological Economics*, 10(3): 209–19.

Sahlins, M., 1976. *Culture and Practical Reason*. Chicago: University of Chicago Press.

Said, E., 1978. *Orientalism*. New York: Vintage.

Schumpeter, A. J., 1934. *The Theory of Economic Development*. Cambridge: Harvard University Press.

Schumpeter, A. J., 2008 [1942]. *Capitalism, Socialism and Democracy*. New York: Harper Perennial Modern Thought.

Scoones, I., 2015. *Sustainable Livelihoods and Rural Development*. Black Point, NS: Fernwood.

Scott, J. C., 1977. *The Moral Economy of the Peasant*. New Haven: Yale University Press.

Scott, D., 1999. *Refashioning Futures*. Princeton, NJ: Princeton University Press.

Seçkin, E., 2015. 'Perakende Sektöründeki Yapısal Dönüşümün Bursa'daki Üretim Piyasası ile Tüketim Piyasasına Yansıması'. *MEGARON*, 10(1): 70–9.

Selwyn, B., 2010. 'Gender Wage Work and Development in North East Brazil'. *Bulletin of Latin American Research*, 29(1): 51–70.

Sen, A., 2009. *The Idea of Justice*. Cambridge: The Belknap Press of Harvard University Press.

Sevilmiş, G., 2014. 'Perakende Sektörünün Yükselişi Devam Ediyor'. AR&GE Bülten, Ocak, http://www.izto.org.tr/portals/0/argebulten/perakendesekt%C3%96r%C3%9C_g%C3%96zdesev%C4%B0lm%C4%B0%C5%9E.pdf (accessed 4 June 2015).

Shand, H., 2012. 'The Big Six: A Profile of Corporate Power in Seeds, Agrochemicals & Biotech'. *Heritage Farm Companion*, Summer (2012): 10–15, http://www.seedsavers.org/site/pdf/HeritageFarmCompanion_BigSix.pdf (accessed 11 February 2016).

Shanin, T. (ed.), 1971. *Peasants and Peasant Societies*. Harmondsworth, Middlesex: Penguin Books.

Sikor, T., 2012. 'Tree Plantations, Politics of Possession and the Absence of Land Grabs in Vietnam'. *The Journal of Peasant Studies*, 39(3–4): 1077–101.

Silvasti, T., 2003. 'The Cultural Model of "The Good Farmer" and the Environmental Question in Finland'. *Agriculture and Human Values*, 20: 143–50.

Slow Food Foundation for Biodiversity, 2013a. 'In Turkey Foça Earth Market Turns One', http://www.slowfoodfoundation.com/pagine/eng/news/dettaglio_news.lasso?-idn=173#.VDW-nBbhuHM/ (accessed 8 October 2014).

Slow Food Foundation for Biodiversity, 2013b. *Social Report 2013*, http://www.slowfood-foundation.org. ING_2013_bilancio_sociale.pdf (accessed 8 October 2014).

Smith, A., 1976 [1759]. *The Theory of Moral Sentiment*. New York: Oxford University Press.

Smith, A., 1991 [1776]. *The Wealth of Nations*. New York: Everyman's Library.

Smith, D. E., 1999. 'From Women's Standpoint to a Sociology for People'. In *Sociology for the Twenty-First Century*, ed. J. L. Abu-Lughod, 65–82. Chicago: The University of Chicago Press.

Solorzano, N., 2003. 'Watershed Conservation Farming "A Friendly Solution to Soils Degradation", FAO, Ministry of Agriculture and Husbandry; Abdo. 8198–1000, San Jose, Costa Rica'. In L. *Conservation Agriculture*, eds L. Garcia-Torres, J. Benites, A. Martínez-Vilela and A. Holgado-Cabrera, pp. 351–54. Dordrecht/Boston/London: Kluwer Academic Publishers.

Somers, R. M., 1992. 'Narrativity, Narrative Identity, and Social Action'. *Social Science History*, 16(4): 591–630.

Somers, M., 1999. 'The Privatization of Citizenship'. In *Beyond the Cultural Turn*, eds V. E. Bonnell and L. Hunt, 121–61. Berkeley: University of California Press.

Sonnino, R., 2007. 'The Power of Place: Embeddedness and Local Food Systems in Italy and the UK'. *Anthropology of Food*, S2, March.

Sönmez, A., 2008. 'The Effects of Violence and Internal Displacement on Rural-Agrarian Change in Turkey'. *Rural Sociology*, 73(3): 370–413.

Sönmez, M., 1998. 'The Story of Eastern and Southeastern Turkey'. *Private View*, 2(6): 28–35.

SPO, 2006. National Rural Development Strategy, http://ekutup.dpt.gov.tr/bolgesel/strateji/UKKS-i.pdf (accessed 13 May 2013).

SPO, 2014. *The Tenth Development Plan, 2014-2018*, http://www.mod.gov.tr/Lists/RecentPublications/Attachments/75/The%20Tenth%20Development%20Plan%20%282014-2018%29.pdf (accessed 26 November 2015).

Standing, G., 1999. 'Global Feminisation through Flexible Labour'. *World Development*, 27(3): 583–602.

Stephan, H. R., 2012. 'Revisiting the Atlantic Divergence over GMOs'. *Global Environmental Politics*, 12(4): 104–24.

Storper, M., 2016. 'Neo-liberal City as Idea and Reality'. *Territory, Politics, Governance*, 4(2): 241–63.

Sugden, F. and S. Punch, 2014. 'Capitalist Expansion and the Decline of Common Property Ecosystems in China, Vietnam and India'. *Development and Change*, 45(4): 656–84.

Svendsen, M., 2001. 'Irrigation Management Transfer in Turkey'. FAO-INPIM International E-mail Conference on Irrigation Management Transfer, ftp://ftp.fao.org/agl/aglw/imt/CSTurkey.pdf (accessed 9 December 2015).

Sztompka, P., 1999. *Trust*. Cambridge: Cambridge University Press.

TAMPF (Türkiye Alışveriş Merkezleri ve Perakendeciler Federasyonu) (n.d.). *Dönüşürken Büyüyen Türkiye Perakende Sektörü*, http://www.tampf.org.tr/wp-content/uploads/donu-surken-buyuyen-turkiye-perakende-sektoru-raporu.pdf (accessed 28 July 2016).

Tanpınar, A. H., 2008 [1949]. *A Mind at Peace*. Brooklyn: Archipelago Books.

Tanpınar, A. H., 2013 [1962]. *The Time Regulation Institute*. New York: Penguin Books.

Tarım Reformu Genel Müdürlüğü, 2013. 'Arazi Toplulaştırma Çalışmaları', http://www.tarim.gov.tr/TRGM/Documents/Toplulaştırma/AraziToplulastirma.docx (accessed 11 February 2014).

Tatlı, U., 2013. 'Yereller, DiaSA'nın ÜLKER oluşunu Yorumladı', 21 Haziran, http://www.perakende.org/guncel/yereller-diasanin-ulker-olusunu-yorumladi-1342792877h.html (accessed 4 June 2015).

T.C. MAVA (T.C. Ministry of Agriculture and Village Affairs), 2000. 'Tarım Satış Kooperatif ve Birlikleri Hakkında Kanun', http://www.tarim.gov.tr/Files/Mevzuat/kanun_son/TKB_Kanunlar/TARIMSATISKOOPERATIFVEBIRLIKLERI.pdf (accessed 23 June 2011).

T.C. MAVA, 2004. 'Tarımsal Üretici Birlikleri Kanunu', http://www.tarim.gov.tr/Files/Mevzuat/kanun_son/TKB_Kanunlar/TARIMSALURETICIBIRLIKLERI KANUNU.pdf. (accessed 23 June 2011).

Tekeli, I., 1977. *Kırda ve Kentte Dönüşüm Süreci*. Ankara: Mimarlar Odası Yayınları No. 18.

Tekeli, İ., 1990.'Osmanlı İmparatorluğu'ndan Günümüze Nüfusun Zorunlu Yer Değiştirmesi ve İskan Sorunu'. *Toplum ve Bilim*, 50.

Tennent, R., and S. Lockie, 2011. 'Production Relations under GLOBALG.A.P'. *Sociologia Ruralis*, 52(1): 31–47.

Terres, J-M., L. N. Scacchiafichi, A. Wania et al., 2015. 'Farmland Abandonment in Europe'. *Land Use Policy*, 49(2015): 20–34.

The Economist, 2012. 'Goodbye Doha, Hello Bali', 8 September, http://www.economist.com/node/21562196 (accessed 28 July 2013).

Theron, J., S. Godfrey, P. Lewis and M. Pienaar, 2005. *Labour Broking and Temporary Employment Services*. Cape Town: University of Cape Town.

Thiers, P., 2006. 'China and Global Organic Food Standards'. In *Agricultural Standards*, eds J. Binden and L. Bush, 193–218. Dordrecht: Springer.

Thomas, E. V., 2008. 'Innovation in Policy'. In *Creating Food Futures*, eds C. R. Farnworth, J. Jiggins and E. V. Thomas, 41–54. Aldershot: Gower.

Thompson, E. P., 1963. *The Making of the English Working Class*. New York: Random House.

Thompson, J., T. Hodgkin, K. Atta-Krah, D. Jarvis, C. Hoogendoorn and S. Padulosi, 2007. 'Biodiversity in Agroecosystems'. In *Farming with Nature*, eds S. J. Scherr and J. A. McNeely, 46–60. Washington DC.: Island Press.

TMMOB, 2004. 'Doğrudan Gelir Desteği', http://www.zmo.org.tr/genel/bizden_detay.php?kod=147&tipi=5 (accessed 1 August 2010).

TMMOB, 2011. *Mesleğimiz, Meslek Alanlarımız, Haklarımız Üzerine*. Ankara: Türk Mühendis ve Mimar Odaları Birliği.

TMO, 2014. 'Turkey Wheat Area-Production-Yield', http://www.tmo.gov.tr/Upload/Document/istatistikler/2013_ing_tables/1_wheat.pdf (accessed 3 March 2014).

Tohumculuk Kanunu (2006). http://www.tarim.gov.tr/Files/Mevzuat/kanun_son/TKB_Kanunlar/TohumculukKanunu.pdf (accessed 22 January 2012).

Tomich, P. T., S. Brodt, H. Ferris, R. Galt et al., 2011. 'Agroecology'. *Annual Review of Environment and Resources*, 36: 193–222.

Triomphe, B. and R. Rajalahti, 2013. 'From Concept to Emerging Practice'. In *Renewing Innovation Systems in Agriculture and Food*, eds E. Coudel, H. Devautour, C. T. Soulard, G. Faure and B. Hubert, 57–76. Wegeningen: Wegeningen Academic Publishers.

Tunçel, H., 2009. 'Geleneksel Ticaret Mekanı Olarak Türkiye'de Haftalık Pazarlar'. *e-Journal of New World Sciences Academy*, 4(2): 35–52.

TÜİK May 2007. Haber Bülteni, Sayı 76, 15 Mayıs.

TÜİK, 2008a. 'Press Release: Agricultural Holdings Crop Production Survey, 2006', 18 Aralık, No. 197, http://www.turkstat.gov.tr (accessed 10 November 2010).

TÜİK, 2008b. '2006 Agricultural Holding Structure Survey 17 December', http://www.turkstat.gov.tr/PreHaberBultenleri.do?id=3977 (accessed 8 December 2013).

TÜİK, 2009. 'Summary of Agricultural Statistics: 1989–2008'. Ankara: Türkiye İstatistik Kurumu.

TÜİK, 2011. 'Press Release: Crop Products Balance Sheets; "Cereals and Other Crop Products Balance Sheets", 2009/10', 21 April, No. 83, http://www.turkstat.gov.tr. (accessed 30 May 2011).

TÜİK, March 2014. *İstatistiklerle Kadın, 2013*, No. 16056, 5 Mart.

TÜİK, February 2015. *İşgücü İstatistikleri, Kasım 2014*, No. 18634, 16 Şubat.

TÜİK, March 2015. *Tarımsal İşletmelerde Ücret Yapısı*, 2014, No.18693, 10 Mart.

TÜİK, May 2015. 'Haber Bülteni: Bitkisel Üretim 1. Tahmini, 2015: Tahıllar ve Diğer Bitkisel Ürünler', 26 Mayıs, Sayı: 18704, http://www.tuik.gov.tr/PreHaberBultenleri.do?id=18704 (accessed 30 Mayıs 2015).

TÜİK, October 2015. 'Crop Production 2nd Estimation, 2015', Press Release, 23 October 2015, http://www.turkstat.gov.tr/PreHaberBultenleri.do?id=28705 (accessed 18 November 2015).

TÜİK, 2016. 'Press Release: Crop Products Balance Sheets: "Cereals and Other Crop Products", 2014-2015', 5 April, No. 21667, htpp://www.turkstat.gov.tr. (accessed 31 March 2017).

TÜİK, n.d. *Hanehalkı İşgücü Araştırması: Bölgesel Sonuçlar, 2004-2013*, İşgücü ve Yaşam Koşulları Daire Başkanlığı.

TZOB, 2005. *Buğday Raporu*, May.

Ulukan, U., 2009. *Türkiye Tarımında Yapısal Dönüşüm ve Sözleşmeli Çiftçilik*. İstanbul: SAV Sosyal Araştırmalar Vakfı.

Vanclay, F. and T. Silvasti, 2009. 'Understanding the Sociocultural Processes that Contribute to Diversity and Conformity among Farmers in Australia, Finland and the Netherlands'. In *Research in Rural Sociology and Development*, vol. 14, eds K. Anderson, E. Eklund, M. Lehtola and P. Salmi, 51–67. Amsterdam: JAI Press.

Vandemoortele, T. and K. Deconinck, 2014. 'When Are Private Standards More Stringent than Public Standards?' *American Journal of Agricultural Economics*, 96(1): 154–71.

van der Ploeg, J. D., 2012. 'Poverty Alleviation and Smallholder Agriculture: The Rural Poverty Report 2011'. *Development and Change*, 43(1): 439–48.

van der Ploeg, J. D., 2013. *Peasants and the Art of Farming*. Halifax and Winnipeg: Fernwood.

van der Ploeg, J. D., 2014. 'Peasant-Driven Agricultural Growth and Food Sovereignty'. *The Journal of Peasant Studies*, 41(6): 999–1030.

Verdery, K., 2003. *The Vanishing Hectare*. Ithaca: Cornell University Press.

Vergara-Camus, L., 2012. 'The Legacy of Social Conflicts over Property Rights in Rural Brazil and Mexico'. *The Journal of Peasant Studies*, 39(5): 1133–58.

Vestergaard, J., 2009. *Discipline in the Global Economy?* London: Routledge.

Vorley, B., 2001. 'The Chains of Agriculture'. IIED and RING Opinion Paper, World Summit on Sustainable Development, htpp://www.ring-alliance.org/ring_pdf/bp_foodag_ftxt.pdf (accessed 3 March 2016).

Wallerstein, I., 1995. *After Liberalism*. New York: The New Press.

Wallerstein, I., 2006. *European Universalism*. New York and London: The New Press.

Wang, H. H., Y. Wang and M. S. Delgado, 2014. 'The Transition to Modern Agriculture: Contract Farming in Developing Economies'. *American Journal of Agricultural Economics*, 96(5): 1257–71.

Wang, H., P. Moustier and N. T. T. Loc, 2014. 'Economic Impact of Direct Marketing and Contracts: The Case of Safe Vegetable Chains in Northern Vietnam'. *Food Policy*, 47(2014): 13–23.

Warner, K. D., 2007. *Agroecology in Action*. London: The MIT Press.

Wattnem, T., 2016. 'Seed Laws, Certification and Standardization: Outlawing Informal Seed Systems in the Global South'. *The Journal of Peasant Studies*, doi: 10.1080/03066150. 2015.1130702.

Watts, M., 1990. 'Peasants under Contract'. In *The Food Question*, eds H. Bernstein, B. Crow, M. Mackintosh and C. Martin, 149–62. New York: Monthly Review Press.

Weatherspoon, D. and T. Reardon, 2003. 'The Rise of Supermarkets in Africa'. *Development Policy Review*, 21(3): 335–55.

Weber, M., 1984 [1930]. *The Protestant Ethic and the Spirit of Capitalism*. London: George Allen & Unwin.

Weber, M., 1947. *The Theory of Social and Economic Organization*. New York: The Free Press.

Weber, M., 1946 [1915]. 'Religious Rejections of the World and Their Directions'. In *From Max Weber*, eds H. H. Gerth and C. Wright Mills, 323–59. New York: Oxford University Press.

Werlhof, C. V., 1988. 'The Proletarian Is Dead: Long Live the Housewife!' In *Women the Last Colony*, eds M. Mies, V. Bennholdt-Thomsen and C. Von Werlhof, 168–79. London: Zed Books.

Weiss, C. R., 2011. 'Consumer Demand for Food Variety'. In *The Oxford Handbook of The Economics of Food Consumption and Policy*, eds J. L. Lusk, J. Roosen and J. F. Shogren, 667–94. New York: Oxford University Press.

White, B., S. M. Borras Jr., R. Hall, I. Scoones and W. Wolford, 2012. 'The New Enclosures'. *The Journal of Peasant Studies*, 39(3–4): 619–47.

Wield, D., J. Chataway and M. Bolo, 2010. 'Issues in the Political Economy of Agricultural Biotechnology. *Journal of Agrarian Change*, 10(3): 342–66.

Wilkinson, J. and S. Herrera, 2010. 'Biofuels in Brazil'. *The Journal of Peasant Studies*, 37(4): 749–68.

Wily, L. A., 2012. 'Looking Back to See Forward'. *The Journal of Peasant Studies*, 39(3/4): 751–75.

Winson, A., 2013. *The Industrial Diet*. Vancouver: UBC Press.

Wittman, H., M. Beckie and C. Hergesheimer, 2012. 'Linking Local Food Systems and the Social Economy? Future Roles for Farmers' Markets in Alberta and British Columbia'. *Rural Sociology*, 77(1): 36–61.

Wolf, E., 1969. *Peasants Wars of the Twentieth Century*. New York: Harper & Row.

Wolford, W., 2005. 'Agrarian Moral Economies and Neoliberalism in Brazil'. *Environment and Planning A*, 37: 241–61.

Wolford, W., S. M. Borras Jr., R. Hall, I. Scoones and B. White, 2013. 'Governing Global Land Deals'. *Development and Change*, 44(2): 189–210.

World Bank, 2001. *Agricultural Reform Implementation Project (ARIP)*, http://siteresources. worldbank.org/TURKEYEXTN/Resources/361711-12063 (accessed 22 August 2010).

World Bank, 2004. *Turkey: A Review of the Impact of the Reform of Agricultural Sector Subsidization.* Washington, DC: The World Bank.

World Bank, 2007. *World Development Report 2008.* Washington, DC: The World Bank.

Wright, E. O., 2010. *Envisioning Real Utopias.* New York: Verso.

WTO, 1995. Legal Text: A Summary of the Final Act of the Uruguay Round, http:// www.wto.org/english/docs_e/legal_e/ursum_e.htm#aAgreement (accessed 7 September 2010).

Yazar, A., M. Kuzucu, I. Çelik, S. M. Sezen and S.-E. Jacobsen, 2014. 'Water Harvesting for Improved Water Productivity in Dry Environments of the Mediterranean Region Case Study: Pistachio in Turkey'. *Journal of Agronomy and Crop Science*, 200: 361–70.

Yıldız, A., 2014. 'Hiç ŞOK'lanmayacak!' *Milliyet Newspaper*, 18 December.

Zucker, L. G., 1986. 'Production of Trust: Institutional Sources of Economic Structure, 1840–1920'. *Research in Organizational Behavior*, 8(1986): 53–111.

Index

A-101 137, 230, **232**, 235–7
accommodation 35, 247; *see also* ambiguity
accumulation 2–3, 6–7, 12, 14, 37,
    96, 104, 176, 183, 209, 251, 253;
    accumulation by dispossession 11, 89;
    capital accumulation 20, 34, 39, 56, 209;
    primitive accumulation 11–13, 176
agency 196, 198, 248–9, 253, 259; *see also*
    agro-labour trader; three goals; the state;
    Perry Anderson
agrarian question 10–11, 38, 97
agrarian transformation 37, 86
Agreement on Agriculture (AOA) 9, 31,
    41, 42, 58
agribusiness 8–9, 12, 23–4, 26, 55, 72, 99,
    115, 120, 132, 216, 218, 227, 251–3,
    255, 258
agricultural biotechnology patents 71
agricultural employment 169–70, 198
agricultural production 9, 13, 16, 22–3, 36,
    38, 42–3, 46–7, 55, 61, 65, 89, 110, 118,
    155, 170, 241; industrial methods 4, 33,
    38, 97, 127, 132, 144, 224, 255; input-
    intensive 1, 32–3, 38, 42, 49, 58, 61, 91,
    93–5, 97–8, 109, 124; productivist 43,
    53, 139, 145
Agriculture Law (No. 5488) 39, 61, 84, 86
agriculture: market-oriented agriculture
    3, 6, 24, 170; new agriculture 1, 6, 8,
    31, 34, 122, 158; state-led agriculture
    212, 242; subsistence agriculture 11,
    97; *see also* conservation agriculture;
    conventionalization
agrifood 2–6, 12, 18–19, 21–2, 24–6, 31–2,
    34, 38–41, 59, 68, 175, 212, 223, 241,
    246–7, 249–50, 252, 254
agro-ecology 131, 136, 259; agro-
    ecological conditions 102, 120, 152,
    249–50, 255, 258

agro-environmental measures 132
agro-industry 24, 61, 98, 247, 254
agro-labour traders 34, 172–3, 175–6, 178,
    183; *see also* çavuş
agro-traders 27–8, 31, 33–4, 94, 145, 147,
    153, 172, 176–7, 181, 187, 197, 212–13,
    215, 217–18, 220, 225, 228–9, 234,
    241–2
AKP 4, 18, 31, 39, 49, 52, 55–6, 58–9, 61,
    153, 238, 252
Akyurt **30,** 221, 231, 237–8, 240
alienation 32, 69, 91, 258; decontextual 69;
    disentanglement 31, 70; fragmentation
    55–6, 70, 235, 252, 258; standardization
    of biological networks 70
Altunbilekler 63, 214–15, 231, 237, 238,
    239, 240, 241
ambiguity 166, 248; ambiguous 251;
    ambiguously 248; *see also* accommodation
ambivalence 34–5, 94, 96, 97, *98*, 100,
    129, 139, 246–9, 256; ambivalent 33,
    103, 132, 139, 166–7, 212; ambivalent
    tensions 132
Anatolia 87; Central Anatolia 26, 44, 45,
    91, 99, 111, 114, 117, 147, 167, 170,
    174; Eastern Anatolia 173, 191, 192;
    Southeastern Anatolia 173, 191
Anatolian 34, 54, 98, 118, 220, 237;
    Anatolian businesspeople 237; Anatolian
    capitalists 230, 237
Anderson, Perry 248–9
Ankara 26–30, 32–4, 44–7, 57–60, 75, 87,
    93, 101, 111, 114, 127, 133, 135, 141–3,
    145, 147, 153, 155–61, 164, 167, 171,
    213–14, 218, 220–1, 223, 226, 229, 231,
    238–40, 245–6, 261–2, 265, 267–9, 271,
    274–5, 277, 279–80
ARIP 42–4, 58, 227
artisanal 138, 141–2, 223, 247

assembly line 200
Atasoy, Yıldız 3, 5–7, 11, 17, 19–21, 23, 25, 39–40, 42–3, 48, 50–1, 53–8, 90, 96, 98–9, 128, 148, 209, 214–15, 227–8, 238–9, 241, 252–3, 256, 262

bakkal 229–31, 236, 241, 244n18
Başgimpa 237, **238**, 239, **240**
Bayer 71–2, 87, 109
Bernstein, Henry 4, 10–11, 16, 38, 54, 59, 61, 97
Beypazarı 26, **27**, 28–33, 73–5, 77, 79–80, 82, 93, 100–1, 103, 108–16, 124, 133–4, 141, 146, 151, 155–6, 169, 177, 179, 180–7, 191, 196, 198–9, 201–3, 205, 208, 219, 221, 237
BİM 135, 137, 230, **232,** 235–7
bio-information 31–2, 69, 71, 73, 78, 91
bio-prospectors 69, 71, 117
biodiversity 6, 12, 68–71, 86–7, 90–1, 95–6, *98*, 132, 136, 139, 144, 154, 247; biodiversity markets 71
biological: characteristics 104; control 136; diversity 61, 92n7; indicators 132; information 70–1; materials 70; networks 70; parts 70; processes 69, 246, 248–9; relationships 69, 258; resource economy 86; resources 68–9; system 69–70
biology: microbiological 69; molecular 69, 70; reductionist understanding 69; synthetic 70; systems 70
biotech seeds 28, 32, 62, 68, 101–3, 141–42, 199; dependency on external chemical inputs 104; deplete the fertility of available soil 104; disease prone 104; germination rates 78, 102, 109; resistance 72, 77–8, 82, 102, 121; water resources 104; *see also* seeds
biotechnology 8, 20, 34, 59, 61, 69, 71–3, 100, 118, 120, 136, 251, 254; agricultural biotechnology 19, 32, 33, 39, 68, 71, 73, 84, 136; agro-biotechnology 88; biotechnology companies 8, 20–1, 28, 32, 34, 62, 71–3, 86, 89, 93–5, 100–1, 116, 249, 250–1; biotechnology intensification 114; biotechnology research 70–1, 87, 88, 249; intellectual property rights 32
Brazil 4, 16–7, 20, 22–4, 36, 55, 63, 84, 176, 225
breeding 69, 76–7, 104–6; companies 73, 81, 92n13; crop 89; plant 73, 76–7, 79–81, 87, 116, 118–19, 157; seed 115
Bretton-Woods 8

Bryceson, Deborah F. 12, 97
Büyükoba, Savcılı 11, **27,** 29–31, 145, 147, 125–3, 162, 164

capacity building: farmers and retailers 213; Kurdish migrant workers 197–8, 209
capital 6–8, 14, 16, 20, 25, 37–9, 52, 56, 59, 65, 91n6, 98, 106, 128, 131, 239, 235, 237–8, 242, 250–1, 254; finance capital 19, 38; human capital 14
capitalism 11, 13, 15–17, 25, 53, 120, 176, 206, 208, 256; cultural contradictions of capitalism 13, 263; modernity 12–13, 16–18, 252
capitalists 15, 237; Anatolian capitalists 230, 237; Islamic capitalists 34, 213, 237; İstanbul capitalists 237; Muslim capitalists 34
capitalized agriculture 6, 32–3, 38, 93, 154, 171–2, 174
CarrefourSA 230–1, **232**, 233, 235
certification 20, 66, 86, 89, 137, 157, 281; GAP certification 28, 63–4, 133–9, 145, 183, 219, 234; organic certification 132, 211; third-party certification 63, 133, 139
chemicals 85, 100, 102, 104, 108–9, 114, 136, 138, 140–1, 143–5, 150, 163–6, 199–201, 206; chemical residues 95, 113, 122, 137
citizenship 7, 177, 222, 251, 278
Cittaslow 90
class relations 21, 34, 242, 251
climate 56, 75, 77, 102–5, 109, 126, 139, 151, 155–6, 163, 200, 223–4, 249; climatically suitable crops 151
co-existence of: diverging perspectives/ farming imaginaries 247–8, 254; heterogeneous 24; marketing strategies 167, 211–2, 246–8, 254; multiple pathways 32–3, 211; multiplicities 254; standards 131, 167, 211; traditional methods 1, 246–8; trust 33, 212
cognitive remaking 251; cognitive orientations 34, 253
cohabitation of: complexities 34; informally functioning 255; small-scale farming/ farming styles 38, 59
commercialization 4–6, 8–9, 11, 13–14, 18, 23, 26, 32, 36–7, 39, 49, 52, 70, 98, 114, 122–3, 127, 155, 157, 162, 167, 174, 177, 211–12, 229, 242, 254–5; multiple pathways 3, 4, 32
commissioners 146, 167, 213–14, 217, 225, 228, 229; *see also* wholesale commissioners

commodification 1, 3–4, 11–12, 18–19, 31, 34, 36–7, 39, 58–9, 69–71, 87, 89, 91, 98, 218, 242, 246–54, 256, 258, 262, 265
commodities 3, 16, 19, 32, 40, 69, 91
commodity chains 19, 63–4, 277
commons 10, 16, 90
competition 2, 7, 13–16, 34, 41–2, 69, 72, 125, 147, 152, 158, 212, 220–1, 230–1, 233–5, 237–8, 240–2
competitive 2–4, 7, 13–14, 17, 24, 32, 34, 38, 41–2, 49, 52, 61, 78, 80, 93, 98–9, 117, 125, 127, 174, 212, 226, 233–5, 239–42, 250, 252, 254; competitiveness 2, 7, 17, 49, 61–2, 64, 95–6
compliance with: industrial agriculture / industrial model 101, 104; new food varieties 80; norms 99, 227; standards 9, 61–4, 66, 68, 83, 86, 132, 234, 242
conformity to/with: agro-industry 98; biotechnology 32; economization 5; efficiency and performance 94; industrial model 33, 98, 247; innovation 96, 100; market-oriented model 3; standards 122, 144; techno-scientific knowledge 97, 99
connection: agro-traders 153; bureaucratic 155; ecology 251; food quality 139; growth projects 99; horizontal 176–7, 187–8, 209; land 55, 258; local 142, 149, 175; marketing 115, 153, 167; natural heritage 139; regional 33, 172, 191, 209; relatives 196; sense-based 12, 140; supermarket 145; sustenance 11; trust 225, 255
conservation agriculture 96, *98*, 132, 154, 268, 278
consumers: choices 62; direct marketing 124; distant 20, 38, 41, 94; food varieties 80, 81, 83, 90; GAP certification 137; industrial agriculture 96; information/ traceability 216–17, 219; participatory certification 131, 133, 153, 161–2, 167, 169, 212, 255; *pazars*/street vendors 152, 153, 160, 221–5; quality standards/food quality/safety 63, 66, 79–80, 119, 122, 139, 167, 221, 234, 254; supermarkets 79, 231, 233–5; taste 82, 121, 163–4, 223, 224, 241; trust 33, 133, 139, 161, 169, 225
continuity with: industrial agriculture 96; market-based value generation 250; Ottoman-republican 36, 52, 54; past 17; science and technology-intensive modernity 35

control over: bio-information 69; food 100; genetic information 247; knowledge system 154; labour process 182 (*see also çavuş*); land 52–3; landscapes 95; nature 257; seeds 89, 90, 94–5, 117, 157; plant 68, 95, 247; plant varieties 116; production 63, 157; product qualification 66; resources 117
conventional: agriculture 136; growers/ farmers/farms 33, 144, 152, 175; horizontal differentiation 152; industrial methods 127, 145, 255; localized competition 147, 152; production 152, 169–70, 211; varieties 152
conventionalization of: customary methods 211; GAP-certified 175, 216; organic agriculture 138, 211
customary knowledge systems 132, 154, 255
crop rotation 135, 138, 142, 144–5, 162, 167
crop varieties 1, 28, 70, 76, 89, 100–1, 116, 141, 148, 167, 249
customary knowledge 132, 134–5, 154, 255; customary methods 211
Customs Union (CU) 31, 39–40
Çağa **27**, 30–1, 105, 129, 145, 152–8, 161–2, 167, 222–3
çavuş 171–2, 176–83, 187–8, 190–1, 196, 204, 218

de-agrarianization 12, 18, 44, 49, 58
de-peasantization 12, 49, 169
dependency on: biotechnology firms 136; inputs 12, 104–5, 164, 224
Descartes, René 256, 266
development: developmentalism 4–5, 8, 13, 18, 21, 34, 93, 155, 237, 256–7, 265; developmentalist 3–5, 18, 21, 31, 53, 55, 94, 96, 161, 246, 250; economic 6, 8, 14–15, 66, 95–6, 125, 156, 247, 249, 273–4, 277; market-oriented 58; state-centric 3–5
Devlet Su İşleri (DSİ) 47–8, 111, 261, 266
direct marketing 124, 138, 140, 161, 167, 221–2, 281
Direct Payment Aid (DPA) 31, 40–4, 58, 86
disease 77–8, 82, 102–5, 110, 121, 133, 136–9, 144, 152, 158, 162–3, 165–6
dispossession 4, 7, 9, 11–14, 17, 251, 252, 262, 272; *see also* accumulation by dispossession
distrust 33, 96, 131, 190–1, 255; distrust of industrially homogenized food 96

divergence from: customary ways 139; industrial model 98–9, 247
diverse economies 250–1, 254, 268
Documentation and the Betterment of Problematic Agricultural Land (STATİP) project 39, 49, 56, 59
Doha Round 9, 31, 41
Dow 71–2, 262
downstream 61, 65, 73, 79, 94, 124
duality of assessments 33, 99, 247, 252
duality of thought 96
DuPont 71–2, 262
Dürüst 187; *Dürüstlük* 187; *see also* trust; trustworthy

earning: export 74; family budget 180; family wage 206; income/money 12, 121–2, 132–3; not paid 193; opportunities 147; wage earning 15, 17; withholding 186; wage gap 197–9; women 195–6
east-west divide 125, 127, 194, 252
ecologically adaptive systems 104
economic: crisis 9, 21, 42–3, 126, 235, 237, 262; development 6, 8, 14–15, 66, 95–6, 125, 156, 247, 249, 273–4, 277; growth 1, 2, 7, 9, 13, 16, 42, 52–3, 59, 91, 94–5, 122, 252–3, 256, 277
economies of scale 96, 122, 174
economization 2–5, 7, 9–10, 12, 14–17, 31, 91, 246, 252–3, 259; calculative rationality 17; cultural modernization 14; entrepreneurial spirit 13–15, 83; efficiency 2, 3, 7, 13, 15; global norm 2; human capital 14; knowledge mode 4; knowledge structure 2, 254; market calculus 16; mobility 14, 248; neoliberal reasoning 3; neoliberalism 2, 252–3, 259; normative project 252; ontological 3, 5; personal enterprise 4, 7, 14–15; productivity 16; rationality 15; self-investing 7, 14, 83, 121, 131, 253; the self 2, 15
ecosystem stewardship 258
edification 194, 209
education 65, 90–1, 100, 118, 165, 178–9, 192, 194, 197, 199, 203–4, 206, 226
European Environment Agency (EEA) 57, 267
efficiency 1–3, 12–18, 32, 42, 55–6, 61, 94–5, 98, 104, 174, 254; *see also* productivity
Eker, Mehdi 56, 74, 129n11, 233, 267
emulation 24, 53, 99, 127, 129, 250, 253

entrepreneurial 3–4, 7, 14, 32, 48, 61, 122, 131, 241, 250, 253
EUREPGAP 62, 215, 234–5, 277; *see also* GLOBALGAP
European 7, 11, 42, 53, 57, 62, 64, 87, 100, 105, 117–18, 120, 123, 125–7, 129, 132, 208, 230–1, 250, 253, 256; capitalism 208, 256, 264; cultural practices 208; modernity 205, 208–9; normative standards 208
European Economic Community (EEC) 40
European Union (EU) 3, 22, 39, 40–1, 58, 62–4, 84–5, 99, 113, 122–3, 132, 167n4, 227, 267
ethnicity 169, 171, 175; *see also* labour
entire household as a labouring unit 34, 172, 186–7, 209
exclusive: access to and management of water sources 47; control over land 53; property rights 69; rights over genetic materials 68; water user's associations 47
exploitation 34, 191, 197, 204, 209, 257, 265

family: family income 183, 206; family-wage 172, 206, 208–9
FAO 70, 267
FAO Treaty 69, 70
farmers: ambivalence 97, *98*, 246, 256; capacities 157; conventional 144, 271; cultivars and landraces 72, 86; GAP-certified 28, 133, 233; large-scale 7, 32, 39, 91, 93, 124–5, 133, 177, 183, 197, 211–12, 215; organic 129, 131, 133; farmers' privilege 86, 89; professional 38, 101, 134, 158; small-scale 1, 20, 44, 58, 89, 97, 131, 139, 144, 154, 169, 212, 218, 220, 223, 242, 254, 263, 270
farmers' conformity with: agro-industry 98; biotechnology 32; industrial innovation 96; industrial quality standards 144, 242; nonconformity 97, 99, 246
farmers' consciousness 248, 254; deliberative interpretive/evaluative judgements 248
farming imaginaries 32, 33, 93–100, 128, 131, 167, 212, 247–8, 250, 252, 254, 256, 259
farming scripts 38, 68, 73, 93
farming: agency 248–9; agro-ecological conditions 258; capitalized farming 32, 42, 91, 93; competitive business 3, 78; contract farming 1, 10, 20, 23, 32, 61–2, 65–6, **67**, 68, 86, 94, 101, 133, 135, 146,

158–9, 227, 233–4, 241–2, 267, 276, 281; experiential knowledge 211; experimental 28, 62; farming pathways 166; good farming 170; heterogeneity 254; income generation 33, 97, *98*, 247, 249; industrial 33, 94, 96, 100, 104, 131, 144, 152, 156; knowledge intensive 258; large-scale 1, 7, 20, 26, 32, 39, 42, 44, 55, 91, 99, 101, 122, 124, 125, 129, 131, 133, 134, 169, 177, 182–3, 186, 197, 211–12, 215, 219, 241; local farming 20, *98*, 136; old-style 253; peasant driven 12, 280; peasant farming 16, 93, 154; practices 16, 30, 32, 38, 42, 44, 73, 91, 93, 96–8, 11, 132, 136, 139, 143, 165, 170, 246, 249, 251, 254; professionalized 159; profit-driven 1, 9, 13, 79, 80; reorganization 32, 73; small-scale 1–2, 37–8, 42, 44, 54, 101, 123, 162, 167; styles of farming 38, 42; subsistence 153, 246; technologically driven 12; traditional farming knowledge 97, 211; unproductive 125; *see also* upstream; downstream
farmland 53, 58–9, 75, 101, 134, 279
Federation of Retailers of Turkey (PERDER) 230, 236–41, 245n4, 275
feminization of agriculture 170–1, 276
fertilizer 43, 61, 83, 113–14, 135, 138, 143–4, 164; inorganic fertilizers 164
fictitious commodities 32, 69, 91
food provisioning 1, 3–5, 20–1, 31–4, 38, 53, 61, 63, 211; contract farming 242; formal 225; informal 225; organized trade 23; *pazar* 225; *pazar* merchants 222; supermarkets 66, 212, 242; traditional food provisioning 19, 21, 23, 211, 222, 235; unorganized trade 23; written contracts 242
food system 96, 137, 224, 268, 276; *see also* food system sustainability
foodshed 224, 272; *see also* local food
foreign-owned global biotechnology companies 95, 249
formal 7, 14, 25, 31–2, 117, 134, 137, 139, 153, 158–62, 167, 169, 173, 198, 204–5, 212–13, 216–18, 220, 225–6
formal institutionalized commercial trust 32
fresh fruits and vegetables (FFVs) 6, 10, 20, 22–4, 41, 45, 63–4, 67, 73–4, 81, 143, 153, 158, 213–14, 233, 234, 272
Friedmann, Harriet 18–19, 40, 154, 268

gang masters 176; *see also* agro-labour traders
GAP Project 39, 61–2, 64; *see also* Good Agricultural Practices (GAP)

gender 34, 169–71, 196, 198, 209, 267, 276; gendered division of labour 200, 277; gendered wages 172, 197–8; paternalism 198; *see also* labour
gene bank 77, 87
General Agreement on Tariffs and Trade (GATT) 8, 31, 40–1, 69
General Directorate of National Property (GDNP) 50–1
genetic diversity 70, 135; genetic information 89, 94–5, 247
geographical indication (GI) 11, 30, 105, 115, 116, 130n15, 153–7, 161, 167n4, 255, 267, 274
geographical proximity 141, 155, 157, 223–4
germplasm 70, 72, 89, 94
GLOBALGAP 9, 32, 62–5, 68, 74, 215, 233–5
global North 6, 19, 25, 41, 71
global South 1, 8–10, 19–21, 36, 41, 55, 64, 70–2, 132, 225
GM/GE/GMO 84–5, 120
Good Agricultural Practices (GAP) 28, 32, 39, 46, 59, 61–5, 118, 122, 131, 133–9, 144–5, 166, 169, 175, 177, 183, 200, 211, 215–19, 229, 233–5, 237, 241–2, 255; *see also* GLOBALGAP; Turkish-GAP
good farmer 170, 272, 278
good food 169, 175, 205, 274
greenhouse 32, 34, 73, 75, 77, 99–100, 114–15, 141–2, 146, 151, 156, 158, 162, 165, 169–70, 173, 176, 182, 198–203, 205; commercial 162; nutrient stress 158; pests-disease control 158; self-owned 162; water-use issues 158
greenhouse workers 198, 200, *201*, 203, 208–9; *see also* gender
Güdül 26–33, 58, 75, 93, 100–1, 105, 107–12, 123, 133, 138–42, 145, 147–56, 158–9, 170, 182–3, 188–9, 191, 195, 197–8, 208, 221–3, 225–6

habit formation 231, 244, 266; habit persistence 231
Harmancık 112, *113*
heirloom 28, 30, 33, 105, 133, 151–8, 160, 162, 223, 255, 271, 274; no commercial substitute 155
hemşeri 172, 187, 191; *see also* labour
heterogeneity 144, 249, 251, 254–5, 263
heterogeneous landscapes 144
historical sensory experience 150

288   *Index*

holistic worldview 35, 249
homo Islameconomicus 253, 262
homogenization 20, 32, 68
horizontally established ties of trust 172–3,
    194; geographic-regional connections
    33, 172; *hemşeri* 172, 187, 191; kin 10,
    16, 33, 172, 183, 187–8, 191, 209;
    migration 33, 172; *see also* labour
household labour 153, 169, 175, 198
human resource management 198, 203–4
Hundred years of vineyards 138
husbandry 131, 167
hüzün (or melancholy) 128–9, 259
hybrid varieties 116, 140, 146–7, 151–2,
    155, 157–8, 163–4
hybridity 131, 162

identification: badge 222; labels 222;
    product 215, 217; public lands 58
income 2, 12, 19, 23, 32–3, 41–3, 60, 95,
    97, *98*, 124, 132–3, 158, 186, 192, 199,
    204–7, 212, 225, 231, 234–5, 247, 249,
    253–4; *see also* profit
Independent Industrialists' and Businessmen's
    Association (MÜSİAD) 237
industrial certainty 215–16, 242
informal: consumer networks 153; economy
    17, 175; labour 172–3, 175–6, 183, 197–8,
    234; labour regimes 209–12; marketing
    155, 167, 169, 219–20, 225–6; markets
    158–62, 211; milk vendors 161; open-field
    work 204; trust 139, 224; sharecropping
    148; *see also* vendors; participatory
    certification by consumers; labour
innovation 15, 32, 38, 42, 68, 71, 78–80,
    83, 93–7, 101–2, 105, 116, 119, 121–2,
    125, 127, 129, 132, 136, 145, 151, 246,
    249, 250, 253, 255, 258, 261, 263–4,
    267–8, 273, 279–80; agro-industrial
    211, 247; productivity-enhancing 95;
    scientific knowledge 95, 97, 99
inorganic: fertilizers 164; pesticides 164
Institution of Support for Agricultural
    and Rural Development (TKDK) 113,
    129n10, 130n11
institutional power barriers 154
institutionalization 2, 6, 9, 49, 56, 59, 95,
    171, 183, 187, 211, 227, 240, 250
instrumental rationality 15, 32, 91, 259; *see
    also* alienation; fictitious commodities
integrity 7, 64, 95–7, 119, 133, 136, 139,
    144, 187, 223, 246, 249, 254–5, 257–9
integrity of: agroecology; biodiversity 96,
    136, 144; biological 249; food culture

97; landscape structure 144, 249, 258–9;
    local landscape 136; smell of food 246;
    soil fertility 95; taste 246; water 95–6
intellectual property rights (IPR) 8, 19, 32,
    61, 68–9, 72, 86–7, 116, 154, 274, 276;
    Consultative Group on International
    Agricultural Research (CGIAR) 70;
    Convention on Biodiversity (CBD)
    69–70; FAO Treaty 69–70; IPR regime
    69–71; IPR-led governance 69, 73
intensification 10, 12, 18, 24, 42, 114, 120,
    125, 167, 254
intensive 1, 32–3, 35, 37–8, 40, 42, 45–9,
    55, 58, 61, 73, 91, 93–8, 101–2, 109–11,
    120, 122, 124–5, 127, 132, 137–8,
    143–4, 153, 174, 250, 254, 258; high-
    tech 32, 94, 101, 120, 124, 127, 224;
    specialized 49, 58, 94
International Federation of Organic
    Agricultural Movements (IFOAM) 132
International Monetary Fund (IMF) 8,
    15, 99
internet-based certification 157
interpretive meanings 209, 253
irrigation: capitalized agriculture 174; drip
    148; fragmented land 148; greenhouses
    199–200; irrigated lands 45, 47–8,
    112; irrigation infrastructure 46, 49;
    irrigation networks 56; irrigation-
    intensive 48, 110, 254; rain-fed
    agricultural lands 45; sprinkler 110, 137;
    see also Devlet Su İşleri DSİ; water-users'
    associations (WUAs)
Islam 121, 126, 265, 268, 275
ISO 62, 234–5, 244

justice: ecological 99; economic 93;
    redistributive 7, 53, 99; social 7,
    237–8, 99

Kaman **27,** 29–30, 33, 145, 147, 152–3,
    162–5
Kamanlar **27**, 30, 145, 147–9, 162, 196
Karacaören **27**, 30–1, 100, *107*, 109, 133,
    138, *142*, 145, 147, 156, 162, 170, 188,
    195–6
kaşıklama (spooning) 202–3
Kayabükü **27**, 28–9, 62, 177
Kırşehir 26, **27**, 29–30, 33–4, 145, 162,
    164, 171, 190, 218, 220
Kısakürek, Necip Fazıl 128, 271
knowledge 4, 11–12, 21, 38, 59, 63, 73,
    89, 91, 93–5, 97, *98*, 99, 101, 105, 134,
    155, 157, 161, 177, 200, 208, 211, 223,

249–51; knowledge culture 42, 94, 97, 100; knowledge structure 2, 94, 96, 100, 246; systems 34, 118, 132, 137, 154, 247–8

köylü 120–2, 213–14; *see also* peasants

Kurdish migrant workers 169, 172, 177–8, *184*, 190–1, 194–5, 198, 209; cultural maturity 194; culturally bounded 209; living conditions 177, 178, 182, 188, 190–1, 198

labour: agricultural labourers 122, 169, 182; agro-labour contractors 33; bounded members of entire households 33, 171; brokerage 171, 177–8; complementary labour forms 204; control 33, 172; discipline 182, 188; family-wage 172, 206, 208–9; gendered 171–2, 198–9, 205, 208–9, 276; horizontally established 33, 172, *173*, 175, 183; Kurdish migrant 101, 169, *170*, 174, 177–8, 182–3; local 170, 172, 182, 198; loyalty 34, 172, 188, 194; management 4, 34, 172, 177, 182, 197; paternalism 173, 176, 182, 197–8, 209; paternalistic 183, 187, 197–8, 209; racialized 171, 198, 208–9; recruitment 175–7, 183, 188; self-discipline 182, 188; skilled labour 182; supervision 172; vertically established 34, 172; wage determination 34, 172, 175, 183, 195, 197–8; working conditions 180, 182, 204, 219, 234, 244; *see also* agro-labour traders, *çavuş*, entire household as a labouring unit

land: access 6, 31, 36, 38, 49, 55, 59, 253; cadastral techniques 36, 49; cadastre modernization and land-registry 51; commodification 36, 262; configuration 31, 36, 39, 42; effective ownership 55; grabbing 11–12; land consolidation 16, 47, 49, 56, **57**, 134, 254; land-consolidation schemes 36, 49, 56–9; land distribution 52; land-titling 36; public lands 31, 36, 50, 51–2, 54–5, 57–9, 91, 147, 254; 'rational land use' 52, 91; registration 36, 49, *98*; the state 7, 36, 37, 39, 47, 49, 50–3, 58, 91, 248; state-led commodification of land 36; state-owned 51–2, 54, 57–8, 147; unregistered public lands 50; use 6, 21, 29, 31, 36–9, 46, 49, 52–3, 55–9, 91, 134, 254; use rights 53, 56

Land Conservation and Usage Law (No. 5403) 39, 49, 55–6

landraces 70, 72, 86, 131, 151, 164

landscape 26, 31, 38, 58–9, 61, 100, 102–5, 118–20, 127, 131, 133, 135–6, 139, 144–5, 151–2, 156, 158, 223–4, 246–7, 249, 251, 255, 258–9; land/soil/plant management 91; management 32–3, 93, 95–7, *98*, 247; planning at a landscape level 120; structure 144, 155, 166, 249, 255, 258

life-sciences 117, 154; companies 69

livelihood 4, 6–7, 10, 12–13, 17, 34, 49–51, 54–5, 58, 61, 93, 129, 150, 153, 159, 172

livestock 6, 22, 31, 43, 56, 64, 73–4, 86, 111, 144, 153, 157–8, 161–2, 218, 222, 227, 233

living universe 257

local: agro-ecological knowledge 118; consumption 29, 101, 140, 225; food 33, 90, 95, 101, 131, 138, 150, 157, 160–1, 163–4, 212, 220, 223–6, 237, 242, 249, 258; supermarkets 230–1, 233, 235, **238**, **240**, 243n14; tastes 164, 223–4, 241, 254; trap 155

local landscape 102, 104, 136, 139, 152, 223, 249, 255

locality 4, 100, 140, 144, 156–7, 167, 220–1, 224, 241, 252, 255; artisanal 138, 141–2, 223, 247; customary ways 131, 139, 142, 255; 'niche' markets 4, 224; production 221; seasonally grown 143, 226; village products 220

locally valued: food cultures 96; taste 96, 223, 246

McMichael, Philip 1, 4, 6, 9, 11, 17, 21, 39–41, 96, 100, 132, 154, 268, 273

Makromarket 63, 231, **232**, 237–9, 241

manure 135, 138, 141, 143–5, 160, 162, 164, 167

marginality 17, 154–5, 160

market economy 2, 12, 14, 24–5, 32, 34, 40, 42, 48, 52–3, 61, 91, 158, 242

Marx, Karl 11, 13, 15, 49, 69, 183, 208, 248, 251, 273

mechanized 181

Meeting of Local Chains 240

melding of old and new 212; *see also* ambivalent attitudes

Meriç, Cemil 127, 273

metabolic rift 12

Metro 19, 62, 73, 230–1, *232*, 236

migrant family *184*, *185*, *186*, *189*, 195–6

migration 10, 17, 33, 54. 170–2, 174, 176, 178–9, 181, 194, 198

Migros 62–3, 135, 137, 159, 228, 230–1, **232**, 233–5, 241

milk 143, 147, 153, 157–9, 161–2,
165–7, 255; livestock farmer 31, 157,
161; marketing 161; Milk Producers
Association 161; producer 157, 159, 161,
167; raw 142–3, 161, 166–7; vendor
159–62, 167, 255
Ministry of Food, Agriculture and
Livestock (MFAL) 22, 43–4, 46, 49,
55–7, 64–7, 73, 85–9, 131, 218, 222,
227, 243, 273–4
mixed associations 35, 247, 250
mixture of formal informal marketing
strategies 167
model: agro-industrial 35–6, 38, 132;
business 82; computer-based 70, 91;
development 34, 39, 40, 42, 73, 127,
212; industrial 98–100, 104, 128,
145, 247; intensive agriculture 48;
market 42, 86, 238; market-oriented
3, 34; performance-oriented 37, 71;
supermarket 1, 21, 34, 212–3, 228;
transnationally advocated 32, 34, 75, 97,
100, 128, 212
modernity 12–14, 16–18, 33, 35, 53, 58,
93–4, 128, 205–6, 208–9, 212, 227,
246, 250, 252, 253, 258, 259; embodied
practice 206, 208; English road to
modernity 13; modernity's fragmentation
252; *see also* capitalism; European
modernization 5, 13–15, 49, 51, 58,
127, 250
mono-cultural production 154
Monsanto 71–2, 87, 92n8, 108–9
muddy terrain 241, 262

national economic development 95–6, 125,
247, 249
national registry of farmers 28, 43, **44**,
58, 160
nationalist 95, 106, 125, 250; east-west
divide 127; Islamic 253; Kurdish 172;
Muslim 98; nationalist imagery 125;
Turkish-Muslim 249
native crops 72, 86, 152
native spirituality 258
native varieties 105–6, 115–16, 119, 126,
140, 142, 151, 154, 163
natural history of the senses 150, 261
nature 2, 7, 15, 25, 36, 59, 93–4, 120, 144,
149, 193, 207, 222, 246, 249, 251–2,
256–9
neoliberal reasoning 2, 3, 5
neoliberal selves 7; capable of enhancing
their investment-capital value 7; as

'entrepreneurial' 2, 7, 14, 83, 122,
131; entrepreneurialized subjects 3;
as 'investment capital' 7; 'personal
enterprises' 4, 7, 14
neoliberalism 2, 7, 17, 31, 37, 237, 252–4,
259, 265, 271, 281
neostatism 59, 60n19
networks 8, 23–4, 33, 56–7, 69, 70, 91, 94,
129, 133, 153, 155, 160–2, 169, 172,
183, 187
normative 2–5, 7, 15, 24–5, 31–3, 93–4,
97, 99, 127, 131, 139, 186–7, 208–9,
238, 246–7, 249–54, 257; normative
conflict 257; normatively grounded
ambivalence 246
notification model (*bildirim modeli*) 216

ontological 3, 5, 11, 26, 48, 58, 75, 82, 96,
251–3, 256, 258–9; anti-economy 17;
ontological precarity 11
ontology 4, 13, 98, 212, 256
open-access rights 68
open-field workers 171, 203–4; non-open-
field workers 171
optimization of performance 32; agro-
industrial notion of agriculture 38,
71, 246; values 75, 78, 82, 91; *see also*
economization
organic 33, 90, 104, 129, 131–6, 138–45,
153, 162, 164–7, 169–70, 175, 211,
216–17, 228, 255; agriculture 132, 136,
138–9, 141, 145, 262–3; farming 135,
136, 166, 271–2, 274; values 138
Organisation for Economic Co-operation
and Development (OECD) 43, 64, 86,
110–11, 275
Ottoman 53–6, 59, 96, 127, 172, 176,
209, 250, 252, 256, 276; Ottoman
land surveys 52; Ottoman-republican
continuity 36

Pamuk, Orhan 128–9, 275
Parent-child relationship 194
participatory certification by consumers 33,
131, 133, 153, 161–2, 167, 169, 212, 255;
see also trust; quality standards
patents 11, 32, 68–2, 86–7, 89, 94, 116,
153–8
paternalism *173*, 176, 182–3, 187–8, 191,
194, 197–8, 203, 209; paternalist labour
regimes 173; personal paternalism 197;
personalized paternalism *173*, 203, 209;
public paternalism *173*, 209; *see also*
labour regimes

pazar 34, 122, 138, 145, 147, 150–3, 159, 164–6, 212, 215, 217, 220, 222–3, 225, 229, 242; merchants 133, 160, 167, 213, 220–2, 255; neighbourhood 34, 153, 160–1, 211, 213, 219–22, 224; producers 33, 225; professional 124; *see also* wholesale markets

peasant farming *see* farming

peasantry 11, 13, 16, 18, 267

peasants 10, 13, 16–17, 39, 52–4, 132, 246, 273, 278, 280–1; *see also köylü*

pedogenesis 103–4, 272

plant improvement 95–6, 154

Polanyi, Karl 11, 13, 48–9, 69, 99, 250, 276; Polanyian 98, 187

poverty 2, 9–10, 17, 44, 126–7, 178, 258

Prediction of Harvest and Drought Tracing in Agriculture (TARİT) program 39, 46, 49, 58

primitive accumulation *see* accumulation

private: companies 47, 49, 87, 214; firms 71; immovables 50; labels 230–1, 233; land 147–8; ownership 157, 60n11; patents 71; plant-genetic resources 68; profit-driven 79; property 16, 52–3, 70, 269–70, 272; sector 49, 71; seeds 68, 70, 87; standards 18–9, 62–5, 68, 227, 236, 266, 280

privatization 13, 17, 48, 157, 212, 272

producers: large-scale 4, 32, 34, 37, 59, 146, 211, 218; professional 79; small/small-scale 1, 4, 7, 12–13, 16–17, 20–1, 23, 26, 33, 36, 41–2, 44–5, 51-2, 54, 59, 64–6, 68, 97, 108, 115, 120–6, 129, 131–3, 144–6, 154–5, 161, 166, 169, 211–15, 218, 222, 224–9, 241–2

producers' unions and cooperatives 67, 97, 123, 212–13, 226–9, 242

product: identity 215–16, 218–19; innovation 32, 68, 73–4, 80, 102; planning 80

productivity 1, 5, 10, 12–18, 42, 48, 55–6, 66, 81, 98, 103–4, 126, 135, 138, 143, 156, 166–7, 174, 227

professional: professional farmers 38, 101, 134, 158; professional farming 100, 137; professional grower 79, 108, 159; professional seedling growing 114; professionalized farming 159; unprofessional form of diversification 158

profit making 247, 249–50

profit-oriented growth 211

property 7, 12, 16, 37, 50, 55, 69, 190; access 7, 12, 31, 37–8, 49, 51, 155, 253; common 6, 31, 38, 49, 51–2; genetic resources 69;

land 12, 248, 253; ownership 37, 269; private 16, 52–3, 70; public 31, 51; regime 69, 70; resources 6, 31, 37–8, 49, 51; rights 50–1, 55, 61, 69; state 52; use 6, 31, 37–8, 49–50, 55, 69; *see also* intellectual property rights (IPRs); geographical indication (GI)

protected plant varieties *88*

quality 48, 62, 66, 78–81, 83, 102, 118–19, 121, 123–4, 131, 133–4, 137, 139, 140, 144, 147, 155, 160–1, 200, 203, 214–15, 223, 234; food 20, 32, 66, 80, 96, 119, 122, 137, 139, 167, 175, 211–12, 216, 219, 221, 234, 241–2, 250, 254–5; inspection certification 219; trust 139, 229, 235, 241–2

quality standards 18, 63, 66, 68, 73, 80, 95, 154, 167, 219, 224, 227, 234, 236, 242; ecological sustainability 20, 132; inspection 219; monitoring 214, 219; *pazar* 167, 212, 242; registration 239; traceability 64, 155, 215, 217, 219, 222; verification 217, 219; wholesale market 229; *see also* trust; Federation of Retailers of Turkey (PERDER); GLOBALGAP

re-contextualization: farming activities 258; integrity of landscapes 258; science and technology 258; real estate 6, 48, 50, 58–9

reconfiguring: class relations 34, 242; commodification 37, 247, 253; farming imaginaries 254; land 6, 49; land access 6, 36, 37, 254; land, labour and food 247; land use 6, 36, 37, 58, 254; social and ecological relationships 5

reconnection 259

registration 28, **67**, 86, 115, 156, 160, 215–20, 222, 225, 239, 242; *see also* land

relationships: biological 69, 258; capitalized model 93; contractual 214; ecological 5, 26, 258–9; employment 181, 187; food 2, 3, 5, 11, 21, 34, 59, 212, 225, 254; food provisioning 212; labour brokering 182–3; place specific 24; treatment of workers 194; trust-based 133

reliable 51, 56; information 20, 64, 174; labour 172, 177, 183; land register 49; workers 187

residence 179, 181, 183, 186, 188; *see also* Kurdish workers, tents

restructuring: agrarian restructuring 44; corporate-led restructuring 11; market-oriented 171; neoliberal restructuring 5, 9, 10, 24, 29, 31, 169, 209 rhythms: meaningful agroecological 259; temporal order 129

Rijk Zwaan **27**, 28, 32, 61–2, 73, 75–7, 81–2, 92n9, 114, 117, 119

Rostow, Walt W. 4, 13–15, 277

Rumi 257

rural 9–14, 16–17, 19, 24, 36, 42, 44–5, 49–50, 54, 58, 86, 95, 118, 154, 170–1, 174, 176–7, 198, 220, 223, 226–8, 237, 242, 258

science 21, 35, 69, 95, 117, 125, 129, 154, 208–9, 250, 258; *see also* techno-scientific

seasonal workers 174, *175*, 179, 191; *see also* Kurdish workers; temporary workers

seed: biotech seed 28, 32, 62, 68, 101–3, 141–2, 199; certification 89; conservation agriculture 96, *98*, 132, 154, 268, 278; customary use 157; dispossession 89; distribution 32; enclosures 89, 266; F1 77, 85, 115–16, 119, 146, 155; farmers' 162; germination 114, 164; heirloom 153–4, 162, 274; hybrid 85, 106, 118–19, 136, 150–2, 162, 164–6, 224; imported 85, 105–6, 118, 163; industrial seed systems 154; industrially hybridized seeds 92n17, 95; locally saved 167; open access 68, 70, 157; peasant farming 154, 165, 246; saving 11, 72, 90, 154; seed industry 32, 72; self-provisioning 11, 31, 68; self-saved 31, 163, 165; store-purchased 143; trade 85, 86

seed-exchange festivals 90

seedlings 21, 78, 90, 114–5, 119, 141–2, 146, 151, 155, 157, 160, 162, 165, 182, 199–201, 203, 207

seedling growing 114–15, 164

Seeds Law (No. 5553) 39, 61, 84, 86–7

segmentation: ethnic 171; gendered 171; labour force 171, 199, 203

Slowfood 90–1, 268, 278; *see also* Cittaslow

smallholder 2, 4, 9–12, 17, 18, 20, 24, 53, 56, 66, 86, 132, 212, 225, 242

Smith, Adam 2, 7, 97–8, 187, 253, 278

social security 175, 187, 198–9, 203–4

social-ecological realization 258–9

soil: degradation 111–2, 164; fertility 10, 95, 103, 106, 126, 133, 135, 144–5, 164–5; nutrient availability 104, 138–9, 165, 167

Southeastern Anatolia Development Project 46, 174

standards: grades and standards 63, 65–6, 68, 267; private standards 18–19, 62–5, 68, 91n5, 227, 236, 266, 280; public standards 68, 91n5, 280; standardization 20, 25, 62, 70, 73, 80–3, 142, 144,

166–7, 215, 234, 236, 242, 265; *see also* quality standards

state, the: conflicting expectations 251; dual nature 251; state capacity 6–8

State Planning Organization (SPO) 47, 54, 111, 216

state's *eminent domain* 52

strategic practice of criticism 100, 247

structural capacities 251

structural impositions 248

subcontract 34, 49, 166–7, 197

subsidy 41, 43

subsistence 4, 6, 9–12, 14, 16, 18–19, 31, 36–7, 39, 41, 15, 51–6, 61, 89, 97, 108, 143, 153, 159, 165, 176, 212, 246, 254; *see also* agriculture; farming

supermarketization 1–35

supermarkets: agro-traders 33–4, 94, 212, 215, 228, 241–2; certification 145, 235; certified crops 134; consumers' preference 80, 83; contract farming 66; contractual relations 133, 146, 214, 227; discount stores 23, 230–1, 233, 235; expansion 6, 19, 21, 34, 229, 242, 262; food appeal 121; grades 63, 65, 68, 101, 267; joint venture 231; large-scale 65; local 230–1, 233, 235, **238**, **240**, 243n14; model 1, 21, 34, 212–3, 228; national 19, 63, 231, **232**, 239; own-brand 20, 236; private label 19, 230–1, 233; private standards 18–19, 62–5, 68, 91n5, 227, 236, 266, 280; quality standards 20, 73, 80, 95, 167, 219, 212, 234, 236, 241–2; seed companies 20–1, 28, 251; socio-technical innovation 83; standardized differentiation 32, 73, 80–1; trust 3, 133, 137, 143, 147, 161, 212, 214, 225, 228–9, 234–5, 242; vertical coordination 68, 228, 242, 276; vertical integration 23, 124, 138; wholesale markets 20, 23, 124–5, 135, 161, 164, 212; *see also* food-provisioning systems; GAP; GLOBALGAP

suppliers 1, 20, 63, 66, 68, 73–4, 124–5, 133, 234, 236, 242, 255; first-tier suppliers 66, 133; preferred suppliers 63, 66; second-tier suppliers 68

supply chain 19, 23–4, 62, 134, 216, 218–19, 222, 225–6; *see also* value chain

sustainability 20, 96, 132–3, 135, 239, 264, 274; food-system sustainability 224

sustainable: agriculture 91, 249; conservation agriculture 132; development 105; ecologically 135; economic growth 9; growth 95; land

and water usage 10; linkages 225; synthesis 258

Syngenta **27**, 28, 32, 34, 62, 71–83, 87, 101–2, 104, 116, 125, 177–80, 187; field-experimentation demonstration days 102; in-soil field experimentation 75; open-field demonstration day 73–5, 119, 178, 187; open-field experiment-based planting 102

synthesis: capitalist 209; European and Turkish-Muslim ways 127; Muslim ways 258; temporal order 129; of two elements 241; universal 252

Tanpınar, Ahmet Hamdi 129, 279

tarım platformları (agricultural platforms) 236

techno-scientific: commercial agriculture 59, 125; development 249, 257; expert knowledge 59, 63, 91, *98*, 266; exploitation of nature 257; growth 75, 103; industrial productivist perspectives 145; innovation 32, 95, *98*, 125, 245–6; intensification of commercial agriculture 125; knowledge 97, 99; management of bio-information 71; management of land 32, 91; management of plants 32; market-economic performance 247; progress ideology 252–3, 256; reorientation of agrifood relations 252; ways 32, 59, 94, 151, 253; *see also* optimization of performance values; economization

technology 32, 35, 50, 64–5, 70, 95, 101, 104, 106, 109, 114, 117, 122, 125, 127, 129, 149, 224, 227, 240, 254, 256, 258

temporary workers 176, 193; *see also* seasonal workers; Kurdish workers

tents 179, 180–1, 184, 186, 190–2, 195, 196, 204, 219; Kurdish labour 179, 219; make-shift 190, 204, 219

terroir 154, 266

Tesco-Kipa 230, 231, **232**

Third Party Certification (TPC) 63, 133, 139; *see also* GLOBALGAP

three goals 249; *see also* agency

TKDK *see* Institution of Support for Agricultural and Rural Development

traceability 63–4, 154–5, 215–17, 219, 222, 224, 234, 242

Trade-Related Aspects of Intellectual Property Rights (TRIPS) 69, 116, 154

traders: *pazar* traders 220, 225; small-scale traders 220; specialized 23; vendors 33, 133, 153, 159, 161–2, 167, 213, 220, 222, 255; wholesalers 20, 21, 228, 236;

see also agro-traders; agro-labour traders; wholesale commissioners

trading-up 231, 234

tradition 14, 54, 120, 197–8, 206, 208–9, 252, 262

traditional bred cultivars 72

traditional retailers 214, 231; *see also* food provisioning

transformative possibilities 259

triangular employment relationship 181, 187

trust: agro-industrial methods 4, 33, 144, 224; agro-industrial processes 131, 166, 218, 255; commercialized 211, 218, 234, 242; consumer trust 139, 161, 169; food quality 137, 242, 255; homogenized food 96; horizontally established relations 175, 209; horizontally established ties 172, *173*, 183; networks 33, 187, 210n4, 255; participatory certification by consumers 33, 131, 133, 153, 161–2, 167, 169, 212, 255; paternalism 173, 187, 188, 191, 194, 197–8; personalized relations 33, 224; personally established 133, 229, 225; rooted in 255; standard food 32, 133; supply chains 33, 235; *see also* distrust

trust-producing structures 211

trustworthiness 68, 133, 161, 187, 191, 255, 259; trustworthy 137, 172, 188

Turkish-GAP 62, 64–5, 68

tutelage 188, 191

upstream 19, 61, 73, 79, 89, 94, 119–20, 124

urban 6, 13, 17, 19, 22, 48, 54, 57–8, 153, 160, 167, 170, 215, 219–20, 223–6, 230–1, 239

Uruguay Round 31, 40, 69, 282; *see also* World Trade Organization (WTO); General Agreement on Tariffs and Trade (GATT)

utilitarian 5, 7, 14, 251, 259; cost-benefit calculation 2, 5; ethics 259; human capital 14; liberal logic 14; logic of utility 257; self-interest 7, 14

ÜLKER 128, 161, 230, **232**, 233, 235–8, 279

value: authentic value systems 252; cultural values 187, 240; divergent value systems 83; ethically grounded behavior 253; Islamic values 256–7; local taste 96, 223–4, 241, 246; locality in ethics 241; market economic values 252; modernity 18, 208, 250, 253; neoliberal value

system 3; non-market values 248, 252, 255; optimization of performance value approach 78; paternalism 187; performance value 2, 18, 55, 75, 78, 80, 82, 91, 122, 125, 131, 249–50, 253; rationality values 32; universal 208; value orientation 2, 78, 131, 144
value chains 213, 228, 235, 239, 263, 265; *see also* commodity chains
variety 9, 10, 21, 68, 70, 77, 79–82, 86, 103, 105, 108, 110, 115, 119–20, 135, 140, 147, 149, 151–8, 163, 165, 221, 224, 256
vendors 161, 167, 220; street vendors 33, 133, 153, 159, 167, 213, 220, 222, 255; vegetable vendors 167; *see also* milk
vertical paternalism 194, 197–8
vertically concentrated wealth 59, 258
vicegerent 257
visual standardization 83

wage: allowance 178, 193, 194; cultural suitability of women 208; method of payment 193; wage determination 34, 172, 175, 183, 195, 197–8; wage labour 13, 146, 169–70, 177, 183, 198; women's wages 206; *see also* family wage
Wallerstein, Immanuel 128, 205–6, 208, 253, 280
water: conservation 31, 111, 137, 167; productivity 138, 156, 167, 274, 282; scarcity 47, 111; stress 110, 274; underground water 76, 100, 115; waste water 113–14; *see also* irrigation
water-users' associations (WUAs) 47–8; *see also* DSİ; irrigation
watershed 28, 111, 224, 278

wealth 2, 7, 13–14, 32, 37, 53, 56, 59, 61, 98, 122–3, 182–3, 209, 249, 251, 253, 256, 258, 278
web of life 251, 256
Weber, Max 15, 32, 91, 208, 248, 253, 259, 281
weed 13, 77, 120, 136–8, 140–1, 143–5, 162, 165, 179–80, 182, 199; weed-management strategies 136
wheat production 44, *45*, *46*
wholesale: commissioners 28, 31, 146, 162, 215, 228; food-provisioning system 21, 222; markets 20, 23, 68, 113, 124–5, 135, 146, 154, 160–1, 164, 212–20, 223, 225, 228, 241, 242; registration system 160, 216–9, 222, 242; retail store 236; terminals 213–14, 217, 241
wild varieties 70, 76–7, 86–7
Wolf, Eric 10, 12, 17, 281
women: domestic work 206; double shift 206
World Bank (WB) 1, 3, 6, 7, 8, 15, 34, 39, 41–3, 47, 49, 51–2, 57, 99, 227, 281
World Trade Organization (WTO) 9, 31, 39, 41–2, 58, 69, 116, 282; *see also* Trade-Related Aspects of Intellectual Property Rights (TRIPS)
written contracts 23, 34, 212, 218, 229, 242

yield 2, 12, 76, 78, 82, 94, 97, 100, 102, 104, 117, 119–21, 135–6, 141, 144, 150, 152, 163–4, 166; yield gap 1, 2, 136, 266–8 4, 7, 13, 16, 20–1, 23, 26, 33, 41–2, 45, 51, 65–6, 120, 122, 124, 129, 131, 133, 144–6, 161, 166, 169, 211–12, 218, 222, 224, 241–2

For Product Safety Concerns and Information please contact our EU
representative GPSR@taylorandfrancis.com
Taylor & Francis Verlag GmbH, Kaufingerstraße 24, 80331 München, Germany